Handbook of Research on Evolving Designs and Innovation in ICT and Intelligent Systems for Real–World Applications

Kandarpa Kumar Sarma
Gauhati University, India

Navajit Saikia
Assam Engineering College, India

Mridusmita Sharma
Gauhati University, India

A volume in the Advances in IT Standards and
Standardization Research (AITSSR) Book Series

Published in the United States of America by
    IGI Global
    Engineering Science Reference (an imprint of IGI Global)
    701 E. Chocolate Avenue
    Hershey PA, USA 17033
    Tel: 717-533-8845
    Fax: 717-533-8661
    E-mail: cust@igi-global.com
    Web site: http://www.igi-global.com

Library of Congress Cataloging-in-Publication Data

Names: Sarma, Kandarpa Kumar, editor. | Saikia, Navajit, 1972- editor. |
    Sharma, Mridusmita, 1988- editor.
Title: Handbook of research on evolving designs and innovation in ICT and
    intelligent systems for real-world applications / Kandarpa Sarma,
    Navajit Saikia, and Mridusmita Sharma, editors.
Description: Hershey, PA : Engineering Science Reference, an imprint of IGI
    Global, [2022] | Includes bibliographical references and index. |
    Summary: "This book discusses emerging areas related to ICT, electronics
    engineering, intelligent systems and allied disciplines with real world
    applications to aid human civilization attempts to mitigate the effects
    of the pandemic situation and the rapid advances in AI, wireless
    communication, sensors, cloud and edge computing, biomedical sciences
    and related domains which promise exciting times"-- Provided by
    publisher.
Identifiers: LCCN 2021042334 (print) | LCCN 2021042335 (ebook) | ISBN
    9781799897958 (h/c) | ISBN 9781799897972 (ebook)
Subjects: LCSH: Expert systems (Computer science) | Human face recognition
    (Computer science) | Khasi language--Discourse analysis--Data
    processing. | Optical detectors. | Solar cells.
Classification: LCC QA76.76.E95 H35545 2022 (print) | LCC QA76.76.E95
    (ebook) | DDC 006.3/3--dc23/eng/20211101
LC record available at https://lccn.loc.gov/2021042334
LC ebook record available at https://lccn.loc.gov/2021042335

This book is published in the IGI Global book series Advances in IT Standards and Standardization Research (AITSSR) (ISSN: 1935-3391; eISSN: 1935-3405)

British Cataloguing in Publication Data
A Cataloguing in Publication record for this book is available from the British Library.

For electronic access to this publication, please contact: eresources@igi-global.com.

Advances in IT Standards and Standardization Research (AITSSR) Book Series

Kai Jakobs
RWTH Aachen University, Germany

ISSN:1935-3391
EISSN:1935-3405

MISSION

IT standards and standardization are a necessary part of effectively delivering IT and IT services to organizations and individuals, as well as streamlining IT processes and minimizing organizational cost. In implementing IT standards, it is necessary to take into account not only the technical aspects, but also the characteristics of the specific environment where these standards will have to function.

The **Advances in IT Standards and Standardization Research (AITSSR) Book Series** seeks to advance the available literature on the use and value of IT standards and standardization. This research provides insight into the use of standards for the improvement of organizational processes and development in both private and public sectors.

COVERAGE

- Future of Standardization
- Descriptive Theory of Standardization
- Standardization for Organizational Development
- Case Studies on Standardization
- Risks of Standardization
- Economics of Standardization
- Standards for information infrastructures
- Managing Standardization Implementation
- Analyses of Standards-Setting Processes, Products, and Organization
- User-Related Issues

IGI Global is currently accepting manuscripts for publication within this series. To submit a proposal for a volume in this series, please contact our Acquisition Editors at Acquisitions@igi-global.com or visit: http://www.igi-global.com/publish/.

Titles in this Series

For a list of additional titles in this series, please visit: http://www.igi-global.com/book-series/advances-standards-standardization-research/37142

Digital Transformation for Promoting Inclusiveness in Marginalized Communities
Munyaradzi Zhou (Midlands State University, Zimbabwe) Gilbert Mahlangu (Midlands State University, Zimbabwe) and Cyncia Matsika (Midlands State University, imbabwe)
Engineering Science Reference • © 2022 • 300pp • H/C (ISBN: 9781668439012) • US $260.00

The Strategies of Informing Technology in the 21st Century
Andrew Targowski (Independent Researcer, USA)
Engineering Science Reference • © 2022 • 557pp • H/C (ISBN: 9781799880363) • US $240.00

Developing Countries and Technology Inclusion in the 21st Century Information Society
Alice S. Etim (Winston Salem State University, USA)
Information Science Reference • © 2021 • 318pp • H/C (ISBN: 9781799834687) • US $205.00

IT Auditing Using a System Perspective
Robert Elliot Davis (Walden University, USA)
Information Science Reference • © 2020 • 260pp • H/C (ISBN: 9781799841982) • US $215.00

Handbook of Research on the Evolution of IT and the Rise of E-Society
Maki Habib (The American University in Cairo, Egypt)
Information Science Reference • © 2019 • 602pp • H/C (ISBN: 9781522572145) • US $245.00

Global Implications of Emerging Technology Trends
Francisco José García-Peñalvo (University of Salamanca, Spain)
Information Science Reference • © 2018 • 323pp • H/C (ISBN: 9781522549444) • US $185.00

Effective Standardization Management in Corporate Settings
Kai Jakobs (RWTH Aachen University, Germany)
Business Science Reference • © 2016 • 418pp • H/C (ISBN: 9781466697379) • US $205.00

Business Process Standardization A Multi-Methodological Analysis of Drivers and Consequences
Björn Münstermann (University of Bamberg, Germany)
Business Science Reference • © 2015 • 448pp • H/C (ISBN: 9781466672369) • US $245.00

701 East Chocolate Avenue, Hershey, PA 17033, USA
Tel: 717-533-8845 x100 • Fax: 717-533-8661
E-Mail: cust@igi-global.com • www.igi-global.com

List of Contributors

Table of Contents

Detailed Table of Contents

Chapter 1

Nazreena Rahman, Kaziranga University, India
Salma Sultana, Kaziranga University, India
Abhinav Kashyap, Kaziranga University, India

In this chapter, the authors have studied different knowledge-based semantic similarity measures that are used to calculate semantic similarity between two words. Further, finding semantic similarity between two words helps in calculating semantic similarity between two sentences. Existing semantic similarity measures do not give the importance to the word's sense or meaning. Therefore, they have proposed a shallow neural network-based semantic similarity measure through which they find its similarity using its sense. It produces word embedding of words in documents using Word2vec on the books of A Song of Ice and Fire.

Chapter 2

Sabyasachi Pramanik, Haldia Institute of Technology, India

If there isn't enough parking within a university's campus, it will take a long time to look for parking. If a university has a number of research stations that are geographically apart from one another, communication occurs between them and the main office using office cars, although occasionally leased vehicles are obtained from a travel agency. The cost of transportation will rise as a result. Similarly, all students who are not from the dormitory are day scholars who come from their homes. Every day they must drive a significant distance to go to the institution in rented automobiles. This chapter deals with the performance solutions in carpooling using machine learning techniques.

Chapter 3

Mrinmay Medhi, Gauhati University, India
Hirakjyoti Goswami, Gauhati University, India

A low-frequency receiver is designed and operated to capture the LF spectrum associated with the atmospheric lighting with an ultimate aim to detect such events. Lightning releases frequencies over a wide band of the electromagnetic spectrum, but the reception of those frequencies are always limited by the prevailing EM noise at the receiving station. Therefore, the EM noise characteristics in the study environment are analyzed through a rigorous noise survey over the band 10kHz-2MHz. Based on the survey, 30-300kHz is selected as the operating frequency of the receiver, and the design and simulations are done accordingly. The receiver was calibrated using a known local AM radio signal of 730 kHz, which was later demodulated to validate the quality and accuracy of reception. The detector is then tested for three real lightning cases. It is seen from the observations that the frequencies 46.6 kHz and 90.13 kHz appeared during the lightning strikes with a maximum gain of 8.7 dB above the noise level.

Chapter 4

Prasanta Bhattacharya, Gauhati University, India

Maps are used to visualize geospatial data, and they help their user to better understand geospatial relationships. From maps, information on distances, directions, and area size can be retrieved, patterns revealed, and relations understood and quantified. Thus, maps and mapped data have been used extensively for spatial planning and management of resources. Located between $260 8/ 45//$ N to $260 9/ 37//$ N latitude and $910 39/ 22//$ E to $910 40/ 32//$ E longitude, the Gauhati University Campus occupies an important position in the western part of rapidly expanding Guwahati city. Considering its unique location, richness in terms of scenic constituents and biodiversity, use and abuse of its landscapes, an attempt has been made in this chapter to put emphasis on the significance of mapping and spatial database generation using GIS, GPS, and visual documentation through photographs for sustainable management of landscape, along with increasing spatial awareness among stakeholders.

Chapter 5

Sujit Chatterjee, Gauhati University, India
Rubi Baishya, Behali Degree College, India
Debashis Saikia, Gauhati University, India
Banty Tiru, Gauhati University, India

The visible light communication (VLC) system is expected to share the load on internet and communication technology (ICT) and be a promising green mode of communication, especially in healthcare applications. In this chapter, a frequency shift keying (FSK)-based VLC system is proposed that caters to the need of biomedical signal transfer. The system is implemented in hardware and is found to be flicker free to bit rates as low as 34bps and shows 82.33% improvement in BER compared to OOK. Using this method, different types of ECG signal are transferred successfully through a 1 W LED through a distance of 3m. The received signal retains the characteristics in terms of the RR interval and beats per minute (BPM) and the correlation between the transmitted and the received is very high (~100%), which is highly desired in transfer of biomedical signals. Future implementations and scope are also discussed in the chapter.

Chapter 6

Kunal Chakraborty, North Eastern Hill University, Shillong, India
Samrat Paul, North-Eastern Hill University, Shillong, India

This chapter presents the tunneling mechanism of electron and hole in the junction between absorbing layer and electron transport layer (ETL), which has an impact on the performance of devices in terms of quantum efficiency. In the present work, SCAPS-1D simulator is used to understand the effect of tunneling mechanism between the layers numerically. The most promising thin film-based lead-free Perovskite solar cells (PSCs) is the tin-based solar cell, which has tuneable band gap between 1.2 to 1.4 eV, and it can be used as both single junction and tandem structures.

Chapter 7

Horacio Alain Millan-Guerrero, Universidad Autónoma de Baja California, Mexico
Jose Antonio Nuñez-Lopez, Autonomous University of Baja California, Mexico
Fabian N. Murrieta-Rico, Universidad Politécnica de Baja California, Mexico
Lars Lindner, Universidad Autónoma de Baja California, Mexico
Oleg Sergiyenko, Universidad Autónoma de Baja California, Mexico
Julio C Rodríguez-Quiñonez, Universidad Autónoma de Baja California, Mexico
Wendy Flores-Fuentes, Universidad Autónoma de Baja California, Mexico

In this chapter, the authors design, simulate, and implement an optimal controller for a rotary pendulum while addressing real-world phenomena. The controller, called linear-quadratic-regulator (LQR), minimizes a cost function based on weights that penalize the system's state error and controller effort. The control objective is to reach the desired system state in an optimal way. The rotary pendulum consists of a pendulum attached to a rotary arm actuated by a motor. It is a great system to design and analyze different types of controllers. This system is underactuated, nonlinear, sensitive to initial conditions, and has 2 DOF. This chapter's main contributions are the mathematical modeling of the system taking into account nonlinear friction, the characterization of the plant using measured data from the physical system using the nonlinear squares and the trust-region reflective algorithms, comparison of linear and nonlinear behaviors, and implementation on real hardware considering discrete phenomena while using hardware-provided tools such as position decoding and PWM generation.

Chapter 8

Risanlang Hynniewta, North Eastern Hill University, India
Arnab Maji, North Eastern Hill University, India
Sunita Warjri, North Eastern Hill University, India

Part-of-speech tagging is a process of assigning each word of a sentence to a part of speech based on its context and definition. POS tagging is a prerequisite tool for many NLP tasks like word sense disambiguity, name entity information extraction, etc. Unfortunately, very little work has been done so far in this line for Khasi Language. The main difficulty lies with the unavailability of an annotated corpus. Hence, a small corpus is created which consists of 778 sentences with 34,873 words, out of which 3,942 are distinct words and a tagset of 52 tags. In this chapter, three methods for POS tagging, namely Brill's tagger, hidden Markov model (HMM)-based tagger, and bidirectional long short-term memory recurrent neural network (Bi-LSTM), have been implemented. Then a comparative analysis is performed, and it is observed that Bi-LSTM performs better in terms of accuracy.

Chapter 9

K. Vinoth Kumar, New Horizon College of Engineering, India
S. Prithi, Rajalakshmi Engineering College, India
Vinodha K., PES University, India

The vast majority of the system security application in today's systems depend on deep packet inspection. In recent years, regular expression matching has been used as an important operator that examines whether or not the packet's payload can be matched with a group of predefined regular expression. Regular expressions are parsed using the deterministic finite automata representations. Conversely, to represent regular expression sets as DFA, the system needs large amount of memory, an excessive amount of time, or an excessive amount of per flow state limiting their practical applications. In this chapter, the intelligent optimization grouping algorithms (IOGA) are discussed to resolve the state blow up problem. As a result of using IOGA, the system provides memory-efficient automata by dispensing the regular expression sets in various groups and optimizing the DFAs.

Chapter 10

Chaya P., GSSS Institute of Engineering and Technology for Women, India
Nandini Prasad K. S., Dr. Ambedkar Institute of Technology, India

Wireless sensor networks (WSN) have emerged as significant technology that has been adopted in various research fields to monitor the physical environments and collect information from the surroundings. However, WSNs are more vulnerable to attacks owing to their significant characteristics, including dynamicity in network topology and resource constraints. Multiple methods have been investigated to efficiently identify the different types of threats and attacks over the WSN. However, most of the existing works focus on a specific type of attack detection and lack in analyzing their performance. This survey highlights the significant functionalities of WSN, applications, and security requirements. From the viewpoint of security measurements, the authors have classified the survey study as security towards data collections and routing in WSN. Also, various security attacks based on protocol stack layers are classified. Finally, the authors have emphasized the significant security challenges in this research field based on the prior studies followed by the conclusion.

Chapter 11

Showkat Ahmad Dar, Annamalai University, India
Palanivel S., Annamalai University, India

FBA (facial-based authentication), a non-contact biometric technology, has been evolving since its inception.. FBA can be used to unlock devices by showing their faces in front of devices. DLTs (deep learning techniques) have been receiving increased interest in FBA applications. Many proposals have used DLTs in this area. This chapter proposes DAEs (denoise auto encoders) for real-time classification of human faces. The proposed scheme balances accuracy with constraints of resource and time. The proposed

DAE technique uses MDCs (mobile device cameras) for FBAs as they can address spoof or Windows-based attacks. The proposed DAE technique eliminates possible attacks on windows by immediately recognizing impostors. Moreover, feature extraction in DAE is dynamic and thus authenticates humans based on their facial images. Facial videos collected from MDCs results in realistic assessments. Spoof attacks using MDCs for bypassing security mechanisms are identified by DLTs in authentication.

    Biswajit Mandal, National Institute of Technology, Durgapur, India
    Partha Sarathee Bhowmik, National Institute of Technology, Durgapur, India
    Tapas Chakrabarti, Heritage Institute of Technology, India

Irrespective of the photo incident angle and lighting condition of a day, DSSC is a kind of photovoltaic device consistent to generate power. Power extracted in diffuse light condition from DSSC is greater than the generated power from a conventional existing photovoltaic cell. This lucrative feature drives many to improve the device performance. To fill the gap between theoretical and practical performance of the device, more study is required on this topic. This study reviews the various methods to prepare DSS cell in each step, working principle, different measuring systems for characterization of the cell, and how those characters affect the final product to achieve its goal.

    Seuji Sharma, Gauhati University, India

The chapter attempts to look at different themes and issues relating to the use of Assamese language on Facebook. This study examines the changes observed at different levels of linguistic analysis. The users have been seen making some changes at phonological level which is associated with the phonemes or sounds in Assamese. Modifications have also been observed regarding the use of sentence structure as well as phrase structure, and the matters related to these areas have been dealt with at a grammatical level. Since linguistic analysis covers a vast area, some specific domains are being dealt with in this chapter, especially from the areas of phonology, morphology, and syntax.

    Jonathan Bishop, Crocels Community Media Group, UK
    Mark M. H. Goode, Cardiff University, UK

This chapter expends the application of the ecological cognition framework to serendipity engineering, seductive hypermedia, user analysis, and socialnomics. It updates the theory to better account for the advances in computational science computational intelligence. In terms of 'serendipity engineering for seductive hypermedia', the chapter looks at how to design information systems to account for the pleasant occurrences that happen in offline environments studied by those in sales and marketing where beneficial outcomes often occur by chance encounters. In terms of 'user analysis using socialnomics', it looks at how a parametric user model based on the ecological framework can be used to understand users of information systems. To do this, a number of socialnomics equations based on the parametric user model are explored, including to calculate probability of seduction and probability of serendipity in an information system. The parametric model presented has great applicability for information and communications technology solution providers.

Chapter 15

High-tech textiles play ever-increasing roles as technology becomes increasingly integrated into our everyday lives. Smart textiles are materials that sense and react to environmental conditions or stimuli. Examples include chromatic materials that change color in response to environmental changes, phase change materials for thermoregulation, and shape-memory polymers that change shape in response to temperature changes. The main technical components used to create fashionable wearables are interfaces, microprocessors, inputs (sensors), outputs (actuators), software, energy (batteries and solar panels), and materials (electronic textiles and enhanced materials). Moreover, the role of 3D printing in fashion has grown substantially, with remarkable increases in awareness and interest in the technology from designers. This is because 3D printing allows fashion designers to remove traditional design limits and produce fascinating designs. Detailed information on "smart fashion," as well as its functions and performance characteristics, is given in this chapter.

Chapter 16

A communication system transmits and receives information from one place to another, where the separation between transmitter and receiver may be of few kilometers or transoceanic distances. Fiber-optic communication is one of such communication systems where optical fibers are deployed for information transmission. The capacity of a fiber-optic communication system is very high since it has large carrier frequency (Capacity~100 THz) in the visible or near-infrared region of the electromagnetic spectrum. The transmission of multiple optical channels over the same fiber has provided a simple way to extend the system capacity. Channel multiplexing can be achieved through time-division multiplexing (TDM) or frequency division multiplexing (FDM). In optical communication, FDM is known as wavelength division multiplexing (WDM). This chapter includes the discussion about the working principle of the WDM system, WDM components, classification of WDM system, and other supporting technologies.

Chapter 17

The massive wastage of water occurs due to irregular heavy rainfall and water released from dams. Many statistical methods are of the previous techniques used to predict water level, which give approximate results. To overcome this disadvantage, gradient descent algorithm has been used. This gives more accurate results and provides higher performance. K-means algorithm is used for clustering, which iteratively assigns each data point to one of the k groups according to the given attribute. The clustered output will be refined for further processing in such a way that the data will be extracted as ordered datasets of year-wise and month-wise data. Clustering accuracy has been improved to 90.22%. Gradient descent algorithm is applied for reducing the error. It also helps in predicting the amount of water to be stored in watershed for future usage. Watershed development appears to be helpful in terms of groundwater recharge, which benefits the farmers. It can also be used for domestic purposes.

Preface

The relentless advances in all areas of Information and Communication Technology (ICT), Intelligent Systems and related domains have continued to drive innovative research. Most of these works have attempted to contribute in some form towards improving human life in general and have become indispensable elements of our day to day life. The evolution continues at accelerated pace while the world faces innumerable challenges including those posed by pandemic situations. The unabated developments in the areas of artificial intelligence (AI), wireless communication, sensors, cloud and edge computing, biomedical sciences and related domains provide ample of research opportunities. Optimization leading to innovation and association with attributes of green technologies provide a wide scope of further improvement. Simultaneously, an all pervasive importance of documenting such research is always a pre-requisite. Moreover, any effort of documenting such outcomes adds catalytic effect for more work with renewed vigour. The emerging perspectives in ICT, Intelligent Systems and related domains while human civilization attempts to mitigate the effects of pandemic situation and the rapid advances in AI, wireless communication, sensors, cloud and edge computing, biomedical sciences and related domains promise exciting times. To document such aspects and provide a platform for discussion and sharing of knowledge among researchers of such areas, a special book volume is required.

The *Handbook of Research on Evolving Designs and Innovation in ICT and Intelligent Systems for Real-World Applications* disseminates details of works undertaken by various groups of researchers in emerging areas related to information and communication technology, electronics engineering, intelligent systems, and allied disciplines with real-world applications. Covering a wide range of topics such as augmented reality and wireless sensor networks, this major reference work is ideal for industry professionals, researchers, scholars, practitioners, academicians, engineers, instructors, and students.

The book volume covers areas as diverse as Artificial Intelligence, Augmented Reality, Face Authentication, Gaming, Information Sciences, Intelligent Systems, Natural Language Processing, Rotary Pendulum, Smart Textile, Visible Light Communication System, Wireless Sensor Network to name a few.

The intended audiences are industry professionals, researchers, scholars, practitioners, academicians, engineers, instructors, and students. It is expected to enrich libraries worldwide. The contents shall serve as ready reckoner to any innovator or researcher or even a beginner willing to delve deep into the area of design and optimization related to real-world systems and applications.

The contents of the book represent a diverse treatment of experimental works and insightful review of available literature.

The Chapter 1, titled "A Sense-Based Semantic Similarity Measure Using a Shallow Neural Network," outlines how Artificial Neural Networks are used to determine semantic similarity measure. The description includes different knowledge based semantic similarity measures which are used to calculate semantic similarity between two words. Further finding semantic similarity between two words helps in calculating semantic similarity between two sentences. Existing semantic similarity measures does not give the importance to the word's sense or meaning. Therefore, we have proposed a shallow neural network based semantic similarity measure through which we can find its similarity using its sense. It produces word embedding of words in documents using Word2vec on books of The Game of Thrones.

In the Chapter 2, the authors first outline the major reason for writing the chapter. It is from some of the issues we experience in our daily lives, such as traffic congestion, a lack of parking spaces, fuel waste, and pollution. If there isn't enough parking within a university's campus, it will take a long time to look for parking. If parking is available outside, employees will have to travel a great distance to access the building, which will take longer. For residential reasons, the identical issue will arise. If a university has a number of research stations that are geographically apart from one another, communication takes occur between them and the main office using office cars, although occasionally leased vehicles are obtained from a travel agency. The cost of transportation will rise as a result. Similarly, all students who are not from the dormitory and are day scholars who come from their homes are considered day scholars. Every day, they must drive a significant distance to go to the institution in rented automobiles. This chapter deals with the solutions in carpooling using machine learning techniques.

The third chapter is related to a low-frequency receiver which is designed and operated to capture the LF spectrum associated with the atmospheric lighting with an ultimate aim to detect such events. Lightening releases frequencies over a wide band of the electromagnetic spectrum, but the reception of those frequencies are always limited by the prevailing EM noise at the receiving station. Therefore, the EM noise characteristics in the study environment are analyzed through a rigorous noise survey over the band 10kHz-2MHz. Based on the survey, 30-300kHz is selected as the operating frequency of the receiver and the design and simulations are done accordingly. The receiver was calibrated using a known local AM radio signal of 730 kHz which was later demodulated to validate the quality and accuracy of reception. The detector is then tested for three real lightning cases. It is seen from the observations that the frequencies 46.6 kHz and 90.13 kHz appeared during the lightning strikes with a maximum gain of 8.7 dB above the noise level.

The next chapter is an important contribution towards cartography and geographical information system (GIS). Maps are used to visualize geospatial data and they help their user to better understand geospatial relationships. From maps, information on distances, directions and area size can be retrieved, patterns revealed, and relations understood and quantified. Thus, maps and mapped data have been used extensively for spatial planning and management of resources. Located between 260 8/ 45// N to 260 9/ 37// N latitude and 910 39/ 22// E to 910 40/ 32// E longitude, the Gauhati University Campus occupies an important position in the western part of rapidly expanding Guwahati city. Considering its unique location, richness in terms of scenic constituents and biodiversity, use and abuse of its landscapes, an attempt has been made in this paper to put emphasis on the significance of mapping and spatial database generation using GIS, GPS and visual documentation through photographs for sustainable management of landscape, along with increasing spatial awareness among stakeholders.

Chapter 5 deals with visible light communication. Visible light communication (VLC) system is expected share the load on Internet and Communication Technology (ICT) and a promising green mode of communication especially in health care applications. In this chapter, a frequency shift keying (FSK) based VLC system is proposed that caters to the need of biomedical signal transfer. The system is implemented in hardware and is found to be flicker free to low bit rates as low as 34bps and shows 82.33% improvement in BER compared to OOK. Using this method, different types of ECG signal are transferred successfully through a 1 W LED through a distance of 3m. The received signal retains the characteristics in terms of the RR interval and beats per minute (BPM) and the correlation between the transmitted and the received is very high (~100%) which is highly desired in transfer of biomedical signals. Future implementations and scope are also discussed in the chapter.

The sixth chapter presents the tunneling mechanism of electron and hole in the junction between absorbing layer and Electron transport layer (ETL) which has an impact on the performance of device in terms of quantum efficiency. In that present work, SCAPS-1D simulator is used to understand the effect of tunneling mechanism between the layers numerically. Most promising thin film based lead-free Perovskite solar cells (PSCs) is tin-based solar cell which has tuneable band gap between 1.2 to 1.4 eV and it can be used as both single junction and tandem structure.

In most applications, it is helpful to control systems and machines in an optimal way, minimizing cost, power, energy, or any other desired parameter. In this chapter, an optimal controller, called Linear-Quadratic-Regulator (LQR), will be implemented for a rotary pendulum. The controller minimizes a cost function based on weights that penalize the system's state error and controller effort. The objective of the controller is to reach the desired system state in an optimal way. The rotary pendulum consists of a pendulum attached to a rotary arm. It is an excellent system to design and analyze different types of controllers. This system is underactuated, nonlinear, sensitive to initial conditions and has 2 DOF. The Chapter 7 covers the mathematical modeling of the rotary pendulum, the characterization of the real plant including the actuator (motor), design of the LQR controller, simulation, and implementation.

Khasi is an important language spoken in the north eastern part of India. The next chapter is related to the Khasi language. Part-of-Speech tagging is a process of assigning each word of a sentence to a part of speech such as nouns, adjectives, verbs, adverbs, based on its context and definition. POS tagging is a prerequisite tool for many NLP tasks like word sense disambiguity, Name Entity information extraction, etc. But unfortunately, very little work has been done so far in this line for Khasi Language. The main difficulty lying with the unavailability of annotated corpus. Hence, a small corpus is created which consists of 778 sentences with 34,873 words, out of which 3,942 are distinct words and a Tagset of 52 Tags. In this Chapter per the authors, an implemention of three methods for POS Tagging namely Brill's Tagger, Hidden Markov Model (HMM) based Tagger and Bidirectional Long Short-Term Memory Recurrent Neural Network (Bi-LSTM) has been implemented, then a comparative analysis is performed and It is observed that Bi-LSTM performs better, in terms of accuracy.

Next is the Chapter 9. The vast majority of the system security application in today's systems depends on Deep packet inspection. In recent years regular expression matching are used as an important operator which examines whether or not the packet's payload can be matched with a group of predefined regular expression. Regular expressions are parsed using the Deterministic Finite Automata representations. Conversely, to represent regular expression sets as DFA the system needs large amount of memory, an excessive amount of time, or an excessive amount of per flow state limiting their practical applications. In this paper the Intelligent Optimization Grouping Algorithms (IOGA) are discussed to resolve the state blow up problem. As a result of using IOGA the system provides memory efficient automata by dispensing the regular expression sets into various groups and optimizing the DFAs.

From the last decades, Wireless Sensor Network (WSN) has emerged as significant technology that has been adopted in various research fields to monitor the physical environments and collect information from the surroundings. However, WSNs are more vulnerable to attacks owing to their significant characteristics, including; dynamicity in network topology and resource constraints. Multiple numbers of methods have been investigated to efficiently identify the different types of threats and attacks over the WSN. However, most of the existing works focus on a specific type of attack detection and lack in analyzing their performance. This survey highlights the significant functionalities of WSN, applications, and security requirements. From the viewpoint of security measurements, have been classified the survey study as security towards data collections and routing in WSN. Also, various security attacks based on protocol stack layers are classified. Finally, the authors have emphasized the significant security challenges in this research field based on the prior studies followed by the conclusion. This constitutes Chapter 10.

Chapter 11 deals with Facial Based Authentications (FBAs) which is a non-contact biometric technology has been evolving since its inception. FBAs can be used to unlock devices by showing their faces in front of devices. DLTs (Deep Learning Techniques) have been receiving increased interests in FBA applications. Many proposals have used DLTs in this area. This chapter proposes DAEs (Denoise Auto Encoders) for real time classification of human faces. The proposed scheme balances accuracy with constraints of resource and time. The proposed DAE technique uses MDCs (Mobile Device Cameras) for FBAs as it can address spoof or windows based attacks. The proposed DAE technique eliminates possible attacks on windows by immediately recognizing impostors. Moreover, feature extraction in DAE is dynamic and thus authenticates humans based on their facial images. Facial videos collected from MDCs results in realistic assessments. Spoof attacks using MDCs for bypassing security mechanisms are identified by DLTs in authentications.

Irrespective of the photo incident angle and lighting condition of a day, DSSC is a kind of photovoltaic device consistent to generate power. Power extracted in diffuse light condition from DSSC is more compared to the generated power from a conventional existing photovoltaic cell. This lucrative feature drives many to improve the device performance. To fill the gap between theoretical and practical performance of the device, more study required on this topic. This study reviews the various methods to prepare DSS cell in each step, working principle, different measuring systems for characterization of the cell, and about how those characters affect the final product to achieve its goal. This is covered in Chapter 12.

Chapter 13 attempts to look at different themes and issues relating to the use of Assamese language on Facebook. Assamese is an important language spoken in North East India. This study examines the changes observed at different levels of linguistic analysis.

Chapter 14 expends the application of the ecological cognition framework to serendipity engineering, seductive hypermedia, user analysis and socialnomics. It updates the theory to better account for the advances in computational science computational intelligence. In terms of 'serendipity engineering for seductive hypermedia,' the chapter looks at how to design information systems to account for the pleasant occurrences that happen in offline environments studied by those in sales and marketing where beneficial outcomes often occur by chance encounters. In terms of 'user analysis using socialnomics,' it looks at how a parametric user model based on the ecological framework can be used to understand users of information systems. To do this number of socialnomics equations based on the parametric user model are explored, including to calculate probability of seduction and probability of serendipity in an information system. The parametric model presented has great applicability for information and communications technology solution providers.

High-tech textiles play ever-increasing roles as technology becomes increasingly integrated into our everyday lives. Smart textiles are materials that sense and react to environmental conditions or stimuli. Examples include chromatic materials that change color in response to environmental changes, phase change materials for thermoregulation, and shape-memory polymers that change shape in response to temperature changes. The main technical components used to create fashionable wearables are interfaces, microprocessors, inputs (sensors), outputs (actuators), software, energy (batteries and solar panels), and materials (electronic textiles and enhanced materials). Moreover, the role of 3D printing in fashion has grown substantially, with remarkable increases in awareness and interest in the technology from designers. This is because 3D printing allows fashion designers to remove traditional design limits and produce fascinating designs. Detailed information on "smart fashion", as well as its functions and performance characteristics, is given in Chapter 15.

A communication system transmits and receives information from one place to another, where the separation between transmitter and receiver may be of few kilometers or transoceanic distances. Fiber-optic communication is one of such communication systems where optical fibers are deployed for information transmission. The capacity of a fiber-optic communication system is very high since it has large carrier frequency (~100 THz) in the visible or near-infrared region of the electromagnetic spectrum. The transmission of multiple optical channels over the same fiber has provided a simple way to extend the system capacity. Channel multiplexing can be achieved through time-division multiplexing (TDM) or frequency division multiplexing (FDM). In optical communication, FDM is known as wavelength division multiplexing (WDM). This chapter includes the discussion about the working principle of the WDM system, WDM components, classification of WDM system, and other supporting technologies. This is discussed in Chapter 16.

The last chapter deals with the wastage of water. The massive wastage of water occurs due to irregular heavy rainfall and water released from dams. Many statistical methods are of the previous techniques used to predict water level which gives approximate results only. To overcome this disadvantage, gradient descent algorithm has been used . This gives more accurate results and provides higher performance. K-means algorithm is used for clustering which iteratively assigns each data point to one of the k groups according to the given attribute. The clustered output will be refined for further processing in such a way that the data will be extracted as ordered dataset of year wise and month wise data. Clustering accuracy has been improved to 90.22%. Gradient descent algorithm is applied for reducing the error. It also helps in predicting the amount of water to be stored in watershed for future usage Watershed development appears to be helpful in terms of groundwater recharge which benefits the farmers. It can also be used for domestic purpose.

The contents are expected to give enough of opportunity to the reader to expand their knowhow and work towards finding better solutions for handling real-world challenges.

The editors are thankful to the anonymous reviewers and the publication team at IGI Global. Their support and guidance from the beginning to the end has been exemplary.

Kandarpa Kumar Sarma
Gauhati University, India

Navajit Saikia
Assam Engineering College, India

Mridusmita Sharma
Gauhati University, India

Chapter 1
A Sense–Based Semantic Similarity Measure Using a Shallow Neural Network

Nazreena Rahman
Kaziranga University, India

Salma Sultana
Kaziranga University, India

Abhinav Kashyap
Kaziranga University, India

ABSTRACT

In this chapter, the authors have studied different knowledge-based semantic similarity measures that are used to calculate semantic similarity between two words. Further, finding semantic similarity between two words helps in calculating semantic similarity between two sentences. Existing semantic similarity measures do not give the importance to the word's sense or meaning. Therefore, they have proposed a shallow neural network-based semantic similarity measure through which they find its similarity using its sense. It produces word embedding of words in documents using Word2vec on the books of A Song of Ice and Fire.

INTRODUCTION

Semantic similarity is a widely used approach to understand the natural language issue in so many NLP tasks such as question answering, recommender system, natural language processing, word sense disambiguation, text segmentation, information retrieval, information extraction, etc. It is the similarity between documents or words based on their meanings or semantic content. It is different from syntactic similarity where we estimate the similarity based on their syntactical representation i.e, their string format. We

DOI: 10.4018/978-1-7998-9795-8.ch001

use WordNet (Pedersen et. al, 2004) as per lexical database for finding the similarity distances between sentences. WordNet contains approximately 57,000 nouns organized into approximately 48,800 synsets.

IMPLEMENTATION OF EXISTING SEMANTIC SIMILARITY MEASURES

We use existing similarity measures to find the distance between sentences. The existing similarity measures that we have used falls under two category: one is path based and other is information content based. Path based measures (Martin, 2009) finds the shortest path between two concepts. We use following path based measures for our experiment:

1. Shortest Path based measure (Rada et al., 1989)
2. Wu and Palmer (Wu and Palmer., 1994)
3. Leacock and Chodorow (Leacock and Chodorow, 1998)

Information Content based measure (Martin, 2009) is concerned with the probability of concept occurring in a text. Following content based measures are used here:

1. Jiang and Conrath (Jiang and Conrath, 1997)
2. Lin (Li et al., 2003)
3. Resnik (Resnik, 1995)

We have taken following three sentences for our experiments:

978-1-5090-4291-3/16/$31.00 2016 IEEE
Sentence 1. Prime Minister visits China.
Sentence 2. Ram visits his uncle's house.
Sentence 3. Narendra Modi visited China.

Now we compare these sentences using WordNet and find out the similarity score between sentence 1 and 3 and sentence 2 and 3. We use the six above mentioned measures to calculate the semantic similarity between them. Each Table shows the particular sense which is taken by WordNet. Finally average semantic similarity is shown in Table XIII.

Using the above measures, we have achieved semantic similarity score, but most of the time they have not used the sense that is appropriate with the context of the word. WordNet takes that sense for which the semantic similarity score is maximum. Different semantic similarity measures have different characteristics. Path based measures take the path length linking the concepts and the position of the concepts into consideration. Their edge or link is used to find the relationships between concept nodes. Most measures are simple. But it is difficult to find the local density of word pairs. IC based measures assumes that similar concepts share more common concepts. These measures are found to be effective than path based measures. However they are not able to determine the structure information of concepts. These measures do not give us the desired sense in context of the sentence.

METHODOLOGY

In NLP, there are many words that have more than one sense (the meaning of a word) and most of the time human brain can figure out what sense is used in the sentence. But it is not the case with machines. Hence it becomes difficult to determine the similarity distance between two sentences if the desired sense of a word is not considered. Word Sense Disambiguation (WSD) is concerned with finding the correct sense of a word used in the sentence.

Here we use word embedding to find semantic similarity between two sentences with respect to its sense and context. We determine similarity between two sentences by comparing the vectors of words in the sentence. It is a representation of a word having multi-dimensional meaning. Word vectors let us gather information from raw text into our model. Words used in similar contexts are closer than the words with different context. Since machines understand numbers and many machine learning algorithms require their input to be vectors of continuous values; they cannot interpret plain text and the input needs to be converted into numbers for the machine to interpret it. Word Embedding converts the text input into numerical values. Each word is mapped to one vector and the learning of the vector values resembles a neural network. Each word is represented by a vector, which has usually tens or hundreds of dimensions.

Table 1. Using path length measure between sentence 1 and 3

Words pair	Sense	Similarity Measure
Prime-Narendra	-	-
Prime-Modi	-	-
Prime-visits	-	-
Prime-China	a number that has no factor but itself and 1; a government on the island of Taiwan established in 1949 by Chiang Kai-shek after the conquest of mainland China by the Communists led by Mao Zedong	0.0909
MinisterNarendra	-	-
Minister-Modi	-	-
Minister-visits	-	-
Minister-China	a person authorized to conduct religious worship; a government on the island of Taiwan established in 1949 by Chiang Kai-shek after the conquest of mainland China by the Communists led by Mao Zedong	0.0909
visit-Narendra	-	-
visit-Modi	-	-
visit-visit	go to see a place, as for entertainment – go to see a place, as for entertainment	1
visit-China	-	-
China-Narendra	-	-
China-Modi	-	-
China-visits	-	-
China-China	a communist nation that covers a vast territory in eastern Asia; a communist nation that covers a vast territory in eastern Asia	1

Neural Word Embeddings

The vectors that are used to represent words are called neural word embeddings. So a neural word embedding represents a word as numbers. 'Shallow' neural networks is a term used to describe neural network that usually have only one hidden layer and one output layer.

Table 2. Using path length measure between sentence 2 and 3

Words pair	Sense	Similarity Measure
Ram-Narendra	-	
Ram-Modi	-	
Ram-visits	-	
Ram-China	a tool for driving or forcing something by impact; high quality porcelain originally made only in China	0.0.1429
visit-Narendra	-	
visitr-Modi	-	
visit-visit	go to see a place, as for entertainment–go to see a place, as for entertainment	1
visit-China	-	
uncle-Narendra	-	
uncle-Modi	-	
uncle-visit	-	
uncle-China	the brother of your father or mother, the husband of your aunt; a government on the island of Taiwan established in 1949 by Chiang Kai-shek after the conquest of mainland China by the Communists led by Mao Zedong	0.1
house-Narendra	-	
house-Modi	-	
house-visits	-	
house-China	(astrology) one of 12 equal areas into which the zodiac is divided – a government on the island of Taiwan established in 1949 by Chiang Kai-shek after the conquest of mainland China by the Communists led by Mao Zedong	1.1429

Table 3. Using Wu and Palmer measure between sentence 1 and 3

Words pair	Sense	Similarity Measure
Prime-Narendra	-	
Prime-Modi	-	
Prime-visits	-	
Prime-China	a number that has no factor but itself and 1; a government on the island of Taiwan established in 1949 by Chiang Kai-shek after the conquest of mainland China by the Communists led by Mao Zedong	0.2857
MinisterNarendra	-	
Minister-Modi	-	
Minister-visits	-	
Minister-China	a person authorized to conduct religious worship; a government on the island of Taiwan established in 1949 by Chiang Kai-shek after the conquest of mainland China by the Communists led by Mao Zedong	0.4444
visit-Narendra	-	
visit-Modi	-	
visit-visit	go to see a place, as for entertainment; go to see a place, as for entertainment	1
visit-China	-	
China-Narendra	-	
China-Modi	-	
China-visits	-	
China-China	a communist nation that covers a vast territory in eastern Asia; a communist nation that covers a vast territory in eastern Asia	1

Recently Mikolov et al. (Mikolov et al., 2013) introduced Word2vec type of word-embedding method that produces embeddings of words in the corpus. This model learns a vector representation for each word using a shallow neural network model. They have proposed a neural network architecture (the skip-gram model) that consists of an input layer, an output layer and a projection layer to predict neighbor words.

Table 4. Using Wu and Palmer measure between sentence 2 and 3

Words pair	Sense	Similarity Measure
Ram-Narendra	-	
Ram-Modi	-	-
Ram-visits	-	-
Ram-China	a tool for driving or forcing something by impact; high quality porcelain originally made only in China	0.7273
visit-Narendra	-	
visit-Modi	-	-
visit-visit	go to see a place, as for entertainment; go to see a place, as for entertainment	1
visit-China	-	
uncle-Narendra	-	-
uncle-Modi	-	-
uncle-visit	-	-
uncle-China	the brother of your father or mother, the husband of your aunt; a government on the island of Taiwan established in 1949 by Chiang Kai-shek after the conquest of mainland China by the Communists led by Mao Zedong	0.4706
house-Narendra	-	-
house-Modi	-	-
house-visits	-	-
house-China	a dwelling that serves as living quarters for one or more families; dishware made of high quality porcelain	0.6

Table 5. Using Leacock and Chodorow measure between sentence 1 and 3

Words pair	Sense	Similarity Measure
Ram-Narendra	-	
Ram-Modi	-	-
Ram-visits	-	-
Ram-China	a tool for driving or forcing something by impact; high quality porcelain originally made only in China	1.743
visit-Narendra	-	
visit-Modi	-	-
visit-visit	go to see a place, as for entertainment–go to see a place, as for entertainment	3.3322
visit-China	-	
uncle-Narendra	-	-
uncle-Modi	-	-
uncle-visit	-	-
uncle-China	the brother of your father or mother, the husband of your aunt; a government on the island of Taiwan established in 1949 by Chiang Kai-shek after the conquest of mainland China by the Communists led by Mao Zedong	1.3863
house-Narendra	-	
house-Modi	-	-
house-visits	-	-
house-China	(astrology) one of 12 equal areas into which the zodiac is divided; a communist nation that covers a vast territory in eastern Asia	1.743

Word2vec takes a large corpus of text and produces a vector space which usually consists of several hundred dimensions, where each unique word in the corpus is assigned a vector in space. Word vectors are in the vector space in a way that words sharing common contexts in the corpus are located near to one another. It does so in either using context to predict a target word (a method known as continuous bag of words, or CBOW), or using a word to predict a target context, which is called skip-gram.

Table 6. Using Leacock and Chodorow measure between sentence 2 and 3

Words pair	Sense	Similarity Measure
Prime-Narendra	-	
Prime-Modi	-	
Prime-visits	-	-
Prime-China	a number that has no factor but itself and 1; a government on the island of Taiwan established in 1949 by Chiang Kai-shek after the conquest of mainland China by the Communists led by Mao Zedong	0.0909
MinisterNarendra	-	
Minister-Modi	-	
Minister-visits	-	-
Minister-China	a person authorized to conduct religious worship; a government on the island of Taiwan established in 1949 by Chiang Kai-shek after the conquest of mainland China by the Communists led by Mao Zedong	0.0909
visit-Narendra	-	
visit-Modi	-	
visit-visit	go to see a place, as for entertainment; go to see a place, as for entertainment	1
visit-China	-	
China-Narendra	-	-
China-Modi	-	-
China-visits	-	-
China-China	a communist nation that covers a vast territory in eastern Asia—a communist nation that covers a vast territory in eastern Asia	1

Table 7. Using Jiang and Conrath measure between sentence 1 and 3

Words pair	Sense	Similarity Measure
Ram-Narendra	-	
Ram-Modi	-	
Ram-visits	-	-
Ram-China	a tool for driving or forcing something by impact; high quality porcelain originally made only in China	0.105
visit-Narendra	-	
visit-Modi	-	-
visit-visit	go to see a place, as for entertainment; go to see a place, as for entertainment	1
visit-China	-	
uncle-Narendra	-	-
uncle-Modi	-	-
uncle-visit	-	-
uncle-China	the brother of your father or mother, the husband of your aunt; a communist nation that covers a vast territory in eastern Asia	1.3863
house-Narendra	-	
house-Modi	-	-
house-visits	-	-
house-China	(astrology) one of 12 equal areas into which the zodiac is divided; a communist nation that covers a vast territory in eastern Asia	1.743

Table 8. Using Jiang and Conrath measure between sentence 2 and 3

Words pair	Sense	Similarity Measure
Prime-Narendra Prime-Modi Prime-visits Prime-China	- - - the period of greatest prosperity or productivity; a communist nation that covers a vast territory in eastern Asia	- 0.0501
MinisterNarendra Minister-Modi Minister-visits Minister-China	- - - a person authorized to conduct religious worship; a communist nation that covers a vast territory in eastern Asia	- - 0.0617
visit-Narendra visit-Modi visit-visit	- - go to see a place, as for entertainment; go to see a place, as for entertainment	- 1
visit-China China-Narendra China-Modi China-visits China-China	- - - - a communist nation that covers a vast territory in eastern Asia; a communist nation that covers a vast territory in eastern Asia	- - - 1

Table 9. Using Lin measure between sentence 1 and 3

Words pair	Sense	Similarity Measure
Ram-Narendra Ram-Modi Ram-visits Ram-China	- - - a tool for driving or forcing something by impact; high quality porcelain originally made only in China	- 0.5699
visit-Narendra visit-Modi visit-visit visit-China	- - go to see a place, as for entertainment; go to see a place, as for entertainment -	- 3.3322 -
uncle-Narendra uncle-Modi uncle-visit uncle-China	- - - the brother of your father or mother, the husband of your aunt; high quality porcelain originally made only in China	- - 0.1
house-Narendra house-Modi house-visits house-China	- - - a dwelling that serves as living quarters for one or more families; a communist nation that covers a vast territory in eastern Asia	- - 1

Table 10. Using Lin measure between sentence 2 and 3

Words pair	Sense	Similarity Measure
Prime-Narendra	-	
Prime-Modi	-	
Prime-visits	-	-
Prime-China	a number that has no factor but itself and 1 a government on the island of Taiwan established in 1949 by Chiang Kai-shek after the conquest of mainland China by the Communists led by Mao Zedong	0
MinisterNarendra	-	
Minister-Modi	-	
Minister-visits	-	-
Minister-China	a person authorized to conduct religious worship; high quality porcelain originally made only in China	1.291
visit-Narendra	-	
visit-Modi	-	-
visit-visit	go to see a place, as for entertainment; go to see a place, as for entertainment	1
visit-China	-	
China-Narendra	-	
China-Modi	-	-
China-visits	-	-
China-China	a communist nation that covers a vast territory in eastern Asia; a communist nation that covers a vast territory in eastern Asia	1

Table 11. Using Resnik measure between sentence 1 and 3

Words pair	Sense	Similarity Measure
Prime-Narendra	-	
Prime-Modi	-	
Prime-visits	-	-
Prime-China	a number that has no factor but itself and 1; a government on the island of Taiwan established in 1949 by Chiang Kai-shek after the conquest of mainland China by the Communists led by Mao Zedong	0
MinisterNarendra	-	-
Minister-Modi	-	
Minister-visits	-	-
Minister-China	a person authorized to conduct religious worship; high quality porcelain originally made only in China	1.3696
visit-Narendra	-	
visit-Modi	-	
visit-visit	talk socially without exchanging too much information; talk socially without exchanging too much information	- 9.862
visit-China	-	
China-Narendra	-	-
China-Modi	-	
China-visits	-	-
China-China	government on the island of Taiwan established in 1949 by Chiang Kai-shek after the conquest of mainland China by the Communists led by Mao Zedong; government on the island of Taiwan established in 1949 by Chiang Kai-shek after the conquest of mainland China by the Communists led by Mao Zedong	

EXPERIMENTAL ANALYSIS AND DISCUSSION

Using Word2vec, we find the similarity using game of thrones dataset (Roy et al., 2014). Following steps are used here:

1. Make the imports required.
2. Download Natural Language Toolkit (NLTK) tokenizer models.
3. Prepare the corpus by combining all the books into one string.

Table 12. Using Resnik measure between sentence 2 and 3

Words pair	Sense	Similarity Measure
Ram-Narendra	-	
Ram-Modi	-	-
Ram-visits	-	-
Ram-China	a tool for driving or forcing something by impact; high quality porcelain originally made only in China	6.3104
visit-Narendra	-	
visitr-Modi	-	-
visit-visit	talk socially without exchanging too much information; talk socially without exchanging too much information	1
visit-China	-	
uncle-Narendra	-	-
uncle-Modi	-	-
uncle-visit	-	-
uncle-China	the brother of your father or mother; the husband of your aunt; a government on the island of Taiwan established in 1949 by Chiang Kai-shek after the conquest of mainland China by the Communists led by Mao Zedong	1.3863
house-Narendra	-	
house-Modi	-	-
house-visits	-	-
house-China	(astrology) one of 12 equal areas into which the zodiac is divided; a communist nation that covers a vast territory in eastern Asia	3.0088

Figure 1. Shallow neural networks

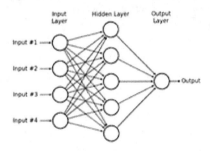

4.   Preprocess the raw data.
5.   Train the Word2vec model.
6.   Train t-SNE
7.   Find semantic similarities between characters of the book and words closest to the given word.

We use a dataset containing five books of Game of Thrones and combine the books into one single corpus:

Improved understanding of many NLP tasks. Using WordNet and its similarity measures, we can find the similarity, but it can work only for a few sentences as we have to specify the sense for each word, which is not possible for large datasets. Using word embedding helps us to solve these problems by converting the words into numerical features and finding how similar they are.

Word2Vec vocabulary length is 17277. Now we explore semantic similarities between characters of the book. Top 10 nearest words to Dragon are shown in Fig. 5

Table 13. Semantic similarity values between sentences

Measure Name	Sentences Sentences	Avg. Similarity Measure
Path Length	Prime Minister visits China & Narendra Modi visited China	0.54545
	Ram visited his uncle's house & Narendra Modi visited China	0.34645
Wu and Palmer	Prime Minister visits China & Narendra Modi visited China	0.6825
	Ram visited his uncle's house & Narendra Modi visited China	0.6994
Leacock and Chodorow	Prime Minister visits China & Narendra Modi visited China	1.7285
	Ram visited his uncle's house & Narendra Modi visited China	0.0478
Jiang and Conrath	Prime Minister visits China & Narendra Modi visited China	0.5259
	Ram visited his uncle's house & Narendra Modi visited China	0.3008
Lin	Prime Minister visits China & Narendra Modi visited China	0.8225
	Ram visited his uncle's house & Narendra Modi visited China	0.6673
Resnik	Prime Minister visits China & Narendra Modi visited China	3.0579
	Ram visited his uncle's house & Narendra Modi visited China	2.9222

Figure 2. Word2vec models

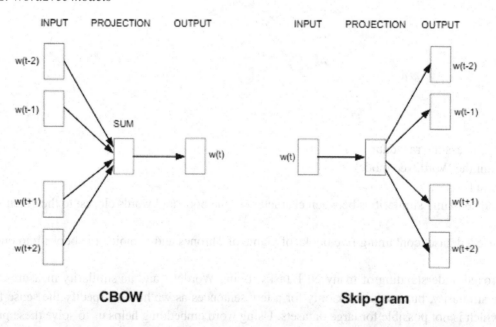

Similarly, Top 10 nearest words to Stark and Top 5 nearest words to Eddard are shown in Fig. 6 and 7. We plot the most similar words to dragons in Fig. 8. Fig. 9 shows the linear relationships between word pairs.

Figure 3. Snippet of the first few raw sentences of the corpus

```
Out[113]: ['This edition contains the complete text of the original hardcover edition.',
           'NOT ONE WORD HAS BEEN OMITTED.',
           'A CLASH OF KINGS\n\nA Bantam Spectra Book\n\nPUBLISHING HISTORY\n\nBantam Spectra hardcover edition published February 199'
           \n\nBantam Spectra paperback edition / September 2000\n\nSPECTRA and the portrayal of a boxed "s" are trademarks of Bantam B
           oks, a division of Random House, Inc.\n\nAll rights reserved.',
           'Copyright © 1999 by George R. R. Martin.',
           'Maps by James Sinclair.',
           'Heraldic crest by Virginia Norey.',
           'Library of Congress Catalog Card Number: 98-37954.',
           'No part of this book may be reproduced or transmitted in any form or by any means, electronic or mechanical, including pho
           ocopying, recording, or by any information storage and retrieval system, without permission in writing from the publisher.',
           'Visit our website at www.bantamdell.com\n\nBantam Books, the rooster colophon, Spectra and the portrayal of a boxed "s" ar
           registered trademarks of Random House Inc.\n\neISBN: 978-0-553-89785-2\n\nv3.0_r1\n\n\n\n\nCONTENTS\n\n\nCOVER\n\nTITLE PA
           E\n\nCOPYRIGHT\n\nDEDICATION\n\nMAPS\n\nPROLOGUE\n\n\n\nARYA\n\nSANSA\n\nTYRION\n\nBRAN\n\nARYA\n\nJON\n\nCATELYN\n\nTYRION\
           \nARYA\n\nDAVOS\n\nTHEON\n\nDAENERYS\n\nJON\n\nARYA\n\nTYRION\n\nBRAN\n\nTYRION\n\nSANSA\n\nARYA\n\nTYRION\n\nBRAN\n\nCATELY
           \n\nJON\n\nTHEON\n\nTYRION\n\nARYA\n\nDAENERYS\n\nBRAN\n\nTYRION\n\nARYA\n\nCATELYN\n\nSANSA\n\nCATELYN\n\nJON\n\nBRAN\n\nTY
           ION\n\nTHEON\n\nARYA\n\nCATELYN\n\nDAENERYS\n\nTYRION\n\nDAVOS\n\nJON\n\nTYRION\n\nCATELYN\n\nBRAN\n\nARYA\n\nDAENERYS\n\nTY
           ION\n\nJON\n\nSANSA\n\nJON\n\nTYRION\n\nCATELYN\n\nTHEON\n\nSANSA\n\nDAVOS\n\nTYRION\n\nSANSA\n\nTYRION\n\nSANSA\n\n
           DAENERYS\n\nARYA\n\nSANSA\n\nTHEON\n\nTYRION\n\nJON\n\nBRAN\n\nAPPENDIX\n\n\nTHE KINGS AND THEIR COURTS\n\nTHE KING ON THE IRO
           THRONE\n\nTHE KING IN THE NARROW SEA\n\nTHE KING IN HIGHGARDEN\n\nTHE KING IN THE NORTH\n\nTHE QUEEN ACROSS THE WATER\n\nOTH
```

Figure 4. Closest words to Stark

```
Out[34]: [(u'Eddard', 0.742438018321991),
          (u'Winterfell', 0.64848792552948),
          (u'Brandon', 0.6438549757003784),
          (u'Lyanna', 0.6438394784927368),
          (u'Robb', 0.6242259740829468),
          (u'executed', 0.6220564842224121),
          (u'Arryn', 0.6189971566200256),
          (u'Benjen', 0.6188897490501404),
          (u'direwolf', 0.614366352558136),
          (u'beheaded', 0.6046538352966309)]
```

Figure 5. Closest words to Eddard

```
Out[52]: [('stark', 0.7335386276245117),
          ('executed', 0.7216434478759766),
          ('beheaded', 0.7134278416633606),
          ('lyanna', 0.6927077770233154),
          ('paramount', 0.6762300729751587)]
```

Figure 6. Training the model

```
2019-04-29 12:01:46,679 : INFO : collecting all words and their counts
2019-04-29 12:01:46,683 : INFO : PROGRESS: at sentence #0, processed 0 words, keeping 0 word types
2019-04-29 12:01:46,784 : INFO : PROGRESS: at sentence #10000, processed 140984 words, keeping 10280 word types
2019-04-29 12:01:46,880 : INFO : PROGRESS: at sentence #20000, processed 279730 words, keeping 13558 word types
2019-04-29 12:01:46,971 : INFO : PROGRESS: at sentence #30000, processed 420336 words, keeping 16598 word types
2019-04-29 12:01:47,058 : INFO : PROGRESS: at sentence #40000, processed 556581 words, keeping 18324 word types
2019-04-29 12:01:47,138 : INFO : PROGRESS: at sentence #50000, processed 686247 words, keeping 19714 word types
2019-04-29 12:01:47,223 : INFO : PROGRESS: at sentence #60000, processed 828497 words, keeping 21672 word types
2019-04-29 12:01:47,315 : INFO : PROGRESS: at sentence #70000, processed 973830 words, keeping 23093 word types
2019-04-29 12:01:47,402 : INFO : PROGRESS: at sentence #80000, processed 1114967 words, keeping 24252 word types
2019-04-29 12:01:47,487 : INFO : PROGRESS: at sentence #90000, processed 1260481 words, keeping 26007 word types
2019-04-29 12:01:47,565 : INFO : PROGRESS: at sentence #100000, processed 1393203 words, keeping 26884 word types
2019-04-29 12:01:47,662 : INFO : PROGRESS: at sentence #110000, processed 1532150 words, keeping 27809 word types
2019-04-29 12:01:47,764 : INFO : PROGRESS: at sentence #120000, processed 1680961 words, keeping 28486 word types
2019-04-29 12:01:47,853 : INFO : collected 29026 word types from a corpus of 1818103 raw words and 128868 sentences
2019-04-29 12:01:47,863 : INFO : Loading a fresh vocabulary
2019-04-29 12:01:47,965 : INFO : effective_min_count=3 retains 17277 unique words (59% of original 29026, drops 11749)
2019-04-29 12:01:47,971 : INFO : effective_min_count=3 leaves 1802699 word corpus (99% of original 1818103, drops 15404)
2019-04-29 12:01:48,135 : INFO : deleting the raw counts dictionary of 29026 items
2019-04-29 12:01:48,138 : INFO : sample=0.001 downsamples 50 most-common words
2019-04-29 12:01:48,141 : INFO : downsampling leaves estimated 1404424 word corpus (77.9% of prior 1802699)
2019-04-29 12:01:48,264 : INFO : estimated required memory for 17277 words and 300 dimensions: 50103300 bytes
2019-04-29 12:01:48,270 : INFO : resetting layer weights
```

Figure 7. Closest words to Dragon

```
Out[73]:  [('headed', 0.6387238502502441),
           ('targaryen', 0.6356745958328247),
           ('dragons', 0.6164939999580383),
           ('daenerys', 0.5989516973495483),
           ('drogon', 0.5886488556861877),
           ('viserys', 0.5796190500259399),
           ('hatched', 0.574368953704834),
           ('lion', 0.5647329092025757),
           ('aegon', 0.5642436742782593),
           ('conquered', 0.5641995668411255)]
```

Figure 8. Plotting similar words to dragons

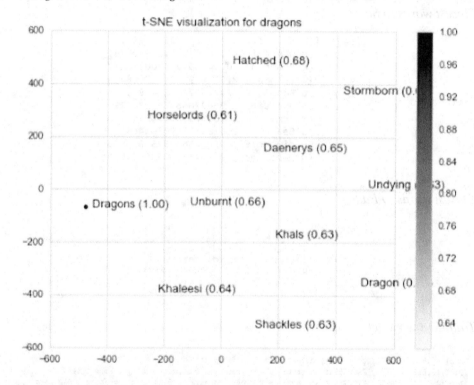

Figure 9. Linear relationships between word pairs

```
Stark is related to Winterfell, as whacking is related to Riverrun
Jaime is related to sword, as guilds is related to wine
Arya is related to Nymeria, as Dracarys is related to dragons

Out[212]:  'Dracarys'
```

CONCLUSION AND FUTURE WORK

Natural Language Processing (NLP) deals with WSD as natural languages are ambiguous. Therefore to understand a sentence properly, we have to understand each word in the sentence to capture the correct meaning portrayed by the sentence. This is also applicable to phrases, paragraphs and large articles. So, resolving WSD allows us to have an improved understanding of many NLP tasks. Using WordNet and its similarity measures, we can find the similarity, but it can work only for a few sentences as we have to specify the sense for each word, which is not possible for large datasets. Using word embedding helps us to solve these problems by converting the words into numerical features and finding how similar they are.

REFERENCES

Jiang, J. J., & Conrath, D. W. (1997). *Semantic similarity based on corpus statistics and lexical taxonomy.* arXiv preprint cmp-lg/9709008.

Leacock, C., & Chodorow, M. (1998). Combining local context and WordNet similarity for word sense identification. *WordNet: An Electronic Lexical Database, 49*(2), 265-283.

Li, Y., Bandar, Z. A., & McLean, D. (2003). An approach for measuring semantic similarity between words using multiple information sources. *IEEE Transactions on Knowledge and Data Engineering, 15*(4), 871–882.

Martin, J. H. (2009). *Speech and language processing: An introduction to natural language processing, computational linguistics, and speech recognition.* Pearson/Prentice Hall.

Mikolov, T., Chen, K., Corrado, G., & Dean, J. (2013). *Efficient estimation of word representations in vector space.* arXiv preprint arXiv:1301.3781.

Pedersen, T., Patwardhan, S., & Michelizzi, J. (2004, July). WordNet: Similarity-Measuring the Relatedness of Concepts. In AAAI (Vol. 4, pp. 25-29). AAAI.

Rada, R., Mili, H., Bicknell, E., & Blettner, M. (1989). Development and application of a metric on semantic nets. *IEEE Transactions on Systems, Man, and Cybernetics, 19*(1), 17–30.

Resnik, P. (1995). *Using information content to evaluate semantic similarity in a taxonomy.* arXiv preprint cmp-lg/9511007.

Roy, A., Guinaudeau, C., Bredin, H., & Barras, C. (2014, May). Tvd: a reproducible and multiply aligned tv series dataset. LREC 2014.

Wu, Z., & Palmer, M. (1994). Verbs semantics and lexical selection. *Proceedings of the 32nd annual meeting on Association for Computational Linguistics–Association for Computational Linguistics.*

Chapter 2
Carpooling Solutions Using Machine Learning Tools

Sabyasachi Pramanik
ⓘ https://orcid.org/0000-0002-9431-8751
Haldia Institute of Technology, India

ABSTRACT

If there isn't enough parking within a university's campus, it will take a long time to look for parking. If a university has a number of research stations that are geographically apart from one another, communication occurs between them and the main office using office cars, although occasionally leased vehicles are obtained from a travel agency. The cost of transportation will rise as a result. Similarly, all students who are not from the dormitory are day scholars who come from their homes. Every day they must drive a significant distance to go to the institution in rented automobiles. This chapter deals with the performance solutions in carpooling using machine learning techniques.

INTRODUCTION

India boasts the world's second-largest geographical area as well as the world's second-largest road network. By 2025, the country's road network will have covered about 5.89 million kilometres. 90% of India's total passenger traffic utilises the road network for communication (Samanta, D. et. al., 2021; Anand, R. et. al., 2022) and transportation. At the same time, the world's vehicle population is more than 0.66 kilometres per square kilometre.

Carpooling (Ma, N., et. al. 2021) is when a group of people wish to use their automobile to go from one home to another, not only to save money but also to preserve the environment from pollution by using less gasoline, and it also provides them joy while travelling. The carpooling services supplied via the website will operate as a barrier between various unknown persons who wish to travel in a shared manner and will only need calculating tips when collectively displacements from their source to each other's destination are required. Carpooling has been shown to be a socially acceptable and environmentally beneficial method of sharing travel travels. It aids in the reduction of carbon dioxide (CO_2) emissions, the reduction of traffic congestion, and the resolution of different parking space concerns,

DOI: 10.4018/978-1-7998-9795-8.ch002

giving us the ability to promote carpooling during times of rising fuel costs and high pollution levels. Because of the fast expansion in transportation, providing common transportation services has become more difficult. Carpooling also helps to save transportation costs such as gasoline, maintenance, toll fees, and the hardship of driving by allowing ordinary people to use one vehicle for communication.

LITERATURE REVIEW

IoT makes use of various devices that are capable of talking and exchanging information among themselves, since this concept allows them to be used in both active and passive configurations. The basic goal of IoT (Liu, S., et. al., 2021) is to create clever intelligent settings or places where objects such as smart cities (Kaushik, D., et. al. 2021), smart homes and smart transportation (Stiles, J., et. al., 2021) are self-aware for unique and inventive applications. In the Internet of Things, each item and entity (thing) is given a unique identification that allows them to receive or send data mechanically from or to a network. Radio-Frequency Identification (RFID (Shaohao, X., et. l al. 2020) sensors (Wei, H. et. al. 2021), actuators (Zenkour, A. M., et. al. 2021), detectors (Gonzo, R.. 2021), and other IoT gadgets are examples. Much of the Internet of Things (IoT) consists of various intelligent computer devices and associated sensor systems that are primarily utilised in vehicle-to-vehicle (V2V) and machine-to-machine (M2M) communication, as well as wearable computing devices for various reasons. The Internet of Things (IoT) is steadily expanding its application sectors in several domains of technology, securing its position in the sphere of transportation and traffic management as well. The main issue in the present situation is the rise in the number of passenger vehicles (i.e. automobiles), which is directly proportional to population growth. As a consequence, substantial issues such as extreme traffic congestion (Moyano, A. et. al. 2021), accidents, noise, and travel time lag have arisen. Car sharing is an improvised means of transportation that allows numerous people to share the trip of a single car regardless of their origin. The major goal is to minimise the overall number of vehicles on the road at any one time while also lowering the cost of travel for each rider. Car sharing is, in reality, the most frequent general paratransit method, in which passengers from various user groups to share a vehicle that follows their pre-determined itinerary. Car sharing facilitates ride sharing using passenger automobiles; it is based on the concept of sharing a single passenger vehicle with others, with the vehicle's owner being a third party (subject to business). As a consequence, most urban users or passengers have the opportunity to travel in a shared vehicle without owning one, and they may do so after acquiring a standardised key card from one of the expressly named approved stations and paying a predetermined wage or reimbursement cost. In comparison to the existing scenario, the IoT notion provides a horizon for automobile sharing. The main objective of the Internet of Things is to provide connection for everyone to everything, 24 hours a day, 7 days a week, and from any location, which is critical for the car-sharing system.

FOCUS OF THE ARTICLE

Congestion caused by automotive traffic is one of the primary challenges in our daily lives in most of our cities and towns. As a result, the quality of life suffers, with negative consequences in the areas of economics (Baker, H. K. et. al. 2021), social welfare, and the environment (Pradhan, D. et. al., 2022). As a result, it will need a lot of work and dedication to study and establish imaginative and determined transportation modes in metropolitan areas in order to achieve a car-free lifestyle, which is one of the primary reasons of traffic congestion in cities. It is now difficult for us to imagine a totally sustainable transportation strategy that will meet our demands. As a result, major cities throughout the globe are confronted with issues such as reducing greenhouse gas emissions and air pollution caused by car traffic congestion. As a result, combining several modes of transportation (also known as combination transport or multimodal transport) is still a big demand in metropolitan areas. To assess the social, environmental, and climate change implications, we must examine the transportation vehicles utilised, as well as the vehicle's energy sources and the infrastructure necessary for transportation implementation. Public transportation infrastructure is one of the greatest ways to deal with and control traffic congestion caused by vehicles, although it has several drawbacks: It is exceedingly expensive to include a technological item like as software, hardware, or mechanical components in the framework of a city's public transportation system. In most cases, public transportation follows a defined geographic itinerary and follows a set schedule. It shows that there isn't a lot of room for change in a particular area of the public transportation system. As a result, many individuals choose to drive their own vehicle or use other private transportation methods over public transit.

In recent years, the outcomes of carpooling have gained enormous notoriety or recognition in the field of sustainable transportation. Carpooling (also known as ridesharing) is nothing more than the sharing of automobile travels in which numerous people, i.e. passengers, may travel in a personal vehicle along the same route. As a result, it combines the convenience of owning a vehicle with the cost-effectiveness of public transit. Two ways are often employed in a vehicle travel in order to utilise it for sharing reasons, among other things:

1.   In the first method, many persons (passengers) who wish to travel the same route may share a seat in their own automobile by swapping drivers.
2.   When a driver wants to assign an unused seat in his or her own vehicle among potential passengers, the seats are merged for payment towards fuel expenditures, with the driver's expenses being returned at the end.

In contrast to the above two techniques, the first one is widely utilised amongst users who wish to travel on the same route with the same source and destination and on the same timetable, and in the following instant, all participants continue to make arrangements regarding the shared ride's details. However, the second technique informs the traveller of a route that is suited for the infrequent traveller. The utilisation of carpooling services has a wide variety of beneficial effects. These are the following:

1.   It essentially means lowering the cost of travel for the driver.
2.   For the rider, it essentially means more adaptability at a lower cost, making it an excellent alternative for public transit.
3.   In terms of the environment, it is primarily intended to reduce air pollution by reducing the number of vehicles used in transportation.
4.   For cities, it is primarily intended to alleviate traffic congestion and the requirement for car parking space.
5.   The shared cost of the journey should be accurately apportioned between the participating driver (who shares his or her own automobile) and the passengers, lowering the overall trip cost for each

of them. It also implies that the driver would not only be able to earn money, but will also be able to recoup his expenditures.

Carpooling services have acted as a bootstrap for our transportation system in recent years, and this has only been possible thanks to the inclusion of web-based platforms that allow passengers and drivers to interact and make necessary arrangements for a shared ride, including the arrangement of a trip schedule with their path on or before the trip. Carpooling services are now accessible as smart phone and tablet apps for hand-held contemporary mobile devices, which are becoming more popular in our culture. Because people are used to accessing the internet using these devices, there are no concerns with using them to access carpooling services. The availability of these devices is solely dependent on the availability and utilisation of a high-quality remote sensor that can deliver context-based information at any time and in any location. A mobile network method is required for a smart phone-based carpooling application to connect and communicate with passengers and drivers who are interested in travelling along comparable routes. The basic principle of this network is that each ride request or offer information must reach a large number of network members who are planning to travel, i.e. the chances of finding a travel companion should be high. As a result, special appreciations are extended to the network's information supplier. Users may also deny the information if they don't want to share their own automobile with individuals who aren't interested in their interests. This sort of problematic scenario in carpooling services causes roadblocks for the global expansion of these businesses (Pramanik, S., et. al., 2020). As a result, the majority of current carpooling systems do not perform as well as expected and must be improved.

Key Aspects of Carpooling

The comparison and matching of requests for rides with offers is only based on temporal and spatial parameters in this case. Knowing the specifics of the categorisation of the temporal and positional aspects of carpooling is critical. In this case, the categorization may be summarised as follows:

1. The term "identical ridesharing" refers to when the rider's source pickup and destination drop-off locations are identical to the driver's source and destination locations.
2. Just when the source pickup and destination drop-off locations are on the driver's real route is inclusive ridesharing considered to occur, however here share trips cover only a portion of the driver's actual journey.
3. When the source pick-up and destination drop-off locations are on the driver's original route, but they do not correspond with the rider's source and destination locations, it is said to be partial ridesharing.
4. Detour ridesharing is defined as when a driver must make a choice to divert their route in order to get at the rider's source location for pickup.

The departure time specified by the drivers as well as the passengers, which most of the time fluctuates, is the real temporal factor that causes irregularities in the whole carpooling process. Since a result, it is crucial to match users based on this attribute, as it is critical in determining the real rider prior to the commencement of a ride. Here, a match is created between the rider's requests and the offers offered by the car-pooler service provider, which is only based on the geographical distance between the rider's route, which determines the pick-up and drop-off times. Another important temporal feature is the flexibility in pick-up timings, which indicates how much time the riders are willing to wait at the time of pick-up and which should be acceptable to everybody without interfering with the rider's trip. It is incredibly simple to plan and discover pick-up and drop-off times for similar ride sharing with little effort and time. However, for other ridesharing services, determining the meeting times via which the car-pooler determines the estimated time of arrival at the pick-up place is quite difficult. Another important temporary factor to consider when calculating the rider-driver matching time is the previous calculation of journey length, which should be determined only on a temporal basis.

Solutions for Stationary Conditions

To use carpooling applications, the intended users must first create a new account by filling out the required information, and then provide their own riding requirements, such as desired source and destination pick up and drop off locations, desired pickup time, and optionally and required time flexibility as per their needs during their trip. Carpooling apps are often run on third-party social networks or via their own websites or apps in order to boost user trust and trustworthiness and enable people to participate in social activities with their senses. In certain carpooling apps, a rating system is employed, which allows users to provide comments on each other at the conclusion of each journey in order to improve carpooling services in a more positive and healthy way for all car-poolers. When carpooling, the trip expenditures may be paid in cash or by automatic payment over the internet once they have shared the costs among themselves. Riders may compensate drivers before or after their journey depending on the distance they travelled in a shared vehicle using this approach.

Carpooling Apps that aren't Mobile

The most frequently recognised ridesharing execution in the present environment is completely based on a "static" approach. Car-poolers submit their requests and offers in this network, which is valid for many hours for future transportation needs, and all criteria should be addressed before the start of journeys. In most cases, while approaching static carpooling, the different possibilities of unanticipated changes in date, time, or other aspects of the shared journey are not considered. The carpooling system in this approach is typically based on the matching of lists that are generally based on the common source and destination matching, where the riders and drivers are expected to communicate regularly in order to make proper arrangements for upcoming trips and then to reach an agreement for the same. The agreement between them should contain the specifications necessary for the rider's pickup and drop off locations, as well as their required meeting time, as well as the real price incurred for riding, as well as the possibility of carrying baggage in it. In most cases, the static carpooling technique produces better results for long-distance trips planned ahead of time, but it does not perform well in metropolitan locations where consumers want additional services and amenities. BlaBlaCar (Wagih, M. et. al. 2021) is now the most frequent and well-known case study of a static carpooling service in Europe.

BlaBlaCar: A Case Study

This section provides comprehensive illumination for a static method to carpooling by detailing the procedure in depth using BlaBlaCar. For resident users, a software provider offers this static ridesharing programme through Internet-enabled mobile phones as well as desktop web browsers. At the time of writing the thesis, this static carpooling process was the world's largest long-distance ridesharing community, with over 60 million members from 22 countries across four continents. BlaBlaCar connects drivers who want to drive and passengers who really want to travel with them. These customers usually wish to organise shared transportation between two cities or within a city, and split the expense of the travel. The targeted users must first register on the desired website and then establish their own profile, which may include information such as the user's personal hobbies, profile responsibilities, community network profile, as well as rating and reviewing. All of its services are available to customers through mobile phones, websites, and its own applications for Android and iOS platforms. BlaBlaCar, like other static ridesharing platforms, needs an agreement to be made for scheduled long-distance travel, where the drivers desire to fill up the empty seats with passengers for extended excursions. Offers may be made to the rider in this service, just as they can to the driver or passenger. The programme enables users to specify source and destination locations by entering or choosing from a list of pre-defined locales. It necessitates the usage of a GPS-enabled mobile phone, via which the user may establish their current position prior to the commencement of the voyage and optionally add one or more waypoints. The driver's and rider's route information are then matched to see who has a similar source, destination, or waypoint. These programmes enable the user to set the desired departure time at the source location, as well as the needed payback amount. The user may then choose his travel companion from a matching list based on their choices, such as source, destination, and timings, as well as the driver's payback amount. When everyone agrees to a shared trip, the driver will pick up the passenger at the agreed-upon time and location. The overall cost of the voyage is shared among the participants, who are responsible for making their own payment by phone or PayPal.

One of the key drawbacks of this strategy is that it does not allow for temporary trip management, and the characteristics are as follows:

1. Initially, users are compared based on their source and destination pairs, or waypoints. As a result, the same ridesharing mode is available here.
2. If feasible, a shared transport may be scheduled in advance, from a few hours to a few days.
3. During the journey, the driver is unable to pick up any riders that cross their route. It's only conceivable if their journeys are perfectly matched, that is, if they have similar stopovers.

Ridesharing in a Dynamic Mode

In comparison to static carpooling, dynamic ridesharing is regarded to be a new sort of carpooling since it is more desirable in metropolitan areas. In this ridesharing system, the rideshare provider used an automated approach to make matches between drivers and passengers in a short period of time. The timing begins here within a very short time gap, ranging from a few minutes to many hours before the actual departure time from the source side. It is the most recent and advanced sort of ridesharing technique, which is being used by a large number of individuals. It definitely outperforms the standard static ridesharing model in a number of ways.

1. Information and communication technology are crucial aspects that play a significant and sensitive role in allowing dynamic ridesharing from a technological standpoint.
2. Ridesharing apps that are always changing

3. When we think about its implementation, we need a lot of new technology to exploit the numerous services given by dynamic ridesharing. The following are some of the most widely utilised technologies:

    a. Both passengers and drivers utilise mobile devices (smart phones) to interact with and access numerous services, as well as to organise everything for a shared trip when it is in portable mode.

    b. A GPS gadget (often found within a smart phone) is used to monitor the driver's movement in order to determine the whereabouts of passengers.

    c. The usage of social media is being used to raise the level of honesty between the driver and the passenger.

Constant Network Connection necessitates that all shared ride arrangements be completed in a timely manner, which may need that the user's mobile device be connected to the Internet 24 hours a day, seven days a week. Many global telecommunication firms now offer such services with continuous mobile connection without fail. The aforementioned current technologies are crucial enablers for the smooth operation of Dynamic Ridesharing. Projects for ridesharing have been launched in the past, but the primary challenge at the time was a lack of such communication tools. All of the aforementioned elements are managed by a reliable network service that can instantly connect a rider with a driver to begin a journey and also assist with the payment process by using suitable optimization algorithms (Pramanik, S. et. al. 2020; Pramanik, S. et. al. 2014). As a result, the following key characteristics of Dynamic Ridesharing have been identified:

1. All of the arrangements for a shared transport may be made on short notice, making it dynamic.
2. Independent drivers, who are not affiliated with any organisation, may participate in this dynamic ridesharing.
3. The motto of dynamic ridesharing is cost-sharing, which results to cost reductions via cost-sharing among both drivers and passengers.
4. At the end of the day, the fundamental goal of Dynamic Ridesharing is non-recurring journeys. Traditionally, carpooling necessitates starting the shared rides work many hours in advance, and the nature of the journeys is essentially repeating, i.e. repeated trips (such as daily travel to workplace with the help of colleagues). It is better suited for on-demand, continuous, planned share rides that may be scheduled in advance in a matter of minutes or hours.
5. The pre-planned sort of shared trip is organised between drivers and passengers entirely in advance, without the need to go to a specific destination.
6. Automated matching automates the whole process without requiring much additional labour, and it does so in a relatively short period of time with little work on the part of the participants. The process of finding a good partner for the journey is not done manually here; rather, the system will match the riders and drivers automatically, allowing them to communicate.

Lyft as an Example

Lyft began in the United States as a Dynamic Ridesharing Organization system based in San Francisco, founded by Logan Green and John Zimmer in 2012. This on-demand ridesharing network system was launched with the goal of making Zimride services more accessible to those looking for shorter journeys within or between cities. Lyft is now utilised in a larger number of cities, such as San Francisco, Texas, Los Angeles, New Jersey, and New York City, among others. Users must download the Lyft programme from the store for their Android and iOS devices in order to utilise it and its services. After that, customers may join up and provide their own cell phone number for communication, as well as choose the best payment option for each journey. When a user wishes to utilise Lyft to take a journey, the driver must first search for a nearby location using an interactive map. When the shared ride arrangement is complete, the passenger may speak with the chosen driver to confirm the accuracy of their information, such as their name, rating, profile photo, and vehicle type. When the journey begins, the riders are picked up from their current position by the designated driver. The overall cost of the shared transport is divided among the tour participants, who then pay using their smart phones and PayPal. The Lyft service's ideology aims to instil trust in its consumers. Riders are obliged to offer their own evaluations to the driver when the journey is over, and only the highest-rated drivers are allowed to spare their seats for further trips. All participants in this procedure must go through a screening process that includes a check of their criminal history, car standards, and drug and alcohol addiction, among other things. One of the system's potential downsides is that riders are picked up from their current position by the drivers. As a result, the proper matching algorithm cannot use partial ridesharing mode. Because the drivers may only pick up the passengers who are closest to them or within a specific distance, the driver's real path is not taken into account for assessment and matching.

Carpooling's Social Benefits

1. The current carpooling system offers a variety of socioeconomic advantages, including:
2. By sharing, the number of miles driven by the vehicle is reduced.
3. Fuel consumption is reduced, as is the quantity of greenhouse gas (GHG) emissions released into the environment.
4. Reduced detrimental effects of air pollution on a variety of societal population categories such as low-income, low-cost and other verified environmental populations.
5. Employers and government organisations both need to save costs.

Vehicle Miles Travelled (VMT)

It is a travel measure that indicates the total number of kilometres travelled by each transportation vehicle in carpooling. According to a research conducted by the Federal Highway Administration (FHA) in the 1970s, the energy crisis was alleviated by 23% in terms of Vehicle Miles Travelled (VMT). Employee Based Trip Reduction and Transportation Demand Management programmes, both of which are capable of performance monitoring and evaluation, are the best practises for supporting VMT reduction targets. Only a few hand count empirical research may be used to investigate the effect of VMT regulations. Workers that engage in a programme had lower VMT, ranging from 4.2 percent to 4.8 percent, than employees who work at the same location and are not required to participate in the programme, according to one research. When Washington State's Commute Trip Reduction Law was introduced, and a research was conducted on it, it was discovered that it had comparable impacts on VMT. It is also discovered that, as a result of this rule, the average VMT decrease per employee at work locations is 6%. According to some estimations, such initiatives may reduce VMT by 4 to 6 percent for office driving (approx. 1 percent in regionally). VMT reduction estimates for a whole region or a metropolitan area are based on precisely two researches. The essential data is obtained directly from businesses for the research in order to calculate the list of commute trips eliminated as per Washington State's Commute Trip Reduction (CTR) programme. According to this research, overall VMT in the four core counties of metropolitan Seattle has decreased by 1.33 percent for all routes and 1.07 percent for all freeways. Because the author of the research considers all sorts of journeys during the morning peak hour, including commute travel to non-participating sites as well as non-commute visits, it indicates a lower effect than prior studies. The Commute Trip Reduction Task Force conducted an individual analytical study for multiple years in 2005 and predicted a 1.6 percent reduction in overall VMT based on the same data set. People are exhibiting interest in carpooling as a result of the decrease in their journey time and expense, according to the preceding findings. This is a significant aspect that has a greater influence on the net VMT of this sort of communication mechanism.

Fuel Consumption is Reduced

In a year, the average fuel consumption of passenger automobile and sports-related vehicles is almost equivalent to 550 and 915 gallons, respectively. According to a research aimed at improving carpooling rules, the most efficient technique is to minimise energy use rather than fully restricting driving. Another research was conducted in the United States of America to determine the possibility of reducing annual gasoline consumption from 0.80 percent to 0.82 percent billion gallons by adding merely one more passenger to each 100 automobiles. According to a recent research, adding one additional passenger to every ten automobiles might result in an annual fuel savings of 7.54 to 7.74 billion gallons. According to another research, carpooling may save 33 million gallons of gasoline per day if a third passenger is added to an average communicative vehicle. Carpooling has a notable regional impact in terms of fuel savings, which may be plainly seen. A research was conducted in the San Francisco Bay Area, where gasoline consumption was reduced from 4, 50,000 to 9, 00,000 gallons per year. It is related to a drop in regular traffic as a result of the reduction in carpooling congestion.

Emissions of Greenhouse Gases (GHGs) are Reduced

Many researchers have undertaken with the goal of reducing greenhouse gas emissions in carpooling systems by reducing the amount of gasoline used. When a rider joins the employer trip reduction programme, a simulation model was provided for predicting about each car-pooler rider to cut personal travel GHG emissions from 4% to 5%. According to a research conducted in the United States, adding one passenger to every 100 vehicles would result in an annual reduction of 7.2 million tonnes of GHG emissions. According to this analysis, adding one passenger to every ten vehicles would result in an annual reduction of 68 million tonnes of GHG emissions. Another research, according to the SMART 2020 report, estimates that if we employ information and communication technology (ICT) for carpooling, such as app-based carpooling, CO_2 emissions may be reduced by 70 to 190 million tonnes per year.

Savings for Government Agencies and Employers

The most cost-effective strategy for carpooling is to improve infrastructure capacity and person throughput in order to alleviate traffic congestion and reduce the need for additional roadway and public transportation capacity. In the City of Seattle, an Ordinance for a Commute Trip Reduction was passed in 2017, contributing to an 11 percent reduction in single-occupant vehicle trips. Another study was conducted on casual carpooling, and the potential capacity of such carpooling was identified as reducing energy consumption for approximately 150 commuters by providing them with a standard express bus service while also lowering the cost.

Financial and Tax Benefits

Carpooling provides a variety of tax and financial advantages to those who participate in it, including businesses and workers. According to the 132(f) provision of the Internal Revenue Code of the United States of America, companies may give tax-free parking, vanpool service, public transportation, and cycling expenditure to their employees. The monthly parking lot, vanpool service, and public transportation benefit maximum is now $260 US Dollars per month, which is subject to annual cost of living increases. Previously, companies paid such perks, but now such commuting expenditures might be removed from the employee's subsidy part by the company. According to the US Levy Cut and Jobs Act of 2017, the government's tax on such activities was repealed. However, the employer may still support these costs, since there is no means to withhold the subsidised share of the commuter's costs. Employees ultimately gain from tax and financial incentives to encourage carpooling.

Trends and Innovations

People's lifestyles are fast changing these days, thus a variety of variables are influencing how they travel and carpool. Some of these critical elements are linked to specific sectors such as technical, mobility, social, and demographic changes.

1. Technological Developments
2. Due to the introduction of many new tools and technologies, i.e. technical trends, carpooling has become increasingly popular in the contemporary day.
3. Cloud computing, geographical area-based navigation systems with associated services, and current mobile phone-based communication technology with associated computer capabilities are some of the most recent technical trends.
4. Growth in data availability, compilation, dissemination, accumulation, and re-broadcasting by cloud source public and private sectors is enabled through public-private partnerships, APIs, and supplemental tools.
5. Carpool passenger services are more convenient when they enable app-based and on-demand transportation choices.

Trends in Mobility

Due to a rise in travel demand and well-managed urban congestion, as well as a decrease in financing for transportation facilities and the urgent need to expand current infrastructure facilities the demand for dispersed and improved occupancy options such as micro-transit, app-based carpooling, and many more is increasing. As a result of customer demand, the number of on-demand transportation options has increased.

Social Developments

There is an increase in the environmental awareness around carbon emissions. Consider a huge region as an economic hub and draw transportation lines around it. As one goes toward urbanisation, one will come to rely on private automobiles. With the aid of mobile internet, there is a growing demand in receiving rapid results and services.

Trends in Demography

People wish to labour for extended periods of time without regard for the distance travelled as a result of population growth and changing lifestyles. When a person's impairment in society grows, they will desire to work to support themselves. As the number of the family grows, they will wish to communicate via their own private transportation cars. People in society desire to work after they retire from their jobs not just to keep themselves engaged (fit) but also to generate money.

Benefits of Carpooling

1. It reduces travel costs and the likelihood of obtaining a personal vehicle for the purpose. A lone traveller may receive some additional company and the fuel price can be divided by taking a shared journey.
2. It cuts down on the journey time. Because shared journeys are quicker on highways, and if there are more than one passenger in the vehicle, the automobile will only go in the lanes with the least amount of traffic. It not only allows one to choose the best route for one's needs, but it also allows one to travel on a budget.

Strategies for Carpooling

Carpooling, often known as car-sharing, is a cost-effective way to save money while simultaneously lowering pollution. It is well-known and widely used in advanced European nations such as the United States, France, Germany, Italy, and Spain. In India, we should put in place various methods to encourage carpooling. To embrace carpooling, the following methods are necessary.

1. It is necessary to legislate for carpooling in order to ensure the legal status of the process in order to protect the interests of car-poolers and their legal rights.
2. By creating a specific carpooling organisation to lead carpooling disinformation, association, and service activities, the government may provide the groundwork for the process. It encourages public carpooling institutions to aid in the growth of carpooling.
3. Initiate and execute a carpooling incentive campaign to increase the percentage of people that carpool on a daily basis.
4. Begin a carpooling pilot study to determine the program's effect and utility.
5. Carpooling process management is dependent on well-managed operations such as determining an accurate pickup time for a specific route after considering all factors.

Carpooling Power Tools

Scala, the programming language used to construct the most popular carpooling system is regarded as the most crucial tool. To create concurrent applications, the same tools, namely Akka, are utilised. Another toolkit, OscarR, is used to handle Operations Research issues, and its most notable features are a constraint programming solver and visualisation capabilities. Finally, the time of the travels between two places was calculated using Google Maps and the MapQuest API.

Scala

Scala (Norwicki, M. et. al. 2021) is derived from the term scalable. This is a general-purpose high-level programming language that was created on the apex of the Java virtual machine platform to support object-oriented programming. It includes functional programming elements and is fully compatible with Java. The most common java features are included, as well as a variety of features from other languages. Scala has a number of extra features, including:

1. The lambda function is a type of function.
2. Type of auto detection
3. Making of lists
4. Calculation that isn't done quickly
5. Matching patterns
6. Classes on a regular basis
7. System with a single root
8. Arguments that are optional
9. Arguments with names
10. Using Scala, it is feasible to write typical programming patterns in a short amount of time. Martin Odersky conceived and developed it in 2004.

Akka

It's written in the Scala programming language. Akka is a free and open source runtime library or toolkit for the JVM that provides a variety of tools for creating powerful reactive, concurrent, message-driven, and distributed applications. The actor is the Akka component that not only runs in distinct threads but also has the potential to execute on many machines. As a result, it employs a variety of Actor-Based Models. These may be used to get Google Maps and MapQuest online APIs (Sharon, T. 2021). Because the request messages are queued and correctly handled by Akka, a group of engineers may contact the distant servers at the same time with less effort.

OscaR

"Scala in OR" is what OscaR stands for. It's a Scala toolkit or package designed specifically for using on the JVM to solve operational research problems. It has a thriving developer community that is working on open source projects. OscaR offers the ability to combine several packages using the following techniques:

1. Constraints Programming (CP)
2. Local Search with Restrictions (CBLS)
3. Linear Programming (LP)
4. Discrete Event Simulation (DES)
5. Optimization without Derivatives
6. Visualization

For the carpooling solution, a constraint programming solver is employed, as well as a visualisation tool: Map Quest and Google Maps. The primary goal of combining Google Maps (Lavorgna, L. 2022) and Map Quest is to create a web API that allows for simple calculation in order to estimate the real time necessary while travelling by automobile from one location to another. It may also be computed locally using the most appropriate geographical data, however it is more readily done utilising various online services, requiring less time and effort. API eliminates the hassle and stress of keeping up with the newest data on roadwork and other traffic-related information.

The following are two essential aspects that are the focus of my study for the above-mentioned issues:

Time: There are several modes of transportation available (Buses, Peer-to-Peer ride-sharing, private transportation). Buses and other public transportation vehicles have set departure and return times. Each time, it navigates a large number of students and staff members. For example, if students and employees finish their job, they will be unable to return home immediately since the bus is running according to their previous timetable. As a result, everyone must wait till the bus does not come.

Cost: Private transportation is too costly for both employees and students. Their travel costs are set within a range, i.e. within a monthly limit; nevertheless, the distance between riders fluctuates. Furthermore, there is a lack of information on the vehicle's owner. Female passengers will not be safe in this car since it lacks a security (Bandyopadhyay, S. et. al. 2021; Bansal, R. et. al. 2021; Pramanik, S. and Raja, S. S., 2020) design. Some drivers of vehicles adjust the car seats to accommodate a large number of students. Combining car owners with female pupils or workers has no purpose or applicability.

CONCLUSION

The main motivation for writing this chapter is from some of the problems we face on a daily basis, such as traffic congestion, parking shortages, fuel waste, and pollution. It will take a long time to hunt for parking on a university's campus if there isn't enough. Employees will have to drive a considerable way to get to the building if parking is accessible outside, which will take longer. The same problem will develop for residential reasons. If a university has a number of research stations that are geographically apart from one another, communication takes place between them and the main office using office automobiles, however leased vehicles from a travel agency are sometimes purchased. As a consequence, transportation costs will climb. Similarly, all day scholars who do not live in the dormitory and arrive from their homes are designated day scholars. Every day, students must travel a long distance in hired cars to go to the facility. The solutions in carpooling utilising machine learning (Dutta, S. et. al. 2021) methods are discussed in this chapter.

REFERENCES

Anand, R., Singh, J., Pandey, D., Pandey, B. K., Nassa, V. K., & Pramanik, S. (2022). Modern Technique for Interactive Communication in LEACH-Based Ad Hoc Wireless Sensor Network. In M. M. Ghonge, S. Pramanik, & A. D. Potgantwar (Eds.), *Software Defined Networking for Ad Hoc Networks*. Springer. doi:10.1007/978-3-030-91149-2_3

Baker, H. K., Kumar, S., & Pandey, N. (2021). Thirty years of *Small Business Economics*: A bibliometric overview. *Small Business Economics*, *56*(1), 487–517. doi:10.100711187-020-00342-y

Bandyopadhyay, S., Goyal, V., Dutta, S., Pramanik, S., & Sherazi, H. H. R. (2021). Unseen to Seen by Digital Steganography. In S. Pramanik, M. M. Ghonge, R. Ravi, & K. Cengiz (Eds.), *Multidisciplinary Approach to Modern Digital Steganography*. IGI Global. doi:10.4018/978-1-7998-7160-6.ch001

Bansal, R., Jenipher, B., Nisha, V., Makhan, R., Pramanik, S., Roy, S., & Gupta, A. (2022). Big Data Architecture for Network Security. In Cyber Security and Network Security. Wiley. doi:10.1002/9781119812555.ch11

Dutta, S., Pramanik, S., & Bandyopadhyay, S. K. (2021). Prediction of Weight Gain during COVID-19 for Avoiding Complication in Health. *International Journal of Medical Science and Current Research*, *4*(3), 1042–1052.

Gonzo, R., & Pokraka, A. (2021). Light-ray operators, detectors and gravitational event shapes. *J. High Energ. Phys.*, *15*. doi:10.1007/JHEP05(2021)015

Kaushik, D., Garg, M., Annu, Gupta, A., & Pramanik, S. (2021). Application of Machine Learning and Deep Learning in Cyber security: An Innovative Approach. InGhonge, M., Pramanik, S., Mangrulkar, R., & Le, D. N. (Eds.), *Cybersecurity and Digital Forensics: Challenges and Future Trends*. Wiley.

Lavorgna, L., Iaffaldano, P., Abbadessa, G., Lanzillo, R., Esposito, S., Ippolito, D., Sparaco, M., Cepparulo, S., Lus, G., Viterbo, R., Clerico, M., Trojsi, F., Ragonese, P., Borriello, G., Signoriello, E., Palladino, R., Moccia, M., Brigo, F., Troiano, M., ... Bonavita, S. (2022). Disability assessment using Google Maps. *Neurological Sciences*, *43*(2), 1007–1014. doi:10.100710072-021-05389-7 PMID:34142263

Liu, S., Liu, X., Wang, S., & Muhammad, K. (2021). Fuzzy-aided solution for out-of-view challenge in visual tracking under IoT-assisted complex environment. *Neural Computing & Applications*, *33*(4), 1055–1065. doi:10.100700521-020-05021-3

Ma, N., Zeng, Z., Wang, Y., & Xu, J. (2021). Balanced strategy based on environment and user benefit-oriented carpooling service mode for commuting trips. *Transportation*, *48*(3), 1241–1266. doi:10.100711116-020-10093-0

Nowicki, M., Górski, Ł., & Bała, P. (2021). PCJ Java library as a solution to integrate HPC, Big Data and Artificial Intelligence workloads. *Journal of Big Data*, *8*(1), 62. doi:10.118640537-021-00454-6

Pramanik, S., & Bandyopadhyay, S. K. (2014). Image Steganography Using Wavelet Transform and Genetic /Algorithm. *International Journal of Innovative Research in Advanced Engineering*, *1*, 1–4.

Pramanik, S., Ghosh, R., Ghonge, M., Narayan, V., Sinha, M., Pandey, D., & Samanta, D. (2020). A Novel Approach using Steganography and Cryptography in Business Intelligence. In A. Azevedo & M. F. Santos (Eds.), *Integration Challenges for Analytics, Business Intelligence and Data Mining* (pp. 192–217). IGI Global.

Pramanik, S., & Suresh Raja, S. (2020). A Secured Image Steganography using Genetic Algorithm. *Advances in Mathematics: Scientific Journal, 9*(7), 4533–4541.

Pramanik, S., & Suresh Raja, S. (2020). A Secured Image Steganography using Genetic Algorithm. *Advances in Mathematics: Scientific Journal, 9*(7), 4533–4541.

Samanta, D., Dutta, S., Galety, M. G., & Pramanik, S. (2021). A Novel Approach for Web Mining Taxonomy for High-Performance Computing. *The 4th International Conference of Computer Science and Renewable Energies (ICCSRE'2021).* 10.1051/e3sconf/202129701073

Sharon, T. (2021). Blind-sided by privacy? Digital contact tracing, the Apple/Google API and big tech's newfound role as global health policy makers. *Ethics and Information Technology, 23*(S1), 45–57. doi:10.100710676-020-09547-x PMID:32837287

Sinha, M., Chacko, E., Makhija, P., & Pramanik, S. (2021). Energy Efficient Smart Cities with Green IoT. In Green Technological Innovation for Sustainable Smart Societies: Post Pandemic Era. Springer.

Wagih, H. M., & Mokhtar, H. M. O. (2021). Ridology: An Ontology Model for Exploring Human Behavior Trajectories in Ridesharing Applications. In M. Al-Emran, K. Shaalan, & A. Hassanien (Eds.), *Recent Advances in Intelligent Systems and Smart Applications. Studies in Systems, Decision and Control* (Vol. 295). Springer. doi:10.1007/978-3-030-47411-9_30

Xie, S., Zhang, F., & Cheng, R. (2021). Security Enhanced RFID Authentication Protocols for Healthcare Environment. *Wireless Personal Communications, 117*(1), 71–86. doi:10.100711277-020-07042-6

Zenkour, A. M., & El-Shahrany, H. D. (2021). Hygrothermal forced vibration of a viscoelastic laminated plate with magnetostrictive actuators resting on viscoelastic foundations. *International Journal of Mechanics and Materials in Design, 17*(2), 301–320. doi:10.100710999-020-09526-6

Chapter 3
Design and Development of a LF Receiver for Detection of Atmospheric Lightning

Mrinmay Medhi
Gauhati University, India

Hirakjyoti Goswami
Gauhati University, India

ABSTRACT

A low-frequency receiver is designed and operated to capture the LF spectrum associated with the atmospheric lighting with an ultimate aim to detect such events. Lightning releases frequencies over a wide band of the electromagnetic spectrum, but the reception of those frequencies are always limited by the prevailing EM noise at the receiving station. Therefore, the EM noise characteristics in the study environment are analyzed through a rigorous noise survey over the band 10kHz-2MHz. Based on the survey, 30-300kHz is selected as the operating frequency of the receiver, and the design and simulations are done accordingly. The receiver was calibrated using a known local AM radio signal of 730 kHz, which was later demodulated to validate the quality and accuracy of reception. The detector is then tested for three real lightning cases. It is seen from the observations that the frequencies 46.6 kHz and 90.13 kHz appeared during the lightning strikes with a maximum gain of 8.7 dB above the noise level.

INTRODUCTION

Lightning is a sudden electrostatic discharge that is established rapidly in the atmosphere where two electrically charged regions temporarily equalize themselves. Lightning creates a wide range of electromagnetic radiations from the very hot plasma created by the electron flow, including visible light. Electrical discharge resulting from lightning can travel several miles in the air creating a hazardous situation for the living beings on earth. When lightning strikes an object, a high electric current flow over the surface of the body. This can result in the immediate death of a living being and the destruction of

DOI: 10.4018/978-1-7998-9795-8.ch003

any property. Therefore, detection and prediction of lightning are very important to mitigate the damage induced by such events. Detection of lightning requires one or more parameters associated with it, especially the ear of an observer or the camera sensors, or the radio receivers. For detection of lightning activities, it is often necessary to have a better knowledge of the EM spectra emitted during intra-cloud (EC) and cloud-to-ground (CG) lightning strikes. Bonnet tried to detect lightning activity by receiving EM spectra emitted during lighting (Bonnet 2020). He observed that during intra-cloud discharge, VHF components are more prominent whereas VLF and LF frequencies are associated with cloud-to-ground discharge (Figure 1: Power spectrum of lightning). The detection of a VHF signal from a lightning activity has some limitations as it is not only rapidly attenuated by the atmospheric condition but also the propagation path is limited by the Earth's curvature. In LF detection (typ. 30 to 300 kHz), the signals can propagate to a large distance (typ. up to 1000 km) as a ground wave where the effects of terrain on propagation are minimal (Bonnet 2020). Orville and his co-workers observed the detection of lightning by using a magnetic direction finder (DF) (Orville, R. *et al.* 1987). The U.S. National Lightning Detection NetworkTM (NLDN) proposed a system that senses the electromagnetic fields radiated by individual return strokes in CG flashes.

Figure 1. Power spectrum of lightning

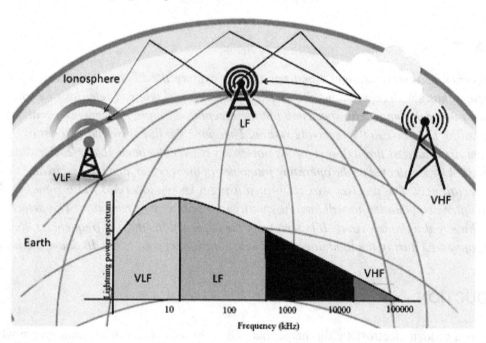

This network provides lightening related information like the stroke location, polarity, and an estimation of the associated peak current (Cummins *et al.* 1998). Musilová *et.al.* 2017 developed a satellite-based VLF network detection of range up to 30 kHz. They utilize a magnetic loop antenna connected to a transducer low pass amplifier and the data is sampled using a microcontroller. A Multiband network system coupled with a GPS module was also employed for the proper detection and location of such events (Leal *et al.* 2016). Lightning detection, based on the satellite-based Optical Transient Detector systems (OTD) was also employed by different groups. But the detection efficiency of the OTD is not appropriate (46-69%) for CG lightning (Nath *et al.* 2009). Therefore, satellite-based information merged with ground-based detection may be significantly useful for lightening related research.

In the present work, an attempt is made to detect lightning activity by receiving LF components emitted by such events. For this, a receiver is designed, simulated & tested for the selected LF band.

The chapter is organized into five sections. The next section addresses the results of the noise survey over the study environment. Section III deals with circuit design & simulation. Section IV covers the results of the testing and detection. Finally, the conclusion & future aspects are discussed in section V.

NOISE SURVEY

To design an efficient RF receiver, it is essential to have a detailed knowledge of all the frequencies available in that region. Therefore, a noise survey is conducted in the working environment to detect all kinds of frequencies up to 2 MHz. The arrangement for this survey is shown in Figure 2: Block Diagram of Noise Survey. A whip antenna of length 0.85m is directly connected to a DSO to receive the EM noise in the time domain. Then the received signal is sampled at 4 MHz and the frequency domain signal is obtained as presented in Figure 3 and Figure 4.

Figure 2. Block diagram of noise survey

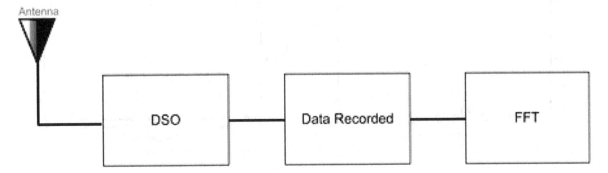

The noise survey was conducted on both days as well as during night hours. During the survey, two prominent signals at 730 kHz and 1 MHz were continuously observed. The source of 730 kHz is the AM radio station, Guwahati. The signal disappears during 9:30 - 13:00 IST and 00:00 - 5:30 IST as the radio station did not broadcast during that time. The 1 MHz signal is from the All-India Radio (AIR) center Guwahati B which was available all the time. From the above observations, a 30 - 300 kHz frequency range was selected for our receiver as that particular band is free from local RF noise and frequency components in that band can travel a large distance.

Figure 3. Daytime observations

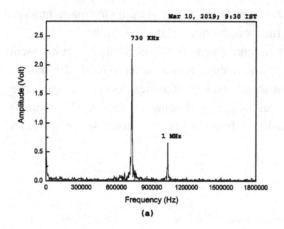
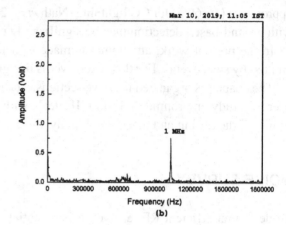

Figure 4. Night-time observations

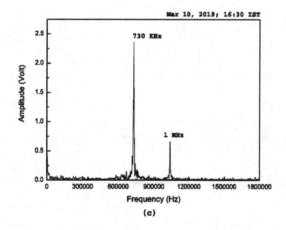
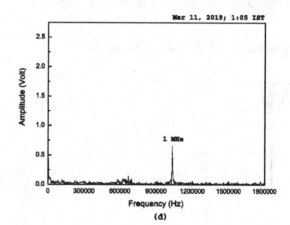

CIRCUIT DESIGN AND SIMULATION

The block diagram of the receiver is shown in Figure 5.

Figure 5. Block diagram of the receiver

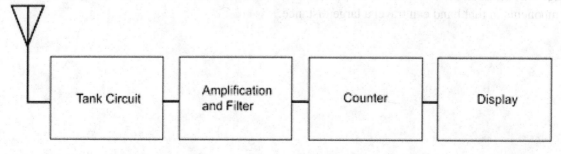

The detector circuit consists of 3 major parts an antenna and a counter. The first part of the detector is a tank circuit which is intended for the selection of the desired frequency. The tank circuit is simulated for different values of L and C to obtain the best resonance level using the following expression,

$$f_c = \frac{1}{2\pi\sqrt{LC}}$$

Where, f_c is the resonance frequency, L and C are the value of inductor and capacitor respectively. The resonance frequency is found to be sensitive to L and C values as presented in Table 1.

Table 1.

L (μH)	C (pF)	f_c (kHz)
600	1061	200
600	471	300
600	265	400

Figure 6. Resonance at 200, 300 & 400 kHz

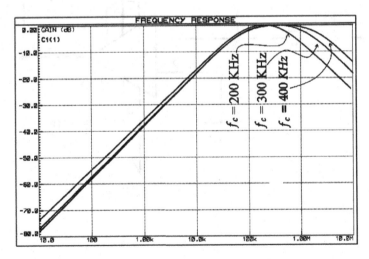

The resonance characteristics for different values of L and C are presented in Figure 6.

The amplification section is realized using high-speed low noise opamp, LM318. The theoretical gain of the circuit is (Figure 7).

$$A = -\frac{R2}{R1}$$

For R2 = 1.5 kΩ and R1 = 500 Ω, the theoretical gain of the amplifier circuit is 9.54 dB. And the frequency response curve is presented in Figure 8. The gain of the amplifier is considerably high in LF.

A demodulator section is added to the receiver to check the accuracy of reception. This section consists of low noise, amplifier NPN transistor BC549 and the demodulated output is acquired from the C4(2) point (Figure 9).

The detector is simulated with a known signal and outputs are collected the output responses are checked at four different points as shown in Figure 9. It is observed that the signals which were retrieved from output 4 have the maximum gain of 70 dB at resonance which is further fed into the ADC and sampled at 40 kHz.

For counting the number of CG strikes, a counter based on AT89C51 is designed and an LCD is connected at the end for the number of events as well as the strength of the strikes.

Figure 7. Amplification circuit

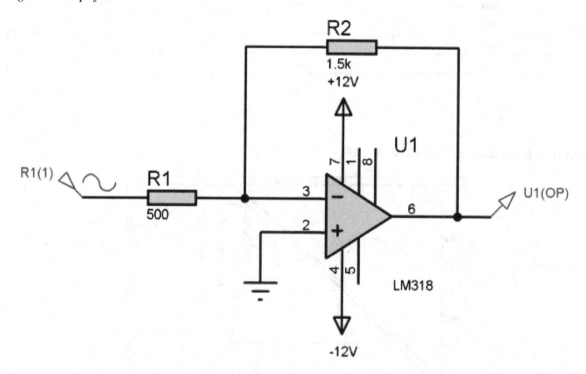

Figure 8. Frequency response curve

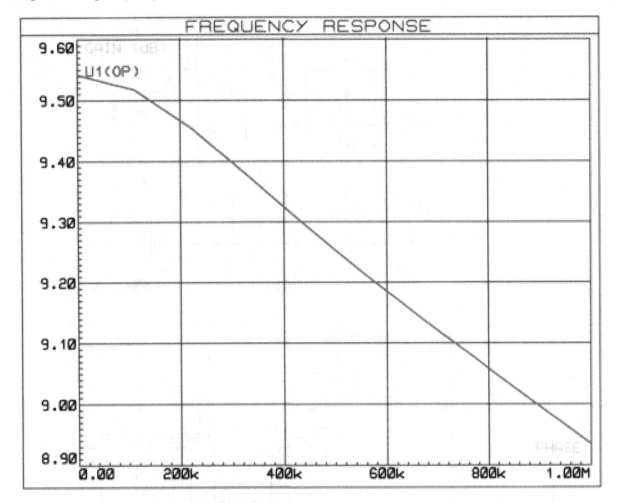

TESTING AND DETECTION

The detector is tested using a known LF signal available in the study environment. For this purpose, the tank circuit is tuned for the reception of 730 kHz (Guwahati Radio Broadcast Station), and the received signal along with the demodulated is are presented in Figure 11. The demodulated audio signal is verified by retrieving the audio information.

The system is operated during the lightning activity on Jun 21, 2019 (Figure 12) where three events were received. The EM noise level before and during the lightning strikes are presented in Figure 12[a], Figure 12[b], Figure 12[c] and Figure 12[d] respectively. It is observed that during the first strikes (10:19 IST), two frequencies 46.6 kHz and 90.13 kHz were received with amplitudes of 2.65V, and 1.5V respectively. During the second and third strikes at 10:27 IST and 10:35 IST, only the 90.13 kHz frequency component is received with an amplitude of 1.5V and 2.7 V respectively.

Figure 9. Circuit used for simulation

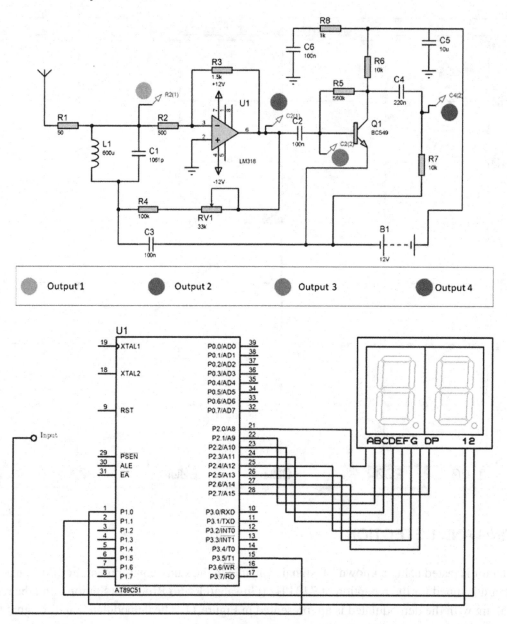

Figure 10. Frequency response curve

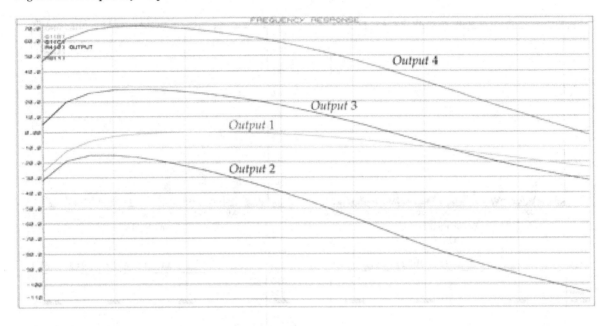

Figure 11. Reception and demodulation of 730 kHz signal

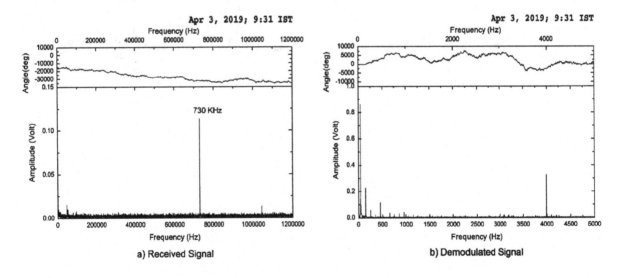

Figure 12. Recorded lightning pulses in comparison with the noise level

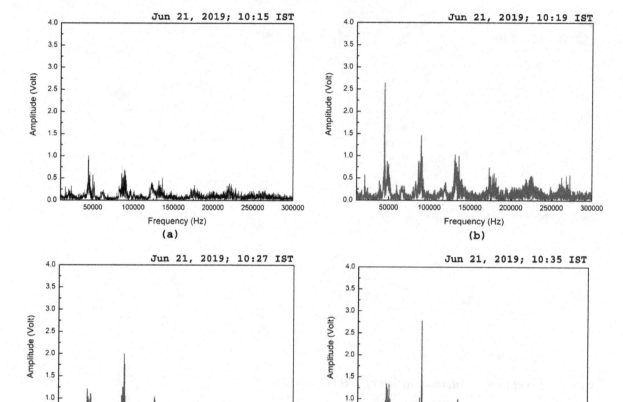

Figure 13. Peak detection in comparison with the noise level

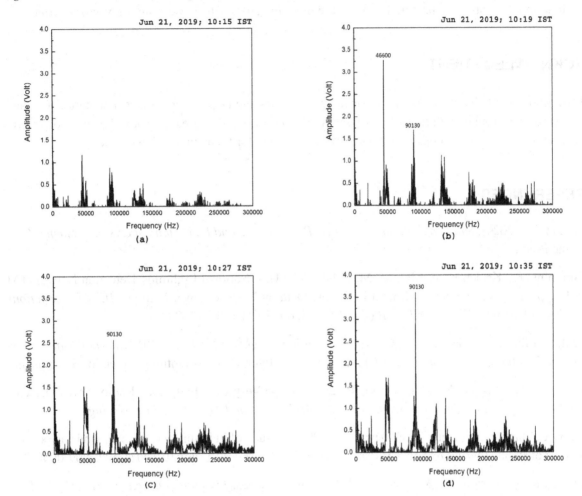

CONCLUSION AND FUTURE ASPECTS

In summary, an LF receiver (30 - 300 kHz) is designed and tested during the occurrence of thunderstorm activity to detect the location and intensity of such events. The strength of such an event can be characterized by the voltage level of the received signals. It is observed that during a CG strike, the detector received some instantaneous frequency components which disappeared just after the occurrence of the event. All the lightning-induced frequencies are received within the frequency band of 40-200 kHz instead of the targeted frequency of 30-300 kHz. This difference between the simulated and experimental frequency ranges may be due to the tank circuit which cuts the edge frequency components after the reception.

Using a magnetic loop antenna, the magnetic field component of the lightning-generated signals can be retrieved. It can be further integrated to achieve the lightning power spectrum. Further, the detector can be upgraded to identify the event's location. For this work, a radio directional finder can be employed along with the receiver. There are reports of detection of the horizontal magnetic field associated with LF radio waves with the help of a cathode-ray direction finder. In this arrangement, orthogonal loop antennas oriented in north-south and east-west directions are used where the azimuth angle to the discharge could be obtained by plotting antenna outputs simultaneously on an x–y plane. Here, the direction of lightning discharge can be obtained from the direction along which the resulting vector is oriented.

ACKNOWLEDGMENT

The authors would like to thank the Department of Physics and Department of Instrumentation, Gauhati University for providing all the necessary facilities to carry out this research work. We are also grateful to Assam Science Technology and Environmental Council for their financial assistance.

REFERENCES

Bonnet, M. (2020). *Status of lightning detection Performance and limitations of existing systems*. Academic Press.

Cummins, K., Krider, E., & Malone, M. (1998). The U.S. National Lightning Detection NetworkTM and Applications of Cloud-to-Ground Lightning Data by Electric Power Utilities. *IEEE Transactions on Electromagnetic Compatibility, 40*(4), 465–480. doi:10.1109/15.736207

Leal, A., Filho, J., Rocha, B., & Sá, J. (2016). *A Multiband Lightning Detector, 2014 International Conference on Lightning Protection (ICLP)*. ChinaILPS 2016 - International Lightning Protection Symposium.

Musilová, M., Šmelko, M., & Lipovský, P. (2017). Cube Very-Low-Frequency Radio Waves Detector and Whistlers. *8th International Conference on Mechanical and Aerospace Engineering*.

Nath, A., Manohar, G., Dani, K., & Devara, P. (2009). A study of lightning activity over land and oceanic regions of India. *Journal of Earth System Science, 118*(5), 467–481. doi:10.100712040-009-0040-7

Orville, R., Henderson, R., & Bosart, L. (1987). *An East Coast Lightning Detection Network*. IEEE.

Chapter 4
Application of Geoinformatics in Mapping and Understanding the Microspatial Environment:
A Case Study of Gauhati University Campus

Prasanta Bhattacharya
Gauhati University, India

ABSTRACT

Maps are used to visualize geospatial data, and they help their user to better understand geospatial relationships. From maps, information on distances, directions, and area size can be retrieved, patterns revealed, and relations understood and quantified. Thus, maps and mapped data have been used extensively for spatial planning and management of resources. Located between 260 8/ 45// N to 260 9/ 37// N latitude and 910 39/ 22// E to 910 40/ 32// E longitude, the Gauhati University Campus occupies an important position in the western part of rapidly expanding Guwahati city. Considering its unique location, richness in terms of scenic constituents and biodiversity, use and abuse of its landscapes, an attempt has been made in this chapter to put emphasis on the significance of mapping and spatial database generation using GIS, GPS, and visual documentation through photographs for sustainable management of landscape, along with increasing spatial awareness among stakeholders.

INTRODUCTION

Maps are used to visualize geospatial data, that is data that refer to the location or the attributes of objects or phenomena located on the earth. Maps help their user to better understand geospatial relationships. From maps, information on distances, directions and area size can be retrieved, patterns revealed, and relations understood and quantified (Kraak and Ormeling, 2004). The Gauhati University Campus, located between 26^0 8/ 45// N to 26^0 9/ 37// N latitude and 91^0 39/ 22// E to 91^0 40/ 32// E longitude, occupies an

DOI: 10.4018/978-1-7998-9795-8.ch004

important position in the western part of rapidly expanding Guwahati city. The campus covers an area of around 2.05 sq km (1547.88 bigha). It is full of wetlands, grasslands, plains, hills, narrow valleys and rivulets. The northern boundary of the campus mostly passes through wetlands, while southern boundary mostly includes hills rising up to an altitude of 168 meters. The national highway 37 passes through the campus in east-west direction (Figure 1).

Though small in extent, three different types of micro-ecosystems, i.e. low granite hills, wetlands (alluvial lowlands) and narrow foothill plains may be identified in the campus and the mutual linkages among them may be discerned even at present. The ecosystems have their distinct contribution to the natural diversity of the campus. Survey reveals that the campus is habitat for more than 100 species of resident and migratory birds (Gauhati University, 2008). The campus is also rich in floral diversity, which is the result of topographical as well as pedological variation. The campus is also reach in respect of wetlands varying in size, from 89612 sq mt to 110 sq mt. They regulate the natural flow and distribution of water within micro-watersheds of the campus and support fish fauna along with resident and migratory water birds.

Considering the significance of understanding the space of Gauhati University campus within a dynamic city environment, an attempt has been made in this paper to address the issue of mapping so that awareness for mapping can be created and necessary data base can be generated.

Figure 1. Gauhati University campus as on 2008, prepared by the author

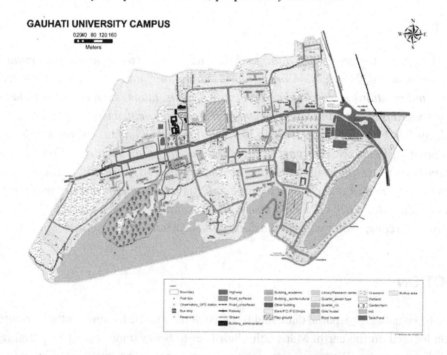

OBJECTIVES

The main objective of the paper is to state the significance of mapping in micro-spatial units like Gauhati University Campus to increase the level of space consciousness among the resident community and authorities concerned. However, the specific objectives are to (i) portray the evaluation of the landscape through the mapped data generated over time (ii) use geoinformatics and increase precision of spatial evaluation process and mapping and (iii) to portray the rapid transformation of land use and land cover and cast light on the consequences there of.

METHODOLOGY

The work followed an exploratory approach to reach the desired end. Primary spatial data has been generated for new landscape constituents like diverted highway with the help of Global Positioning System. Point and line data has been so generated along the mid-point of the diverted highway. Based on actual field measurement of the breath of the road (15 mt in one way), buffering has been done in GIS environment to have the areal extent of the 30 mt wide road the passes through the northern part of the campus. Buffering is a process of creation of a zone of interest around a spatial entity (Heywood, Cornelius and Carver, 2003). Secondary data has been generated from the campus map prepared by Department of Geography, 1993 and contour map redesigned design by the department in 1993, based on the map of Gauhati Development Authority, 1960. Topographic map No 78 N/12 of survey of India surveyed in the session of 1911-12 and 1969-70 was also consulted to have an idea of the landscape from the past. Apart from it, high resolution satellite images (1mt) for 1995 and 2010 (in visible band) from Google Earth was consulted to update the situation. Around 28 magnified images of the area were initially downloaded, control points are generated through GPS and mosaic has been prepared using the Eardas Imagine raster GIS software. Co-ordinates for prominent control points are also derived from Google Earth to avoid error in spatial modeling. As, handheld GPS generates co-ordinates with an accuracy level of around 5 meter, GPS was not found to be appropriate to generate coordinates for control points to map micro-spatial unites like Gauhati University Campus. Finally, images are geo-referenced using Universal Transverse Marketor's Projection (UTM) and World Geodetic System-1984 (WGS 1984) datum, accepted globally for survey and spatial measurement. It was done in Arc GIS environment, considering its flexibility in respect of outputs. Apart from it, information has been derived from local oral history along with report prepared by Gauhati university Plantation Committee has also been consulted in the process. Photographic documantation of the landscape has also been carried out.

ANALYSIS

Mapping the Campus: A Historical Perspective

The past environment of the Gauhati University campus was covered and under the one inch to a mile British topographical survey scheme during 1911-12. As in comparison to the area, the scale was quite small and leaving less space to know details of this micro environment. However, a few dwelling units are shown in the northern fringe of the area, in the localities like- Sodilapur, Bamun Bori, etc. However, the Lachit *Gor* (rampart) was portrayed in details in the westerner fringe of the area. The hillocks of the southern side were shown by contours in feet. Except it, to the north of the hillocks, there lies agricultural field and low-laying areas, bearing an altitude of around 90 feet from MSL. In fact, most of the areas of the northern front belong to *Devatoor* land of the temple Kamakhya. Comparatively higher grounds, adjacent to hillocks were covered with thick bamboo breaks and leopards used to venture in search of cattle and goat of the villagers. Locals used to refer the place as *kahar bakara*.

After allocation of the land to start with the Gauhati University in 1948 the landscape took a new shape. Feeder road arteries were added. Comparatively raised areas are selected for construction of academic and administrative buildings, hostels, residential quarters and market places. Law laying areas are avoided as much as possible to maintain balance between development and natural setting. All such development initiative was carried out according to the Master Plan for Gauhati University, prepared by Gauhati Development Authority in 1960. Detailed mapping has been done at a scale of 1:500. However, basic emphasis was laid on documentation of the topographic details of the area with the help of contours. Terrain details are plotted for hilly area by using contours at 4 feet interval and 1 foot for the plains of the university landscape. The sincere effort of the surveying authority and the pioneers of the university planners can able to provide us an organized landscape of the campus. However, lend filling during congress session in 1952 and construction of Saraighat bridge over the river Brahmaputra in 1965 and introduction of a raised highway portion, linking the bridge, converted many low-lying agricultural field presale to wetlands with varying depth. Keeping in mind the oriental perspective of nature association, new plantation drive for both the native and alien varieties were also encouraged, that converted and enriched the campus landscape in terms of biodiversity amides a haphazardly growing city like Guwahati.

With the gradually growing developmental needs, Gauhati University authority deemed it appropriate to map the campus accommodating the new developments in early 1990s. The Department of Geography, Gauhati University was entrusted to accomplish the task in the later part of 1992. Seven teacher and thirty five students were actively engaged in the survey using plane table for the plain and theodolite for the hilly area to map the campus. It took around 15 days to cover the area and prepare the draft map. The author was also entrusted to lead a team that surveyed the central and north eastern part of the campus. Every details of the campus, including telephone and electric posts, major trees along with detail projections of each and every administrative and academic buildings, hostels, residential units, culverts, streams are plotted, keeping the applied aspects of such mapped data and their future use. The map was finalized in February 1993 at a scale of 1:2000 (1cm to 20 mt) and handed over to GU authority. Subsequently, university entrusted the duty to convert the contour map prepared by Gauhati Development Authority from its 1:500 format to a manageable one. In 1993 the map was converted to a scale of 1: 2000. Unfortunately, no effort has been made by the university in subsequent years to use such valuable inputs for planning, except putting it in front of the university main gate for location hunt.

Mapping in Digital Environment

Geoinformatics is a combination of RS, GIS and GPS technologies that allows the user to generate, process, manipulate and display spatial data by modeling the earth. Remote Sensing and Global Positioning System provides spatial data and Geographic Information System offers the necessary platform in digital environment to process spatial data and create the required earth model to display in the form of maps. Some specific models available in GIS environment are quite effective in surveying and measurement. Considering such application possibilities, analogous data of Guwahati university campus, i.e. map prepared in 1993 along with high resolution RS data (1mt) acquire from Google earth for the session of 2005 and 2010 has been incorporated and analyzed in GIS environment. As these images and map not offer the upcoming highway along the northern part of the campus (the project initiate in 2011),

GPS survey has conducted to fix road alignment and length. Breadth of the road was fixed by buffering process that is creation of a zone around the central line along the road.

Boundary layer of information has been generated from the map of the campus prepared in 1993. As the map was the outcome of actual ground survey, boundary marks are accepted as accurate. However, boundary mark/wall was also not defined for a portion of about 30 meter in northern part of the campus in the wester part of Saraighat colony and in the southern fringe along the hillock, strait line between defined marks in the north and straight ling along the crest of the was considered as boundary of the campus in 1993. Same principle has been followed in boundary demarcation process in digital surveying and mapping. For updating changes satellite images for 2005 and 2010 has also incorporated in the process. Altogether five broad area layers was generated, viz. boundary, built-up area, pond, wetland and hill. The algorithm pArea.area was executed to calculate area component under each category in square meter unit. Thus, area under the Gauhati university campus was found be 2070765.40 sq mt (2.07 sq km/ 1547.88 bigha). The built-up category, which covers all developed area currently under use and having possibilities of use represent around 49 per cent of the campus area (Table.1). The category includes areas under 17 km of road artery, areas under all sorts of buildings, playgrounds, parks, gardens, etc. The second important constituents of Gauhati University landscape is found to be wetlands, which cover around 26 per cent of the total area (Fig.2), followed by hill (23.56 per cent) and pond (0.91 per cent).

Figure 2. Status of wetlands and pond in GU campus, 2008

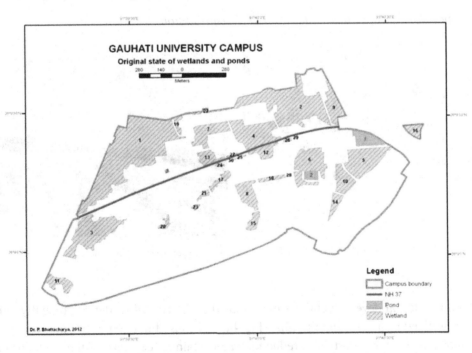

Table 1. Land-use in Gauhati University campus, 2008

Sl. No.	Category	Area		PC to total area
		Sq. meter	Bigha	
1	Built-up area	1017185.71	760.34	49.13
2	Wetland	546777.10	408.71	26.40
3	Hill	487935.77	364.73	23.56
4	Pond	18866.82	14.10	00.91
Total		2070765.40	1547.88	100.00

Source: Based on assessment of the author, 2008

Transformation of Land Use

Rapid transformation of the campus land use has been seen over the last couple of years, basically due to construction of National highway diversion along the northern portion of the campus. As this part of the campus was covered by wetlands, many of them are quite rich in terms of nutrients and depth (up to 6 meter) even use to support migratory water birds during winter (Fig. 3a). These wetlands are drastically transformed from 2011 onwards (Fig.3b).

Figure 3. Support to migratory birds and wetland transformation

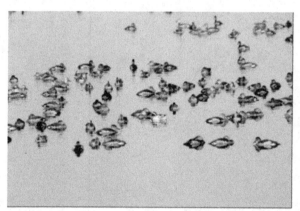

A: Migratory birds in wetland No.2, picture by the author on 02.03.2009

B: Same spot in wetland No.2, picture by the author on 06.05.2011

Apart from it, internal development process initiated at the cost of wetlands gradually reduced the habitat of rare wetland birds like Pintail Snipe (Fig 4a) and caused frequent artificial flood in the campus during monsoon season. Drastically reducing water retaining capacity of the wetlands caused by unplanned earth filling, without due consideration of local terrain and ecology will be a major cause of concern in the coming years (Fig 3b).

Figure 4. Effect of reducing wetlands

A: Habitat lost for Pintail Snipe or Gallinago Stenura in wetland No 6. picture captured by the author on 07.03.2009

B: Artificial flooding in GU model school campus due to unplanned filling at wetland No. 6; picture captured by the author on 11.05.2013

The highway diversion along with internal development process in the Guwahati University campus at the cost of basically the wetlands will have far reaching consequences (Fig. 5). The artificially raised highway platform, encircling the northern low-laying front of the campus has already transformed the gradient and natural drainage mechanism. Such development also instrumental in increasing groundwater level, decreasing plinth heights of most of the residential and other buildings planned at built at the physical setting of 1960s. For the entire 1.6 km raised stretch, provision of only a single culvert have been left in the north-western part of the campus. The water from the micro-catchment of the western front, which used to pass through the culvert of national highway, near Bodo Department has already been coughed. Apart from wetlands, the hill and pond components (in the extreme eastern part) of the landscape also suffered in this process. However, lost in the category of built-up area is found to be minimal (Table 2). Loss in built-up category need to be readdressed, as road boundaries are not properly marked in the field. Apart from it, if the area claimed by the highway authority is 30 mt from the centre of the newly constructed highway (as stated by estate officer of the university) and acquired proposed land of another 30 meters (inbuilt) in the periphery of the highway, then the breadth of the land strip for the road will be 60 meter in its entire length. Under such circumstances, lost are will be 185 bigha, instead of 92.8 bigha measured at present. Such issues need to be addressed properly in appropriate forum, so that the university gets necessary compensation against land loss, if not yet paid.

Figure 5. Nature of spatial transformation in GU campus

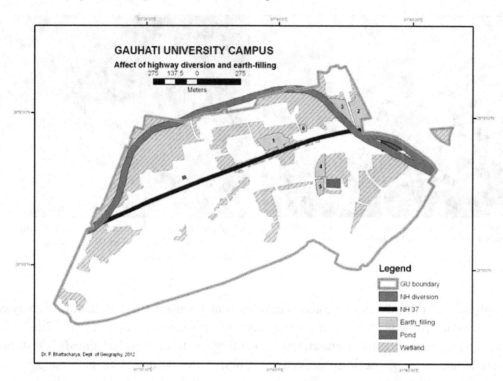

Table 2. Transformation and loss of space due to highway diversion in GU campus (2008-12)

Sl. No	Category	Area, 2008 (sq mt) / % to total	Area, 2012 (sq mt) / % to total	Area loss (in sq mt)	Area loss (in bigha)	% to total loss
1	Built-up area	1017185.71 (49.12)	1017000.00 (52.24)	185.71	00.14	00.15
2	Wetland	546777.10 (26.40)	443597.78 (22.78)	103179.32	77.13	83.11
3	Pond	18866.82 (00.91)	5548.14 (00.29)	13318.68	9.95	10.72
4	Hill	487935.77 (23.56)	480469.1 (24.68)	7466.67	5.58	06.02
	Total	2070765.40 (100)	1946615.20 (100)	124150.20	92.80*	100.00

Source: based on the assessment of the author, 2012 * Additional 92.80 bigha are acquired by NHAI for future expansion of highway lane (inbuilt), which is already handed over by the university. Then total land lost will be 185 bighas.

Apart from the landscape transformation due to highway diversion, a few important wetlands, especially wetland no. 4 and 6 (Fig. 2 and 5) has also been transformed at the cost of recent developmental activities of the university. Original area of wetland no. 4 was found to be 39403.95 sq meter in 2008, with an average depth of 5 meters. The area was reduced to 23,584.46 sq meters with a loss of 15,855.49 sq meters. Thus it lost the water retaining capacity of around 79,227 cubic sq meters. A new academic building has been built in the developed ground and earth filling process is going on in the wetland. The wetland no. 6 was partly renovated to ponds to accommodate the SAP project associated with Department of Zoology. However, the wetland have lost 20,225.92 sq meter (43707.83-23481.91) due to earth filling in the western periphery of the SAP aquaculture ponds, which reduced water holding area of the wetland and leads to occasional flooding in the vicinity unless water thoroughfare between the two schools is maintained.

CONCLUSION

Maps are used to visualize geospatial data and they help their user to better understand geospatial relationships. Considering the unique location of Guwahati university campus in respect of its rich scenic constituents and biodiversity assets, emphasis has been given in mapping and spatial database generation for sustainable management of landscape. It is believed that spatial database generated through the process with help in increasing spatial awareness among stakeholders. It may also caste highlight on use and abuse of the fragile landscape of the area.

REFERENCES

Baruah, P.P., & Bhattacharya, P. (2012). *Status of Wetlands in Guwahati University Campus.* Gauhati University.

Gauhati University. (2008). *Plantation for Conservation of Biodiversity and Eco-restoration in Gauhati University Campus.* Project proposal prepared by Committee for Scientific Plantation of Trees in Gauhati University Campus.

Heywood, I., Cornelius, S., & Carver, S. (2003). *Introduction to Geographical Information Systems.* Pearson Education.

Kraak, M. J., & Ormeling, F. (2004). *Cartography: Visualization of Geospatial Data.* Pearson Education.

Chapter 5
Development of a Visible Light Communication System for Electrocardiogram Signal Transfer in Biomedical Applications

Sujit Chatterjee
Gauhati University, India

Rubi Baishya
Behali Degree College, India

Debashis Saikia
Gauhati University, India

Banty Tiru
Gauhati University, India

ABSTRACT

The visible light communication (VLC) system is expected to share the load on internet and communication technology (ICT) and be a promising green mode of communication, especially in healthcare applications. In this chapter, a frequency shift keying (FSK)-based VLC system is proposed that caters to the need of biomedical signal transfer. The system is implemented in hardware and is found to be flicker free to bit rates as low as 34bps and shows 82.33% improvement in BER compared to OOK. Using this method, different types of ECG signal are transferred successfully through a 1 W LED through a distance of 3m. The received signal retains the characteristics in terms of the RR interval and beats per minute (BPM) and the correlation between the transmitted and the received is very high (~100%), which is highly desired in transfer of biomedical signals. Future implementations and scope are also discussed in the chapter.

DOI: 10.4018/978-1-7998-9795-8.ch005

INTRODUCTION

Internet and Communication Technology (ICT) has proved to be instrumental in providing health care, not to patients but health workers alike. The World Health Organization (WHO) has also recognized ICT as a key and utmost priority for health care (Aslan et al., 2018). This is more so when the world is fighting against an unprecedented COVID19 pandemic. Incorporation of innovative methods in health care is the need of the hour and requires exploring new methods of communication and monitoring that is secured and readily available. Use of ICT has exploded in the recent years and led to acute bandwidth (BW) shortage due to the crowding of the radio frequency (RF) part of the electromagnetic spectrum. RF cause electromagnetic interference (EMI) in the nearby electronic devices, and therefore not suitable in critical areas (Singla et al., 2017). There is therefore restriction in the use of RF in hospitals, petrochemical plants and airplanes. In health care centers, RF has been known to cause malfunctioning of the medical instruments, and to jeopardize the entire monitoring system. Such an incidence is undesirable as this will compromise with the health of the patients, leading to leading to adverse effect (Tang et al., 2009) that may be fatal. A most promising option for communication can be Optical Wireless Communication (OWC). OWC may be in the infrared (750nm- 1mm) or in the visible light region (380-750nm). The communication in the visible band is known as Visible Light Communication (VLC) and uses the same source used to illuminate the room for communication also. The advantage of VLC over RF is that visible light has 10^4 times larger BW than RF and does not cause any EMI with the other instruments. This makes it safer to use in critical areas. Moreover, the communication is secured owing to limited coverage (bounded by the room) and is also license free (Khan, 2017). Use of VLC in these centers can provide the required BW for dealing with a large data. VLC can also give the opportunity for caregivers to monitor the physiological status of the patients, activity and movement very closely. Other applications of VLC can be in smart homes. Smart homes are alternate options for the elderly to get health care even without going to the health care centers in the comfort of their homes. In the next three decades, the population of aged people is expected to increase drastically from 7.5% to 14.9% for males and 9.5% to 18.5% for females. Such a growth will make it impossible for hospitals and health care centers to accommodate all of them and smart home can be another option (Alam et al., 2012). VLC can have an important role to play in this smart home as the available lighting can be used to monitor the health status of the occupants.

VLC is now possible due to the fast switching action of light emitting diodes (LEDs) at a very higher rate than a human eye can detect. These LEDs are available in all rooms and slowly replacing other lighting options like CFL and florescent light due to its long life and better efficiency. The receiver of a VLC system requires an electro-optic photo detector like a PIN photodiode (PD) for reception and detection of the message signal. At present, there are two standards that govern the available VLC devices: The Visible Light Communication Consortium (VLCC) in Japan and the IEEE Standard (Khan, 2017).

Though medical field is one of the most promising applications of VLC, the work done is this area is very less. The chapter is about the use of VLC for medical applications. The chapter starts with the importance of VLC as a communication option for green technology. A literature review of the application of VLC in biomedical applications is then presented. A typical cannel modeling common to a VLC system is then performed and the characteristics studied. A frequency-shift keying (FSK) VLC prototype is proposed which is seldom used in VLC. The same is implemented in hardware and the performance estimated. This prototype is used for an electrocardiogram (ECG) signal transfer and the results discussed. The chapter then recommends solutions to the problems faced and proposes future work and concludes.

REVIEW OF VLC AS GREEN COMMUNICATION, CHALLENGES, USE IN BIOMEDICAL APPLICATIONS AND SCOPE OF THE CHAPTER

VLC as a Green Technology Option

Exponential growth of ICT and Internet of Things (IoT) has made it to be one of the highest consumers of electric power by utilizing nearly 4.6% of the world electricity in 2021. This will alarmingly increase more in the coming years (Chen et al., 2011). In 2007, the CO_2 footprint of ICT was nearly 2% (Gelenbe & Caseau, 2015) and it is predicted that by 2030, there will be an increase of 23% in the release of greenhouse gases. This can even be worse and go up-to 50% (Rehman et al., 2019). These carbon footprints have initiated technologies aiming green communication also (Chen et al., 2011). As such, it is required to maximize the output of available infrastructure like illumination technologies and use it for communication. LEDs consume 75% less power and last 25% more than incandescent lamps. This is a very positive scenario because it is expected that by 2020, nearly 75% of all the other illumination devices are replaced by these power efficient LEDs. VLC therefore has a huge prospect expected to take the load of ICT requirements at least in the illuminated spaces. For this, health care centers are the most promising due to associated advantages discussed earlier.

Challenges in VLC

VLC has to overcome many challenges like flicker, dimming, shadowing, multiple path and multiplexing for extended usage. Availability of a limited modulation scheme like On-Off-Keying (OOK), pulse modulation techniques like Pulse Position Modulation (PPM), Expurgated PPM (EPPM), Pulse Position Pulse Width modulation (PPM-PWM), Pulse amplitude modulation (PAM), Variable Pulse Position Modulation (VPPM) and Pulse Dual Slope Modulation (PDSM) make the options very narrow for providing suitable solutions to the problems void of complexity (Rajbhandari et al., 2017). Flicker is a problem faced by VLC in low bit rates or in long runs of ones or zero. Due to slow variation of the intensity level of light, the same can be easily recognized by the human eye. Long time exposure of flicker is dangerous to the eyes and it may damage eyesight. Flicker in the range of 3-70 Hz causes epileptic seizure and that in the range of 70-200 Hz causes malaise, headache and impaired vision. The IEEE 802.15.7 standard recommends flicker below 200Hz must be avoided (Rajagopal et al., 2012). Most of the methods use codes (example RLL, polar code, finite state machine (Fang et al., 2017) etc. that at times require complex synchronizing for implementation. A minimum flicker of 200 bps has been reported in (Mejia et al., 2017) using FSM and 60 bps using FSK (Chatterjee & Tiru, 2020). Even the multiplexing schemes are few like Orthogonal Frequency Division Multiplexing (OFDM), code division multiplexing (CDMA), wavelength division multiplexing or WDM, Color Shift Keying (CSK) and polarization division multiplexing (PDM have many limitations like in the number of channels and are complex.

VLC in Biomedical Applications

Biomedical signals arise from some physiological activities of the physical mechanisms of biological systems. These physiological activity can be of varied types arising from nerves, brain, heart, speech, etc. Some signals are blood pressure, pulmonary artery pressure, central venous pressure, ECG, photoplethysmography (PPG), cardiac output, electroencephalography (EEG) and body temperature having approximate frequency 60Hz, 50Hz, 50Hz, 0.1-250Hz, 30Hz, 20Hz, 0.1-100Hz and 0.1Hz respectively (Paksuniemi et al., 2005). In hospitals, monitoring of patients is usually done via wireless LAN (WLAN). This mode is, however unsecured and the BW required is very large. Use of VLC can provide the required BW, with an added advantage of security.

ECG (Tan et al., 2013), EEG (Dhatchayeny et al., 2015) and PPG (Tan & Chung, 2014) signal has been successfully transferred via VLC using RGB LED or white LED using OOK. Table 1 gives a comparison of the work. However, the distance achieved is very small (<100cm) and many dependencies like angular coverage, three dimensional (3D) coverage and the effect of flicker has not been done and some require mandatory synchronization. In another work, patient monitoring with a wearable arrangement has been implemented with VLC as downlink and infrared (IR) as a plausible uplink (Cahyadi et al., 2015). Patient information can also be transferred with the biomedical signals (Tan et al., 2013). A number of multiple access schemes have been proposed to increase the bit rates and enable multiple accesses. Three types of bio-signal (ECG, PPG and temperature) has been transmitted using Time Hopping (TH) scheme (An & Chung, 2016). A total of three one color LED was used for transmission. In another work (Orovic et al., 2021), six different biomedical signals, namely ECG signals were transferred using sparse code division multiplexing (SCDM). Three channel access was also done using RGB LEDs (Dhatchayeny et al., 2015). Some papers have also suggested hybrid communication (HYC) schemes with Power Line Communication (PLC) (Ma et al, 2017; Yang et al., 2017).

Focus of This Chapter

In this work, we propose a FSK based VLC system that has better efficiency than the OOK and removes the use of codes for flicker mitigation. FSK has advantages over other modulation schemes like PAM, OFDMA, CSK, VPPM because in these modulation schemes, the information is in the amplitudes and cause flicker due to high peak to average power ratio (PAPR). However, in FSK, as the information is in the frequency, it is immune to dimming, flicker free and more stable (Chow et al., 2018).Though FSK modulation is known to decrease flicker (Chatterjee & Tiru, 2020) and has been explored in many variants, but the same has not been analyzed in depth. In this paper, a VLC prototype has been developed that uses FSK modulation for VLC and successfully transfers ECG signal through a distance of ~3m can be extended to ~10m using simple circuitry and a 1W LED. The system has been analyzed for flicker mitigation, bit error rate (BER), distance and angular coverage, and correlation between the transmit and the receive ECG signal. As many as 13 types of ECG signals are used to validate the setup. FSK modulation has huge prospects in implementing frequency division multiplexing (FDM) as another option for multiple access.

Table 1. Review of VLC applications in biomedical signal transfer

Parameters	(Tan et al., 2013)	(Dhatchayeny et al., 2015)	(Tan & Chung, 2014)	This work
LED Wattage	3W	NA	1W	1W
Distance	50cm	50cm	100cm	~3m and can be extended to 9m
Synchronization	Mandatory	Not Required	Mandatory	Not Required
Modulation	OOK-NRZ	OOK-NRZ	OOK-NRZ	FSK
Angular coverage	NA	NA	NA	25-30 degree
Complexity	High	Medium	High	Low
3D coverage	NA	NA	NA	Done
Effect of flicker	NA	NA	NA	Done
Biomedical signals	ECG	EEG	PPG	13 ECG signal

VLC CHANNEL MODELING

Figure 1. The VLC Channel model (a) A typical channel model for four LED case (b) The parameters for a one LED system

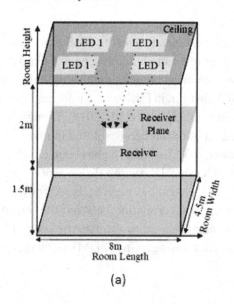
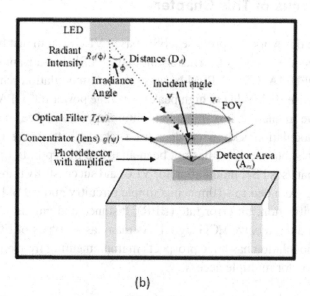

(a)   (b)

A general experimental arrangement of a VLC system consists of a number of LEDs placed on the ceiling and a detector on the receiving floor as shown in Figure 1(a). Figure 1(b) shows the geometry of a single transmitter where the PD may be preceded by an optical filter and a concentrator lens (Komine & Nakagawa, 2004). Light is emitted from the LEDs in different directions and the luminous intensity at an angle ϕ is given by (1)

$$I(\phi) = I(0)Cos^m(\phi) \tag{1}$$

The horizontal illuminance at a point (x,y) is given by (2)

$$E_{hor} = \frac{I(0)\cos^m(\phi)}{D_d^2 \cdot \cos(\psi)}$$

(2)

Where ϕ is the angle of irradiance, $I(0)$ is the central luminous intensity, Dd is the distance between the LED and the director surface and ψ is the angle of incidence. The LED can be assumed to be a Lambertian emitter where the radiant intensity also called the radiant flux per unit solid angle is proportional to the cosine of the angle between a normal to the surface and the observation direction. The radiation intensity for such a source can be taken as (3) (Zeng et al., 2008)

$$R(\phi) = \left[\frac{m+1}{2\pi}\right]\cos^m\phi$$

(3)

In (1), m is the order of the Lambertian emitter that can be calculated by (4)

$$m = \frac{\ln 2}{\ln\left(\cos\phi_{\frac{1}{2}}\right)}$$

(4)

In (3), $\phi_{1/2}$ is called the transmitter semi angle at half power. In the line of sight (LOS) propagation, light from the transmitter reach the PD directly without reflection from the walls. However, in diffuse channel, light reaches the PD after reflections from the walls of the room. The DC channel transfer function of the LOS channel is given by (5)

$$H(0) = \begin{cases} \frac{A_{rx}}{d^2}R_0(\phi)\cos(\psi); 0 \leq \psi \leq \psi_c \\ 0; \psi > \psi_c \end{cases}$$

(5)

Where A_{rx} is the area of the PD, d is the distance between the transmitter and the receiver, ψ is the angle of incidence and ψ_c is the field of view of the PD. If there are a number of LED arrays, them the received power in the direct path is given by (6)

$$P_{rx,LOS} = \sum_{i=1}^{LEDs} P_{tx}H_{LOS}^i(0)$$

(6)

At the receiver, the light is passed through an optical filter and a lens acting as a concentrator and the received power is related to the LOS and the diffused channel given by (7)

$$P_{rx} = \left(P_{LOS} + P_{diff} \right) * T_f^o \left(\psi \right) g_f^l \left(\psi \right) \tag{7}$$

In (7), $T_f^o \left(\psi \right)$ is the transmission coefficient of the optical filter, $g_f^l \left(\psi \right)$ is the gain of the concentrator lens and P_{diff} is the received diffuse power that depends on the reflecting walls and surface. The Signal to Noise (SNR) is given by (8) where R is the Responsivity of the PD in A/W

$$SNR = \frac{\left(RP_{rx} \right)^2}{\sigma_{total}^2} \tag{8}$$

In (8), σ_{total}^2 is the total noise variance and is the sum of the shot noise variance $\left(\sigma_{shot}^2 \right)$ and the amplifier noise variance $\left(\sigma_{amplifier}^2 \right)$ as in (9)

$$\sigma_{total}^2 = \sigma_{shot}^2 + \sigma_{amplifier}^2 \tag{9}$$

The noise is dependent on the noise bandwidth, the noise power of ambient light, data rate, noise bandwidth factor and amplifier bandwidth. In order to evaluate the typical characteristics of a VLC channel, a room of size (5x5x3.5) m³ is assumed with a one LED system. The height of the LED from the receiving floor is taken to be 2m. Typical characteristics of the system are given in Table 2. The calculation is performed without the use of optical filters and lens. Using these parameters, illuminance (Komine & Nakagawa, 2004), and the received signal power at the PD, the channel gain, and SNR are evaluated. Figure 2 gives the typical characteristics for the parameters and it is seen that the received power is very low which can however provide a high SNR of nearly ~45dB in the center and cause high expected bit rates of the LED.

Figure 2. The 3D characteristics of a one LED system (a) the horizontal luminous intensity (b) The received power at the photo-diode (b) The channel gain and (b) The Signal to Noise Ratio

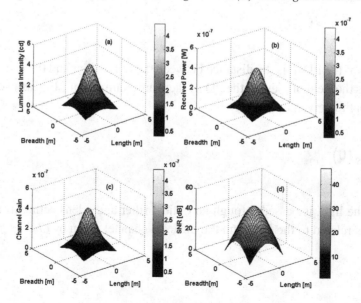

Table 2. Parameters of the System used for channel modeling

Parameter	Specification
Room Size	5m*5m*3.5m
Desk height from the LED plane	2m
Amplifier bandwidth	15MHz
No of LED	1
Single LED power	1W
Semi angle at half power	60 deg.
Detector Physical area of the PD	7.5mm^2
Ambient light photocurrent	5840μA
Noise bandwidth factor (I_2)	0.562
Responsivity of the PD	0.64W/A
Central Luminous Intensity	0.73cd (say)

EXPERIMENTAL SETUP FOR VLC USING FSK AND ANALYSIS

Experimental Setup for VLC-FSK

The block diagram of the experimental setup for VLC using FSK is shown in Figure 3. It consists of a transmitter and a receiver module with a VLC channel between them. The transmitter consists of a source of a message signal (digital/analog like ECG) that is FSK modulated using the modulator (FSKM) producing X_t. If the signal is analog then a suitable analog to digital converter (ADC) is used to produce the transmitted bits D_t. The modulated signal is amplified by the LED driver and that in turn drives the LED whose output is Y_t. The receiver consists of a PD connected to a transimpedance amplifier (TIA), an amplifier and comparator combination and a FSK demodulator (FSKDM). The FSKDM converts the amplified received signal Y_r to the demodulated signal X_r. The demodulator circuit is followed by a filter and comparator combination that regenerates the received bits (D_r). A XR2206 ICs having space and mark frequency (f_s, f_m) is used as a FSKM. The driver used is a (Chatterjee & Tiru, 2018) shunt over-drive and under-drive arrangement. This arrangement is known to provide higher speed than the normal shunt driver. The photo-emitter is a white LED specifically a yellow phosphor coated blue LED which produces white light. This LED is made of 1W Indium Gallium Nitride (InGaN) chip coated with cerium (III) –doped yttrium aluminum garnet (Ce-YAG) phosphide that converts blue light to white. The PD used is a BPW34 which has dimensions of 5.4 x 4.3 x 3.2 mm^3 and has radiant sensitive area of 7.5 mm^2. The dark current of the PD is roughly to 2nA and is sensitive to visible and near IR. The PD is used in reverse biased using a reverse bias of 12V as the reverse breakdown is given by 60V. A Phase locked loop (PLL) IC, LM565 is used as a FSKDM with center frequency and lock range given by F_c and ΔF_L respectively. All the amplifiers/TIA/comparators are constituted of LM356 IC. A suitable data logger is used to observe the received analog signal. A director/reflector and a lens may be used with the LED and PD, respectively and as such, experiments are done using four conditions as shown in Figure 3(b). These conditions are namely *Setup 1* (with director/with lens), *Setup 2* (with director/without lens), *Setup 3* (without director/with lens) and *Setup 4* (without director/without lens). In the figure 'D' represents the presence of director, 'L' the presence of lens and 'X' represents the absence of director/ lens. The presence of the director leads to greater directionality and the lens concentrates the received signal. The director has an angle of 40^0 and the lens has a focal length of 19cm.

Figure 3. (a) The block diagram of a VLC system using FSK (b) Different LED and photodiode configuration (b) The four LED configurations, x=8, y=4.5m

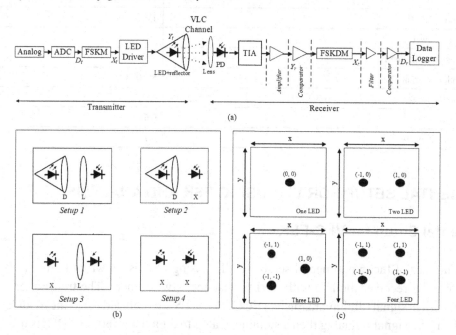

Analysis of the VLC-FSK Prototype and Comparison with OOK

In order to check the efficiency of the FSK system for VLC, the minimum bit rate for flicker (MBF), the dependence of BER on distance and angle and the three dimensional (3D) room coverage is analyzed and compared with OOK.

Flicker Mitigation

For this, the transmitted signal is a TTL signal having different frequencies from a signal generator. The signal can be taken as a bit stream '0101...' or hexadecimal 'UU'. The frequency of the TTL signal is changed and the frequency MBF is found out. Table 3 shows the MBF for different modulating frequencies of the FSKM. As seen from the table, the MBF is lesser in FSK compared to OOK. As the frequency of the carrier is increased, the bit rate decreases and can be as small as 34 bps which is 67.5% lower than that for OOK (160 bps) (Chatterjee & Tiru, 2020). In FSK modulation, each high or low of the digital signal is represented by a high f_s or f_m that causes the LED to switch at a much faster rate than the digital bit itself. This causes the flicker to disappear even at low bit rates.

BER Verses Angle and Distance

For this, the f_s and f_m are taken to be 7 kHz and 9 kHz respectively, with $F_{cl}=8.5kHz$ and $\Delta F_{LI}=3kHz$ for the PLL. The angular coverage is taken at the receiving floor at a vertical separation of 2m with a bit rate equal to 1.2 kbps which is beyond the flicker rate. Figure 4 shows the plots for the four setups considered. It is seen from the figures that for all the cases, the BER is less in FSK compared to OOK. The BER of OOK is in the range 10^{-3}-10^{-2} while in FSK is 10^{-4} to 10^{-3}. On an average, the improvement in BER is 82.33% in FSK compared to OOK in the maximum distance and maximum angle condition. The *Setup 1* shows the best coverage in the distance (~10m) and the *Setup 3*, in angle (90^0). The *Setup 4* shows the worst coverage in the distance (3.15m) with an angular coverage of ~25^0. The *Setup 4* is used for further analysis because it shows the worst performance and it is likely that the LED for room lighting is without a director and the PD without a lens.

Three Dimensional Room Coverage

The three dimensional BER for a typical room of area (8x4.5x3.5m) m^2 is also estimated for OOK and FSK system. The LEDs are placed 2 m above the receiving floor (Figure 1) in four configurations (x,y): at (0,0) for a 1 LED, (-1,0)/ (1,0) for a 2 LED, (1,0)/(-1,1)/(-1,-1) for a 3 LED and (1,1)/ (-1,1)/(-1,-1)/ (1,-1) for a 4 LED system where |1|=1m. For this, the *Setup 4* is used. Figure 3(c) shows the position of the LEDs in all the cases. Each of the LEDs are driven by separate driver system. Figure 5 shows the 3D plots of the distributions of the BER for each case. It is seen in all the cases, the FSK system shows a lesser BER and better coverage than the FSK counterpart. The average FSK is as much as 64.28% as those without in the 4 LED conditions. The room coverage of 1 LED, 2 LED, 3LED and 4LED system is approximately 2x2m², 4x4m², 4.5x4,5m² and 5x4.5m² respectively. Though the FSK system has led to a decrease in BER, it does not improve the angular and distance coverage.

Table 3. Bit rate at which flicker is removed in OOK and FSK modulation

Modulation	Frequencies (f_s, f_m) kHz For FSK	Bit rate at which the flicker disappears (MBF)	Percentage improvement over OOK (%)
OOK	---	160bps	
FSK	1, 2	120	25
FSK	3.7, 4.1	80	50
FSK	5, 6.5	60	62.5
FSK	7, 9	52	67.5
FSK	8.5,10	48	70
FSK	9, 11	44	72.5
FSK	13, 15	34	78.75

Figure 4. The BER verses distance and angle for OOK and FSK for different setups (the Y axis all figure is BER)

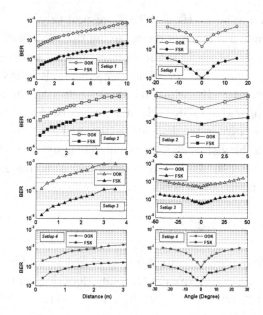

Figure 5. The 3D coverage of BER in a room for a 1LED, 2LED, 3LED and 4LED system using OOK and FSK

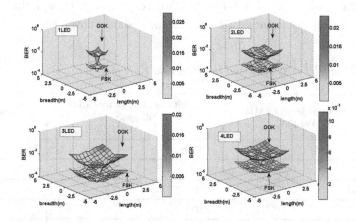

ECG SIGNAL TRANSFER USING FSK USING VLC

Experimental Setup for ECG Signal Transfer using VLC

The block diagram of the experimental setup for transmission and reception of ECG signal via VLC is shown in Figure 6. The source of ECG signal is a simulator (SKRIP SE2503). This simulator generates 13 different types of ECG signals with different characteristics corresponding to normal and abnormal cases. The ECG signals are denoted by S, S1, ….S12 for easy reference. These are S (*normal*), S1 (*Bradycardia*), S2(*Tachycardia*), S3(*Ventricular Tachycardia*), S4 (*Artial Fibrillation*), S5 (*Paced Rhythm*), S6(*Heart block*), S7(*Bigeminy*), S8(*Missed Beat*), S9(*Fusion Beat*), S10(*R on T wave*), S11(*Ventricular Fibrillation*) and S12(*Asystole*). The characteristics of the signal are specified in terms of the RR interval and bits per minute (BPM) ranging from 14-132 BPM. The RR Interval is an important parameter of ECG signal analysis and the distance between the consecutive R to R peaks in the signal. The BPM can be evaluated from the RR Interval as given by (10) (Andrae & Edler, 2015):

$$Heart\ rate\left(beats\ per\ minute\right) = \frac{60}{RRInterval\left(s\right)} \tag{10}$$

Figure 6. The block diagram of the experimental setup for ECG signal transfer over VLC

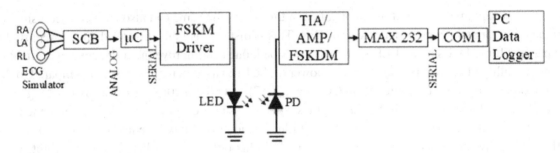

The ECG simulator has probes or pins related to the right arm (RA), the left arm (LA) and the right leg (RL). The output of the simulator is connected to a signal conditioning IC namely AD8232. The signal conditioning block (SCB) does the necessary signal conditioning and converts the signal acquired by the three probes to ECG signal. This is fed to one of analog input pins of an Arduino Uno board. This board has an inbuilt microcontroller µC known as ATmega328P and has a maximum sampling rate of 9615Hz. The µC board is capable of transmitting bits having baud rate 300 to 115200. However a baud rate of 1200 is used here. The microcontroller (µC) has a 10 bit ADC capable of converting an analog voltage into a 10 bit number from 0 to 1023 and has a number of pins (A0-A5) for analog input. The serial bit stream (D_t) produced by the µC is used as input to the FSKM with f_s=7kHz and f_m=9kHz. The received light at the PD is suitably demodulated by the PLL and converted to serial bit stream using the FSKDM and MAX232 combination. The bits are logged on to the data logger software in the computer through the COM port. The received bit is analyzed using the Labview (LabVIEW, NI) environment using the biomedical signal toolbox enabling the RR interval and the BPM to be evaluated. For each type of signal, the correlation (r_{tx}) between the transmit (Tx) and the receive (Rx) is also estimated and noted. A successful VLC system should give a high value of r_{tx} which depicts that the signal is successfully transferred with negligible amount of distortion. This would allow correct analysis of the characteristics of the vital signal at the receiver that is very important for biomedical signal communication.

Results

The setup used for ECG signal transfer is *Setup 4* being the worst condition analyzed. The ECG signal transfer is transferred successfully through a 1LED system to a maximum distance of 3m. Table 4 gives the results of the analysis with the different types of signal transmitted. Figure 7 shows the snapshot of the data logger in the Labview environment, showing signal S and S1. It is seen from the figures and the table that the shape of the signal remains unchanged with a high correlation between Tx and Rx with an approximate $r_{tr}\sim1$ (mean of 0.99995). The error in all the cases is of the order of 10^{-4} but still retains the shape of the signal. The error in the received bits may increase the noise in the signal which can be removed by proper signal processing.

SOLUTIONS AND RECOMMENDANTIONS

Though a maximum distance of 3m is obtained in this work, the same can also be increased using additional director and a lens with decreased BER. This is distance is much greater than that reported in the papers (Table 1). Using a 4LED system as described, one can improve the room coverage, enabling greater mobility of the receiver system. The power of the LED used here is very small compared to that used in other papers (for example 3W in (An et al., 2017) and 60x60 20mW LED array in (Zeng et al., 2008). Use of a higher power LED or LED arrays will increase the coverage and also decrease the BER. This is permissible because a minimum average illumination of 300lux is required for a room (David, 2014) and the system tested gives an illumination of ~70lux only with a 50lux background light. There is thus more room for improvement that will lead to better performance. The work focuses on low bit rates, but the same can be implemented for high bit rate also. The advantage of this method is that does a way of use of codes and synchronization as is common to other modulation schemes. The MBF is also much smaller than available schemes (Mejia et al., 2017). The use of low bit rate by a single channel has increased the plausibility of multiplexing a large number of channels for multiple channel transfer. The use of different f_s and f_m for multiple channels and conversion to frequency modulation after adding up all the signals will lead to a new method of multiplexing with lower PAPR. Incorporating such variability to the OOK such as duty cycle, rise time, fall time, etc., can enable the system to support dimming facility. Continuous data stream in a particular channel from a particular sensor for a specific vital signal can have a specific data header that can be properly identified after the demodulation. This will increase the capacity of the VLC system, for multichannel data transfer.

Figure 7. Snapshot of the data logger (received) showing signals (a) S: normal hear beat (b) S2: Bra-dycardia showing the RR interval and BPM

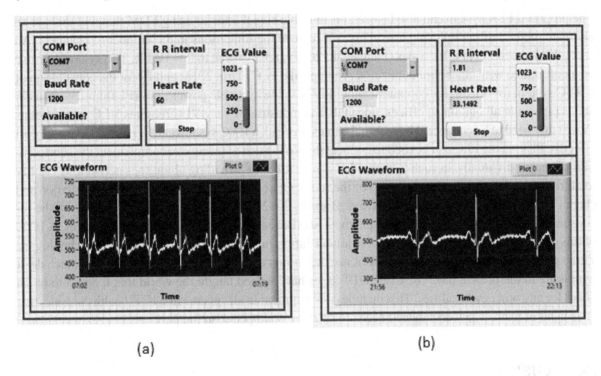

(a)　　　　　　　　　　　(b)

Table 4. The efficiency of various test channel for ECG signal transfer for FSK using setup 4

SI no	ECG signal (S-S12)	BER (x10⁻⁴)	r_{txl}	BPM Tx	BPM Rx
1	S: Normal	3.10	0.999830	60	60
2	S1: Bradycardia	3.12	0.999976	33.14	33.14
3	S2:Tachycardia	2.11	0.999989	133.33	133.33
4	S3:Ventricular Tachcardia	3.63	0.999942	120	120
5	S4:Artial Fibrillation	4.10	0.999961	66.6	66.6
6	S5:Paced Rhythm	2.98	0.999943	66.6	66.6
7	S6:Heart Block	2.62	0.999984	33.14	33.14
8	S7:Bigaminy	3.62	0.999912	76.92	76.92
9	S8:Missed Beat	3.41	0.999974	33.14/66.66	33.14/66.66
10	S9:Fusion Beat	2.59	0.999966	66.66	66.66
11	S10:R or T wave	2.61	0.999935	66.66	66.66
12	S11:Ventricular Fibrillation	2.42	0.999978	NA	NA
13	S13: Asystole	3.41	0.999956	14.01	14.01

FUTURE DIRECTIONS

The proposed FSK system can also be used for multiple signal transfer using FDM that will provide an alternate method of multiplexing also. This will remove the limitations in the number of channels (An et al., 2017) need of complex codes (Fang et al., 2017) and also lead to low PAPR. The system can also be incorporated with other communication schemes like PLC (Tiru, 2015) and IR for the constitution of a HYC system for full duplex communication. PLC use the available power lines (PLs) for data transfer and is present in all buildings, offices, hospitals and industries. Every VLC requires VLC access points (VAP) that need to be connected by external cables. Instead, a HYC system can be developed where cost effective PLs via the PLC can be used to connect the VAP. Such a system can complement the shortcomings of each individually. In such a setup, PLC can be used for providing ubiquitous networking facility to all rooms and the VLC to all the areas of the room. Of course new methods of noise cancellation and channel modelling (Tiru et al., 2015; Tiru & Boruah, 2012; Chatterjee et al., 2020) will need to be incorporated with the PLC part as the simple methods (Barua & Tiru, 2006) will not be efficient. A HYC of this nature will maximize the output of available infrastructure like PL and illumination technologies. These green communication will help decrease the carbon and environmental footprint, the much dealt with issue in the present day. The COVID19 crises have indeed taught the world that it needs to be on guard for any other eventualities. This includes development in all spheres like ICT, health care, etc. that goes hand in hand. The world indeed needs to be more equipped than the past.

CONCLUSION

This chapter discusses the use of VLC in biomedical signal transfer. An elaborate review of the current work in this area is done. A channel modelling is performed to get an idea of the typical characteristics of VLC system. A FSK is proposed and implemented in hardware and has better performance than OOK as far as flicker mitigation and BER is concerned. The method is used for ECG signal transfer and is found to be successful up-to considerable distances. Based on the results and expectable performance, it can be stated that VLC can have promising performance in such a critical environment. Such an implementation will surely lead to green communication and technologies for the betterment of human life. Implementing such a system can surely be used in health care centers to deal the new challenges by health system in this current situation.

ACKNOWLEDGMENT

The authors are grateful to the FIST program of DST, New Delhi for the funding of some equipment for the work and the Department of Instrumentation and USIC for providing some of the instruments.

REFERENCES

Alam, M. R., Reaz, M. B. I., & Ali, M. A. M. (2012). A Review of Smart Homes—Past, Present, and Future. *IEEE Transactions on Systems, Man and Cybernetics. Part C, Applications and Reviews*, *42*(6), 1190–1203. doi:10.1109/TSMCC.2012.2189204

An, J., & Chung, W. (2016). A novel indoor healthcare with time hopping-based visible light communication. In *Proceedings of IEEE 3rd World Forum on Internet of Things (WF-IoT)* (pp. 19-23). 10.1109/WF-IoT.2016.7845438

An, J., Pham, Q. N., & Chung, W. Y. (2017). Single cell three channel wavelength division multiplexing in visible light communication. *Optics Express*, *25*(21), 25477–25485. doi:10.1364/OE.25.025477 PMID:29041214

Andrae, A. S., & Edler, T. (2015). On global electricity usage of communication technology: Trends to 2030. *Challenges.*, *6*(1), 1–41. doi:10.3390/challe6010117

Aslan, J., Mayers, K., Koomey, J. G., & France, C. (2018). Electricity intensity of Internet data transmission: Untangling the estimates. *Journal of Industrial Ecology*, *22*(4), 785–798. doi:10.1111/jiec.12630

Barua, A. G., & Tiru, B. (2006). Variation of width of the hysteresis loop with temperature in an emitter-coupled Schmitt trigger. *Indian Journal of Pure and Applied Physics*, *44*, 482–485.

Cahyadi, W. A., Jeong, T., Kim, Y., Chung, Y., & Adiono, T. (2015). Patient monitoring using Visible Light uplink data transmission. In *Proceedings of International Symposium on Intelligent Signal Processing and Communication Systems (ISPACS)* (pp. 431-434). 10.1109/ISPACS.2015.7432810

Chatterjee, S., Baishya, R., & Tiru, B. (2020). Estimating the Characteristics of the Forward Voltage Gain Scattering Parameter of Indoor Power Line Channel Using Only Input Port Measurement. *Wuxiandian Gongcheng*, *29*(4), 644–653. doi:10.13164/re.2020.0644

Chatterjee, S., & Tiru, B. (2018). Optimization of the components of a visible light communication system for efficient data transfer. In *Proceedings of IEEE EDKCON Conference* (pp.373-378). 10.1109/EDKCON.2018.8770450

Chatterjee, S., & Tiru, B. (2020). Development of a visible light communication system for reducing flicker in low data rate requirement. *Int. J. Nanoparticles*, *12*(1/2), 59–72. doi:10.1504/IJNP.2020.106001

Chen, T., Chang, C.-Y., Wang, C.-L., & Chen, Y.-S. (2011). Green technologies for wireless communications and mobile computing. *IET Communications*, *5*(18), 2595–2597. doi:10.1049/iet-com.2011.0852

Chow, C. W., Shiu, R. J., Liu, Y. C., Liao, X. L., Lin, K. H., Wang, Y. C., & Chen, Y. Y. (2018). Using advertisement light-panel and CMOS image sensor with frequency-shift-keying for visible light communication. *Optics Express*, *26*(10), 12530–12535. doi:10.1364/OE.26.012530 PMID:29801291

Dhatchayeny, D. R., Sewaiwar, A., Tiwari, S. V., & Chung, Y. H. (2015). Experimental Biomedical EEG Signal Transmission Using VLC. *IEEE Sensors Journal*, *15*(10), 5386–5387. doi:10.1109/JSEN.2015.2453200

Fang, J., Che, Z., & Jiang, Z. L. (2017). An Efficient Flicker-Free FEC Coding Scheme for Dimmable Visible Light Communication Based on Polar Codes. *IEEE Photonics Journal, 9*, 1-10. Advance online publication. doi:10.1109/JPHOT.2017.2689744

Gelenbe, E., & Caseau, Y. (2015). The impact of information technology on energy consumption and carbon emissions. *Ubiquity, 1*(June), 1–15. doi:10.1145/2755977

Holmes, D. (2014). Lighting for the Built Environment: Places of Worship. CIBSE.

Khan, L. U. (2017). Visible Light Communication: Applications, Architecture, Standardization and Research Challenges. *Digital Communications and Networks, 3*(2), 78–88. doi:10.1016/j.dcan.2016.07.004

Komine, T., & Nakagawa, M. (2004). Fundamental analysis for visible-light communication system using LED lights. *IEEE Transactions on Consumer Electronics, 50*(1), 100–107. doi:10.1109/TCE.2004.1277847

Ma, H., Lampe, L., & Hranilovic, S. (2017). Hybrid visible light and power line communication for indoor multiuser downlink. *Journal of Optical Communications and Networking, 9*(8), 635–647. doi:10.1364/JOCN.9.000635

Mejia, C. E., Georghiades, C. N., Abdallah, M. M., & Al-Badarneh, Y. H. (2017). Code design for flicker mitigation in visible light communications using finite state machines. *IEEE Transactions on Communications, 65*(5), 2091–2100. doi:10.1109/TCOMM.2017.2657518

Orovic, I., Stanković, S., & Beko, M. (2021). Multi-base compressive sensing procedure with application to ECG signal reconstruction. *EURASIP Journal on Advances in Signal Processing, 18*(1), 18. Advance online publication. doi:10.118613634-021-00728-4

Paksuniemi, M., Sorvoja, H., Alasaarela, E., & Myllyla, R. (2005). Wireless sensor and data transmission needs and technologies for patient monitoring in the operating room and intensive care unit. In *Proceedings of IEEE Engineering in Medicine and Biology 27th Annual Conference* (pp. 5182-5185). 10.1109/IEMBS.2005.1615645

Rajagopal, S., Roberts, R. D., & Lim, S. K. (2012). IEEE 802.15.7 visible light communication: Modulation schemes and dimming support. *IEEE Communications Magazine, 50*(3), 72–82. doi:10.1109/MCOM.2012.6163585

Rajbhandari, S., McKendry, J. J. D., Herrnsdorf, J., Chun, H., Faulkner, G., Haas, H., Watson, I. M., O'Brien, D., & Dawson, M. D. (2017). A review of gallium nitride LEDs for multi-gigabit-per-second visible light data communications. *Semiconductor Science and Technology, 32*(2), 1–40. doi:10.1088/1361-6641/32/2/023001

Rehman, S. U., Ullah, S., Chong, P. H. J., Yongchareon, S., & Komosny, D. (2019). Visible Light Communication: A System Perspective-Overview and Challenges. *Sensors (Basel), 19*(5), 1153. doi:10.339019051153 PMID:30866473

Singla, A., Sharma, D., & Vashisth, S. 2017. Data connectivity in flights using visible light communication. In *Proceeding of International Conference on Computing and Communication Technologies for Smart Nation (IC3TSN)* (pp. 71-74). 10.1109/IC3TSN.2017.8284453

Tan, Y. Y., & Chung, W. Y. (2014). Mobile health-monitoring system through visible light communication. *Bio-Medical Materials and Engineering, 24*(6), 3529–3538. doi:10.3233/BME-141179 PMID:25227066

Tan, Y. Y., Jung, S. J., & Chung, W. Y. (2013). Real time biomedical signal transmission of mixed ECG Signal and patient information using visible light communication. In *Proceedings of 35th Annual International Conference of the IEEE Engineering in Medicine and Biology Society (EMBC)* (pp. 4791-4794). 10.1109/EMBC.2013.6610619

Tang, C. K., Chan, K. H., Fung, L. C., & Leung, S. W. (2009). Electromagnetic Interference Immunity Testing of Medical Equipment to Second- and Third-Generation Mobile Phones. *IEEE Transactions on Electromagnetic Compatibility, 51*(3), 659–664. doi:10.1109/TEMC.2009.2021524

Tiru, B., & Boruah, P. K. (2012). Modeling power line channel using ABCD matrices for communication purposes. In *Proceedings of International Conference on Future Electrical Power and Energy Systems Lecture Notes in Information Technology* (*vol. 9*, pp. 374–379). Academic Press.

Tiru, B. (2015). Exploiting power line for communication purpose: Features and prospects of power line communication. In Proceedings of Intelligent Applications for Heterogeneous System Modeling and Design (pp. 320–334). doi:10.4018/978-1-4666-8493-5.ch014

Tiru, B., Baishya, B., & Sarma, U. (2015). An analysis of indoor power line network as a communication medium using ABCD matrices effect of loads on the transfer function of power line. Lecture Notes in Electrical Engineering. *Advances in Communication and Computing., 347*, 171–181. doi:10.1007/978-81-322-2464-8_14

Yang, L., Li, J., & Zhang, J. (2017). Hybrid visible light communications (VLC) and PLC system. In *Proceedings of Opto-Electronics and Communications Conference (OECC) and Photonics Global Conference (PGC)* (pp. 1-2). 10.1109/OECC.2017.8114968

Zeng, L., O'Brien, D., Minh, H. L., Lee, K., Jung, D., & Oh, Y. (2008). Improvement of Date Rate by using Equalization in an Indoor Visible Light Communication System. In *Proceedings of 4th IEEE International Conference on Circuits and Systems for Communications* (pp. 678-682). 10.1109/ICCSC.2008.149

Chapter 6
Effect of Intra–Band Tunneling on the Performance of Lead– Free Sn–Based Perovskite Solar Cell Using SCAPS–1D Simulator

Kunal Chakraborty

North Eastern Hill University, Shillong, India

Samrat Paul

North-Eastern Hill University, Shillong, India

ABSTRACT

This chapter presents the tunneling mechanism of electron and hole in the junction between absorbing layer and electron transport layer (ETL), which has an impact on the performance of devices in terms of quantum efficiency. In the present work, SCAPS-1D simulator is used to understand the effect of tunneling mechanism between the layers numerically. The most promising thin film-based lead-free Perovskite solar cells (PSCs) is the tin-based solar cell, which has tuneable band gap between 1.2 to 1.4 eV, and it can be used as both single junction and tandem structures.

INTRODUCTION

When sun light illuminated into the Sn based perovskite solar cell, Sn^{2+} degraded to Sn^{4+} and produce environment friendly material SnO_2. Initially Sn based solar cell has achieved 6% (Khoshsirat, 2015; Heriche, 2017) and so far the highest efõciency has been recorded to 9.6% (Mostefaoui, 2015). If we analyze the performance parameters of Sn based solar cell, we will get it has higher current density (J_{SC}, mA/cm²) which is above 25 mA/cm² and lower open circuit voltage (V_{OC}, V) which is below 0.5 V as it has low band gap value. In our present research paper, an alternative structure of two absorbing material $MASnI_3$ and $CsSnI_3$ is used as absorbing layer in proposed $TiO_2/MASnI_3$ or $CsSnI_3$/Spiro-OMetAD/Au

DOI: 10.4018/978-1-7998-9795-8.ch006

based device where tunnelling of electrons and holes are allowed between the absorbing material and TiO$_2$ layer and it has recorded above 25% of power conversion efficiency (PCE, %).

DEVICE ARCHITECTURE: PARAMETERS AND SIMULATION

Device Parameters

In our proposed work TiO$_2$ and Spiro-OMetAD is used as Electron transport layer (ETL) and Hole transport layer (HTL) with a band gap of 3.2 eV for TiO$_2$ and 3 eV for Spiro-OMetAD successively. Here, Table 1 shows the various properties of solar cell device parameters (Adewoyin, 2019; Bishnoi, 2018; Bansal, 2016; Khoshsirat, 2015). The absorbing material is placed between the ETL and HTL layer. A schematic view of proposed planar structure is shown in Fig. 1 (a) and band diagram of each layer for the two device is shown in Fig. 1 (b), Fig. 1 (c) respectively.

Table 1. Details of the device material parameters

Properties	Spiro-OMetAD	TiO$_2$	MASnI$_3$	CsSnI$_3$
Thickness (nm)	35	50	40	35
Band gap, E$_g$ (eV)	3.0	3.26	1.23	1.27
Electron affinity, E$_a$ (eV)	2.45	3.70	4.17	4.47
Relative Permittivity, ε_r	3.0	55.0	10.0	18.0
Donor density, N$_D$ (1/cm^3)	-	4.0×10^{14}	-	-
Acceptor density, N$_A$ (1/cm^3)	1×10^{18}	0	1×10^{18}	1×10^{19}
Electron mobility, μ_n (cm^2/V$_s$)	2×10^{-4}	100	1.6	4.37
Hole mobility, μ_p (cm^2/V$_s$)	1×10^{-4}	25	0.2	4.37

Numerical Simulation

This work is executed under 300 K operating temperature under 1.5 AM illumination of light with 1000 W/m2 Solar power which is available in the SCAPS-1D simulator software (Adewoyin, 2019).

RESULTS AND DISCUSSION

Impact of Tunneling on the Device Performance

Tunneling of an electron and hole for an active layer is a quantum-mechanical mechanism. The tunnelling is applied between the active layer and HTL through that quantum-mechanical mechanism. In SCAPS simulation, we have uses five layers and each layer has different electrical properties. Tunneling is executed through a potential barrier and when the tunneling is applied between the layers both the electrons which is exists at the top of the barrier (carrying higher energy level) and bottom of the bar-

Figure 1a. Schematic view of proposed device structure

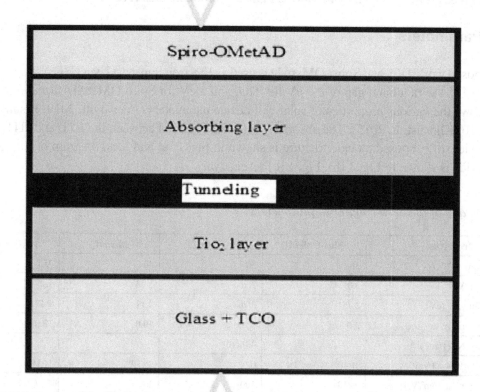

Figure 1b. Band diagram of MASnI₃ layer

Figure 1c. Band diagram of CsSnI₃ layer

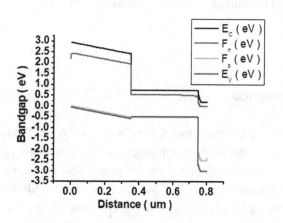

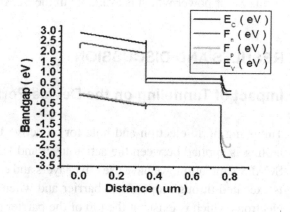

rier (carrying lower energy level) cross the interface. Such excess emission of electrons leads to more absorption of light and as a result better conversion efficiency is achieved. In our case, Fig. 2 (a), Fig. 2 (b), Fig. 2 (c) and Fig. 2 (d) shows the cumulative recombination current density (J_{SCLR} or I_{SCLR}) from left to right and cumulative recombination current density (J_{SCRL} or I_{SCRL}) from right to left respectively for the MASnI$_3$ and CsSnI$_3$ absorbing layer at maximum power point (MPP) with and with out tunnelling mechanism (Khoshsirat, 2015). It is observed that both the J_{SCLR} and J_{SCRL} is increases with open circuit voltage for the MASnI$_3$ active layer which is indicating at lower voltage the back recombination current density is decreases and as a result at lower open circuit voltage a large number of electrons and hole pair are produced. Similarly, for the CsSnI$_3$ layer as the voltage increases the back recombination current density is increases (Bube,1983). To get the higher PCE at low value of open circuit voltage, the short circuit current density is increases. Table 2 shows the device performance value after tunnelling mechanism between the HTL and absorbing layer.

Table 2. Device performance with and without tunneling

Materials	Tunneling	PCE (%)	J_{SC} (mA/cm²)
MASnI$_3$	without	23.2	32.8
MASnI$_3$	with	25.3	35.8
CsSnI$_3$	without	23.7	30.9
CsSnI$_3$	with	25.0	33.0

Effect of Tunneling on Materials Electrical Properties

It is possible to analyze the some of basic electrical measurements like C-V and G-V (Marshall, 2016; Chakraborty, 2021) through SCAPS-1D simulator where C is the capacitance value, and G is conductance. If we observed the Fig. 3 (a) and Fig. 3 (b), the value of C is decreasing and G is increasing with the open circuit voltage for the both the absorbing layer MASnI$_3$ and CsSnI$_3$ as the short circuit current is increases. Short circuit current density increases due to the recombination of excess electron and hole pair at the interface.

Figure 2a. Cumulative recombination current density for MASnI$_3$ layer (Without tunneling)

Figure 2b. Cumulative recombination current density for MASnI$_3$ layer (with tunneling)

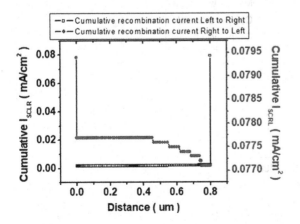

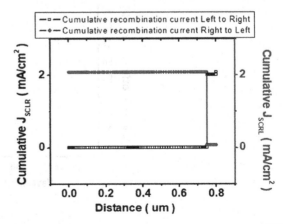

Figure 2c. Cumulative recombination current density for CsSnI₃ layer (without tunneling)

Figure 2d. Cumulative recombination current density for CsSnI₃ layer (with tunneling)

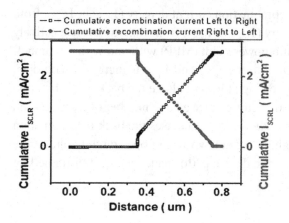
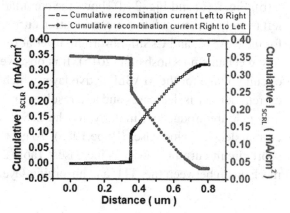

Figure 3a. C-V and G-V graph for MASnI₃ layer

Figure 3b. C-V and G-V graph for CsSnI₃ layer

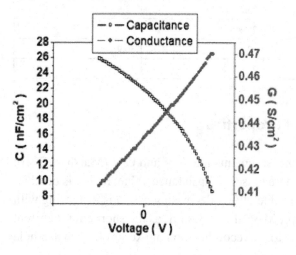
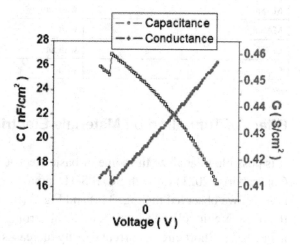

Figure 4. QE spectrum for MASnI₃ and CsSnI₃ layer

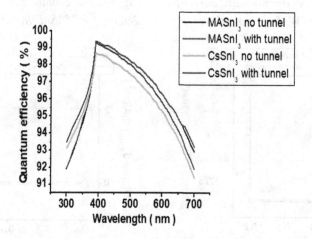

Effect of Tunneling on Quantum Efficiency

QE (quantum efficiency) signifies the area of the absorbing layer wavelength (Jalalian, 2019) is transferred into the electron-hole pair (Chakraborty, 2019). The Fig. 4 shows that between 350 nm to 400 nm the value of QE is higher for both absorbing layer, it implies the collection of electron-hole pair is higher in that region and after the 400 nm region the value of QE is started to decrease.

CONCLUSION

Present work is covered the tunnelling of electrons and holes and its effect on the performance, electrical properties of the solar cell active layer. It shows tunnelling mechanism on layer's thickness enhance the energy level and in our studies we have applied tunnelling mechanism at 400 nm thickness. We may also apply that mechanism in other thickness level to analyze the various performance parameters.

ACKNOWLEDGMENT

We are thankful to the University of Gent, Belgium for providing the SCAPS-1D software for our studies.

REFERENCES

Adewoyin, A. D., Olopade, M. A., Oyebola, O. O., & Chendo, M. A. (2019). Development of CZTGS/CZTS tandem thin film solar cell using SCAPS-1D. *Optik (Elsevier)*, *176*, 132–142. doi:10.1016/j.ijleo.2018.09.033

Bansal, S., & Aryal, P. (2016). Evaluation of new materials for electron and hole transport layers in perovskite-based solar cells through SCAPS-1D simulations. *IEEE 43rd Photovoltaic Specialists Conf.*, 747–750.

Bishnoi, S., & Pandey, S. K. (2018). Device performance analysis for lead-free perovskite solar cell optimization. *IET Optoelectronics*, *124*(4), 185–190. doi:10.1049/iet-opt.2017.0135

Bube, R. H., & Fahrenbruch, A. L. (1983). *Fundamentals of solar cells* (1st ed.). Academic Press.

Chakraborty, K., Choudhury, M. G., & Paul, S. (2019). Numerical study of Cs_2TiX_6 (X=Br⁻, I⁻, F⁻ and Cl⁻) based perovskite solar cell using SCAPS-1D device simulation. *Solar Energy*, *194*, 886–892. doi:10.1016/j.solener.2019.11.005

Chakraborty, K., Choudhury, M. G., & Paul, S. (2021). Study of Physical, Optical and Electrical Properties of Cesium Titanium (IV) Based Single Halide Perovskite Solar Cell. *IEEE J. of Photovoltaics*, *11*(2), 386–390. doi:10.1109/JPHOTOV.2021.3050268

Heriche, H., Rouabah, Z., & Bouarissa, N. (2017). New ultra thin CIGS structure solar cells using SCAPS simulation program. *Int. J. of Hydrogen Energy*, *42*(15), 9524–9532. doi:10.1016/j.ijhydene.2017.02.099

Jalalian, D., Ghadimi, A., & Kiani, A. (2019). Modeling of a high-performance bandgap graded Pb-free HTM-free perovskite solar cell. *The European Physical Journal Applied Physics*, *87*(1), 1–8. doi:10.1051/epjap/2019190095

Khoshsirat, N., & Yunus, N. A. M. (2013). Numerical simulation of CIGS thin film solar cells using SCAPS-1D. *IEEE Conf. Sustainable Utilization and Development in Engineering and Technology*, 63–67. 10.1109/CSUDET.2013.6670987

Khoshsirat, N., Yunus, N. A. M., Hamidon, M. N., & Shafie, S. (2015). Analysis of absorber layer properties effect on CIGS solar cell performance using SCAPS. *Optik (Elsevier)*, *126*(7-8), 681–686. doi:10.1016/j.ijleo.2015.02.037

Marshall, K. P., Walker, M., Walton, R. I., & Hotton, R. A. (2016). Enhanced stability and efficiency in hole-transport-layer-free CsSnI$_3$ perovskite photovoltaics. *Nature Energy*, *1*(12), 1–9. doi:10.1038/nenergy.2016.178

Mostefaoui, M., Mazar, H., & Khelifi, S. (2015). Simulation of high efficiency CIGS solar cells with SCAPS-1D software. *Energy Procedia (Elsevier)*, *74*, 736–744. doi:10.1016/j.egypro.2015.07.809

Chapter 7
Full–State Control of Rotary Pendulum Using LQR Controller

Horacio Alain Millan-Guerrero
Universidad Autónoma de Baja California, Mexico

Jose Antonio Nuñez-Lopez
Autonomous University of Baja California, Mexico

Fabian N. Murrieta-Rico
https://orcid.org/0000-0001-9829-3013
Universidad Politécnica de Baja California, Mexico

Lars Lindner
https://orcid.org/0000-0002-0623-6976

Universidad Autónoma de Baja California, Mexico

Oleg Sergiyenko
https://orcid.org/0000-0003-4270-6872
Universidad Autónoma de Baja California, Mexico

Julio C Rodríguez-Quiñonez
Universidad Autónoma de Baja California, Mexico

Wendy Flores-Fuentes
https://orcid.org/0000-0002-1477-7449
Universidad Autónoma de Baja California, Mexico

ABSTRACT

In this chapter, the authors design, simulate, and implement an optimal controller for a rotary pendulum while addressing real-world phenomena. The controller, called linear-quadratic-regulator (LQR), minimizes a cost function based on weights that penalize the system's state error and controller effort. The control objective is to reach the desired system state in an optimal way. The rotary pendulum consists of a pendulum attached to a rotary arm actuated by a motor. It is a great system to design and analyze different types of controllers. This system is underactuated, nonlinear, sensitive to initial conditions, and has 2 DOF. This chapter's main contributions are the mathematical modeling of the system taking into account nonlinear friction, the characterization of the plant using measured data from the physical system using the nonlinear squares and the trust-region reflective algorithms, comparison of linear and nonlinear behaviors, and implementation on real hardware considering discrete phenomena while using hardware-provided tools such as position decoding and PWM generation.

DOI: 10.4018/978-1-7998-9795-8.ch007

INTRODUCTION

Underactuated systems have fewer actuators than degrees of freedom. This type of system has advantages such as more straightforward mechanical design, better performance, fewer sensors, low cost, and higher energy efficiency. However, there are also disadvantages such as complex dynamics and the inability to follow arbitrary trajectories.

Underactuated systems are a topic of high interest in current research due to their possible medical and industrial applications with human-like robots and other non-human bio-inspired robots. One example of an exciting application are electromechanical prosthetics (Liu, Huda, Sun, & Yu, 2020).

In this chapter, the underactuated system that will be discussed is the Rotary Pendulum. This dynamical system is nonlinear and highly sensitive to initial conditions and perturbations. It also suffers from complex nonlinearities such as break-away friction and mechanical backlash; these complex nonlinearities can become a real problem. Depending on the pendulum's mechanical properties, these nonlinearities may be linearized or not.

Two typically nonlinear effects must be considered when using low-quality DC motors: the break-away and the cogging torque (Lindner, et al., 2017). In tribology, the break-away torque is generally referred to as Static Friction, which firstly was described by Amonton's law and Coulomb's friction law (Gohar & Rahnejat, 2008). The cogging torque is part of the Dynamic Friction (Popov, 2010). Due to the break-away and the cogging torque, a minimum armature voltage must be applied to prevent the motor from stopping. Hence, the motor shaft will always be positioned with an error representing a residual error, not zero. In order to reduce the positioning error, a high-quality DC motor with less break-away and without cogging torque must be used (Lindner, et al., 2016). The high-quality DC motor Maxon RE-Max29 uses an ironless winding for their rotors, which do not possess a cogging torque and uses high-quality ball bearings, which reduce the break-away torque. These motors can be operated constant and linear even at low rotational speeds. Therefore, the shaft of these high-quality DC motors can be positioned more accurately and with higher resolution than the shaft of low-quality DC motors (Lindner, et al., 2016).

For this chapter, the rotary pendulum was identified and modeled using the Stribeck friction model; the respective parameters were estimated using MATLAB's bounded design optimization "Parameter Estimation" tool (Parameter Estimation, 2021). This tool estimates model parameters and initial states using several optimization techniques. It only requires the system's model and measurement data of the real plant to estimate its parameters.

Different linear and nonlinear control methods and algorithms can be used to stabilize the pendulum at the unstable equilibrium point, which makes this system a valuable testbench for conducting experiments with different control approaches and compare their performance. In this chapter, the control will be performed using a full-state LQR controller. There are other methods for controlling the pendulum, such as adaptive neural networks (J. Moreno-Valenzuela, 2016) and sliding mode controllers (Wadi, Lee, & Romdhane, 2018).

The linear quadratic regulator (LQR) controller is a full state feedback controller with the difference that the eigenvalues' location of the system depends on a cost function. This cost function weights the controller effort cost such that the resulting controller minimizes control cost (Moreno-Valenzuela, Aguilar-Avelar, Puga-Guzmán, & Santibáñez, 2016).

MAIN OBJECTIVE OF THE CHAPTER

This chapter's objective is to design, simulate, and implement an LQR controller that stabilizes the rotary pendulum in the upward direction. The controller is implemented on an STM32 microcontroller. The implementation takes advantage of the dedicated hardware the STM32 provides to decode the sensors' angular positions, control the motor via a PWM signal and execute the control loop in a precisely timed manner. This simplifies the C code of the LQR controller, leaving the CPU only for calculating the control signal and other important tasks such as angular velocity estimation.

FUNDAMENTALS

Mathematical Model of the Rotary Pendulum

The mathematical modeling of the pendulum is based on Magnus Gäfvert's work (Gäfvert, 1998) and depicted in following Figure 1.

Figure 1. Schematic of the rotary pendulum

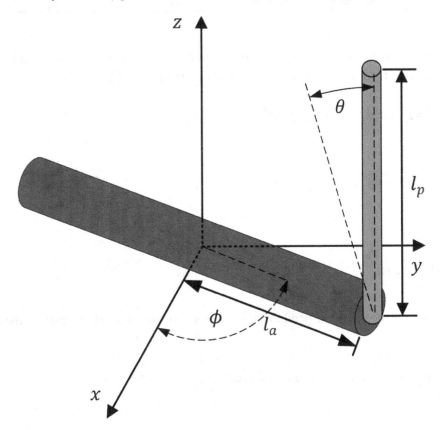

In order to avoid confusion and misunderstandings, it is important to define how the parts of the system shown in Figure 1 will be named. The whole system will be called *Rotary Pendulum*. The cylinder that rotates around the *Z* axis on the *XY* plane will be called *Pendulum's Arm,* and its angular position will be the ϕ angle. Lastly, the rod attached at the end of the *Pendulum's Arm* will be called just *Pendulum,* and its angular position will be the θ angle.

All angular positions, angular velocities, and the rest of the parameters of the system are summarized in Table 1. using S.I units.

Table 1. Table of parameters of the rotary pendulum

Parameter	Description	Units
l_a	Pendulum's Arm length	*m*
l_p	*Length from ϕ joint to θ joint*	*M*
ϕ	Angular position of the actuated joint	rad
θ	Angular position of the underactuated joint	rad
m_a	Mass of the pendulum's arm	*kg*
m_p	Mass of the pendulum	*kg*
J	Moment of inertia as seen from the actuated joint	*kg•m²*

The position at the end of the pendulum can be described as a function of the angular positions ϕ and θ using trigonometry with the following equations (Gäfvert, 1998):

$$r_x\left(l_a,l_p,\phi,\right)=l_a\cos(\phi)-l_p\sin(\,)\textit{sin}(\phi) \tag{1}$$

$$r_y\left(l_a,l_p,\phi,\right)=l_a\sin(\phi)+l_p\cos(\,)\textit{sin}(\phi) \tag{2}$$

$$r_z\left(l_a,l_p,\phi,\right)=l_p\cos(\,) \tag{3}$$

To get the speed at the top of the pendulum, it is needed to take the derivative; thus, the above equations become:

$$v_x\left(l_a,l_p,\phi,\right)=-l_a\sin(\phi)\dot{\phi}-l_p\cos(\,)\textit{sin}(\phi),\,-l_p\sin(\,)\cos(\,)\dot{\phi} \tag{4}$$

$$v_y\left(l_a,l_p,\phi,\right)=l_a\sin(\phi)\dot{\phi}+l_p\cos(\,)\textit{cos}(\phi),\,-l_p\sin(\,)\sin(\phi)\dot{\phi} \tag{5}$$

$$v_z\left(l_a, l_p, \phi,, \right) = -l_p \sin\left(,\right), \dot{} \tag{6}$$

Now, after obtaining the position and velocity equations, the motion equations must be obtained using the Lagrangian, the Hamiltonian, Newton's *F=ma*, or any other method desired.
The obtained motion equations were:

$$\left(\pm + {}^2 \sin^2,\right)\ddot{\phi} + {}^3 cos, \ddot{\theta} + 2\,{}^2 cos, sin, \dot{\phi}, \dot{} - {}^3 sin,, \dot{}^2 = \ddot{A}_\phi \tag{7}$$

$${}^3 cos, \ddot{\phi} + {}^2 \ddot{\theta} - {}^2 cos, sin, \dot{\phi}^2 - {}' \sin, = \ddot{A}, \tag{8}$$

Where *α*, *β*, *γ*, and *δ* are constants used to simplify the motion equations. They depend on the physical parameters of the rotary pendulum, such as the moment of inertia of the arm, mass, etc. Said constants will not be derived in this chapter to keep equations compact.

It is also convenient to express the motion equations as a set of first-order differential equations. This becomes useful for system dynamics simulations.

$$\frac{d}{dt}\phi = \dot{\phi} \tag{9}$$

$$\frac{d}{dt}\dot{\phi} = \frac{1}{\pm^2 - {}^{3\,2} + \left({}^{2\,2} + {}^{3\,2}\right)\sin^2,}$$
$$\left[{}^{2\,3}(\sin^2, -1)sin, \dot{\phi}^2 - 2\,{}^{2\,2}cos, sin, \dot{\phi}, \dot{} + {}^{2\,3}sin,, \dot{}^2 - {}^{3}{}' cos, sin, + {}^2 \ddot{A}_\phi - {}^3 cos, \ddot{A}, \right] \tag{10}$$

$$\frac{d}{dt}, = \dot{}, \tag{11}$$

$$\frac{d}{dt}\dot{} = \frac{1}{\pm^2 - {}^{3\,2} + \left({}^{2\,2} + {}^{3\,2}\right)\sin^2,}\left[{}^2(\pm + {}^2 \sin^2,)cos, sin, \dot{\phi}^2 + 2\,{}^{2\,3}(1 - \sin^2,)sin, \dot{\phi},\right.$$
$$\left. - {}^{3\,2}cos, sin,, \dot{}^2 + {}'(\pm + {}^2 \sin^2,)sin, - {}^3 cos, \ddot{A}_\phi + (\pm + {}^2 \sin^2,)\ddot{A}, \right] \tag{12}$$

DC Motor Model

The starting point is the model of a DC motor's electrical and mechanical behavior with permanent magnets under neglecting nonlinear effects, such as break-away and cogging torque. Thereby $v_{in}(t)$ represents the DC motor armature voltage, $i_{in}(t)$ the armature current, L_a the armature inductance, R_a the armature resistance, J the rotor moment of inertia, c the viscous damping friction constant, $\theta(t)$ the actual angular position, $\dot{\theta}(t)$ the actual angular speed and $T(t)$ the produced motor torque. Transforming the differential equations of the mathematical model of the motor DC into the frequency domain by Laplace-Transformation with initial values zero the transfer function $G(s)$ can be derived. Furthermore, this model is presented by the following equation (13) and Figure 2.

$$G(s) = \frac{V_{in}(s)}{\varphi(s)} = \frac{K_{ma}}{(R_a + s \cdot L_a)(c + s \cdot J) + K_{ma}K_b} \tag{13}$$

Figure 2. DC motor model neglecting nonlinear effects

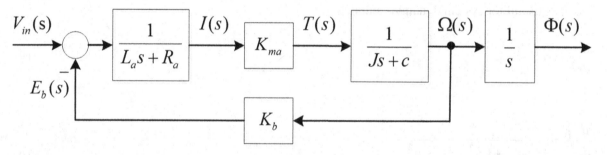

Thereby, $V_{in}(s)$ represents the motor armature voltage, $I(s)$ the armature current, $T(s)$ the motor torque, $\Omega(s)$ the actual angular speed, $\Theta(s)$ the actual angular position in the frequency-domain, G(s) represents the complete system transfer function of the DC motor that relates the output $\Theta(s)$ and the input V_{in}, K_{ma} represents the torque constant which relates the mechanical torque with the electric current flowing through the DC motor, and K_b represents the back electromotive force (back-EMF) constant, which relates the angular velocity taken by the DC motor shaft with the back-EMF. Additionally, two constants were derived, the electrical $T_E = \dfrac{L_a}{R_a}$ and the mechanical time constant $T_M = \dfrac{J}{c}$. Due to the S.I. units being consistent with the conservation of energy, the fact $K_{ma}=K_b$ is assumed (Virgala, Frankovský, & Kenderová, 2013).

The equation of the mechanical section for the DC Motor, which is represented by a transfer block in Figure 2, can be expressed as follows:

$$J \cdot \ddot{\varphi}(t) = T(t) - c \cdot \dot{\varphi} \tag{14}$$

To integrate a nonlinear friction model, the motor damping linearly given by $c \cdot \dot{\theta}$ is replaced by a nonlinear friction torque $T_f\left(\dot{\theta}\right)$, which represents a function of the DC motor actual angular speed $\dot{\theta}(t)$.

$$J \cdot \ddot{\theta} = T(t) - T_f\left(\dot{\theta}\right) \tag{15}$$

Rewriting the mechanical equation (14) of the DC Motor with a nonlinear classical friction model described in (28) or (29); the following equation is obtained:

$$J \cdot \ddot{\theta} + F_v \cdot \dot{\theta} = T(t) - f\left(\dot{\theta}\right) \tag{16}$$

, where J is the inertia, $\dot{\theta}$ the angular velocity, F_v the viscous friction coefficient, $T(t)$ the motor torque, and $f\left(\dot{\theta}\right)$ the nonlinear friction component. If the friction model proposed for the system includes only the Coulomb friction and the viscous friction, the mechanical equation leads to:

$$f\left(\dot{\theta}\right) = F_C \cdot sgn\left(\dot{\theta}\right) \tag{17}$$

In otherwise, if it is considered to use the Stribeck friction for modeling the friction torque, the mechanical equation yields:

$$f\left(\dot{\theta}\right) = \left(F_C + \left(F_S - F_C\right) \cdot e^{-\left(\dot{\theta}/v_s\right)^2}\right) \cdot sgn\left(\dot{\theta}\right) \tag{18}$$

In this chapter, the LQR controller discussed uses a torque signal in Newton-meters to control the plant. However, in the real plant, the motor does not have a 1 to 1 voltage-torque ratio, so a torque-voltage transfer function is needed to apply the correct control signal. Therefore, from the block diagram in Figure 2, it can be seen that the motor converts voltage to torque using the following transfer function:

$$\frac{T}{V_{in}} = \frac{K_{ma}/L_a}{s + R_a/L_a} = \frac{K_{ma}}{sL_a + R_a} \tag{19}$$

In the derivation of the model, the electrical dynamics are neglected in comparison to the mechanical dynamics due to a much faster electric response, i.e., $T_A \ll T_M$. Mostly that is the case of modern used DC motors; for example, the Maxon Motor RE-max29 offers $T_A = 0.0813ms$ and $T_M = 4.4473ms$. Therefore, the transfer function becomes:

$$\frac{T}{V_{in}} = \frac{K_{ma}}{R_a} \tag{20}$$

Solving for V_{in} the following equation is obtained:

$$V_{in} = T \frac{R_a}{K_{ma}}$$

(21)

Where T is the desired torque, V_{in} is the input voltage needed to get the desired torque, R_a is the armature resistance and K_{ma} represents the torque constant.

More information about the electromechanical behavior mathematical model and parameter identification of the DC motor can be widely found in the relevant literature (Lyshevski, 1999), (Chapman, 2003), and (Virgala, Frankovský, & Kenderová, 2013).

Rotary Encoder

Angular Position Measurement

The angular positions of the ϕ and θ axes are measured using a quadrature incremental rotary encoder. The rotary encoder outputs two digital signals out of phase by 90°, signal A and signal B. Every time one of the two signals changes polarity, a step is counted up or down by the TIM$n_{-CN}T$ counter depending on the direction of rotation. The direction of rotation can be detected from the sequence of transitions of the A and B channels.

Figure 3. 3D model of the incremental rotary encoder

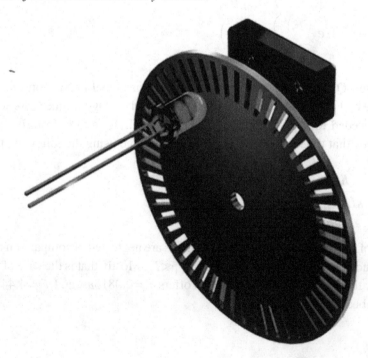

From Figure 3, the working principle of a rotary encoder can be easily understood. The LED is constantly shining a light on the encoder disk, and depending on the position of the disk, the slits on the disk will allow the light to continue its path to the sensor. The black sensor has two light detectors separated by 90 electrical degrees; each detector is a channel. In Figure 4, both channels, A and B, are shown.

The signals generated by the sensor will have a period proportional to the encoder's disk speed, and the direction of motion can be determined by the phase between channel A and B; if the phase is 90°, the encoder is rotating in a certain direction, if the phase is -90° the direction of rotation is the opposite.

Position can be obtained by integrating velocity or by counting single pulses when channel A or B change polarity.

Figure 4. Example of encoder operation

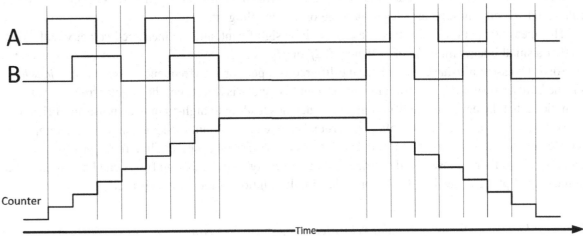

The angular positions of the rotary encoders can be decoded via software using interrupts or polling. However, the STM32 microcontroller can also decode the position via hardware using the timers in *Encoder interface mode*. This has the benefit of an extremely fast update rate f_{TIM} plus, it does not require CPU resources. The CPU reads the $TIM_{n\_}CNT$ counter value when needed to get the current angular position. In this mode, channels A and B are connected to the TIM_n pins in the STM32. Two timers are needed, one for each axis. The timers need to be configured in *Encoder interface mode*; the timer configuration is shown in the Timers Configuration subsection.

As it can be seen in Figure 4, each time a channel changes polarity, the counter is incremented or decremented depending on the current and previous state of the A and B channels. The logic required to determine if the counter has to be incremented or decremented is implemented on the hardware of the STM32.

Angular Velocity Estimation

Due to the fact that the control loop is executed at a constant frequency, the angular velocity can be simply calculated as:

$$\acute{E} = \frac{,[k]-,[k-1]}{Ts} \tag{22}$$

Where ω is the angular velocity in steps per second, θ is the angular position of the axis in steps, k *is* the sample index and Ts ₁s the inverse of the sampling frequency fs.

It is crucial to consider the measurement phenomena that may occur when the controller is implemented on a discrete device such as a microcontroller. An important example of such a phenomenon is velocity estimation. Suppose angular position is measured with a discrete sensor such as an incremental encoder. In that case, velocity can be obtained by taking the discrete derivate of the position. However, it is crucial to take into account that due to the nature of discrete derivates, the calculated velocity will be an integer multiple of the sampling frequency, just as equation (22) shows.

It can be seen from that equation that due to the fact that the numerator will always be an integer, the calculated velocity must be an integer multiple of the sampling frequency.

This means that at low velocities, the error will be significant, and the measured velocity will either be 0 or a small integer multiple of f_s such as f_s, $2f_s$ or $3f_s$.

Also, it is essential to have in mind that the differential operator has a frequency response of $s=j\omega$ where s is the Laplace operator, j is the unit imaginary number, and ω is (this time) the angular frequency. It can be noticed that the derivate amplifies higher frequencies leading to high-frequency noise amplification.

Before implementing the controller, it is crucial to take into account such phenomena; for example, to reduce the error at low velocities, a simple solution can be to reduce the sampling frequency to the detriment of controller response speed. Also, a low pass filter or more elaborate filters can be implemented at the cost of phase delay. For this chapter, the simple solution of reducing fs is used.

Figure 5. Ideal and measured angular velocities and percentage error

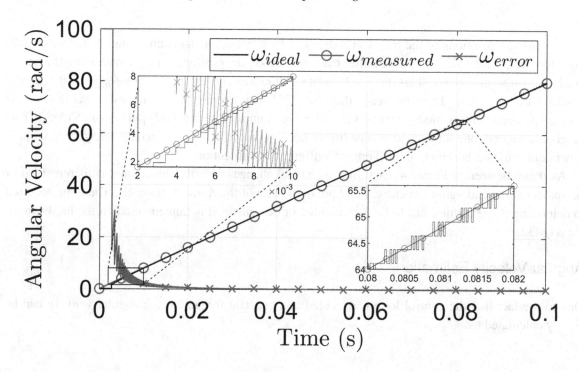

In Figure 1, a simulation of the measurement of velocity was performed. ωi_{deal} represents the actual velocity of the rotary encoder shaft and $\omega me_{asured\,r}$ epresents the velocity estimated by the microcontroller using the formula (41). As it can be seen, velocity $\omega mea_{sured\,ca}$ n only be represented using discrete values. The percentage error signal, $\omega err_{or,\,w}$ as calculated using the following formula:

$$\omega_{error} = \frac{\omega_{measured} - \omega_{ideal}}{\omega_{ideal}} \cdot 100\% \qquad (23)$$

As Figure 1 shows, the percentage error is significant (greater than 5%) for angular velocities smaller than 6rad/s given the rotary encoder steps per revolution and the sampling period, T_s.

Friction Phenomena

Friction is a complex physical phenomenon that acts against relative motion between two surfaces in contact. This phenomenon is a significant obstacle to the search for effective control of an electrome-chanical system, such as the rotary pendulum controlled with a DC motor. The phenomenon of friction is still not completely understood. Over the years, many friction phenomena have been observed and tried to be captured in models. This section starts with an overview of the friction models proposed in literature over the years. Then, the second part of this section discusses the method currently used to perform friction model identification.

Classical Friction Models

There are many different purposes for friction modeling. Reasons are, for example, getting insight into the physical aspects, friction compensation, or simulation. In this subsection, the so-called static models will be discussed. The models are relatively simple and can predict the global quantitative behavior of friction. Generally, the friction force calculated by the classical models depends on the velocity. What model is needed depends on the purpose, on the needed effect of the model in describing the friction phenomena, and on the needed model efficiency.

The empirically observed friction phenomena led to the models of Coulomb (Olsson, Åström, Canudas de Wit, Gäfvert, & Lischinsky, 1998) and terms such as viscous and static friction (Armstrong-Hélouvry, Dupont, & Canudas De Wit, 1994). Models describing one or more of these phenomena are often referred to as the classical models.' The main idea of classical models is that friction force opposes the motion of the object. With the simplest model, it is common to assume that friction force F_f represents a function of the relative sliding velocity v. In (Morin, 1833) was introduced the idea of static friction, stating that such friction can be described satisfactorily not only as a function of velocity but also of the applied torque. Static friction counteracts external forces below a certain level before the initial sliding; static friction is greater than the Coulomb friction (Olsson, Åström, Canudas de Wit, Gäfvert, & Lischinsky, 1998). The friction force for zero velocity is a function of the externally applied torque F_e. This can be modeled by:

$$F_{f_s}\left(v, F_e\right) = \begin{cases} F_e & \text{if} \quad v = 0 \quad \text{and} \quad \left|F_e\right| > F_s \\ F_s \cdot \text{sgn}\left(F_e\right) & \text{if} \quad v = 0 \quad \text{and} \quad \left|F_e\right| \le F_s \end{cases} \qquad (24)$$

where $sgn(\bullet)$ is the standard signum function defined as

$$\text{sgn}(x) = \begin{cases} -1 & \textbf{if} \quad x < 0 \\ 0 & \textbf{if} \quad x = 0 \\ 1 & \textbf{if} \quad x > 0 \end{cases} \tag{25}$$

and F_s represents the break-away friction force, which is assumed to be constant. As for Coulomb friction, it is present when $v \geq 0$, which does not depend on F_e and can be described as

$$F_{f_c}(v) = F_C \cdot sgn(v) \tag{26}$$

where F_C represents the Coulomb friction level, and the friction force is proportional to the normal load F_N by a kinematic friction coefficient μ that depends on the characteristics of the contact surfaces, i.e. $FC_{=}\mu\bullet FN$. The term viscous friction is used for a force component caused by the viscosity of lubricants used between the sliding surfaces, which is usually described as:

$$F_{f_v}(v) = F_v \cdot v \tag{27}$$

where F_v represents the viscous friction coefficient. It is common to combine the Coulomb friction and the viscous friction effects as follows:

$$F_f(v) = F_C \bullet sgn(v) + F_v \bullet v \tag{28}$$

The Stribeck friction describes the interaction of two lubricated surfaces when sliding on each other, defined by Richard Stribeck, thereby defines a characteristic speed friction-torque curve, containing three regimens. The Stribeck friction represents a function of the relative speed between these two lubricated surfaces:

$$F_f(v) = \left(F_C + (F_S - F_C) \cdot e^{-|v/v_s|'} \right) \cdot sgn(v) + F_v \cdot v \tag{29}$$

where F_s, F_C and F_v are the static, Coulomb, and viscous friction components, respectively, v_s is the Stribeck velocity threshold and δ is a random exponent of the Stribeck model. Several parameterizations of (29) have been proposed in (Armstrong-Hélouvry, Dupont, & Canudas De Wit, 1994).

Figure 6. Stribeck friction curve

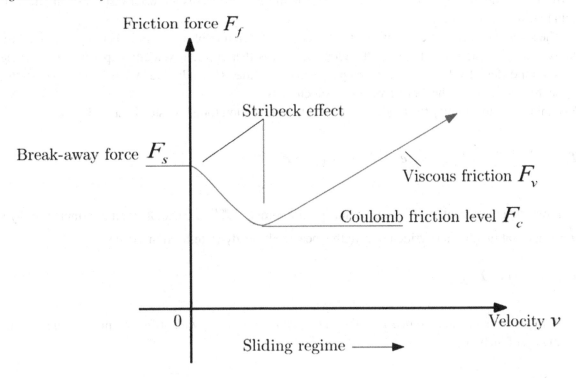

Friction Model Identification Method

The parameters of the classical friction models will be identified experimentally for the DC motors of the rotary pendulum. An overview of the identification procedures proposed in the literature is given (Lischinsky, Canudas De Wit, & Morel, 1999).
The general equation of motion for the DC motor used in the rotary pendulum is given by

$$U(i) - T_{load} - T_f = I \cdot \ddot{\theta} \tag{30}$$

   The friction model identification process has the goal to describe the measured friction torque adequately $T_{f,ss}^{meas}$ using the modeled friction torque $T_{f,ss}^{mod}$. This is done by adjusting the model parameters. The input torque $U(i)$ and the position θ in equation (30) are measured. From the position, the velocity $\dot{\theta}$ and acceleration $\ddot{\theta}$ are calculated. The static load torque T_{load} and the inertia I of the system must be known; they can be deduced from datasheets or determined experimentally (review section 5). Note, that most identification structures in literature are based on set-ups for which gravitational forces do not appear in the equation of motion. To use the identification structures in this work, the gravitational forces (denoted as $T_{load}(\dot{\theta})$ here) must be included. A second note to make is that in this subsection, the equation of motion of the motor is used as a starting point towards friction identification. Therefore, the friction force F_f is replaced by the friction torque T_f since this is the torque the motor must deliver to overcome friction. Also, the angular position θ and its derivatives are used instead of the translational position and its derivatives.

The static parameters are relatively easy to identify. Literature offers various techniques to identify the parameters. The general idea of the identification is that constant velocity experiments are done for several different velocities, for which parameters are fitted (Canudas De Wit & Lischinsky, 1996), (Susanto, Babuška, Liefhebber, & van der Weiden, 2008).

Assuming $\delta=2$ to simplify the model given by (**29**), the friction torque in steady-state $Tf_{,ss}$ is

$$T_{f,ss}\left(\dot{}\right)=\left(F_C+\left(F_S-F_C\right)\cdot e^{-\left(\dot{}/v_s\right)^2}\right)\cdot \text{sgn}\left(\dot{}\right)+F_v\cdot\dot{} \tag{31}$$

From the experiments, the experimental friction torque $T_{f,ss}^{meas}$ is calculated. At constant velocity ($\ddot{\theta}=0$), equation (30) is rewritten to give the measured, steady-state friction torque

$$T_{f,ss}^{meas}=U\left(i\right)-T_{load} \tag{32}$$

With known static load torque T_{load}, the static parameters are now identified by minimizing the following cost function $\mathcal{J}$.

$$\mathcal{J}=\Sigma\left(T_{f,ss}^{meas}-T_{f,ss}^{mod}\left(\dot{}\right)\right) \tag{33}$$

There are two options for determining the parameters since equation (31) is nonlinear. The first option is to use a design optimization tool and include the list of parameters to be identified. The second option is to compute the cost function (33) for several values in the respective range where the parameters are expected to be and select the value that results in the lowest cost function value.

The first option is used; the model parameters were determined using the bounded design optimization MATLAB's "Parameter Estimation" tool (Parameter Estimation, 2021). This tool uses optimization techniques to estimate model parameters and initial states from test data. It computes and minimizes the error between the simulated and measured output. The estimation is complete when the optimization method finds a local minimum (Parameter Estimation, 2021). This knowledge is then given to the design optimization tool using proper bounds on the parameter. The use of the design optimization algorithm may require more calculation time and computational power. However, the parameter estimation tool will be used in this work since these factors are not an issue.

CHARACTERIZATION AND PARAMETER ESTIMATION

Parameter estimation consists of approximating the dynamical system's constants using a mathematical algorithm that tries to reduce as much as possible the difference between experimental data and simulation data generated with the mathematical model that describes the system's dynamics.

Parameter estimation requires three steps before the estimation. The first step is the mathematical modeling of the system's dynamics. The second step is experimentation with the real plant measurement of the plant's dynamics. The third step is data preparation, in this step the data obtained in the second step is prepared so that it matches the simulation time duration, the experiment starts at $t=0$, unwanted noise is reduced, etc.

The mathematical algorithms used to approximate the parameters were the minimum nonlinear squares and the trust-region reflective algorithm.

DC Motor Parameter Estimation

To obtain the DC motor parameters, a step response experiment was captured and analyzed. The signals measured for that experiment were the motor's angular velocity and the armature current. The angular velocity was measured using a rotary encoder, and the armature current was measured as a voltage signal with an oscilloscope using a 1Ω shunt resistor. The input signal is shown in Figure 7.

Figure 7. Input voltage applied to the motor for the parameter estimation

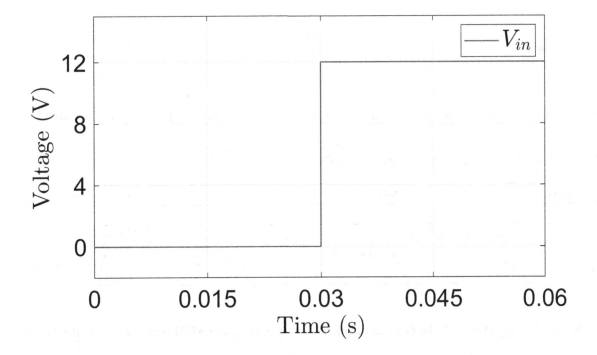

Furthermore, the current measurement taken with the oscilloscope is shown in Figure 8.

Figure 8. Current measurement taken with the oscilloscope using a 1Ω shunt resistor

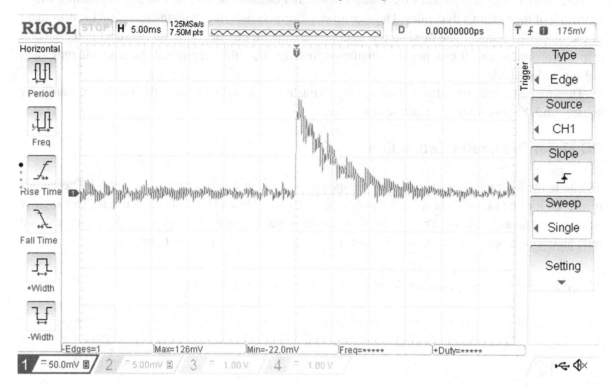

After running the parameter estimation algorithm, the estimated values were summarized in Table 2:

Table 2. Table of estimated parameters of the DC motor

Parameter	Description	Value	Units
K_{ma}	Torque Constant	168×10^{-3}	$Nm \bullet A^{-1}$
J	Rotor Moment of Inertia	1.18×10^{-6}	$kg \bullet m^2$
c	Motor damping Viscous Friction Constant	1.24×10^{-6}	$Nm \bullet s \bullet rad^{-1}$
K_b	Back Electromotive Force (Back-EMF) Constant	168×10^{-3}	$V \bullet s \bullet rad^{-1}$

Notice that $K_{ma} = K_b$ due to the fact that the motor's model assumes no EM energy losses and S.I units are being used.

Furthermore, the parameters measured directly were the armature resistance $R_a = 104\Omega$, and La=8.48e-3 H.

After obtaining the motor's parameters, a simulation with said parameters was done, the results were compared to the measured current signal of the real motor taken with the oscilloscope and the shunt resistor.

Figure 9. Comparation of measured and simulated current signals after the parameter estimation

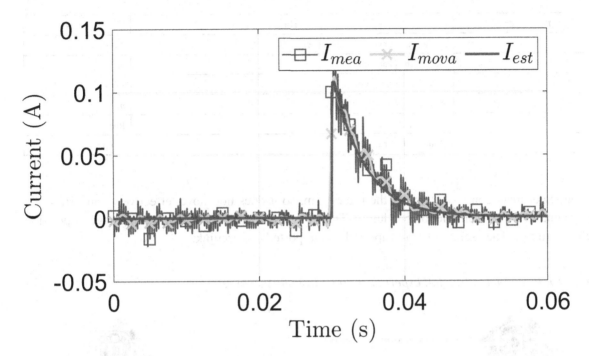

As it can be seen in Figure 9 the estimation of the motor's parameters was successful. I_{mea} refers to the measured current signal taken with the oscilloscope, I_{est} refers to the current signal of the simulated motor with the estimated parameters and I_{mova} is just a moving average of the I_{mea} signal for clarity purposes. The I_{mea} signal is noisy due to the fact that the oscilloscope was measuring millivolt voltages.

The noise does not represent a problem due to the fact that the mathematical model of the motor cannot replicate such noise. What will happen is that the parameter estimation algorithm will try to reduce the quadratic error between the I_{est} and I_{mea} signals by varying the parameters of the motor's model and will eventually converge to a solution that coincides with the I_{mea} signal but without the noise.

Pendulum Friction Estimation

In order to perform the pendulum's friction estimation, equation (34) was modeled in *Simulink*; the model takes into account nonlinear friction and nonlinear dynamics. Then, a free-fall experiment was done with the real pendulum, and the parameters were calculated as explained in section 5 using *Simulink*.

$$\frac{d^2,}{dt} + »\frac{d,}{dt} + \frac{mgL}{I_s}\sin(,) = 0 \tag{34}$$

Where the parameters of equation (34) are summarized in Table 3:

Table 3. Parameters of the pendulum

Parameter	Description	Units
λ	Friction, as shown in equation (**18**)	$Nm \bullet s \bullet rad^{-1}$
m	Mass of the pendulum	m
g	Acceleration of gravity	$m \bullet s^{-2}$
L	Pendulum's length	m
θ	Angular position	Rad
I_s	Moment of inertia	$kg \bullet m^2$

The experiment consists of fixing the rotary arm, so it does not move, effectively converting the rotary pendulum into a simple rod pendulum. Then, the pendulum falls from a starting angular position of $\theta = 90°$ to rest. The oscillations are captured and imported to Simulink.

Figure 10. Pendulum in free-fall experiment going from $\theta = 90°$ to rest

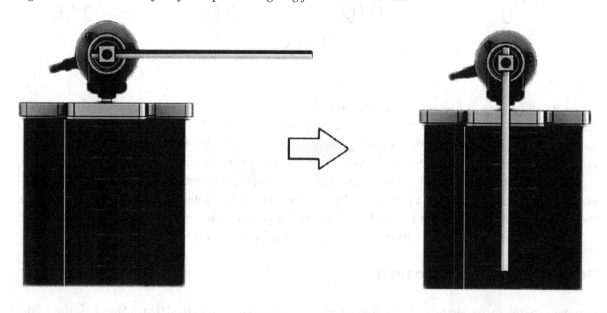

Figure 11. Comparison between measured pendulum and simulated with friction

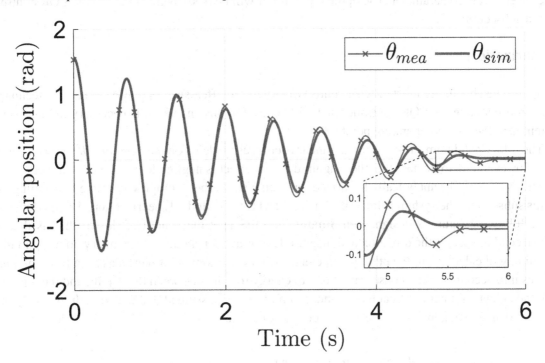

After running Simulink's parameter estimation algorithm, the estimated parameters simulate with great accuracy the real pendulum behavior, as shown in Figure 11. θm_{ea} is the measured angular position and θsi_{m_i}s the position of the simulated pendulum with the estimated parameters.

The estimated parameters obtained in this experiment are summarized in Table 4:

Table 4. Parameters of the pendulum friction estimation experiment

Parameter	Description	Value	Units	Obtention
F_{vp}	Pendulum viscous Friction Constant	66.55e-6	$Nm \bullet s \bullet rad^{-1}$	Estimated
F_{cp}	Pendulum Coulomb friction constant	516.57e-6	Nm	Estimated
m	Mass of the pendulum	0.03	m	Measured
g	Acceleration of gravity	9.81	$m \bullet s^{-2}$	Measured
L	Pendulum's length	0.14	m	Measured
I_s	Pendulum moment of inertia	169e-6	$kg \bullet m^2$	Calculated from geometry

LQR CONTROLLER DESIGN

The objective of the controller is to stabilize the pendulum optimally. Optimality is user-defined, and it can depend on the energy effort of the controller, the time required to reduce the error to 0, or any other user-specified parameter. The optimal controller will be described in detail in the LQR controller design subsection.

Linearization

In order to be able to use most of what control theory has to offer, such as powerful analysis techniques and controllers like the LQR controller that will be used in this chapter, it is necessary to linearize the system near the desired operating point.

The rotary pendulum suffers from nonlinear friction as modeled on the *Friction Phenomena* subsection. However, due to the fact that the magnitude of its effect is negligible, it can be linearized.

The system can be analytically linearized, but doing so can be a complex and time-consuming task. In this subsection, the system is linearized using MATLAB's Model Linearizer app. The model shown in the following figure is designed on Simulink's SimScape; the benefit of this method is that it is only needed to specify the direction and magnitude of gravity, pendulum's geometry, joints, and mass. Simulink will calculate all the other parameters, such as the moment of inertia as seen from the joints. It takes into account energy conservation due to energy transfers between the ϕ joint and the θ joint. In both the analytical mathematical model and in Simulink, it is assumed that the pendulum's body has a constant density so moments of inertia can be easily calculated.

Figure 12. SimScape model of the rotary pendulum

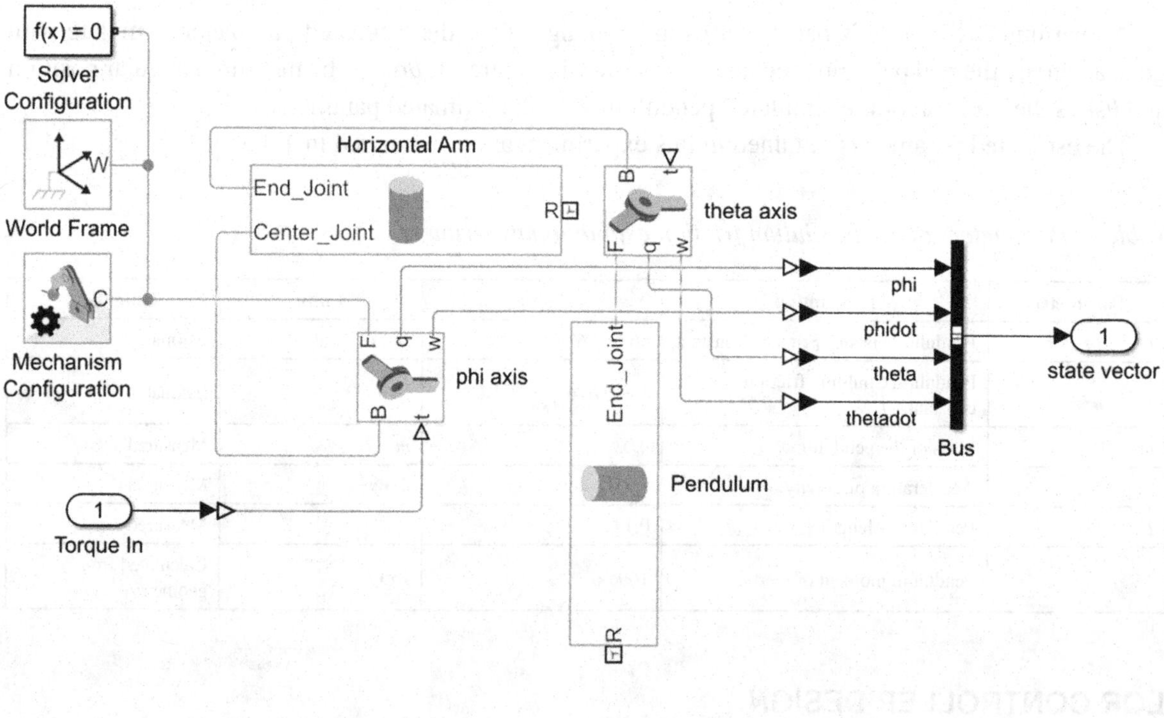

The *SimScape* model was linearized at the upright position. That is all four states, both angular positions, and both velocities equal to 0. The only input is the torque $\tau\phi_a$t the pendulum's horizontal arm joint and the outputs are the four states, $\phi, \dot{\phi}, \theta$ and $\dot{\theta}$.

For the state-space representation, the state vector **x** is the following:

$$\mathbf{x} = \begin{bmatrix} x_1 \\ x_2 \\ x_3 \\ x_3 \end{bmatrix} = \begin{bmatrix} \phi \\ \dot{\phi} \\ , \\ , \end{bmatrix} \tag{35}$$

The resulting linearized system is in the state-space representation:

$$\dot{\mathbf{x}} = \mathbf{A}\mathbf{x} + \mathbf{B}\mathbf{u} \tag{36}$$

$$\mathbf{Y} = \mathbf{C}\mathbf{x} + \mathbf{D}\mathbf{u} \tag{37}$$

Where $\dot{\mathbf{x}}$ is the time derivative of the state vector, **y** is the output vector, **A** is the system matrix, **B** is the input matrix, **C** is the output matrix, and **D** the feedthrough matrix.
The linearized state-space system is the following:

$$\mathbf{A} = \begin{bmatrix} 0 & 1 & 0 & 0 \\ 0 & 0 & -\dfrac{\delta\gamma}{\alpha\beta - \gamma^2} & 0 \\ 0 & 0 & 0 & 1 \\ 0 & 0 & \dfrac{\alpha\delta}{\alpha\beta - \gamma^2} & 0 \end{bmatrix} \tag{38}$$

$$\mathbf{B} = \begin{bmatrix} 0 \\ \dfrac{\beta}{\alpha\beta - \gamma^2} \\ 0 \\ -\dfrac{\gamma}{\alpha\beta - \gamma^2} \end{bmatrix} \tag{39}$$

$$\mathbf{C} = \begin{bmatrix} 1 & 0 & 0 & 0 \\ 0 & 1 & 0 & 0 \\ 0 & 0 & 1 & 0 \\ 0 & 0 & 0 & 1 \end{bmatrix} \qquad (40)$$

$$\mathbf{D} = \begin{bmatrix} 0 \\ 0 \\ 0 \\ 0 \end{bmatrix} \qquad (41)$$

Where α, β, γ and δ represent parameters based on the pendulum's mass, the moment of inertia, etc. Similar to Gäfvert's work (Gäfvert, 1998).

After substituting the α, β, γ and δ parameters for their numeric value based on the rotary pendulum that was built, the resulting state-space matrices are the following:

$$\mathbf{A} = \begin{bmatrix} 0 & 1 & 0 & 0 \\ 0 & 0 & -2.65 & 0 \\ 0 & 0 & 0 & 1 \\ 0 & 0 & 112.09 & 0 \end{bmatrix} \qquad (42)$$

$$\mathbf{B} = \begin{bmatrix} 0 \\ 114.23 \\ 0 \\ -133.26 \end{bmatrix} \qquad (43)$$

$$\mathbf{C} = \begin{bmatrix} 1 & 0 & 0 & 0 \\ 0 & 1 & 0 & 0 \\ 0 & 0 & 1 & 0 \\ 0 & 0 & 0 & 1 \end{bmatrix} \qquad (44)$$

$$\mathbf{D} = \begin{bmatrix} 0 \\ 0 \\ 0 \\ 0 \end{bmatrix} \tag{45}$$

To validate that the linearized system has similar dynamics compared to the full nonlinear SimScape (or analytical) version, a free-fall experiment was done. The initial conditions were $\theta=0.01$rad, all other system states equal to 0.

Figure 13. Comparison between the linearized plant and the nonlinear model with $\boldsymbol{\theta}(0)=0.01$ rad

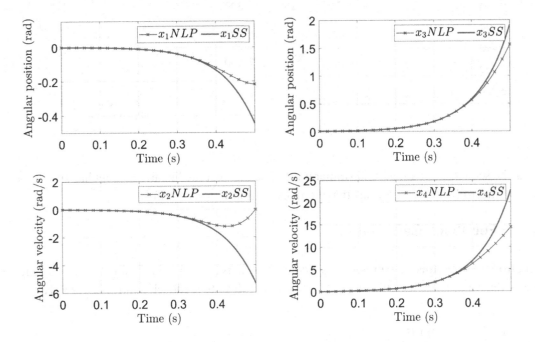

The crossed lines, $x_n NLP$, correspond to the nonlinear model and the continuous lines, $x_n SS$, correspond to the linearized plant. x_n corresponds to the nth system state as shown in equation (35). It can be seen that the linearized system has almost exact dynamics until the models diverge at $t=0.3$, more time than enough for the LQR controller that will be built to stabilize it.

Another experiment was done with initial conditions $\theta=0.15$rad, and all other system states 0.

Figure 14. Comparison between the linearized plant and the nonlinear model with $\boldsymbol{\theta}(0)=0.15$ *rad*

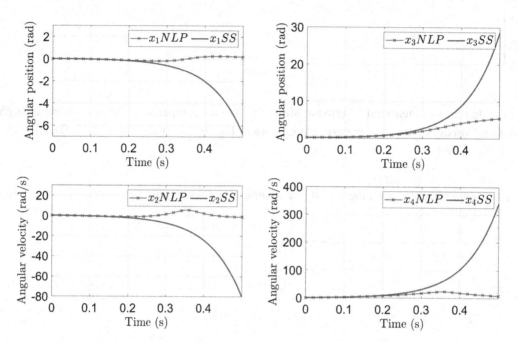

It can be seen that dynamics hold similar until . The fact that the linearized plant has similar behavior to the nonlinear plant from to means that the linearization was successful.

Optimal Feedback Gain Matrix

The controller used in this chapter is the LQR controller. This controller is obtained by finding a feedback matrix **K** that minimizes the cost function J given the full state feedback control law $u= -\mathbf{Kx}$.

$$J = \int_0^\infty \left(\mathbf{x}^T\mathbf{Qx} + \mathbf{u}^T\mathbf{Ru} \right) dt \tag{46}$$

Q and **R** are weight matrices that penalize the cost of state error and control effort, respectively.

The **Q** and **R** matrices values are chosen by the designer depending on the desired controller performance and actuator cost. Since the rotary pendulum is cheap to control given that it is not a mobile device or has limited energy reserves; identity **Q** and **R** matrices were chosen.

The resulting system with the feedback matrix **K** is:

$$\dot{\mathbf{x}} = \left(\mathbf{A} - \mathbf{BK} \right)\mathbf{x} \tag{47}$$

To analytically obtain the **K** matrix it is needed to solve for **S** in the algebraic Ricatti equation (Willems, 1971).

$$0 = A^TS + SA - SBR^{-1}B^TS + Q \qquad (48)$$

Then, to find **K** it is needed to solve the following equation:

$$R^{-1}B^TSx = Kx \qquad (49)$$

Alternatively, the **K** matrix can be easily obtained with *MATLAB* using the command lqr(SYS,Q,R,N). The resulting feedback gain matrix for the specific parameters of the rotary pendulum discussed in this chapter is:

$$K = \begin{bmatrix} 1 & 1.22 & 23.84 & 2.49 \end{bmatrix}$$

This feedback optimal gain matrix, **K**, is only valid for points at or near the point at which the plant was linearized.

Controllability Analysis

Using Kalman stability criteria, it is possible to determine the controllability of the linearized state-space system obtained in the *Linearization* subsection. In order to determine the controllability, it is only needed to compute the controllability matrix, C, and calculate its rank. If the rank is equal to n, where *n* represents the number of state variables; the system is controllable.

All this can be summed up in the following equation:

$$rank(C) = rank\left(\begin{bmatrix} B & \vdots & AB & \vdots \cdots \vdots & A^{n-1}B \end{bmatrix}\right) = n \qquad (50)$$

If equation (50) holds true, the system is controllable.
Using *MATLAB*'s ctrb() command, the following controllability matrix, C, is obtained:

$$C = \begin{bmatrix} 0 & 0.0114 & 0 & 0.0353 \\ 0.0114 & 0 & 0.0353 & 0 \\ 0 & -0.0133 & 0 & -1.4937 \\ -0.0133 & 0 & -1.4937 & 0 \end{bmatrix} \qquad (51)$$

Now, using *MATLAB*'s rank() command, the rank of the C matrix is obtained:

$$rank(C) = 4 = n \qquad (52)$$

Given that $rank(C) = n$ the system is controllable.

It is important to consider that the system that has just been proved as controllable is the linearized plant at **x**=[0000]. The full nonlinear system may be uncontrollable at some states; for example, it is easy to imagine that at any state in which the angle $\theta=\pm90°$ is not possible to control θ given that term $\gamma cos\theta\ddot{\phi}$ in equation (**8**) will always yield 0 when $\theta=\pm90°$.

Given that the LQR controller will maintain the rotary pendulum's states near the state at which the system is linearized, nonlinear controllability analysis is not needed.

SIMULATIONS

Two *Simulink* simulations were done to ensure the LQR controller does its job properly before implementing it on the microcontroller. The simulations were done for both the linearized state-space version of the pendulum and the full nonlinear version of the pendulum, as shown in Figure 15 and Figure 16. Both simulations assume no friction on none of the pendulum's axes.

Figure 15. Simulink model of the linearized pendulum with the LQR controller in closed-loop

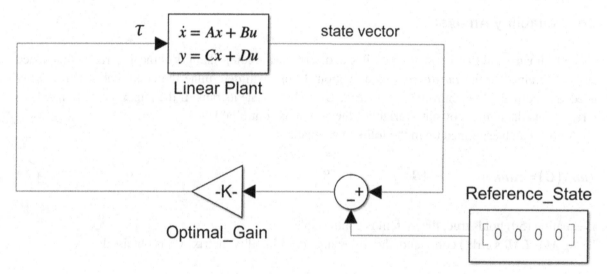

Figure 16. Simulink model of the nonlinear pendulum with the LQR controller in closed-loop

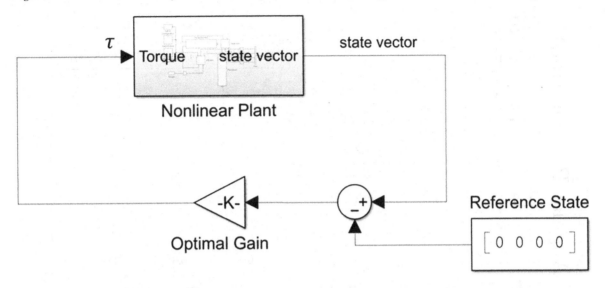

In order to avoid confusions and misunderstandings, the linearized plant in Figure 15 will be referred to as *linear plant, state-space plant,* or more compactly SS_{sim} on figure legends. SS_{sim} for State-Space-Simulation.

The nonlinear plant shown in Figure 16 will be referred to as a *nonlinear plant, SimScape plant,* or more compactly NL_{sim} on figure legends. NL_{sim} for Non-Linear-Simulation.

Also, the real physical plant will be referred to as a *real plant, physical plant,* or more compactly *"exp"* plant. *"exp"* for experimental.

Simulation 1

In this simulation, the desired state is the following:

x = [0 0 0 0]

The initial conditions for this simulation are:

x(0) = [0 0 0.15 0]

The results are the shown in Figures 17 and 18.

Figure 17. Closed-loop response of both linear and nonlinear plants for the first simulation for the **ϕ** *angle*

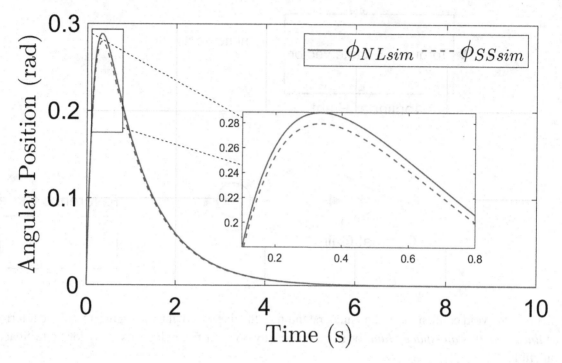

Figure 18. Closed-loop response of both linear and nonlinear plants for the first simulation for the **θ** *angle*

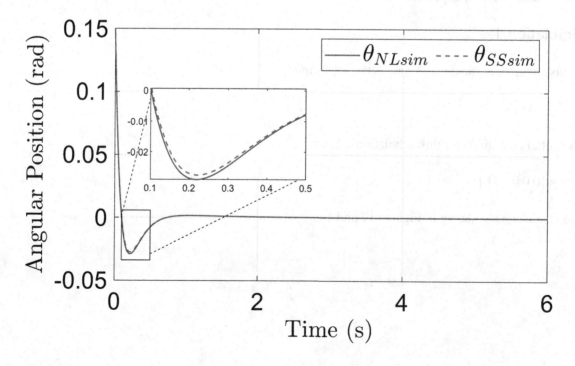

In this simulation, the dynamical behavior of the nonlinear *SimScape* plant state-space plant is simulated—both plants in closed-loop with the (also simulated) LQR controller.

$\phi_{NL_{sim}}$ represents the ϕ angle of the nonlinear simulated S*imScape* plant (see Figure 16), this plant includes nonlinear rotary pendulum dynamics, but friction is neglected.

$\phi_{SS_{sim}}$ represents the ϕ angle of the linearized plant in the state-space representation (see Figure 15), this plant does not include nonlinear rotary pendulum dynamics and only behaves similar to the real (and simulated nonlinear) plant near the point at which it was linearized (x=[0000]).

As it can be seen in both Figure 17 and Figure 18, the linear and nonlinear plants have almost the same behavior; the controller achieves stability at the desired system state within 5 seconds.

Simulation 2

In this simulation, the desired state is the following:

$$\dot{\mathbf{x}} = \begin{bmatrix} \pi\,000 \end{bmatrix}$$

The initial conditions for this simulation are:

$\mathbf{x}(0) = [0\ 0\ 0\ 0]$

The results are shown in Figures 19 and 20.

Figure 19. Closed-loop response of both linear and nonlinear plants for the second simulation for the ϕ angle

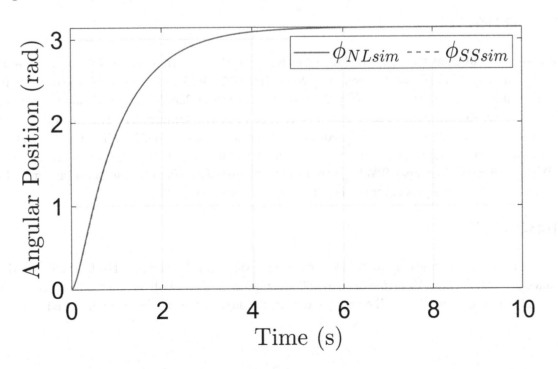

Figure 20. Closed-loop response of both linear and nonlinear plants for the second simulation for the θ angle

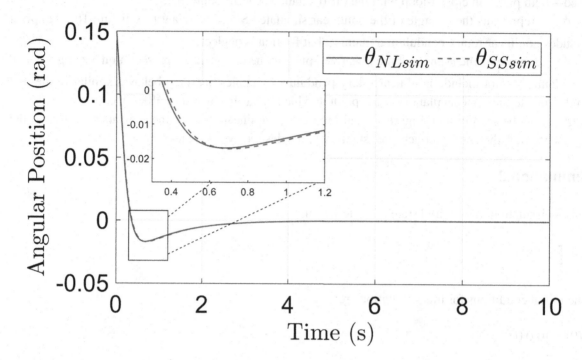

Linear and nonlinear plants show similar behavior; again, the controller achieves stability at the desired system state within 5 seconds.

IMPLEMENTATION

The optimal feedback matrix that was obtained using the method shown in the *LQR Controller* subsection was implemented in C and deployed to an *STM32H755ZI* ARM microcontroller. The motor which applies torque to the ϕ joint is a *MAXON RE-max 29* part number *226783;* the used motor driver is an *L298N* dual full-bridge driver. The control loop runs at a constant frequency fs The angular positions are updated at a constant frequency fT_{IM} and saved on hardware counters T$IM1$ $_C$$NT$ and T$IM2$ $_C$$NT;$ the former timer counter stores the angular position ϕ and the latter stores θ. The motor is controlled using a PWM signal with a frequency fPWM $_M$oreover, the direction of rotation of the motor is determined by the polarity of the two inputs of the driver, CH1 and CH2 (see Figure 23).

STM32H755ZI

The used microcontroller to control the rotary pendulum was an STM32H755ZI. It is based on the ARM architecture, and the main CPU runs at up to 480 MHz. It has 2MB of flash memory and 1MB of RAM. It has 22 timers, of which two will be used to decode the angular positions of the joints, and one more will be used to generate the PWM signal to control the motor. It also has 4 USARTs for communication, 3 ADCs, and 2 D/A converters, among lots of other features.

One timer will be used to generate the interrupts every T_s seconds. This assures that the control loop is executed precisely and also simplifies the code.

NUCLEO-H755ZI-Q

The board that was used is the NUCLEO-H755ZI-Q. These boards feature an integrated ST-LINK debugger/programmer over USB. The board has one custom user button, three user LEDs, an ethernet connector, and USB OTG/FS, which will be very useful for real-time communication and data logging between the PC and the microcontroller.

The board has 144 pins, as shown in Figure 21.

Figure 21. NUCLEO-144 board. [User Manual]

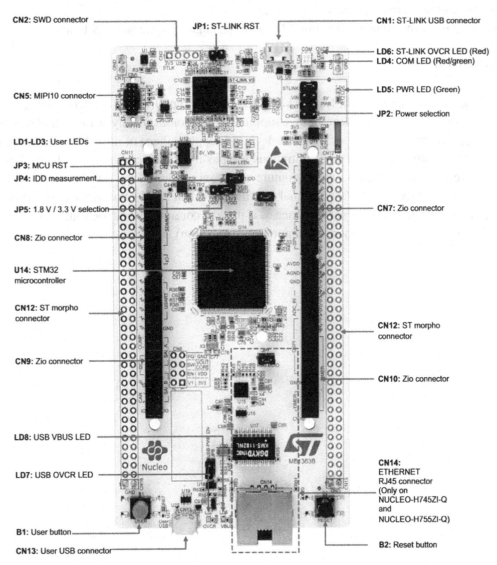

S.I Angular Positions and Velocities

The angular positions measured with the rotary encoders are in *steps* units and need to be converted to S.I units. For example, $4000 steps = 2\pi$ rad in S.I units.

After the conversion is done, the control signal is calculated using the previously obtained optimal gain matrix **K**.

The rotary encoders that were used have a resolution of 4000 steps per revolution. To convert the angular position to S.I. units, the following relation is used:

$$\theta = \theta_{enc} \frac{2\pi}{4000} \tag{53}$$

Where θ is the new angular position in S.I units and θ_{enc} is the old angular position in steps.

As equation (53) shows, for this particular 4000 steps encoder, the minimal nonzero angular position that can be measured is approximately $1.57 \cdot 10^{-3}$ rad.

The velocity is estimated using equation (22) with the angular positions in S.I. units.

PWM Generation

The control signal calculated with the feedback gain matrix **K** is a continuous signal. However, the L298N driver uses a MOSFET H bridge, so the voltage supplied to the motor can only be discrete. The voltage of the motor, V_{MOT}, can only be $0V - V_H$ or V_H where V_H is the supply voltage of the L298N H Bridge Driver.

To be able to control the motor in a continuous way, as if it had a continuous voltage source, it is possible to take advantage of the Low-Pass nature of the motor due to the rotor's mechanical inertia. Using a Pulse-Width-Modulated (PWM) signal with an equivalent RMS value of the desired continuous control signal will result in similar performance as if it had a continuous voltage source. The frequency of the PWM signal is f_{PWM} (see Timers Configuration subsection).

Figure 22. Pulse-width modulated signal

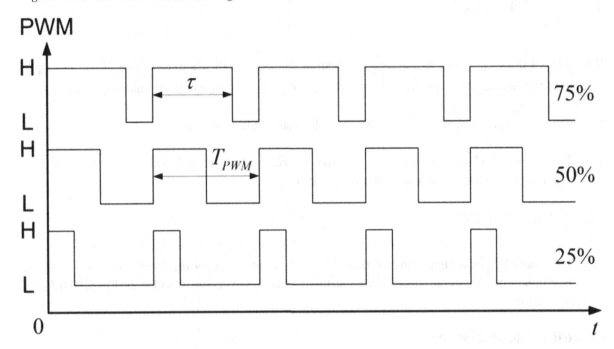

The Pulse-Width is modified by changing the signal's duty cycle, resulting in an RMS equivalent value of a continuous signal. For example, a PWM signal with a peak voltage of 10V and a 33.3% duty cycle will result in an equivalent RMS value of 3.33V, and the motor will have a similar performance as if it had a 3.33V DC continuous supply. This only applies as long as f_{PWM} is much greater than the highest eigenvalue of the angular frequency of the motor. In other words, the time constant of the motor must be much greater than the PWM period.

Timers Configuration

All timers update at f_{TIM}=200 *MHz*.
   The control loop code runs with the timers configured in the following manner:

1. TIM_{16} is in PWM Mode, it has a period $T_{TIM_{16}} = 10000$.

   1. TIM_{16} has a PWM frequency:

$$f_{PWM} = f_{TIM16} = \frac{f_{TIM}}{T_{TIM16}} = \frac{200\,MHz}{10000} = 20\,KHz \tag{54}$$

   The formula used to calculate the needed PWM Duty Cycle as a function of the desired voltage is the following:

$$\mathbf{D}_{uty} = \frac{V}{V_H} \cdot TIM_{16\_}CCR \tag{55}$$

Where D_{uty} is the $T_{TIM_{16}}$ value required for the desired voltage, V is the desired voltage, V_H is the supply voltage of the H-Bridge Driver and $TIM_{16\_}CCR$ is the capture-compare register value of the timer that will be used to generate the PWM signal.

Note that D_{uty} is not a percentage value, D_{uty} is a value ranging from 0 to $T_{TIM_{16}}$.

2.   2. TIM_3 and TIM_4 are configured in *Encoder Interface Mode*, they decode the ϕ and θ angular positions respectively and update at a frequency of:

$$f_{TIM_3} = f_{TIM_4} = 200\,MHz$$

3.   The timer TIM_{15} is configured in *Interrupt Mode* and executes the control() function every T_s seconds. This function executes the control loop. The function is shown in more detail in the PSEUDOCODE subsection.

Electrical Block Diagram

The following diagram shows the connection of the STM32 microcontroller, the motor, the motor driver, and the rotary encoders required to measure the pendulum's arm and pendulum angular positions.

Figure 23. Block diagram of the electrical circuit

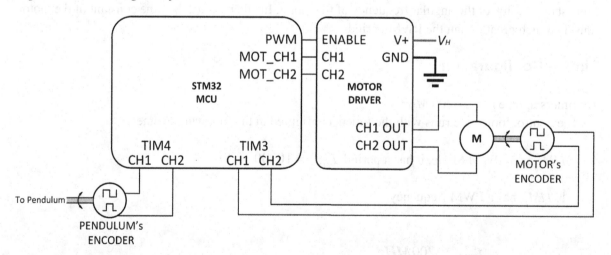

On the bottom-left side of Figure 23, the pendulum's encoder is connected to the θ joint. The motor's encoder is connected to the motor, which is the ϕ joint.

PSEUDOCODE

The following pseudocode represents the tasks the STM32 microcontroller is required to do in order to control the pendulum with the LQR controller that was obtained in the LQR Controller Design subsection.

Figure 24. Pseudocode of the implemented controller

```
configure_clock();      //Configures and initializes MCU clock
configure_timers();     //Configure timers as required
initizalize_timers();   //Initializes timers
initizalize_values();   //Initializes values as required

control(){  //This control function executes continuously every Ts seconds
measure_positions(&phi,&theta); //Gets current pos from Timers
estimate_velocities(&phi,&theta); //Estimates currents velocities
ctrl = Calculate_control_signal(phi,phidot,theta,thetadot);
//Calculate ctrl signal using K matrix
apply_control(ctrl);    //Apply control signal to the PWM output to the Motor
}
```

The code just initializes the clock. Initializes the timers to the required configurations, for example, PWM mode, encoder interface mode, interrupt mode, etc. Initializes the required variables with the initial velocities equal to 0, initial positions equal to 2^{15} to prevent wrapping overflow and underflow.

The implemented controller in the following manner:

The control loop control() function executes every T_s seconds.

The measure_positions (&phi, &theta) function takes the shown parameters as arguments, measures the positions (reads TIM_3 and TIM_4 counter registers), convert them to S.I. units, and saves them to the phi and theta variables.

The estimate_velocities (&phi, &theta) takes the positions' pointers as arguments, calculates the velocities using the discrete derivative, converts them to S.I. units, and saves the velocities to the phidot and thetadot variables. Note that it does not require the velocities as parameters, just the positions.

The calculate_control_signal (phi, phidot, theta, thetadot) calculates the optimal torque required to stabilize the pendulum using the optimal gain matrix, **K** obtained in the LQR Controller Design subsection.

The apply_control (ctrl) function calculates the needed PWM Duty Cycle required to generate the torque calculated with the previous function. It also deals with the motor polarity depending on the sign.

The torque is converted to voltage using the torque-to-voltage transfer function shown in equation (**20**).

More simply, the previous function converts torque to duty cycle in the following manner:

$$\tau o_{ptimal} ® Vc_{ontinuous} ® Du_{ty}$$

Where τo_{ptimal} is the torque calculated by the function calculate_control_signal(…)using the optimal gain matrix, K, $Vc_{ontinuous}$ is the non-discrete voltage calculated using the torque-to-voltage transfer function shown in equation (**20**) and Du_{ty} is the duty cycle that produces a voltage equivalent to the $Vc_{ontinuous}$ voltage.

STABILIZATION EXPERIMENTS

Experiment 1

The Experiment 1 that will be done is similar to simulation 1 in the "SIMULATIONS" subsection. It consists of starting the experiment at a nonzero starting condition near the desired state, and the LQR will try to reach the desired equilibrium state.

In this experiment, the desired state is the following:

x = [0 0 0 0]

The initial conditions for this experiment were:

x(0) = [0 0 0.15 0]

The results are shown in Figure 25.

Figure 25. Comparison of experiment 1 with the real physical plant and the simulated plants

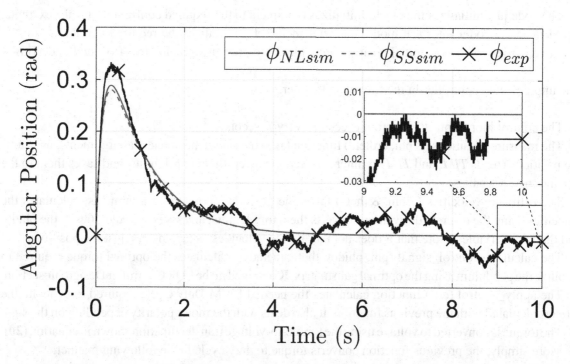

In this experiment, the dynamical behavior of the real plant and the real controller implemented in the STM32 was compared to the simulated plants.

$\phi_{NL_{sim}}$ represents the ϕ angle of the nonlinear simulated plant (see Figure 16), this plant includes nonlinear rotary pendulum dynamics, but friction is neglected.

$\phi_{SS_{sim}}$ represents the ϕ angle of the linearized plant in the state-space representation (see Figure 15), this plant does not include nonlinear rotary pendulum dynamics and only behaves similar to the real plant near the point at which it was linearized (x=[0000]).

ϕe_{xp} represents the ϕ angle of the real plant with the real controller. The measurements were taken with the STM32 and sent to the PC for plotting.

Figure 26. Comparison of experiment 1 with the real physical plant and the simulated plants

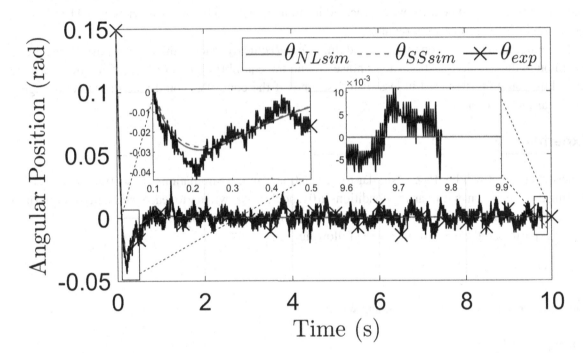

$\theta_{NL_{sim}}$ represents the θ angle of the nonlinear simulated plant (see Figure 16), this plant includes nonlinear rotary pendulum dynamics, but friction is neglected.

$\theta_{SS_{sim}}$ represents the θ angle of the linearized plant in the state-space representation (see Figure 15), this plant does not include nonlinear rotary pendulum dynamics and only behaves similar to the real plant near the point at which it was linearized (x=[0000]).

θe_{xp} represents the θ angle of the real plant with the real controller. The measurements were taken with the STM32 and sent to the PC for plotting.

Conclusions of Experiment 1

The implementation of the LQR controller on the STM32 microcontroller was successful. The pendulum achieved stabilization, as can be seen in Figure 25. The real plant exhibits highly nonlinear effects such as break-away friction on both axes. As it can be seen in Figure 25, the real plant has a similar behavior from $t=0s$ to $t=2s$, after that, nonlinear friction effects of the θ joint make the pendulum rebound causing the pendulum arm (ϕjoint) to change direction in order to keep the pendulum stable. It can be seen that in the real plant, the ϕ angle curvature changes from negative to positive at t=2s while in the simulated plants curvature remains negative for all t>0.5s.

Also, measurements of the real plant are noisy; this is due to the fact that the sample-and-hold effect of the discrete controller produces high-frequency components, given that the motor can only change its voltage every Ts $_s$econds and can only have discrete voltage levels as explained in the Timers Configuration subsection.

Near the end of the experiment, at t=9.8s the rotary pendulum reached stability and stopped. As it can be seen in the subplot of Figure 25, the ϕ joint reached 0 velocity but with a steady-state error of -0.01rad. This steady-state error was replicated in simulations with break-away friction and break-away torque, and similar results were obtained.

In Figure 26, it can be seen that the pendulum (θjo*int*) quickly reaches the upward position at around 1s *a*lthough the angular position shows noise around the equilibrium point of ±0.15rad. In theory the pendulum could be stabilized in less than 2 seconds if the controller could take into account highly nonlinear phenomena.

Experiment 2

Experiment 2 that will be done is similar to Simulation 2 in the Simulations subsection. It consists of starting the experiment with starting conditions **x**(0) and the LQR will try to reach the desired equilibrium state. This experiment is similar to a step response (of ϕ) but with π magnitude.
In this experiment, the desired state is the following:

x = [π 0 0 0]

The initial conditions for this experiment were:

x(0) = [0 0 0 0]

The results can be found in Figures 27 and 28.

Figure 27. Comparison of experiment 2 with the real physical plant and the simulated plants

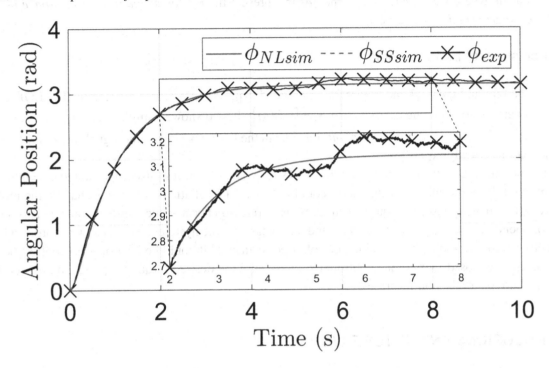

Figure 28. Comparison of experiment 2 with the real physical plant and the simulated plants

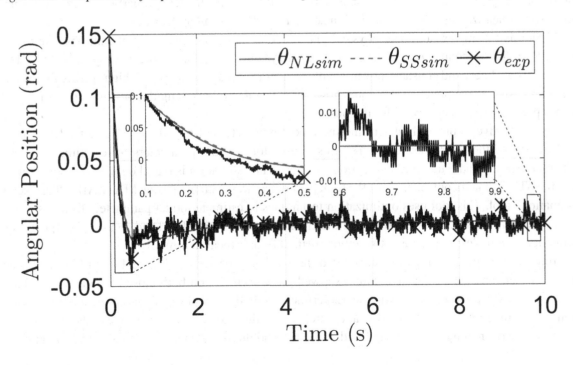

Just as in experiment 1; NL_{sim}, SS_{sim} and "*exp*" represent the *nonlinear plant*, the *state-space plant*, and the *experimental plant*, respectively.

Conclusions of Experiment 2

As can be seen in Figure 27 and Figure 28, the second experiment was also successful. The LQR controller managed to reach the desired state $\dot{\mathbf{x}} = \begin{bmatrix} \pi\,0\,0\,0 \end{bmatrix}$. It also showed similar behavior to the simulated *state-space plant* and *nonlinear plant*. Just like in the first experiment, the signals are noisy for the same reasons already explained.

The nonlinear effects produce oscillations and steady-state error. It is also important to take into account that full torque control of the motor could reduce said oscillations. In all this chapter, the motor was controlled using a linear torque to voltage transfer function because the constant load was assumed. Motor phenomena like dead voltage zones and nonlinearities like hysteresis or break-away torque when velocity is close to 0 may be reducing controller performance. It could be beneficial to control motor torque using a closed-loop torque controller to make sure the desired torque is applied, no matter the load and no matter the nonlinearities.

CONCLUSIONS AND FUTURE WORK

The rotary pendulum is a nonlinear dynamic system. It is also highly sensitive to initial conditions and perturbations. This system suffers mathematically complex nonlinearities such as break-away torque, cogging torque, and mechanical backlash; these nonlinearities can become a real problem if precise control of the system is desired. Depending on the pendulum's mechanical properties, these nonlinearities may be linearized or not, as explained in section "LQR Controller Design."

Friction is a complex nonlinear physical phenomenon that represents a significant obstacle to the search for effective control of an electromechanical system. The inherent break-away torque of a DC motor prevents linear and constant movement of the motor shaft at low speeds. A high-quality DC motor was used to reduce the break-away torque; however, a residual relative angular positioning error is still always present due to mechanical limitations.

It is imperative to precisely determine the model parameters of the Maxon DC motor RE-max29 used to control the rotary pendulum. For this, the motor's model parameters were estimated in the "Characterization and Parameter Estimation" section. The estimation is based on measurements taken with the STM32 microcontroller; then, the final parameters were obtained using MATLAB's "Parameter Estimation" tool. This tool uses optimization techniques to estimate model parameters from test data. It tries different parameters while reducing the error between the simulated and measured outputs. The estimation is complete when the optimization method finds a local minimum.

From the experiments, it can be concluded that, as it can be seen in Figure 17 and Figure 19, the linearized version of the rotary pendulum showed great accuracy on both closed loop and open loop when operating near the equilibrium state. Experiments with the real physical plant were also successful even though the LQR controller is a linear controller, and the plant is not. This is due to the fact that the magnitude of the nonlinearities is small; other rotary pendulums that were built that had big magnitude nonlinearities near the equilibrium state like backlash and big break-away friction showed poor controller performance when controlled using the LQR; limit-cycles, and even instability occurred in some cases.

In the "Stabilization Experiments" subsection, two experiments were performed with the real rotary pendulum plant. The experiments were compared with the simulations and showed similar behavior, meaning the mathematical model of the rotary pendulum was accurate, and the implementation of the controller was successful. Both experiments showed that the LQR successfully stabilizes the pendulum and reaches the desired state; all this with little to no steady-state error and some high frequency and small magnitude oscillations due to the real plant nonlinearities and discrete sampling phenomena. The experiments showed areas that need to be improved, like using a closed-loop torque-controlled motor (not making the assumption that the motor is linear and using a transfer function), better modeling of the real plant, a nonlinear controller, and even a swing-up algorithm/controller.

In future work, a nonlinear controller could be designed taking into account nonlinearities such as break-away friction, backlash, and motor nonlinearities. Such controller could also implement the swing-up of the rotary pendulum intrinsically, or a special-case swing-up stage could be implemented, and then when the pendulum is near the equilibrium state, another controller could take control of the rotary pendulum. This nonlinear controller could be designed using the rotary pendulum's equations (that include nonlinear phenomena), or the dynamical model could be constructed with a memory-based model that includes all the nonlinear phenomena that are difficult to model mathematically.

REFERENCES

Armstrong-Hélouvry, B., Dupont, P., & Canudas De Wit, C. (1994). A survey of models, analysis tools and compensation methods for the control of machines with friction. *Automatica, 30*(7), 1083–1138. doi:10.1016/0005-1098(94)90209-7

Åström, K. J., & Murray, R. M. (2008). *Feedback systems: An introduction for scientists and engineers.* Princeton University Press.

Canudas De Wit, C., & Lischinsky, P. (1996). Adaptive friction compensation with partially known dynamic friction model. *IFAC Proceedings Volumes, 29*(1), 2078-2083. 10.1016/S1474-6670(17)57978-1

Chapman, S. (2003). *Electric Machinery Fundamentals.* McGraw-Hill.

Gäfvert, M. (1998). *Modelling the Furuta Pendulum.* Lund Institute of Technology, Department of Automatic Control. Lund Institute of Technology.

Gohar, R., & Rahnejat, H. (2008). *Fundamentals of Tribology.* Imperial College Press. doi:10.1142/p553

Lindner, L., Sergiyenko, O., Rivas-López, M., Ivanov, M., Rodríguez-Quiñonez, J. C., Hernández-Balbuena, D., . . . Mercorelli, P. (2017). Machine vision system errors for unmanned aerial vehicle navigation. In *2017 IEEE 26th International Symposium on Industrial Electronics (ISIE)* (pp. 1615-1620). IEEE Xplore. 10.1109/ISIE.2017.8001488

Lindner, L., Sergiyenko, O., Rodríguez-Quiñonez, J. C., Rivas-Lopez, M., Hernandez-Balbuena, D., Flores-Fuentes, W., Natanael Murrieta-Rico, F., & Tyrsa, V. (2016). Mobile robot vision system using continuous laser scanning for industrial application. *Industrial Robot: An International Journal*, *43*(4), 360–369. doi:10.1108/IR-01-2016-0048

Lischinsky, P., Canudas De Wit, C., & Morel, G. (1999). Friction compensation for an industrial hydraulic robot. *IEEE Control Systems Magazine*, *19*(1), 25–32. doi:10.1109/37.745763

Liu, P., Huda, M. N., Sun, L., & Yu, H. (2020). A survey on underactuated robotic systems: Bio-inspiration, trajectory planning and control. *Mechatronics*, *72*, 102443. doi:10.1016/j.mechatronics.2020.102443

Lyshevski, S. E. (1999). Nonlinear control of mechatronic systems with permanent-magnet DC motors. *Mechatronics*, *9*(5), 539–552. doi:10.1016/S0957-4158(99)00014-8

Moreno-Valenzuela, J. C. A.-A.-G. (2016). Adaptive Neural Network Control for the Trajectory Tracking of the Furuta Pendulum. IEEE.

Moreno-Valenzuela, J., Aguilar-Avelar, C., Puga-Guzmán, S. A., & Santibáñez, V. (2016). Adaptive Neural Network Control for the Trajectory Tracking of the Furuta Pendulum. *IEEE Transactions on Cybernetics*, *46*(12), 3439–3452. doi:10.1109/TCYB.2015.2509863 PMID:28113230

Morin, A. J. (1833). New friction experiments carried out at Metz in 1831–1833. *Proceedings of the French Royal Academy of Sciences*, *4*(1), 128.

Olsson, H., Åström, K. J., Canudas de Wit, C., Gäfvert, M., & Lischinsky, P. (1998). Friction Models and Friction Compensation. *European Journal of Control*, *4*(3), 176–195. doi:10.1016/S0947-3580(98)70113-X

Parameter Estimation. (2021, September 11). Retrieved from https://la.mathworks.com/discovery/parameter-estimation.html

Popov, V. L. (2010). *Contact Mechanics and Friction: Physical Principles and Applications*. Springer-Verlag. doi:10.1007/978-3-642-10803-7

Susanto, W., Babuška, R., Liefhebber, F., & van der Weiden, T. (2008). Adaptive Friction Compensation: Application to a Robotic Manipulator. *IFAC Proceedings Volumes*, *41*(2), 2020–2024. 10.3182/20080706-5-KR-1001.00343

Virgala, I., Frankovský, P., & Kenderová, M. (2013). Friction Effect Analysis of a DC Motor. *American Journal of Mechanical Engineering*, *1*(1), 1–5. doi:10.12691/ajme-1-1-1

Wadi, A., Lee, J.-H., & Romdhane, L. (2018). Nonlinear sliding mode control of the Furuta pendulum. In *2018 11th International Symposium on Mechatronics and Its Applications (ISMA)* (pp. 1–5). IEEE Xplore. 10.1109/ISMA.2018.8330131

Willems, J. (1971). Least squares stationary optimal control and the algebraic Riccati equation. *IEEE Transactions on Automatic Control*, *16*(6), 621–634. doi:10.1109/TAC.1971.1099831

KEY TERMS AND DEFINITIONS

Breakaway Torque: This is the torque needed to start the rotational motion necessary to cause an object to rotate around an axis. In most cases, more torque is required to create the rotational motion than is needed to keep it going once it has begun. The amount of break-away torque required to move something is determined in part by static friction.

Cogging Torque: This is the torque needed to overcome the opposing torque created by the attractive magnetic force between magnets on the rotor and the iron teeth of the stator. There are multiple rotor positions within a revolution where the cogging torque is high. By design, motors that use ironless winding for their rotors do not have cogging torque.

H-Bridge Motor Driver: This electronic circuit represents a switch-mode power amplifier generally used to reverse the polarity/direction of the DC motor. It is essential to transmit electrical power for the applied actuator in the motion control system. Still, it can also be used to 'brake' the motion system, where the motion comes to a sudden stop as the system control input is effectively disconnected from the power source.

Microcontroller: This is a programmable integrated microcircuit capable of executing commands stored in its memory. It is composed of several functional modules that fulfill a specific task. A microcontroller includes a computer's three main functional units: central processing unit, memory, and input/output ports. Currently, these types of devices are widely used in industry or research due to the fact that they offer great value.

Motion Control System: Comprises the integration of different components of various disciplines such as mechanical, electronic, and control. Each of these performs a unique role in achieving precise motion control and improving the system's efficiency. Despite various design uncertainties, the control objective is to synthesize a control input to track the desired motion trajectory as closely as possible. Selecting the right motion control components concerning the system design is crucial as it largely determines the machine's performance or the automated system.

Rotary Pendulum: This consists of a driven arm that rotates horizontally inside the *XY* plane and a pendulum attached to the edge of the driven arm. The pendulum is free to turn in a plane that is perpendicular to the pendulum's arm and coincides with the edge of said arm. It is an example of a complex non-linear oscillator. Such systems are of interest in control system theory. The rotary pendulum is underactuated and highly non-linear due to the gravitational forces and the coupling arising from the Coriolis and centripetal forces.

Underactuated Systems: Are systems in which the control input cannot arbitrarily change the state of the system. As a consequence, unlike in fully actuated systems, the underactuated systems cannot be commanded to follow arbitrary trajectories.

Chapter 8
Implementation and Analysis of Different POS Tagger in Khasi Language

Risanlang Hynniewta
North Eastern Hill University, India

Arnab Maji
North Eastern Hill University, India

Sunita Warjri
North Eastern Hill University, India

ABSTRACT

Part-of-speech tagging is a process of assigning each word of a sentence to a part of speech based on its context and definition. POS tagging is a prerequisite tool for many NLP tasks like word sense disambiguity, name entity information extraction, etc. Unfortunately, very little work has been done so far in this line for Khasi Language. The main difficulty lies with the unavailability of an annotated corpus. Hence, a small corpus is created which consists of 778 sentences with 34,873 words, out of which 3,942 are distinct words and a tagset of 52 tags. In this chapter, three methods for POS tagging, namely Brill's tagger, hidden Markov model (HMM)-based tagger, and bidirectional long short-term memory recurrent neural network (Bi-LSTM), have been implemented. Then a comparative analysis is performed, and it is observed that Bi-LSTM performs better in terms of accuracy.

INTRODUCTION

Part Of Speech (POS) is the process of assigning each word of a sentence in a corpus to a part of speech such as nouns, adjectives, verbs, adverbs, etc. based on its context and definition. POS Tagging techniques are mainly classified into:

DOI: 10.4018/978-1-7998-9795-8.ch008

- **Supervised Tagging**: Supervised Tagging is based on a correctly tagged corpus. Here, in this method, it facilitates the system to learn the rules or disambiguation of words.
- **Unsupervised Tagging**: In contrast to supervised, unsupervised POS Tagging models do not require any pre-tagged corpus, but they make use of estimation techniques to intrinsically generate tag sets, transformation rules, etc. Both supervised tagging and unsupervised tagging can have the following subtypes:
  - **Rule-Based Tagger** (Brill 1995): The approach of Rule-based tagger Initially is used in a language where a specific set of rules were formulated to determine the part of speech tag of each word. However, even with having enough set of rules, Rule-Based Tagger fails to assign tags to unknown words. Hence this system fails when they face unknown words. Hence a set of rules are needed to be formulated when encountered with unknown words to achieve good accuracy.
  - **Stochastic Tagger**: In Stochastic Tagger, it uses a statistical model to tag the input text (corpus). Stochastic taggers are made based on previously tagged data. Tagger can be built by providing training on already tagged annotated text (corpus). Unlike Rule-based Tagger, these taggers are more promising to tag both known and unknown words, but the correctness of tagging depends on the size of tagged training corpus data. However, for words that are not encountered in the training set, this approach uses probability to assign a tag.

Background

The need of Part Of Speech Tagging Part-of-Speech tagging is not always the solution to all NLP problems. It is, however, as mentioned before, a prerequisite tool to simplify many different complex problems. The following are some of a few applications of POS tagging in NLP tasks.

1. Text to speech conversion:

Let us look at the Example 1, the given sentence:

Example 1: *U khun jong phi u khun ia ka kali.*

The word khun is being used twice in this sentence and has two different meanings here the first khun is a noun meaning son, while the second khun is a verb meaning turn i.e here the word khun have different pronunciation and also have different meanings (heteronym). Therefore, It is paramount to know which word is being used to pronounce the text correctly. It is for this particular reason that text-to-speech systems usually perform POS-tagging before synthesizing the given text to speech.

2. Word Sense Disambiguation:

Words sometimes occur in different senses as different parts of speech. Example 2:

Example 2.1: Ka trei kam.
Example 2.2: Ka kam treh ban leit.

The word kam in Example 2, in these two sentences has different senses, but specifically, the word kam in the first Example 2.1 sentence is a noun and in the second Example 2.2 sentence is an auxiliary verb. Basic word sense disambiguation is possible if we can tag words with their appropriate POS tags. Now, Word-sense disambiguation (WSD) is knowing which sense of a word i.e, which meaning is used in a sentence when the word has many meanings. The Example 1 and 2 are just a few of the various applications where POS tagging is required. There are other applications also which require POS tagging, like Machine Translation, Question Answering, Speech Recognition,etc.

TRANSFORMATION BASED LEARNING

The general framework of Brills corpus-based learning is called Transformation based Learning (TBL) (Brill, 1995). The name reflects the fact that the tagger is based on transformations or rules,and learns by detecting errors.Roughly, the TBL, (see Figure 1), begins with an unannotated text as input which

Figure 1. Error-driven learning module

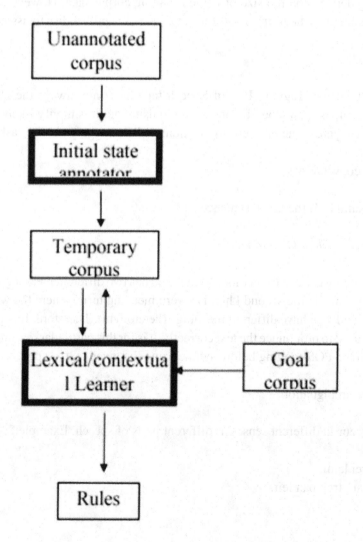

passes through the initial state annotator. It assigns tags to the input in some fashion. The output of the initial state annotator is a temporary corpus which is then compared to a goal corpus which has been manually tagged. For each time the temporary corpus is passed through the learner, the learner produces one new rule, the single rule that improves the annotation the most (compared with the goal corpus), and replaces the temporary corpus with the analysis that results when this rule is applied to it. By this process the learner produces an ordered list of rules. The tagger uses TBL twice: once in the lexical module deriving rules for tagging unknown words, and once in the contextual module for deriving rules that improve the accuracy. Both modules use two types of corpora: the goal corpus,derived from a manually annotated corpus, and a temporary corpus whose tags are improved step by step to resemble the goal corpus more and more.

Confusion Matrix

Inorder to evaluate the performance of any supervised learning particularly here the Transformation Based Learning there is a specific table layout called as the confusion matrix, also known as an error matrix which gives a visualization of the performance of any supervised learning algorithm.

Transition and Emission Probability

Transition probability (Seong, 2018) can be defined as the probability of a POS tag at position i+1 given the previous tag at position i i.e,

P(tag i + 1 | tag i)

Emission probability (Seong, 2018) can be defined as the probability of the observed word given a particular tag i.e,

P(word | tag)

VITERBI ALGORITHM

Viterbi algorithm is a dynamic programming algorithm for finding the most likely sequence of hidden states called the Viterbi Path,which results in a sequence of observed events.It is also commonly used in speech recognition and speech synthesis.

Bidirectional LSTM

Bi-direcional LSTM (Bengio et al,. 2016) duplicate the first layer of the recurrent layer in the network so that there are now two layers side-by-side, then providing the input sequence as it is to the first layer and providing are reversed copy of the input sequence to the second layer.In its core LSTM, preserves information from inputs that has already passed through it using the hidden state. In Unidirectional LSTM it only preserves information of the past because the only inputs it has seen are from the past, whereas using bidirectional it will run the inputs in two ways, one from past to future and one from future to the past and what is different in this approach from unidirectional is that Bi-LSTM runs backwards can preserve information from the future and using the two hidden states combined is able in any point in time to preserve information from both past and future.For example lets, try to predict the next word in a sentence, on a high level what a unidirectional LSTM will see is

Example 3: • The boys went to ...

And will try to predict the next word only by this context however, In bidirectional LSTM we will be able to see information further down for example

- *Forward LSTM: The boys went to .....*
- *Backward LSTM: .....and then they got out of the pool*

we can see from Example 3 that using the information from the future it could be easier for the network to understand what the next word is

IMPLEMENTATION OF DIFFERENT POS TAGGER IN KHASI LANGUAGE

In this Chapter per the authors they have found that very less work has been done on PoS Tagging of Khasi language. Therefore, there is an acute crisis of standard corpus, the authors have firstly built their own small corpus from Khasi newspaper. Then they have implemented the different Taggers and compared each method based on experimental results. The main objectives of the proposed work are as follows:

- **Designing of TagSet:** A set of all POS tags used in a corpus is called a TagSet. TagSets for different languages are different, they can be completely different for unrelated languages and very similar for similar languages, but it is not always the rule. TagSets can also be of a different level of detail. Basic tagsets may only include tags for the most common parts of speech (N for noun, V for verb, A for adjective etc.). It is, however, more common to go into more detail and distinguish between nouns in singular and plural, verbal conjugations, tenses, and much more. Here, some of the specialized TagSets to accommodate our needs have been used. These tagsets are explained in detail in (Warjri et al,. 2018). (see Table 1) presents the tagset used in the corpus.
- **Create a Corpus and Manually Tagging It:** For English there are a number of already existing Corpus that can be used for POS Tagging for example like the Brown Corpus and PennTreebank but since there is no Corpus for Khasi the authors have to create a Corpus and correctly tagged it and with appropriate design Tagset. This corpus is created excluding linguistics expert validation, it consists of 778 sentences with 34,873 words, out of which 3,942 are distinct words.
- Training: Train The Corpus using the three Methods:
  1. Transformation-Based-Learning (Brill's).
  2. Hidden Markov Model (HMM) with Viterbi algorithm.
  3. Bidirectional LSTM.

Designing of Tagset

The TagSet along with its description is given in the following Table:

Table 1. Table of proposed tagset

Serial No.	Tag	Description
1	PPN	Proper Noun
2	CLN	Collective Noun
3	MTN	Material Noun
4	ABN	Abstract Noun
5	EM	Emphatic Pronoun
6	RLP	Relative Pronoun
7	ITP	Interrogative Pronoun
8	DMP	Demonstrative Pronoun
9	POP	Possessive Pronoun
10	VB	Verb
11	CAV	Causative Verb
12	TRV	Transitive Verb
13	ITV	Intransitive Verb
14	DTV	Ditransitive Verb
15	ADJ	Adjective
16	CMA	Comparative Adjective
17	SPA	superlative Adjective
18	AD	Adverb
19	ADT	Adverb of Time
20	ADM	Adverb of Manner
21	ADP	Adverb of Place
22	ADF	Adverb of Frequency
23	ADD	Adverb of Degree
24	IN	Preposition
25	1PSG	1st person singular common gender
26	1PPG	1st person plural common gender
27	2PG	2nd person singular/plural common gender
28	2PF	2nd person singular/ plural feminine
29	2PM	2nd person singular/ plural masculine
30	3PSF	3rd person singular Feminine
31	3PSM	3rd person singular masculine
32	3PPG	3rd person plural common gender
33	3PSG	3rd person singular common gender
34	VPT	verb present tense
35	VPP	verb present progressive

Continued on following page

Table 1. Continued

Serial No.	Tag	Description
36	VST	verb past tense
37	VSP	verb past perfective participle
38	VFT	verb future tense
39	MOD	modalities
40	NEG	Negation
41	COC	coordinating conjunction
42	SUC	subordinating conjunction
43	CRC	correlative conjunction
44	CN	cardinal number
45	ON	ordinal number
46	QNT	quantifiers
47	CO	copula
48	INP	Infinitive participle
49	PAV	passive voice
50	FR	Foreign words
51	SYM	symbol
52	COM	complementizer

Creation of Corpus

For English, there are a number of already existing Corpus that can be used for POS Tagging for example like the Brown Corpus (Bird et al., 2009) and PennTreebank but since there is no Corpus for Khasi the authors have to create a Corpus and correctly tagged it. To create a Corpus the authors just compile a few words from the local newspapers but Correctly Tagging them is tedious, time-consuming and very difficult. Currently, with some help the authors are able to create a small corpus which consists of 778 sentences containing 34,873 words out of which 3,942 are distinct words is created, this small annotated corpus is created based on Political context and they have collected it from a local newspaper Mawphor.

Steps Used for Tagging by Each Approaches

- *Brill*
  - First, the authors divide the corpus into two parts i.e, training 90% and testing 10% of the corpus. To the training dataset, then they separate the word from the word/tag pair and give it to the combination of taggers which is set as default tagger namely regex, unigram, bigram and trigram to tag initially.
  - Next they, then import a set of rules or templates. Here per the authors, they have used fntbl37() template which brill tagger can use to correctly assign a tag to the word when compared with the annotated corpus. This is done recursively until no further rules can be applied or the tagged corpus is approximately the same with the annotated corpus.

- Finally they now take the tagger which is trained from the previous step and tagged the 10% remaining testing corpus and take this result and give it to the function name evaluate() (Bird et al., 2009) to give the accuracy.

- ***HMM with Viterbi Algorithm***
  - Firstly, the authors tagged the text which is to be given for testing by hand.
  - Here the authors use trigram for part of speech tagging. Secondly, they take the annotated corpus and calculate both the transition probability and emission probability.
  - Now, they take the text to be tagged along with the transition and emission probability and give it to the Viterbi algorithm as parameters which returns the sequence of most probable tags having the maximum probability.
  - Taking the result from the Viterbi algorithm and comparing them with the already tagged taken from the first step and calculate the accuracy using the following formula:

- ***Bi-directional LSTM***
  - First, the creation of the model similar to that of Bogdan (2018) is modelled.
  - Next the authors then train the model using fit() function by providing the appropriate parameters like number of epochs, percentage of the validation set, testing data, batch size, and the output size.
  - Next they get the sequence of tags for the testing data using the predict() function which gives the output.
  - Finally they now use the evaluate() function which is present in the already created model to give the accuracy and the Result of all the three methods is presented in the Result (see Table 2)

RESULTS

The authors have implemented basically three methods for Part Of Speech Tagging in Khasi Language. They are namely Brill's, Hidden Markov Model with Viterbi Algorithm and Bidirectional LSTM. Table II shows the accuracy level of all three methods. They have used 34,873 words and compared those methods based on accuracy. As per the authors, they have found that Bidirectional LSTM has the highest accuracy of 93.62, whereas Brill's Tagger has the accuracy of 90.12 percent and Hidden Markov Model has the accuracy of 60.64 percent.

Table 2. Comparison between different POS tagger in Khasi

Serial No	Name of the Tagger	Accuracy
1	Brill's	90.12%
2	Hidden Markov Model (HMM) with Viterbi	60.64%
3	Bidirectional-LSTM	93.62%

Figure 2. Confusion matrix of Brill's tagger

	1PPG	1PSG	3PPG	3PSF	3PSG	3PSM	ABN	AD	ADF	ADJ	ADP	ADT	CAV	CLN
1PPG	<8>	.	.	.	.	.	.	.	.	.	.	.	.	.
1PSG	.	<5>	.	.	.	.	.	.	.	.	.	.	.	.
3PPG	.	.	<203>	.	.	.	.	.	.	.	.	.	.	.
3PSF	.	.	.	<432>	.	.	.	.	.	.	.	.	.	.
3PSG	.	.	.	.	<1>	.	.	.	.	.	.	.	.	.
3PSM	.	.	.	.	.	<184>	.	.	.	.	.	.	.	.
ABN	.	.	.	.	.	.	<183>	2	.	.	.	.	.	.
AD	.	.	.	.	.	.	1	<107>	.	1	.	.	.	.
ADF	.	.	.	.	.	.	.	1	<7>	.	.	.	.	.
ADJ	.	.	.	.	.	.	1	4	.	<78>	.	.	.	.
ADP	.	.	.	.	.	.	.	.	.	.	<2>	.	.	.
ADT	.	.	.	.	.	.	.	.	.	.	.	<17>	.	.
CAV	.	.	.	.	.	.	.	.	.	.	.	.	<57>	.

The figure 2 is just a small portion of the 52 x 52 size Confusion Matrix of Transformation Based Learning and the tags which are present in the row are the reference tags while those which are present in the columns are the test tags or the output tags. The numbers embedded in < > are the true positives (tp). And from the figure 2, it is seen that one of the ADJ from reference was wrongly tagged as ABN from the tagged output. For that instance, it counts as one false positive for ABN and one false negative for ADJ.

CONCLUSION

In this Chapter, a small corpus has been created which was not validated by linguistics experts. In the Result (see Table 2), the authors saw that Hidden Markov Model (HMM) tagger achieves an accuracy of 60 percent which is comparatively low as compared to the other two taggers i,e. Brill's and Bi- directional LSTM which achieve an accuracy of approximately 90 percent. The possible reason for achieving different accuracies in the result are as follows:

- Due to the small corpus size, as it is known that Hidden Markov Model (HMM) is a stochastic tagger and as all taggers of this type, the correctness of tagging depends on the size of tagged training corpus data.
- The tag assigned for Hidden Markov Model does not guarantee that it is a correct tag because they are language independent therefore it sometimes assigns a sequence of tags that are not valid according to rules of the Khasi language.

FUTURE WORKS

The authors future work includes the following:

- Increasing the number of words i.e, accumulating more data for the corpus and of better quality.
- Introducing more Tagset for better and proper classification.
- Part of Speech (POS) Tagging the words taken from a captured Image.

REFERENCES

Ayana, A. G., & University, H. (2015). *Towards improving Brill's tagger lexical and transformation rule for Afaan Oromo language.* Hawassa University.

Bagul, P., Mishra, A., Mahajan, P., Kulkarni, M., & Dhopavkar, G. (2014). Rule based POS tagger for Marathi text. *The Proceedings of International Journal of Computer Science and Information Technologies, 5*(2), 1322–1326.

Barman, A. K., Sarmah, J., & Sarma, S. K. (2013, April). Pos tagging of Assamese language and performance analysis of CRF++ and FNTBL approaches. In *2013 UKSim 15th International Conference on Computer Modelling and Simulation* (pp. 476-479). IEEE.

Bird, S., Klein, E., & Loper, E. (2009). *Natural language processing with Python: analyzing text with the natural language toolkit.* O'Reilly Media, Inc.

Bogdan. (2018). *Part of speech tagging using an lstm network.* https://nlpforhackers.io/lstm-pos-tagger-keras/

Brill, E. (1995). Transformation-based error-driven learning and natural language processing: A case study in part-of-speech tagging. *Computational Linguistics, 21*(4), 543–565.

Goodfellow, I., Bengio, Y., & Courville, A. (2016). *Deep learning.* MIT Press.

Hwang. (2018). *Part-of-Speech Tagging with Trigram Hidden Markov Models and the Viterbi Algorithm.* https://stathwang.github.io/part-of-speech-tagging-with-trigram-hidden-markov-models-and-the-viterbi-algorithm.html

Khan, W., Daud, A., Khan, K., Nasir, J. A., Basheri, M., Aljohani, N., & Alotaibi, F. S. (2019). Part of speech tagging in urdu: Comparison of machine and deep learning approaches. *IEEE Access: Practical Innovations, Open Solutions, 7*, 38918–38936. doi:10.1109/ACCESS.2019.2897327

Megyesi, B. (1998). *Brill's rule based part-of-speech tagger for Hungarian* [Master's thesis]. University of Stockholm.

Mishra, N., & Mishra, A. (2011, June). Part of speech tagging for Hindi corpus. In *2011 International Conference on Communication Systems and Network Technologies* (pp. 554-558). IEEE. 10.1109/CSNT.2011.118

Pakray, P., Pal, A., Majumder, G., & Gelbukh, A. (2015, October). Resource building and parts-of-speech (POS) tagging for the Mizo language. In *2015 Fourteenth Mexican International Conference on Artificial Intelligence (MICAI)* (pp. 3-7). IEEE. 10.1109/MICAI.2015.7

Prabha, G., Jyothsna, P. V., Shahina, K. K., Premjith, B., & Soman, K. P. (2018, September). A deep learning approach for part-of-speech tagging in nepali language. In *2018 International Conference on Advances in Computing, Communications and Informatics (ICACCI)* (pp. 1132-1136). IEEE. 10.1109/ICACCI.2018.8554812

PVS, A., & Karthik, G. (2007). Part-of-speech tagging and chunking using conditional random fields and transformation based learning. *Shallow Parsing for South Asian Languages*, *21*, 21–24.

Sarkar, K., & Gayen, V. (2012). A practical part-of-speech tagger for Bengali. In *2012 Third International Conference on Emerging Applications of Information Technology* (pp. 36-40). IEEE. 10.1109/EAIT.2012.6407856

Singh, J., Joshi, N., & Mathur, I. (2013). *Part of speech tagging of Marathi text using trigram method.* arXiv preprint arXiv:1307.4299.

Singha, K. R., Purkayastha, B. S., & Singha, K. D. (2012). Part of Speech Tagging in Manipuri: A Rule based Approach. *International Journal of Computers and Applications*, *51*(14).

Singha, K. R., Purkayastha, B. S., & Singha, K. D. (2012). Part of Speech Tagging in Manipuri with Hidden Markov Model. *International Journal of Computer Science Issues*, *9*(6), 146.

Tham, M. J. (2012, March). Design considerations for developing a parts-of-speech tagset for Khasi. In *2012 3rd National Conference on Emerging Trends and Applications in Computer Science* (pp. 277-280). IEEE. 10.1109/NCETACS.2012.6203274

Tham, M. J. (2013, September). Preliminary investigation of a morphological analyzer and generator for Khasi. In *2013 1st International Conference on Emerging Trends and Applications in Computer Science* (pp. 256-259). IEEE. 10.1109/ICETACS.2013.6691433

Tham, M. J. (2018, December). Challenges and issues in developing an annotated corpus and hmm pos tagger for Khasi. *The 15th international conference on natural language processing.*

Warjri, S., Pakray, P., Lyngdoh, S., & Kumar Maji, A. (2018). Khasi language as dominant part-of-speech (pos) ascendant in NLP. *International Journal of Computational Intelligence & IoT*, *1*(1).

Chapter 9
Intelligent Systems in Latest DFA Compression Methods for DPC

K. Vinoth Kumar

iD https://orcid.org/0000-0002-3009-1658

New Horizon College of Engineering, India

S. Prithi

Rajalakshmi Engineering College, India

Vinodha K.

PES University, India

ABSTRACT

The vast majority of the system security application in today's systems depend on deep packet inspection. In recent years, regular expression matching has been used as an important operator that examines whether or not the packet's payload can be matched with a group of predefined regular expression. Regular expressions are parsed using the deterministic finite automata representations. Conversely, to represent regular expression sets as DFA, the system needs large amount of memory, an excessive amount of time, or an excessive amount of per flow state limiting their practical applications. In this chapter, the intelligent optimization grouping algorithms (IOGA) are discussed to resolve the state blow up problem. As a result of using IOGA, the system provides memory-efficient automata by dispensing the regular expression sets in various groups and optimizing the DFAs.

INTRODUCTION

Today, a computer network has become an essential part of our day by day life. Internet has a fast growth from the most recent decade with increasing requirement of society on it. Internet provides a wide range of benefits to society however it is infected by many security attacks that disrupt the functionality of networking and computing infrastructure. To enhance the security of the network a large number of

DOI: 10.4018/978-1-7998-9795-8.ch009

devices are introduced. Network Intrusion Detection Systems (NIDS) are amongst the foremost broadly used for this purpose. Snort and Bro are two open source NIDS examples that have been broadly used to safeguard the network.

Network Intrusion Detection Systems use Deep Packet Inspection (DPI) for a variety of applications that enhances security like spam, monitoring and detecting viruses, malevolent traffic, unauthorized access and attacks. The main role of deep packet inspection is to permit Network Intrusion Detection System to effectively match the details of the network packets with respect to signature attacks and thereby be aware of malicious traffic. Formerly, string matching algorithms were used to match the signature attacks. There is an increasing obstacle in network attacks that has possessed the society of research to investigate a best string matching or signature representation. In spite of this a large research community suggests the regular expression as a dominant signature representation. Regular expression consists of a character sets that identify a search pattern. Regular expressions are grammars that denote the regular language. Regular expression matching is a traditional problem of computer science and technology. The authors made productive developments to promote the research of regular expression in algorithms and theories. There are mainly two primary requirements that must be satisfied for any regular expression representations. They are time efficiency and space efficiency. Space efficiency specifies the size of the system representation and it must be less so that it guarantees that it fits inside the main memory of NIDS. Time efficiency specifies the amount of time that is required by the NIDS to process every byte of network traffic and it must be little so as to permit a large degree of traffic to match rapidly.

When compared with the simple string patterns regular expressions are considered to be very expressive and hence they are capable to represent an ample collection of payload signature. However to implement regular expressions need greater memory space and bandwidth. On the other hand the crucial task with these extremely fast regular expressions is to trim down the usage of memory and its bandwidth.

Regular expressions are usually evaluated by finite automaton which is a mathematical framework of a system that comprises of inputs and outputs. The system initially begins at the start state and it can be in any one of the finite states. Based on the previous input characters read the state of the system understands the systems behavior for the subsequent input string. The finite automata can be categorized into Non Deterministic Finite Automata (NFA) and Deterministic Finite Automata (DFA) depending on the prime technology and current resources. The foremost dissimilarity among NFA and DFA is that for each character that is read in packet payload NFA can have multiple state transitions while DFA can have only one state transition. Owing to this NFA has a time complexity of $O(m)$ where m is the number of states while DFA requires a large amount of memory for the same packet payload.

A significant team of research work has been concentrated on compression strategies which aim towards decreasing the memory space that are required to represent DFAs. The set of regular expression when compiled to a single DFA frequently leads to state blowup problem with an enormous or even to impractical memory consumption. One way to alleviate this difficulty is to share out the collection of regular expression into many groups and to build independent DFAs for each group. Intelligent Optimization Grouping Algorithms (IOGA) can be utilized effectively to overcome the issue of state blow up problem by obtaining the comprehensive deal among the number of groups and utilization of memory. One such way to solve the state blow – up problem and to provide an efficient finite automaton is to diminish the number of DFA states. In the rest of the paper the various existing compression techniques that are used to reduce the DFA states are analyzed and the ways through which Intelligent Optimization Grouping Algorithms can be efficiently used to solve the state explosion problem are discussed.

The remainder of the manuscript is structured as follows. Section II deliberates about the regular expression model and types of regular expressions. Section III discusses and evaluates the various state compression techniques that are used to reduce the DFA states and section IV discusses about grouping the regular expression using Intelligent Optimization Grouping Algorithms and section V delivers the concluding remarks.

THE REGULAR EXPRESSION MODEL

Pattern Matching is a technique of finding a string in a text based on a specific search pattern. The search pattern can be effectively described using regular expression. Thus regular expression matching plays a vital role in pattern matching. To better understand the regular expression matching in network intrusion detection system the different types of regular expression representation and its characteristics has to be studied. The most widely used NIDS open source tool is Snort rule set thus in this paper some of the important types of regular expression that are used frequently in Snort rule sets are discussed. In the following section, the various types of regular expression and its characteristics are discussed in the way their complexities are mounted.

EXACT-MATCH STRINGS

Exact-match strings are the simplest patterns that are mostly found in the rule set. The size of patterns in an exact match string is fixed and it occurs in the input text exactly as it is appeared. The rule set which contains exact match strings exposes two vital properties. The first vital property is that DFA based solutions using Aho-Corasick algorithm or the Boyer-Moore algorithm can be efficiently utilized given that their size depends on the number of characters that are present in the pattern set. Secondly, optimization that depends on the hashing schemes can be used for a maximum length pattern size and it does not measure for arbitrarily long strings. When analyzing the properties the exact match string algorithm is not so expressive and if an assaulter appends padding in the regular expression then it can't identify malicious packets. However, the advantage of the exact match string regular expression is that it is easy to implement and can accomplish a high matching speed when compared with other types of regular expressions.

CHARACTER SETS AND SIMPLE WILDCARDS

Character sets and simple wildcard regular expression are basically found in two structures either as [s1-sjsksl] expressions, or as \s, \d, \a, \S, \D, \A. In the first structure the set incorporates all characters between s1 and sj, sk and s1 and in the second structure the set comprises of all space characters (\s), all digits (\d), all alphanumerical characters (\a), and their complements (\S, \D, \A). A wildcard is represented through a non-escaped dot and these sub-patterns represent a set of exact-match strings. As a rule, character sets and wildcards do not permit for immediate utilization of the Aho-Corasick algorithm or the Boyer-Moore algorithm and of hashing schemes. Regardless, in spending the time and cost for mounting the pattern set size it is better to perform a thorough enumeration of the exact match strings and to produce a less complicated case that do not disrupt the properties of exact match strings.

SIMPLE CHARACTER REPETITIONS.

The next type of regular expression is the simple character repetition which looks like the ch+ and ch* structure, where ch is any character of the alphabet. It does not surpass the number of characters in the pattern set and maintains the same size of the DFA. However, it is impractical to permit in-depth details of exact string match to reduce the regular expression because there are an unlimited number of such strings. However, in a finite automaton hashing schemes are employed as a loop transition.

CHARACTER SETS AND WILDCARD REPETITIONS

In character sets and wildcard repetitions the various regular expression are compiled into a single DFA providing a memory blast in the size of DFA. Thus it provides an additional complexity. Subsequently, hashing techniques cannot be applied to this problem and also a single DFA cannot be a possible solution. An obtainable solution is to group rules into multiple rules and form parallel DFAs. This technique might reduce the consumption of memory but result in increased memory bandwidth. Precisely N number of DFAs depends on an N-fold growth in the memory bandwidth. NFA can be used as an alternative by exchanging off the utilization of memory with the requirements of memory bandwidth.

COUNTING CONSTRAINTS

Counting constraints implies the combination of simple character repetition and character sets and wild-cards repetitions. The upper bound of counting constraints might or might not be constrained. As seen in the above implications a simple character repetitions having a constrained upper bound has a potential to do an in-depth enumeration of the exact match strings. As mentioned in a single regular expression when converted into NFA and then to DFA can prompt to exponential state blow up. DFA techniques are impractical to design with counting constraints. Thus the counting constraints with bounded repetition are desirable to replace with unbounded repetition.

LITERATURE SURVEY

Deep packet inspection processes the complete packet payload and identifies a set of predefined patterns. In recent years, contemporary systems replace set of strings with regular expressions, because of their higher flexibility and expressive power. To make a pattern matching process fast and memory competent, many DFA compression techniques are carried out. In this section the merits and demerits of the various deterministic finite automata compression techniques and their performances are discussed.

DETERMINISTIC FINITE AUTOMATA (DFA)

A DFA consists of five tuples (Q, Σ, δ, q_0, F) where Q represents the set of finite states, Σ denotes the finite set of input alphabets, δ the transition function which takes a state and an input character as parameters and returns a state, q_0 denotes the start state and F represents the set of accepting states. In case of networking applications Σ contains 2^8 symbols from an extensive ASCII code. A primary characteristic of DFA is that only one state can be active at a time. It does not have multiple state transitions. However it is infeasible to build a regular expression for the most repeatedly used rule set. Especially when the regular expression contains repeated wildcards it becomes difficult to build a DFA which contains a minimum number of states. It takes only one main memory accesses per byte. A hypothetical study was done and the worst case scenario illustrated on the study shows that a single regular expression of size m is represented as a NFA with a complexity of O(m) states. The same expression when transformed into a DFA generates O($å^m$) states. In a DFA the processing complexity for every input character is O(1) however when all the m states are active at the same time the complexity of NFA is O(m^2).

Fang Yu et al. (2006) proposed a DFA - based implementation called multiple DFAs (MDFA). It is an alternative DFA representing a set of regular expressions. The input string is compared against an MDFA by simulating every constituent DFA to determine whether there is a match or not. When compared with DFA, MDFAs are more compact because there is over a multiplicative raise in the number of states. Since all the elements of DFAs are matched against the input string the matching speed of MDFAs are slower than that of the DFAs. The regular expression matching speed of MDFA is about 50 to 700 instances higher than that of the NFA - based implementation and they are mainly used in the Linux L7-filter Bro and Snort system . On a DFA-based parser it achieves 12- 42 times speedup. The speed of pattern matching is almost at a gigabit rates for certain pattern sets.

Todd J. Green et al. (2004) constructed lazy DFA in which the finite states, finite inputs and state transitions are equivalent to NFA at runtime, but they cannot be considered the same at compile time. In the lazy DFA the states and transitions form a subset of the standard DFA and they are much smaller than that of the standard DFA. The drawbacks of this technique are it leads to a high warm-up cost and large memory consumption.

NON DETERMINISTIC FINITE AUTOMATA (NFA)

The working principle of NFA is same as DFA except that the transition function δ works by transiting to a new state from a state on an input alphabet. In a NFA multiple states can be simultaneously active at a time. The number of states in NFA that are essential to express a regular expression is equal to the number of alphabets that are required in the generation of regular expression. Therefore, Sidhu et al. (2004) proposed a NFA based approach which improved the usage of memory. In NFA several states are active in parallel and it has multiple transitions thus it required multiple parallel operations in memory. At the same time all the states in NFA can be active which needs an excessive amount of memory bandwidth.

In, Sidhu et al. (2004) were the first to use the NFA to construct regular expressions for the given input string using FPGAs. To match a regular expression of size m, a serial machine requires O(2^m) memory and requires the time complexity of O(1) per input character. However, the authors proposed a method that requires O(m^2) space but process a character of text in O(1) time. Additionally, they presented a simple and fast algorithm that rapidly constructs the NFA for the given regular expression. To construct an NFA rapidly is crucial because the NFA structure depends upon the regular expression, which is known only at runtime. Liu Yang et al. (2011) developed a novel technique that employed Ordered Binary Decision Diagrams (OBDDs) in order to improve the time-efficiency of NFAs. An OBDD is represented using arbitrary Boolean formulae. In order to increase the competence of state - space exploration algorithms model checkers used OBDDs. NFA-OBDDs were evaluated with three sets of regular expression. The first set comprises of 1503 regular expressions which were obtained from the Snort HTTP signature rule set. The next set contains 2612 regular expressions and the third set contains 98 regular expressions, which were found from the Snort HTTP and FTP signature rule sets. NFA-OBDDs are between 570x–1645x faster when compared with NFAs and uses almost the same amount of memory as that of NFA. NFA-OBDDs improved the efficiency of time of NFAs without conceding their efficiency of memory.

DELAYED INPUT DFA (D²FA)

Sailesh Kumar et al. (2006) constructed D²FA by converting a DFA by means of incrementally substituting many state transitions with a single default transition. The D²FA is represented by a directed graph, whose nodes are termed as states and whose edges are termed as transitions. Transitions perform a move to a new state based on the present state and the character that is read from a finite set of input alphabet Σ. Each state has not more than one unlabeled active transition known as default transition. There is one start state and for each and every state, a set of matching patterns is defined.

The authors conducted test on the regular expression obtained from Cisco Systems, Snort rule sets, Bro NIDS rule sets, and in the Linux layer-7 filter application protocol classifier. From these regular expression sets, DFAs were constructed with a small number of states and the set splitting techniques proposed by Yu et al. (2001) were applied. The regular expressions were divided into different sets so that every set created a small DFA. Then from the Cisco regular expressions 10 sets of rules were created and the footprints of total memory were reduced to 92 MB, with an aggregate of 180138 states, and lesser than 64K states were obtained from every individual DFA. Then the Linux layer-7 expressions were split into three sets, and it obtained a total of 28889 states. Further the Snort set consisted of 22 complex expressions ware split further into four sets and the state was unpredictable. The regular expressions found from Bro rule set were simple and efficient therefore they compiled all of them into a single automaton.

This approach drastically decreased the number of distinct transitions among states. For a set of regular expressions drawn from current business and academic systems, a D²FA representation reduced state transitions by more than 95%. For instance, using D²FA, the space requirements used in deep packet inspection appliances of Cisco Systems were reduced to less than 2 MB. Unluckily the use of default transition decreased throughput as there was no use of input in default transition and memory has to be accessed to retrieve the next state.

CONTENT ADDRESSED DELAYED INPUT DFA (CD²FA)

S Kumar et al. (2006) designed the Content Addressed Delayed Input DFA (CD²FA), that matches the throughput of the conventional uncompressed DFAs. In a conventional uncompressed DFA implementation the numbers are represented as states and the characteristic information of the given state are found out using the number specified in the table entry. The main function of CD²FA is that the state identifiers are replaced with content labels which specify the small portion of data that are stored in the table entry. The default transition that matches the present input characters are skipped using content labels. The table entry for the next state are found out using content label by means of hashing techniques.

A CD²FA deals with the consecutive states of a D²FA utilizing the content labels. This process provides the chosen information that is available in the state traversal approach and avoids unnecessary memory accesses. The number of main memory accesses required by CD²FA is equal to those required by an uncompressed DFA. Because of the lower memory footprint and high cache hit rate the throughput of uncompressed DFAs is improved. With an unassuming 1 KB data cache, CD²FA attains two times higher throughput than that of an uncompressed DFA and in the meantime only 10% of the memory is needed by table compressed DFA. Subsequently, the regular expressions are implemented by CD²FA very economically and the throughput and scalability of the system is enhanced.

The effectiveness of a CD²FA is evaluated experimentally on the regular expression sets from Cisco Systems, which contains more than 750 reasonably complex regular expressions in the Snort rule sets and Bro NIDS rules sets, and in the Linux layer-7 application protocol classifier. The authors created Cisco rules of ten sets with a total of 180138 states, and the number of states of each DFA is less than 64000 states. Then the Linux expressions were split into three sets with a total of 28889 states. Snort rules were divided into four sets which contains 22 regular expressions. Bro NIDS regular expressions were not divided because they are very simple. CD²FA constructed from the Creation Reduction Optimization (CRO) algorithm achieved a memory reduction of around 2.5 to 20 times higher. The memory utilization reductions of CD²FA are 5 to 60 times higher than that of an uncompressed DFA

HYBRID FINITE AUTOMATA (HFA)

M. Becchi and P. Crowley (2007a, 2007b) have introduced hybrid DFA-NFA state reduction solution. A hybrid DFA-NFA solution combines the strengths of NFA and DFA. When the automaton is constructed, NFA encoding is done on any node that contributes toward state blowup, while the rest of the states are converted into DFA nodes. The end result incorporates the memory utilization of NFA, and integrates the memory bandwidth requirements of a DFA. The size of the automaton is maintained by intruding the subset construction operation of NFA states that takes place when converting NFA to DFA and the growth causes state explosion. The critical states are easily determined by doing the above case. The subset construction operation is intruded with an intermediate state that results in a hybrid automaton which contains DFA-like states, NFA-like states which are not expanded and the border state. The border states are considered to be a part of both a DFA and an NFA. Some of the useful properties of Hybrid FA are that the DFA - state is the start state; the NFA part of the automaton remains inactive till a border state is reached; and there is no backward activation of the DFA coming from the NFA.

The key factor is that the hybrid finite automaton is the first automaton that evaluates all the types of regular expression found in Snort NIDS rule set and is implemented efficiently in real-world rapid systems. The hybrid finite automata uses default transitions and content addressing to encode the system and this leads to a variation in the storage requirements from 21KB up to 3MB. In reality, the default transition technique used in hybrid automaton eliminates approximately 98-99% of the DFA transitions, while the content addressing method implies the usage of state identifiers wide by 64 bit.

The main uniqueness of a hybrid finite automata that it provides an unassuming memory storage requirement that is equivalent to a NFA solution, the memory bandwidth requirement of HFA in average case is also same as that of a single DFA solution, and in worst case it is linear containing dot-star condition and counting constraints. To balance memory and throughput, a new method Deep Classification – DFA (DC-DFA) was proposed by Wei et al. (2013). DC-DFA is a compact representation that is based on hybrid finite automata which combines the advantages of NFA and DFA. It is supported mainly for large scale regular expression matching. Grade One classification approach is used to reduce the memory usage of DC-DFA and uses deep classification approach to improve the throughput of DC-DFA. The experiments evaluated on DC-DFA shows that in case of very large state explosion, DC-DFA reduces DFA states by 75% and improves the utilization of memory more efficiently and maintains high system throughput.

HISTORY BASED FINITE AUTOMATA (H-FA)

When multiple partially matching signatures are present in the DFA, the system becomes inefficient and yields to the state blow-up problem. To overcome this scenario the authors S Kumar et al. (2007) proposed an improved Finite State Machine. The approach builds a machine which retains a lot of information, and stores the data in a small and high-speed cache memory known as history buffer. This type of system is named as History-based Finite Automaton (H-FA) which reduces space up to 95%.

Every transition is associated with a condition that depends upon the associated action and state of the history which decides whether to insert or delete the state from the history set, or both. H-FA is thus represented as a 6-tuple $H = (S, s_0, \Sigma, A, \delta, H)$, where S represents the finite set of states, s_0 denotes the start state, Σ specifies the input alphabet, A represents the set of accept states, the transition function δ, and H represents the history. The transition function δ functions by taking in an input alphabet, a state, and a history state as its arguments and returns a new state and a new history state.

$$\delta: S \times \Sigma \times H \circledR S \times H$$

The history buffer enhances the implementation of the H-FA and its automaton is similar to that of a DFA and contains set of states and transitions. For a single character there can be multiple transitions and leaves from a state but during execution only one of these transitions is taken, and that is resolved after investigating the details of the history buffer.

The performance was evaluated and experiments were conducted on the regular expressions used in the Cisco Systems. The rule sets from Cisco Systems contains over 750 reasonably complex regular expressions. The regular-expression signatures used in the open source Snort NIDS rule set, Bro NIDS rule set, and in the Linux layer-7 application protocol classifier were also considered. Linux layer-7 protocol classifier contains seventy rules and a Snort rule set contains more than 1500 regular-expressions. The Bro NIDS contains 648 regular-expressions and the results for the HTTP signatures were present.

The number of conditional transitions is very small and causes state blow-up. The outgoing transitions of a DFA are around 256 and in most of the H-FAs there are less than 500. Hence the number of transitions increases nearly by double and there is a decrease in the number of states and conversely there is a significant reduction in memory. The size of H-FA that is registered in history buffer depends upon the partial matches. But limitation of this approach is that it has a restricted number of transitions for each input character with a huge size of transition table and a slow inspection speed.

HISTORY BASED COUNTING FINITE AUTOMATA (H-cFA)

When there is a length restriction of l on a sub expression of a given regular expression, the number of states that is needed by the sub expression gets multiplied by l. S Kumar et al. (2007) designed a machine called as H-cFA which can count such events thereby avoiding state explosion.

In H-cFA the length restriction is replaced with a closure and the closure is represented by a flag that is present in the history buffer. A counter is added for every flag in the history buffer. The flag is set by setting the counter to the length restriction rate by the conditional transitions while the flag is reset by resetting these transitions. Besides, the flag which is set are attached with the counter value 0 which denotes an additional condition. During the execution of the machine, for every input character the value of every single positive counter is decremented.

This basic change is to a great degree compelling in reducing the number of states, particularly when long length restrictions strings are present. H-cFA is exceptionally effective in implementation of the Snort signatures because it contains many long length restriction strings. It is very effective in reducing the memory consumption. If there is no use in the counting capability of H-cFA there is a massive memory blowup in the composite automaton for Snort prefixes.

EXTENDED FINITE AUTOMATA (XFA)

Randy Smith et al. (2008) designed a state based Extended Finite Automata (XFAs) which is augmented with a finite set of auxiliary variables in the standard DFA which is used to recollect different sorts of information that is relevant to the signature matching and to collect the explicit instructions that are attached to states in order to update these auxiliary variables. A state based extended finite automaton is a 7-tuple $(S, V, \Sigma, \delta, U, (s_0, v_0), A)$, where

- S represents the finite set of states,
- Σ represents the set of input alphabets,
- $\delta: S \times \Sigma \circledR S$ is the transition function,
- V represents the finite set of variables,
- $U : S \times V \circledR V$ is the update function which describes how the data value is updated on states,
- (s_0, v_0) is the initial configuration which represents a start state s_0 and an initial variable value v_0,
- $A \circledR S \times V$ is the set of accepting configurations.

XFAs is a simplified version of standard DFAs which includes a finite set of possible variable values and are attached to states that operates with the variable during matching. Variable values along with a state are generalized to each of the initial states, transient state and accept state. In particular, individual XFAs are constructed and they are combined by means of standard techniques.

Randy Smith et al. (2008) have also proposed an edge based XFA. This work gives an informal categorization to the state blow up problem and is focused on algorithms to build XFAs from regular expressions. Semantically, edge based XFAs are equal to state-based XFAs, but a lot of states are required for state-based XFAs. Conversely, state based XFAs provide an efficient result for matching, combination and optimization algorithms.

For the test set Snort signature set were used which were obtained in March 2007. Randy Smith et al. (2008) collected at different time interval live traffic traces at the edge of the network, and each trace contained HTTP packets between 17,000 and 86,000. The performances were measured with the count of CPU cycles for each payload that are leveled to seconds per gigabyte (s/GB). The performance was evaluated by carrying the experiments on a standard Pentium 4 Linux workstation that runs at three GHz with three gigabyte of memory. The time complexity of Edge based XFAs is similar to DFAs and the space complexity is just like NFAs. When compared to DFA based system XFAs use 10 instances less memory and accomplish 20 instances higher matching speeds.

Michela Becchi et al. (2008) proficiently handled counting constraints and back-references and proposed an advanced automation. This type of automaton covers all the patterns from the most expressive and popular Snort NIDS rule-set. When the regular expressions are represented with counting constraints in DFA form there is a huge rise in memory space. When there is an increase in the number of repetitions it is infeasible to design DFA. To solve the issues the authors have introduced the idea of the counting automaton. The automaton designed with counting constraints aims to minimize the consumption of memory and bandwidth requirements. In particular, XFA size does not depend on the number of repetitions, the main memory access count that is required for each counter and does not depend on the number of active counter instances. The value of the induced alphabet becomes larger and secondly, there is an excessive increase in the size of the DFA. To solve this in the authors have proposed Extended Hybrid FA which compiles several regular expressions into a single automaton.

The experimental results were evaluated on the Bro v0.9 rule set and Snort rule sets. First, they were able to compile a large number of complex regular expressions which contains simple regular expression with repeated character values, disjunctions of sub patterns, dot-star terms, and counting constraints and back references. Second, there was a decrease in the size of the NFA. Third, there was a reduction in the memory bandwidth in converted hybrid-FA representation and there was a need of an extra 156KB-16MB to hold the head- DFAs. The limited memory utilization makes a way to deploy the automata with static Random Access Memory (SRAM) in an Application Specific Integrated Circuit (ASIC) implementation that allows an excess memory access rate of 500MHz. A XFA has used number of automata alterations to eliminate restricted transitions which is limitation of HFA. XFA is confined to single supplementary state for each regular expression and it is unsuitable for tricky regular expressions.

DELTA FINITE AUTOMATA (δFA)

D Ficara et al. (2008) proposed a compressed DFA called as Delta Finite Automata. The interpretations that were obtained from the above techniques are that most default transitions stay close to the start state and a state that is defined by its transition set represents the accepted rule and for a given input character most of the transitions are directed to the same state. Based on these interpretations the δFA was designed.

The last interpretations state that most states that are adjacent contribute a considerable portion of the same transitions and hence it is sufficient to store the difference between these adjacent states. Therefore a transition set of the current state is been preserved and stored in a table which represents the supplementary structure. The number of states and transitions used by the algorithm is reduced and the study shows that nearly all adjacent states share a few common transitions and it is sufficient to store only differences between them. Essential characteristic of the delta finite automata is that it required only a single state transition for each character, thus allowed a fast string matching.

In a δFA, an arbitrary number of transitions are obtainable and therefore each state does not have a stable size and consequently there is a necessity in state pointers, which are normally standard memory addresses. Char - State compression technique based on input characters was proposed which exploited the relationship of few input characters with many states which reduced the number of bits required for each state pointer. This compression scheme has been included into the delta finite automata algorithm which provided a reduction in memory with an insignificant rise in the state lookup time.

Domenico Ficara et al. (2011) proposed a compact representation that was an extension of the work which deletes most of the neighboring states that share the common transitions and keeps only the different ones. Instead of specifying the transition set of a state concerning its direct parents, this requirement can be relaxed to obtain the adoption of 1-step ancestors which increases the chances of compression. The finest method to exploit the Nth-order dependence is to describe the state transitions among child and ancestors as impermanent. This, during the construction problem leads to NP-Complete problem. Therefore, to make it simpler a direct and negligent approach is chosen. The real rule-sets result shows that the there is no much difference between the simple approach and from the optimal construction. This technique shares the same property of many other existing approaches and they are orthogonal to the various discussed existing algorithms such as XFAs and H-cFA and allows for higher compression rates.

Second Order Delta Finite Automata (δ²FA)

δ²FA is an extended version of δFA. An as alternative of specifying the state transition set relating to its direct parents, there is an increased probability of compression with the acceptance of 2-step ancestor's. Before proceeding with the construction process of δ²FA [9] δFA has to be constructed and that value should be used as input. The subsets of nodes are considered in which a transition for a given character are defined temporarily.

In a δ²FA the table lookup is not similar to that of δFA. The main difference between δ²FA and δFA is that there is an anxiety about the temporary transitions and the temporary transitions are not stored in the local transition set. Therefore, the lookup time complexity of δ²FA is almost same as that of a δFA and memory consumption is better than δFA. δ²FA takes advantage of the 2nd order precedence among states and by implementing the concept of temporary transition it reduces the number of transitions. Only a single state transition per character is required by δ²FA thus it allows for fast string matching and higher compression rates.

DUAL FINITE AUTOMATA

Cong Liu et al. (2013) proposed a new approach called as dual finite automata (dual FA). The dual FA consists of an Extended Deterministic Finite Automaton (EDFA) and a Linear Finite Automaton (LFA). Dual FA consumes only a smaller memory when compared to DFA and the number of main memory access is very low when compared against the various discussed existing compressed DFAs. For instance it needs one or two main memory access for every byte in the payload. This is because by using linear finite automata the dual FA efficiently controls unbounded repetitions of wildcards and character sets.

This technique mitigates the state blow up problem. First, the NFA states that are not dependent to a large number of other states and those states that cause state exploitation are identified. Then, these NFA states are implemented using linear automaton. Subsequently the rest of the NFA states are compiled into a single extended DFA, which reduces the NFA states. Finally, by considering the fact that these two mechanisms cannot work separately, an interaction mechanism is implemented. EDFA has an additional feature compared with DFA to support the interaction mechanism.

The experimental results evaluated on dual finite automata demonstrate that LFA is very efficient in dropping the number of states and transitions. The number of states is reduced for up to four orders of magnitude when compared with that of DFA and the number of transitions is reduced for two orders of magnitude in contrast with MDFA. In dual FA there is only a rare increase in the number of main memory accesses, but in a MDFA there is a rapid increase in the number of main memory accesses as the number of DFAs increases.

Lastly one of the limitations of dual FA is that the number of LFA states cannot be large. When the dual finite automaton is implemented in personal computer, the effects in large number of LFA states considerably have lot of computational overhead. When large number of LFA states is existed in dual FA a larger per-flow state occurs, the storage size of the transition table becomes large and memory bandwidth also becomes large. The dual FA offers an effective solution among memory storage and memory bandwidth, and the implementation becomes very easy. When compared with DFA and MDFA the simulation results shows that in dual FA there is a drastic decrease in the storage demand and the memory bandwidth is almost close to that of DFA.

DETERMINISTIC FINITE AUTOMATA WITH EXTENDED CHARACTER SETS (DFA/EC)

Cong Liu et al. (2014) have proposed a novel approach called Deterministic Finite Automata with Extended Character Sets(DFA/EC) which doubles the size of the character set and considerably reduces the number of states. The DFA/EC can be efficiently implemented by dividing the design into two parts. The first part comprises of a compact DFA with a size m, which requires only one main memory access in its transition table for every byte in the packet payload. The second part consists of an efficient complementary program does not require any main memory access because it runs in the main memory without using the table lookup.

When compared with the above discussed existing compression techniques, the inspection speed of DFA/ EC is increased significantly by assigning the minimum value of one to the number of main memory accesses. The size of the inspection programs that are stored completely in the cache memory is kept small. Cong Liu et al. (2014) conducted experimental results and the inspection program's speed was deliberated with C++ and JAVA implementations in a Unix machine with 16 Gigabyte of 1333 MHz DDR3 memory and with a 2.66 GHz Intel Core i5 CPU. In both C++ and JAVA implementations DFA/ EC showed the fastest results, and when compared with DFA, DFA/EC were over ten times faster and were two times faster than MDFA in Java implementation. Thus DFA/EC is efficiently implemented on ASIC hardware or GPUs with less cache memory and more computation resources.

The memory bandwidth requirement of DFA/EC is much lesser than MDFAs and is very close to DFA. When considering the rule-sets exploit-19 and web-misc-28, DFA/EC can dramatically reduce the number of main memory accesses of DFA. When compared to DFA the number of states in a DFA/

EC is about four orders of magnitude smaller and when compared to 2DFA it is around two orders of magnitude smaller than a 2DFA, and it is an order of magnitude smaller than a 4DFA, and is almost similar to that of an 8DFA. When compared to DFA the number of transitions of DFA/EC is almost four orders of magnitude smaller, when compared to 2DFA is it around two orders of magnitude smaller, with that of 4DFA it is 3 times smaller and 8DFA is comparable to DFA/EC.

The experiments are evaluated with the Snort rule-sets and the results shows that DFA/ECs are very compact and achieve high inspection speed. Particularly, in best case the DFA/ECs are more than four orders of magnitude lesser than DFAs. When compared with DFA, DFA/ECs require significantly lesser memory bandwidth. A DFA/EC is theoretically modest, implementation and upgrading is made easy due to faster construction speed.

DISCUSSIONS AND PROPOSED APPROACH

The various existing DFA compression techniques discussed in section 3 was analyzed to improve the memory consumption and to provide an efficient finite automata. The main reason that was analyzed from these existing DFA compression techniques for the number of states to get increased is due to the state explosion problem. The problem with exponential state explosion can be efficiently alleviated by grouping the regular expression. Grouping the regular expression falls into two cases. The first one is when the number of groups is known, the number of states in DFA can be minimized and second is when the maximum number of DFA states is known, the number of groups can be minimized. Though total number of groups and total number of DFA states plays major criteria in minimizing the memory, only either of these two cases cannot be concentrated in minimization process. Minimizing the number of groups will lead to state explosion and minimizing only the number of states will end up with large number of subdivided group count. Therefore to analyze the performance of the regular expression grouping method both these cases should be equally focused in correspondent with the various practical demands.

Grouping the regular expression can be done by Intelligent Optimization Grouping Algorithms. To provide memory efficient deterministic finite automata, DFA compression techniques can be used along with the Intelligent Optimization Grouping Algorithms. Intelligent Optimization Grouping Algorithms such as Tabu Search (TS), Simulated Annealing (SA), Ant Colony Optimization (ACO), Swarm Intelligence (SI) and Particle Swarm Optimization (PSO) can be used effectively to solve the state blow-up problem by obtaining the overall most favorable distribution between the consumption of memory and number of groups. By recursively analyzing each feasible optimization outcome an exact optimum solution can be effortlessly acquired.

In Figure 1 the overall structure of the proposed approach which reduces DFA states by grouping the regular expression using the Intelligent Optimization Grouping Algorithms is shown. The payload files extracted from the rule sets such as Snort, Bro NIDS, and Linux L-7 filter are used as input. The set of regular expressions are determined using packet payload files. Initially the parameters for the algorithms are assigned and the initial population is generated by randomly distributing the regular expression on the search space. The performance is evaluated according to the Intelligent Optimization Grouping Algorithms such as Simulated Annealing (SA), Swarm Intelligence (SI), Ant Colony Optimization (ACO), Particle Swarm Optimization (PSO), Tabu Search, etc. Based on the performance the parameters such as search space, population, position, velocity etc are adjusted and the process is continued until the optimal groups are formed or until the maximum iteration is obtained.

Once the optimal solution is obtained and the regular expressions are grouped, the finite state automata is designed based on the discussed existing DFA compression technique and is integrated with the DPI search engine to identify the packets that hold the viruses, unauthorized access and attacks such as TCP connection attacks, fragmentation attacks and application attacks. Intelligent Optimization Grouping Algorithms applied on the discussed existing DFA compression techniques for deep packet inspection will provide memory efficient automata with an improved network intrusion detection throughput through the use of DPI techniques and improved malicious packet detection.

The experiments are evaluated in future on the proposed approach for the various performance metrics, and the expected outcome is compared with the various discussed existing DFA Compression techniques. Figure 2 shows the memory consumption, memory bandwidth, throughput and compression rate for the different DFA compression techniques. It depicts that the proposed approach will produce reduced memory consumption, better memory bandwidth, high throughput and better compression rate.

Figure 1. Overall structure of proposed approach

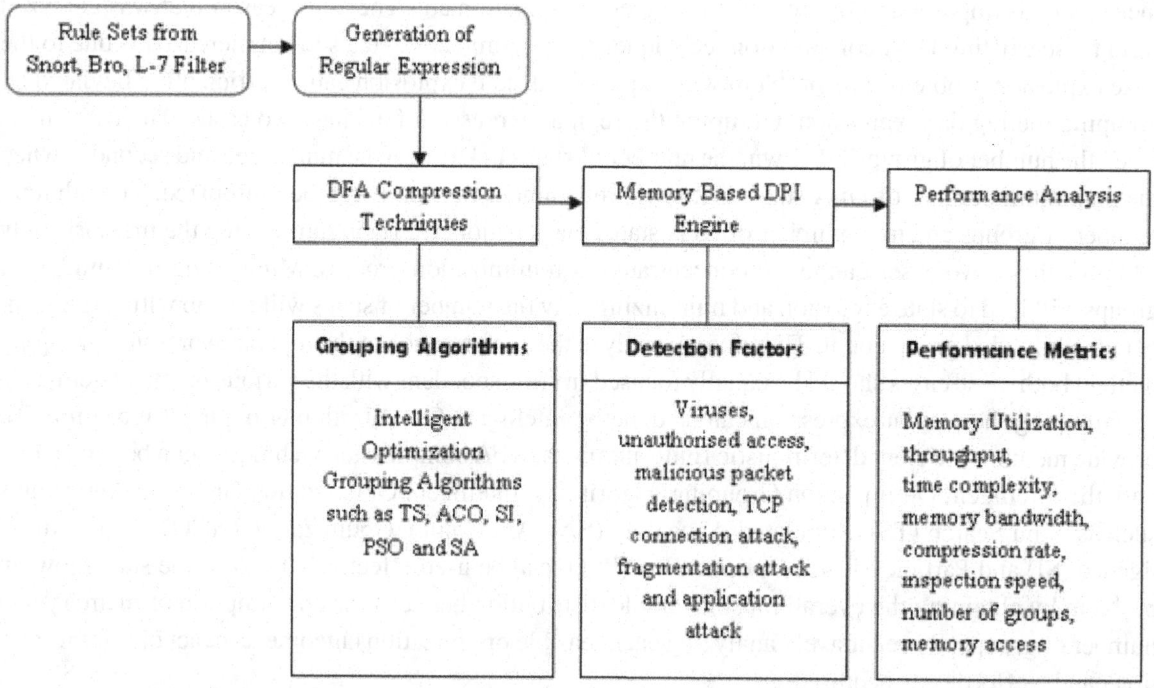

Figure 2. Memory consumption, memory bandwidth, throughput and compression rate for different DFA compression techniques

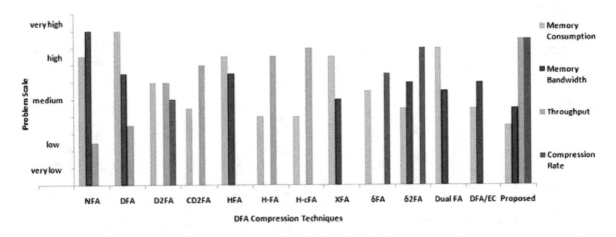

Figure 3 illustrates the performance measures of the main memory access time and the time complexity for the various DFA compression techniques and shows that the proposed approach will produce increased number of memory access time per input byte and will improve the time complexity.

Figure 3. Time complexity and main memory access time for different DFA compression techniques

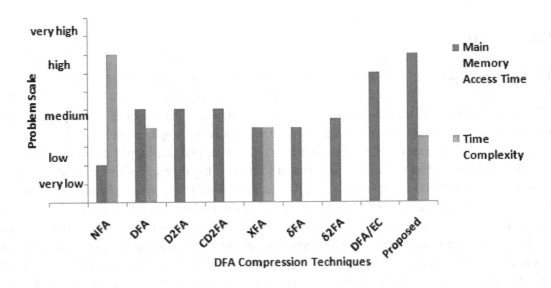

Figure 4 shows the inspection speed of intrusion detection and the regular expression matching speed for the various DFA compression techniques. It illustrates that the proposed approach will produce fast matching speed and high inspection speed of intrusion detection.

Figure 4. Inspection speed and matching speed for different DFA compression techniques

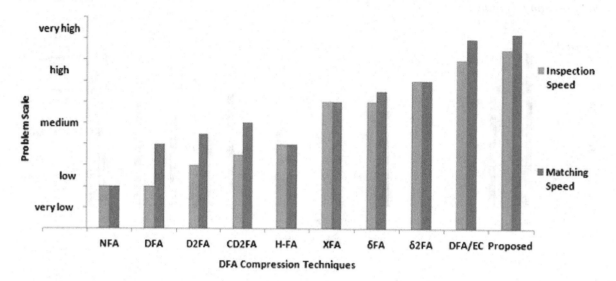

Thus the future experiments evaluated on the proposed approach using Intelligent Optimization Grouping Algorithms will provide an optimally efficient automaton when compared with the discussed existing DFA compression techniques and will also improve the throughput of network intrusion detection through the use of DPI techniques and will enhance the malicious packet detection.

CONCLUSION

In this chapter, the different compression representations for Deterministic Finite Automata such as NFA, DFA, MDFA, Lazy DFA, NFA- OBDD, HFA, H-FA, H-cFA, XFA, D²FA, CD²FA, δFA, δ²FA, Dual Finite Automata and DFA/EC are presented. MDFA increases the matching speed of the regular expression approximately to 50 to 700 times above the NFA-based implementation and achieves the speedup of up to 12-42 times over a DFA-based parser. For all practical applications the size of the lazy DFA remains little but the limitation is that it leads to a high warm-up cost and large memory consumption. NFA-OBDDs improve the time efficiency of NFA. The memory storage requirement of HFA is comparable to those of an NFA; its memory bandwidth is similar to that of a DFA, but the regular expressions that contains counting and dot-star conditions consumes high memory. H-FA reduces space close to 95% but has a vast size of transition table and a slow inspection speed. On the other hand H-cFA is extremely efficient in implementing long length restriction signature patterns. XFAs matching speed is around 20 times higher than a DFA and consumes 10 times lesser memory than DFA. The δFA substantially diminishes the number of transitions and number of states and needs only a single state transition for each character thus providing fast string matching. When compared to δFA, δ²FA provides an effective improvement in memory utilization and lookup speed. D²FA representation reduces the transitions between states by more than 95% and decreases the space requirements to less than 2 MB but the usage of default transitions decreases throughput. Memory reduction achieved by CD²FA is between 2.5 to 20 times better when compared to a compressed DFA and 5 to 60 times higher when compared with uncompressed DFA. The number of main memory access of Dual FA is much quicker than the other existing techniques. When compared to other existing techniques DFA/EC tremendously increases the data packet inspection speed and provides only one main memory access. Each of the state compression techniques that were studied has certain strengths and limitations. Thus any one of these compact representation DFAs can be used along with Intelligent Optimization Grouping Algorithms to provide memory efficient deterministic finite automata that can be used for deep packet inspection.

REFERENCES

Becchi, M., & Crowley, P. (2007a). A Hybrid Finite Automaton for Practical Deep Packet Inspection. *Proceedings of the ACM Conference on Emerging Networking Experiments and Technologies.*

Becchi, M., & Crowley, P. (2007b). An Improved Algorithm to Accelerate Regular Expression Evaluation. *Proceedings of the 3rd ACM/IEEE Symposium on Architecture for Networking and Communications Systems*, 145-154.

Becchi, M., & Crowley, P. (2008). Extending Finite Automata to Efficiently Match Perl-Compatible Regular Expressions. *Proceedings of the ACM International Conference on Emerging Networking Experiments and Technologies.*

Ficara, D., Di Pietro, A., Giordano, S., Member, S., Procissi, G., Vitucci, F., & Antichi, G. (2011). Differential Encoding of DFAs for Fast Regular Expression Matching. *IEEE/ACM Transactions on Networking*, *19*(3), 683–694.

Ficara, D., Giordano, S., Procissi, G., Vitucci, F., Antichi, G., & Pietro, A. D. (2008). An Improved DFA for Fast Regular Expression Matching. *Proceedings of the ACM SIGCOMM Computer Communication Review*, *38*(5), 29-40.

Kumar, S., Chandrasekaran, B., Turner, J., & Varghese, G. (2007). Curing Regular Expressions Matching Algorithms from Insomnia, Amnesia and Acalculia. *Proceedings of the ACM/IEEE Symposium Architecture for Networking and Communication Systems*, 155-164.

Kumar, S., Dharmapurikar, S., Yu, F., Crowley, P., & Turner, J. (2006) Algorithms to Accelerate Multiple Regular Expressions Matching for Deep Packet Inspection. *Proceedings of the Conference on Applications, Technologies, Architectures, and Protocols for Computer Communications*, *36*, 339-350.

Kumar, S., Turner, J., & Williams, J. (2006). Advanced Algorithms for Fast and Scalable Deep Packet Inspection. *Proceedings of the ACM/IEEE Symposium Architecture for Networking and Communication Systems*, 81-92.

Kumar, S., Turner, J. S., Crowley, P., & Mitzenmacher, M. (2007) HEXA: Compact Data Structures for Faster Packet Processing. *Proceedings of the International Conference on Network Protocols*, 246-255.

Liu, C., & Wu, J. (2013). Fast Deep Packet Inspection with a Dual Finite Automata. *IEEE Transactions on Computers*, *62*(2), 310–321.

Sidhu, R., & Prasanna, V. K. (2004). Fast Regular Expression Matching using FPGAs. *Proceedings of the 9th Annual IEEE Symposium on Field-Programmable Custom Computing Machines*, 227-238.

Smith, R., Estan, C., & Jha, S. (2008b). Faster Signature Matching with Extended Automata. *IEEE Symposium on Security and Privacy*, 187-201.

Smith, R., Estan, C., Jha, S., & Kong, S. (2008a). Deflating the Big Bang: Fast and Scalable Deep Packet Inspection with Extended Finite Automata. *Proceedings of the ACM SIGCOMM 2008 Conference on Applications, Technologies, Architectures, and Protocols for Computer Communications*, 207-218.

Yang, L., Karim, R., Ganapathy, V., & Smith, R. (2011). Fast Memory-Efficient Regular Expression Matching with NFA-OBDDs. *Computer Networks: The International Journal of Computer and Telecommunications Networking*, 55(15), 3376–3393.

Yu, F., Chen, Z., Diao, Y., & Lakshman, T. (2006). Fast and Memory- Efficient Regular Expression Matching for Deep Packet Inspection. *Proceedings of the ACM/IEEE Symposium on Architecture for Networking and Communications Systems*, 93-102.

Yu, F., Chen, Z., Diao, Y., Lakshman, T. V., & Katz, R. H. (2001): Fast and Memory-Efficient Regular Expression Matching for Deep Packet Inspection. *Proceedings of the ACM/IEEE Symposium Architecture for Networking and Communication Systems*, 93-102.

Chapter 10
Investigation of Threats, Vulnerabilities, Attacks, and Approaches in Wireless Sensor Networks

Chaya P.
GSSS Institute of Engineering and Technology for Women, India

Nandini Prasad K. S.
Dr. Ambedkar Institute of Technology, India

ABSTRACT

Wireless sensor networks (WSN) have emerged as significant technology that has been adopted in various research fields to monitor the physical environments and collect information from the surroundings. However, WSNs are more vulnerable to attacks owing to their significant characteristics, including dynamicity in network topology and resource constraints. Multiple methods have been investigated to efficiently identify the different types of threats and attacks over the WSN. However, most of the existing works focus on a specific type of attack detection and lack in analyzing their performance. This survey highlights the significant functionalities of WSN, applications, and security requirements. From the viewpoint of security measurements, the authors have classified the survey study as security towards data collections and routing in WSN. Also, various security attacks based on protocol stack layers are classified. Finally, the authors have emphasized the significant security challenges in this research field based on the prior studies followed by the conclusion.

INTRODUCTION

From the past decades, there has been tremendous growth in the adoption of wireless devices and infrastructure (Aliu et al., 2013). Wireless sensor networks (WSNs) is core technology in the Internet of Things and plays a significant role to offer optimal services through sensor devices, i.e., smart home,

DOI: 10.4018/978-1-7998-9795-8.ch010

manufacturing as per industry 4.0 vision, smart transportation, environment monitoring, smart grids and many more (Atzori et al., 2010), (Gubbi et al., 2013). A typical WSN contains sink nodes along with multiple distributed sensor nodes which collect and forwards the data packets to perform various tasks. Built-in WSNs provide reliable data delivery for IoT based applications such as smart healthcare applications, which monitors, analyze, and diagnose the illness. In the application, WSNs provides useful information to the physicians and considered as a significant factor for successful diagnosis. However, distributed WSNs are susceptible to network failures owing to signal interference, which could decrease the quality of service (QoS) (Weber, 2010), (Al-Karaki & Kamal, 2004). Therefore, supporting reliable data delivery becomes a challenging problem in WSNs. Many multi-path optimal routing strategies to offer reliable deliveries in the context of WSNs ().

Moreover, the transmission of data packets takes over multiple paths and hops to receivers. So more transmission contentions and signal interferences lead to the additional transmission failures in the network. These efforts go in vain by very small efforts initiated by the malicious nodes by participating into the network. Therefore, study of security in many various dimensions is an essential research domain in WSN.

Though the concern of data privacy and security issues in the area of disasters management is a popular topic (Erdelj & Akyildiz, n.d.) as initially most of the application were related to such application, However, most of the surveillance applications lack the data privacy and security tools; hence it is crucial to evaluate the security concept. Some of the significant challenges to protect and secure the WSNs from the malicious attackers are listed below:

- *Energy optimization* Indeed, high security with minimum energy consumption policies utilized and strongly influenced by constraints and capabilities of the sensor node.
- The maximum quantity of energy obsessive by the sensor node is during the data transmission. *Security* is essential to transmit the data securely as well as store the data securely.
- The *network topology* poses vulnerabilities to the attackers for both active and passive attack as unlike a wired network, where firewall enhances privacy and security, threats in wireless network attains from various directions and may target any sensor node over the network infrastructure.
- *Minimal resources:* In the WSNs, every sensor nodes contains limited resources, including hardware constraints, energy, processing capability, and memory space. Due to the large scale and distributed topology configuration, processing signals at the receiver end to compensate for attenuation of the signal, the energy consumption by the sensor node communication is very high. Therefore, all previous research studies focus was on energy optimization problem.
- *Rekeying:* The lifetime of the shared key may expire, and it is essential to re-establish.

The primary motive of this study is to represent a comprehensive research study on WSNs security by considering most prior work in the state of art of threats and attacks in WSNs. The different types of vulnerabilities and threats are identified and introduced operational paradigms for WSNs configuration (Xie et al., 2018). The present study overviews existing security protocols concerning data security and routing security and present a comparative analysis among them.

Chapter Organization: Section-II discusses the different types of threats and security challenges over the WSNs. Section-III briefly discuss the process and role of PKC against wireless attacks. Section-IV provides a literature study on existing security solutions towards data collection and routing protocols, including advantages and limitations. Section-V highlights the open research challenges identified from existing studies. Section-VI provides the conclusion of the study.

THREATS AND SECURITY CHALLENGES IN WSNS

There are different types of vulnerabilities, threats, and attacks occur to corrupt and break the network security. As a result, network equipment can breakdown and loss of energy. A typical malicious node comprises with network security and tries to damage the entire networking system. Conceptually, wireless network security attacks are categorized into two class's namely Active attacks and Passive Attacks where the malicious node gains the actionable information to the network resources (Table 1 represents the comparative analysis).

1. Active Attacks: - These are the attacks in which an attacker can try to change the actual information or builds false information. To stop such type of attacks, it is not easy because of the high range of physical and software liability. Instead of avoiding these attacks, it emphasizes in the detection of threats and recovers the system. The pictorial representation of active attack scenario is represented in Figure 1.

Usually, an active attack needs external effort because of dangerous implication. Whenever a malicious node tries to attack, the victim should be alerted about it. Generally, these attacks are in three different forms viz; interruption (Unauthorized user attempts to create as another entity) (Jawandhiya et al., 2010), alteration (modification of original information) (Zhou et al., 2008) and fabrication (unauthorized user gains access to the network and lock the authorized user out) (Wang et al., 2006). The major impacts of active attacks are: to disrupt the network operations, degrades the overall network performance, modification in data transmission, collapse the communication link between the neighboring nodes (Mohammadi & Jadidoleslamy, 2011).

Figure 1. Scenario of active attack

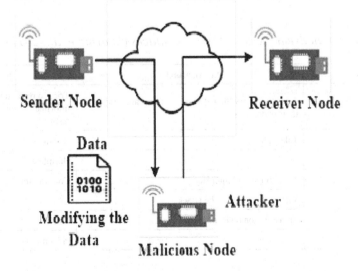

Passive Attacks: -In this scenario, attacker spoils in unauthorized eavesdropping, it just monitors the data transmission and collects the information (Sharma & Ghose, 2010). The pictorial representation of passive attack is shown in Figure 2.

Figure 2. Scenario of passive attack

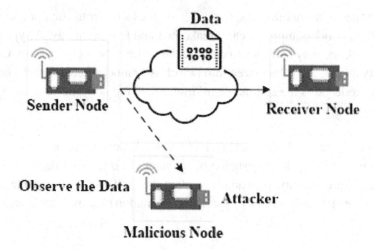

The passive attacks are quite difficult to identify because the attacker does not modify any data or system configuration. Thus, the attacked node isn't able to identify any information about the attack. Though these kinds of attacks may be prevented from cryptographic methods where data is encrypted in secret language at the sender side, and it is again converted into user readable language at the receiver end. This method can maintain security and prevent the data from malicious attacks.

There are two kinds of passive attacks; i) release of data contents and ii) traffic analysis. Typically, the data traffic is forward and received conventionally, and both sender and receiver don't know about the third party have read or observed the traffic pattern. The main objectives are -data eavesdropping, information accessing and gathering, degradation in network performance, compromised with privacy and confidentiality (Mohammadi & Jadidoleslamy, 2011; Sharma & Ghose, 2010).

Table 1. Key difference of active attacks and passive attacks (Sharma et al., 2017)

Key difference	Active attacks	Passive attacks
objective	Tries to modify the network resources and affect their operations	Tries to read and utilize the system information but doesn't affect any resource
Alteration in message	Takes place	Doesn't change
Harm to the resources	Damages the system	Harmless
Threat	Availability and integrity	Confidentiality
Prevention	Victim alerts about the attack	Unaware about the attack
Attacker role	Transmission takes place by physical devices	Traffic analysis
Emphasis	Detection	Prevention

APPROACHES USING PUBLIC-KEY CRYPTOGRAPHY

This section mainly discusses the terminology of public-key cryptography (i.e. PKC) and security mechanism. In the literature, several PKC algorithms have been introduced and adopted to improve network security.

Public Key Cryptography (PKC)

PKC is a cryptographic method that uses a set of both keys, i.e., public key (widely utilized as the owner wants) and private key (user authenticate). It is an asymmetric cryptographic approach where two different parties use different keys for encryption and decryption. Figure 3 shows the PKC process as follows: -

Figure 3. Process of PKC

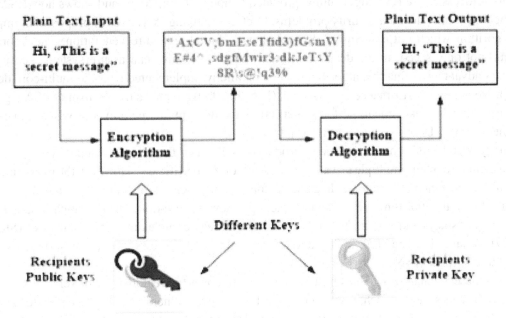

Security against wireless attacks using PKC approach:

- *Encryption and Decryption* can allow the two parties to cover-up the data which needs to be exchanged to each other. The principle of modern cryptography is to encrypt the message based on the key value, which is further utilized to send an encrypted message or decrypt the received message.
- *Threat detection* allows the recipient to check whether it has not been changed during information transmission. Any endeavor to change or insert information is detected.
- *Authentication process* allows the recipient to decide its source by confirming the sender identity.

The different research studies assumed that the data size, code size, processing time and energy optimization make it undesirable for PKC methods including Diffie-Hellman approach (Joshi et al., 2015), Ronald Rivest, or Adi Shamir, and Leonard Adleman (RSA) algorithm (Zhou & Tang, 2011) to be applied for WSN security improvement. Additionally, PKC algorithms are primarily utilized for key exchange or digital signatures.

In PKC, D-H method allows two parties to generate a secret key (i.e., Bob and Alice). Alyani et al. (Alyani, 2012) show the process of how the D-H algorithm performs a key exchange mechanism, and it is applied over the logical key hierarchy structure which is additionally utilized to improvise the key management scheme by modifying the fundamental logical structure. Bodur and Kara (Bodur & Kara, 2017) illustrated a crucial D-H exchange mechanism for logical key hierarchical structure and provided knowledge about how the common secret key can be obtained for both the parent node and user node.

Unlike the D-H algorithm, the RSA algorithm is also designed for message encryption and digital signatures. At present, the RSA algorithm is mainly utilized to enhance message integrity. The implementation process of the RSA algorithm is provided (Zhou & Tang, 2011) and shows how RSA could be applicable to mitigate data security problems. Li et al. (Li, Qing, & Li, 2010) proposed an improved RSA algorithm which outperforms in decryption and digital signature generation. The improvised algorithm not only speed up the decryption performance even also can assure system security. The significant advantage is that this algorithm can be parallelly implemented over the multi-core devices, and improve security performance. Brown et al. (Brown, 2000) adopted a mechanism of RSA algorithm which takes the very less time to perform encryption and decryption operations in WSNs and exposes the vulnerability to Denial of Service (DoS) attacks.

Security-based PKC scheme has been introduced by Raya et al. (Raya & Hubaux, 2007), in which each sensor node contains multiple private keys and authorizes certificates. However, the major drawback is that this scheme cannot handle the huge scale applications owing to its computational complexities. Liu et al. (Lu et al., 2008) investigated an efficient privacy preservation scheme which produces short time anonymous keys and certificates and reduces the storage complexities. In the study of (Studer et al., 2009), (Zhang, Lu, Lin et al, 2008), and (Ying et al., 2013) have proposed a hash-based security protocol to deal with WSN security problems.

Identity-based signature schemes have investigated to cover the real identity of vehicles (Biswas & Misic, 2013). This security mechanism is effective, but it can be vulnerable to leak the private key (Lo & Tsai, 2016). Lo et al. (Biswas & Misic, 2013) proposed an authentication mechanism using ECC method. In order to perform high-security different researchers (He et al., n.d.), (Lin et al., 2008) proposed privacy preservation protocols using identity-based signature approach. In these schemes, public keys are utilized to identify the object. Zhang et al. (Zhang, Lu, Lin et al, 2008) proved that the identity-based signature scheme is vulnerable to reply attack. Hence to overcome this issue, authors introduced a new privacy preservation protocol using digital signature for VANET.

The most recent research work of Qun et al. (Lin, Yan, Huang et al, 2018) introduced a linear homomorphic identity-based signature scheme which performs the linear calculations upon authenticated data. Also introduced a new proxy signature-based method which allows authorized user to handover the signature authority to proxy user. However, an asymmetric cryptography approach contains a group signature scheme allows the Road Side Units (RSUs) to verify the messages from vehicles (Douceur, 2002). RSUs based authentication method using the hash function is proposed to secure the vehicular communication systems (Zhang, Lin, Lu et al, 2008). In (Jiang et al., 2009), Jung et al. proposed an

RSU based privacy preservation scheme that allocates unidentified credentials to vehicles which help to reduce the network overhead.

In the study of (Hussein et al., 2017) and (Hayouni et al., 2014), the authors have discussed the various cryptographic algorithms, and their drawbacks with respect to the security challenges and attacks at different layers of WSN. Lu et al. (Lu et al., 2014) illustrated a model of secure data transmission over the cluster-based WSNs. The proposed approach provides security with less energy consumption by employing a digital signature scheme. Wenjun et al. (Liu et al., 2012) have analyzed the scope and challenges of security protocols based on comparison of WSNs. Also introduced a multi-path routing method for WSNs which balances the energy consumption level and improve the network efficiency. In another research study of Lo and Liu (Lo & Liu, 2013), proposed a secure routing protocol against the black-hole attacks. The experimental results showed that the proposed protocol outperforms up to 2.6 times in terms of data delivery ratio. The table-2 highlights the most common PKC methods with security requirements and limitations.

Table 2. The most common PKC methods with security requirements and limitations

Reference No.	Public Key Cryptographic (PKC) Solutions	Security Requirements	Drawbacks	Attack Alleviation
(Studer et al., 2009), (Ying et al., 2013), (Lin et al., 2008)	unsigned keys and credentials	Certification, privacy preservation	Computational overhead	Eavesdropping, replay attacks.
(Zhang, Lu, Lin et al, 2008), (Biswas & Misic, 2013), (Lo & Tsai, 2016),	Identity-based proxy signatures	Authentication, Non repudiation, privacy preservation	Vulnerable to leak private key	DoS, impersonation attacks.
(Lo & Tsai, 2016)	ECC (Elliptic curve cryptography)	Certification, privacy preservation	Vulnerable to reply attack	Dos, replay attacks.
(Lin et al., 2008), (Jiang et al., 2009)	RSUs based signature schemes	Certification, privacy preservation	Compromise with RSUs and disclosure the information	Impersonation, data routing attacks
(Zhang, Lin, Lu et al, 2008), (Hussein et al., 2017)	Smart cards for identification	Certification, privacy preservation	Storage complexity	Sybil, Impersonation attack.

RELATED WORK

Majority of the research study towards secure routing schemes in WSNs is introduced using a key management policy of cryptography. Therefore, this section discusses the most prominent existing cryptographic methods conducted for addressing routing security challenges in WSNs.

Data Security in WSNs

Generally, WSN is susceptible to numerous attacks due to its dynamic topology, self-organization, and constrained resources. Wireless attacks may cause network variance, which can be reflected in data aggregation from the network resources. The aggregated data is useful and can be employed to recognize malicious attacks. Xie et al. (Xie, 2018) have studied about data security-related challenges and solution strategies, which could be valuable to detect security attacks and figure out the threats and intrusions. Generally, secure data are produced from various WSNs applications, including smart city, intelligent healthcare systems, and many more. Based on security protocols, valuable data can be secured from sensor devices, e.g., fingerprint scanning machine.

To overcome data security challenges, different security mechanisms have been developed by the researchers to provide the security in WSN such methods are Key management, certification and authentication, re-keying, cluster head selection scheme and many more (Ganesh & Amutha, 2013), (Huang et al., 2014). SLEACH protocol is proposed to improve network overhead. The aim was to prevent selective forwarding, hello flooding, and sinkhole attacks. Nevertheless, traditional cryptographic methods like encryption and SLEACH are constrained by storage size and faces network failure problems. To address the challenges of traditional encryption methods in terms of data security and storage size-related problems in WSN, ECC is introduced to offer higher security with minimum key size.

In the study of Zhou et al. (Zhou et al., 2014), homomorphic encryption method allows the cluster heads to collect the encrypted data without decryption, and it performs data aggregation in short delay. Elminir et al. (Elhoseny et al., 2016), proposed ECC and homomorphic encryption scheme to allow secure data transmission over the WSN. The main reason of the study is to enhance the lifespan the network, ECC scheme is utilized to produce both private and public keys for sensor nodes. The proposed encryption algorithm built on GASONEC algorithm (Elhoseny et al., 2014) that uses a genetic algorithm to establish network topology and reduces the energy consumption rate after the data transmission process.

Even though the existing methods to identify the various attacks have been researched and illustrated in the prior studies, none of them offer a significant study on secure data collection and data analytics for detecting malicious attacks in WSNs. Few literature studies focused on secure data collection (Zhou et al., 2018), (Li et al., 2018) and data analytics (Jing et al., 2019), Ad-Hoc network (Liu et al., 2018) and cellular phones (Lin, Yan, Chen et al, 2018). Although et al. (Venkatraman et al., 2013) discussed various attacks occurs in WSNS, but they didn't consider the protocol to identify the malicious attacks. However, in the study of Xie et al. (Xie et al., 2011) proposed an attack detection model which categorized the anomaly detection approaches. However, the drawback is that the authors didn't concern about data security didn't evaluate performance. However, the prior methods lack in the detection of vulnerabilities, threats, and attack with the attention to data security and data analytics.

Routing Security in WSNs

Routing protocols are most significant to secure the WSNs, and they are considered as fundamental constraints for the entire network. In the literature, various routing protocols have been illustrated and classified them based on their functionalities and routing topology example; linear routing protocols, hierarchical routing protocols, and location-based routing protocols (Semchedine et al., 2017), multipath routing schemes, and quality of services (QoS) (Basaran & Kang, 2009) respectively. SLEACH is widely adopted for secure routing of WSNs in which cluster heads are selected in a distributed order

(So & Byun, 2017). Another research work of Wang et al. (Wang & Li, 2019) has proposed the shortest path secure routing algorithm to overcome the compromise nodes with energy consumption. The simulation results showed that the proposed approach outperforms in the finding of the shortest route with ensuring data transmission security. Shi et al. (Shi et al., 2019) discussed QoS aware routing issues in WSNs. Also designed a novel approach of malicious node detection in which classifies the malicious attacks that arise from packet collisions and channel errors.

Paper (Zaki, 2018) presented a computational model for the next generation of QoS routing protocol, which allocates an optimal route to ensure the QoS and support large scale IoT applications. Also, they presented analytical computation for bit error rate and critical path loss model which determine the trust level between the frequently utilized sensor nodes. Chen et al. (Lyu et al., 2019) have designed a selective authentication model which defend from DoS attacks, fulfill the need for authenticity and reliability of WSNs. A distributed validation scheme is introduced to cooperate the authentication model with selective routing. Pattabiram and Sundararajan (Kasthuribai & Sundararajan, 2018) have introduced a QoS aware energy-efficient multi-path secure routing model for MANET. From this model energy-efficient, multi-path routes are elected over the network. The selected optimal path established secure route using cuckoo search algorithm.

QoS based communication arises many challenges owing to the enhancing applications of WSNs. In this regards, Bapu and Gowd (Bapu, 2017), have presented a novel approach of link quality-based routing method. The opportunistic routing strategy selects the relay nodes which improve the entire network lifetime. Another QoS based multi-path routing protocol is proposed by Deepa and Suguna (Deepa & Suguna, 2017). This solution strategy allows the multiple paths between the source nodes to the sink node.

Consequently, if one of the paths fails, transmission can be performed through an alternative path. This process improves the data delivery ratio with optimal latency. Also proposed protocol offers high throughput with minimum delay and enhances the network overhead. Table 3 has an analysis of various security attacks occurs at different layers of network protocol based on the nature of the attacker and network threat model.

Table 3. Classification of various security attacks occurs at different layers of WSNs

Attack type	Security requirement	Layer	Type of Threat	Active/Passive attack
Flooding attack	Interruption	Network layer	Availability	Active attack
Replay attack	Interruption, Interception	Network layer	Availability, confidentiality	Active attack
Sinkhole attack	Modification, Fabrication	Network Layer	Integrity, Confidentiality, Availability	Active attack
Spoofing attack	Interruption, Interception	Network Layer	Authenticity, availability	Active attack
Sybil attack	Interruption, Interception	Network Layer	Authenticity, availability	Active attack
Selective forwarding attacks	Interruption, Interception	Network Layer	Confidentiality, Availability	Active attack
Session hijacking	Interruption	Transport Layer	Availability	Active attack
Maliciounode attack	Interruption	Application Layer	Availability	Active attack
Traffic analysis	Interception	Network Layer	Confidentiality	Passive attack
Packet Tracing	Interception	MAC Layer	Confidentiality	Passive attack
Jamming attack	Modification	MAC layer	Integrity, Availability	Active attack
Blackhole attack	Interruption, interception	Network Layer	Integrity, Confidentiality, Availability	Active attack
Redundant data sorting attack	Interruption, Modification	Application Layer	Integrity, availability	Active attack
Timesynchronization attack	Interruption	Application Layer	Availability	Active attack
Packet dropping attack	Interruption	Network layer	Availability	Active attack
Transmission Failure	Modification	Network Layer	Integrity, Confidentiality, Availability	An active, passive attack
Passive data collection	Modification,	Physical Layer	Integrity, Confidentiality, Availability	Active attack
Node duplication	Modification	Physical Layer	Integrity, Availability	Active attack

Most of the research studies considered specific performance metrics including energy conservation, network lifetime, packet delivery ratio, delay, throughput, computation and communication cost. Also, some survey papers mainly focused on specific attack type and lacked in performance analysis with respect to the dynamic feature of network topology and other performance metrics (Jing et al., 2019; Li et al., 2018; Lin, Yan, Chen et al, 2018; Liu et al., 2018; Venkatraman et al., 2013; Xie et al., 2011). From the literature study, have find various measurements which talk about attack detection methodology and security measurement over the WSN. The proposed comprehensive survey study illustrates brief overview and provides significant contributions towards WSN security system by considering various performance metrics, methodologies, and simulation tools. The following figure 4 shows the statistical analysis of existing research work towards WSN security which mainly considers some significant performance parameters. The study summarized the various threats and security attacks and respective solution strategies using cryptographic approach. In the last have segregated the most prominent research papers and considered authors contributions with unique methodologies and experimental analysis. From the statistical analysis can figure outs that, most of the existing studies majorly focused on energy conservation factor, while very less research work is completed in the field of reduction of communication and computation cost. The reduction of communication overhead is the significant research topic in the state of art of WSN security. WSN has very less resources, and security system introduced additional communication overhead. Hence it is crucial to expand a security mechanism to strengthen the network lifetime during communication process.

Figure 4. Statistical analysis of existing research work with respect to various performance parameters.

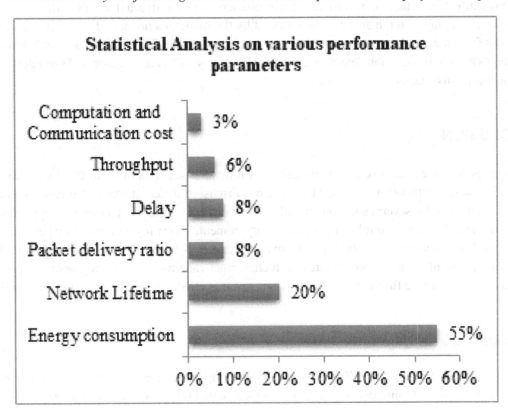

RESEARCH CHALLENGES

Selecting an efficient PKC cryptographic scheme for WSNs is a fundamental requirement to offer higher security services over the network. However, the selection of appropriate protocol depends upon the network topology, communication, and computation capability of the network. This section highlighting the significant research challenges ranging from cryptographic algorithms to network design.

In WSNs, sensor nodes are extremely resource-inhibited in conditions of memory size, computational speed, bandwidth, and energy. These resource constraints degrade the rate of cryptography and authentication which can be implemented over the sensory nodes. Thus, it is crucial to expand a robust cryptography algorithm to support multiple resource constraints and improvise the network overhead.

The traditional PKC have defined that public key operation can be practical in WSNs. However, private key operations are very expensive based on computation and energy consumption rate to achieve in a sensor network.

Key generation algorithms are implemented to maximize the vehicles speed up to 50m/h, but their key generation rate is minimal (Zhu et al., 2017). More focus is required in the development of VANETs to achieve faster key generation operation with high security.

The lightweight cryptographic algorithms play a significant role to mitigate the security challenges for upcoming technology, e.g., vehicular security systems and traffic analysis. Hence there is a major requirement to understand the vulnerabilities, threats, and finding a security solution to enhance the security level at WSNs.

Additionally, WSNs faces the physical security challenges and individual sensor node in the network are physically deployed in the area can be accessed by the malicious node, and then may be subject to the attacks from the attacker to compromise the weaker sensor node. To mitigate such malicious activities, there is a need for intrusion detection model for WSN to significantly secure and prevent the WSNs from the malicious attacks.

CONCLUSION

In this comprehensive study, we have summarized two major categories of security attacks (i.e., active attacks and passive attacks) in WSNs. The study has discussed different types of threats and security challenges followed by several solutions by adopting the public critical cryptographic approach, their advantages, and limitations to fulfill the security requirement. To evaluate the security performance of existing methods, have pointing out the performance parameters in terms of security in data collection and routing protocols. We explored the research challenges ranging from cryptographic algorithms to WSN design and provide future research directions towards effective security measurement in WSNs.

REFERENCES

Al-Karaki, J. N., & Kamal, A. E. (2004, December). Routing techniques in wireless sensor networks: A survey. *IEEE Wireless Communications*, *11*(6), 6–28. doi:10.1109/MWC.2004.1368893

Aliu, O., Imran, A., Imran, M., & Evans, B. (2013, February). A survey of self organisation infuture cellular networks. *IEEE Communications Surveys and Tutorials*, *15*(1), 336–361. doi:10.1109/SURV.2012.021312.00116

Alyani, N. (2012). The Improvement of Key management Based OnLogical Key Hierarchy by Implementing Diffie Hellman Algorithm. *Journal of ETCIS*, *3*, 3.

Atzori, L., Iera, A., & Morabito, G. (2010, October). The Internet of Things: A survey. *Computer Networks*, *54*(15), 2787–2805. doi:10.1016/j.comnet.2010.05.010

Bapu, B. R. (2017). Link Quality Based Opportunistic Routing Algorithm foQoSOS: Aware Wireless Sensor Networks Security. *WPC*, *97*(1), 1563–1578.

Basaran, C., & Kang, K.-D. (2009). *Quality of Service in Wireless Sensor Network s*. Springer London. doi:10.1007/978-1-84882-218-4_12

Biswas, S., & Misic, J. (2013). A cross-layer approach to privacypreserving authentication in WAVE-enabled VANETs. *IEEE Transactions on Vehicular Technology, 62*(5), 2182–2192. doi:10.1109/TVT.2013.2238566

Bodur, H., & Kara, R. (2017). Implementing Diffie-Hellman key exchange method on logical key hierarchy for secure broadcast transmission. In *2017 at CICN* (pp. 144–147). IEEE. doi:10.1109/CICN.2017.8319374

Brown, M. (2000). PGP in Constrained Wireless Devices. *Proc.9th USENIX Security Symp.*

Deepa & Suguna. (2017). An optimized QoS-based clustering with multi-path routing protocol for Wireless Sensor Networks. *Journal of King Saud University-Computer and Information Sciences.*

Douceur, J. R. (2002). The sybil attack. Lecture Notes in Computer Science, 2429, 251–260. doi:10.1007/3-540-45748-8_24

Elhoseny, Yuan, Yu, Mao, El-Minir, & Riad. (2014). Balancing energy consumption in heterogeneous wireless sensor network using genetic algorithm. *IEEE Communications Letters.*

Elhoseny, M., Elminir, H., Riad, A., & Yuan, X. (2016). A secure data routing schema for WSN using elliptic curve cryptography and homomorphic encryption. *Journal of King Saud University-Computer and Information Sciences, 28*(3), 262–275. doi:10.1016/j.jksuci.2015.11.001

Erdelj & Akyildiz. (n.d.). *Help from the Sky: Leveraging UAVs for Disaster Management.* Academic Press.

Felemban, E., Lee, C. G., & Ekici, E. (2006, June). MMSPEED. *IEEE Transactions on Mobile Computing, 5*(6), 738–754. doi:10.1109/TMC.2006.79

Ganesh, S., & Amutha, R. (2013). Efficient and secure routing protocol for wireless sensor networks throug SNR based dynamic clustering mechanisms. *Journal of Communications and Networks (Seoul), 15*(4), 422–429. doi:10.1109/JCN.2013.000073

Gubbi, J., Buyya, R., Marusic, S., & Palaniswami, M. (2013). Internet of Things (IoT): A vision, architectural elements, and future directions. *Future Generation Computer Systems, 29*(7), 1645–1660. doi:10.1016/j.future.2013.01.010

Hayouni, Hamdi, & Kim. (2014). A Survey on Encryption Schemes in Wireless Sensor Network. *ASEA.*

He, Zeadally, Xu, & Huang. (n.d.). An efficient identity based conditional privacy-preserving authentication scheme for vehicular ad hoc networks. *IEEE Transactions on IFS, 10*(12), 2681–2691.

Huang, L., Jie, L., & Guizani, M. (2014). Secure and efficient data transmission for cluster-based wireless sensor networks. *IEEE Transactions on Parallel and Distributed Systems, 25*(3), 750–761. doi:10.1109/TPDS.2013.43

Huang, X., & Fang, Y. (2008). *Multiconstrained QoS multi-path routing in wireless sensor networks.* Academic Press.

Hussein, Barges, & Jameel. (2017). Security Issues in Wireless Sensor Network. *Journal of JMESS, 3*(6).

Jawandhiya, Ghonge, Ali, & Deshpande. (2010). A Survey of MANET Atacks. *IJEST, 2*(9), 4063-4071.

Jiang, Y., Shi, M., Shen, X., & Lin, C. (2009). BAT: A robust signature scheme for vehicular networks using Binary Authentication Tree. *IEEE Transactionon on WC, 8*(4), 1974–1983.

Jing, X. Y., Yan, Z., & Pedrycz, W. (2019, 1). Security Data Collectio and data Analytics in the Internet: A Survey. *IEEE Communications Surveys and Tutorials, 21*(1), 586–618. Advance online publication. doi:10.1109/COMST.2018.2863942

Joshi, P., Verma, M., & Verma, P. R. (2015). Secure authentication approach using Diffie-Hellman key exchange algorithm for WSN. In *2015 ICCICCT* (pp. 527–532). IEEE. doi:10.1109/ICCICCT.2015.7475336

Kasthuribai, P. T., & Sundararajan, M. (2018). Secured and QoS Based Energy-Aware Multipath Routing in MANET. *WPC, 101*(4), 2349–2364. doi:10.100711277-018-5820-4

Li, G. Q., Yan, Z., Fu, Y. L., & Chen, H. L. (2018). Data Fusion for NetworkIntrusion Detection: A review. Security and Communication Networks, 1-16.

Li, S., Neelisetti, R. K., Liu, C., & Lim, A. (2010). Efficient multi-path protocol for wireless sensor networks. *International Journal of Wireless and Mobile Networks, 2*(1), 110–130.

Li, Y., Qing, L., & Li, T. (2010). Design and implementation of an improved RSA algorithm. *2010 International Conference on EDT*, 390-393.

Lin, H. Q., Yan, Z., Chen, Y., & Zhang, L. F. (2018, March). A Survey on Network Security-Related Data Collection Technologi. *IEEE Access: Practical Innovations, Open Solutions, 6*, 18345–18365. doi:10.1109/ACCESS.2018.2817921

Lin, Q., Yan, H., Huang, Z., Chen, W., Shen, J., & Tang, Y. (2018). An ID-based linearly homomorphic signature scheme and itsapplication in blockchain. *IEEE Access: Practical Innovations, Open Solutions, 6*, 20632–20640. doi:10.1109/ACCESS.2018.2809426

Lin, X., Sun, X., Wang, X., Zhang, C., Ho, P.-H., & Shen, X. (2008). TSVC: Timed efficient and secure vehicular communications the privacy-preservingng. *IEEE Transactions on WC, 7*(12), 4987–4998. doi:10.1109/T-WC.2008.070773

Liu, G., Yan, Z., & Pedryczc, W. (2018, March). Data Collection for Attack Detectionand Security Measurement in Mobile Ad Hoc Networks: A Survey. *Journal of NCA, 10*(5), 105–122.

Liu, W., Zhang, S., & Fan, J. (2012). *A diagnosis-based clustering and multi-path routing protocol for WSN.* IJDSR.

Lo, N. W., & Liu, F.-L. (2013). A Secure Routing Protocol to Prevent Cooperative Black Hole Attack in MAN. *ITES, Springer New York, 234*, 59–65.

Lo, N.-W., & Tsai, J.-L. (2016). An efficient conditional privacypreserving authentication scheme for vehicular sensor networks without pairings. *IEEE Transactions on ITS, 17*(5), 1319–1328.

Lu, Jie, & Guizani. (2014). Secure and Efficient Data Transmission for Cluster-Based WSN. *IEEE Transactions on Parallel and Distributed Systems, 25*(3).

Lu, R., Lin, X., & Zhu, H. (2008). ECPP: Efficient conditional privacy preservation protocol for secure vehicular communications. *Proceedings of the 27th IEEE INFOCOM '08*, 1229–1237. 10.1109/INFO-COM.2008.179

Lyu, C., Zhang, X., Liu, Z., & Chi, C.-H. (2019). Selective Authentication Based Geographic Opportunistic Routing WSN for IOT Against DoS Attacks. *IEEE Access: Practical Innovations, Open Solutions*, *7*, 31068–31082. doi:10.1109/ACCESS.2019.2902843

Mohammadi & Jadidoleslamy. (2011). A Comparison olink-layerer attacks on WSN. *GRAPH-HOC, 3*(1).

Raya, M., & Hubaux, J.-P. (2007). Securing vehicular ad hoc networks. *Journal of Computer Security*, *15*(1), 39–68. doi:10.3233/JCS-2007-15103

Semchedine, F., Saidi, N. A., Belouzir, L., & Bouallouche-Medjkoune, L. (2017). QoS-Based Protocol for Routing in Wireless Sensor Networks. *WPC, 97*(3), 4413–4429. doi:10.100711277-017-4731-0

Sharma, K., & Ghose, M. K. (2010). *Wireless Sensor Networks: An Overview on its Security Threats*. IJCA.

Sharma, M., Tandon, A., Narayan, S., & Bhushan, B. (2017). *Classification and analysis of security attacks in WSNs and IEEE 802.15. 4 standards: A survey. In ICACCA*. IEEE.

Shi, P., Gu, C., & Jing, Z. (2019). QoS Aware Routing Protocol Through Cross-layer Approach in Asynchronous Duty-Cycled WSNs. *IEEE Access: Practical Innovations, Open Solutions, 7*, 57574–57591. doi:10.1109/ACCESS.2019.2913679

So, J., & Byun, H. (2017). Load-Balanced Opportunistic Routing for Duty-CycledWireless Sensor Networks. *IEEE Transactions on Mobile Computing, 16*(7), 1940–1955. doi:10.1109/TMC.2016.2606427

Studer, A., Bai, F., Bellur, B., & Perrig, A. (2009). Flexible, extensible, and efficient VANET authentication. *Journal of Communications and Networks (Seoul), 11*(6), 574–588. doi:10.1109/JCN.2009.6388411

Venkatraman, Daniel, & Murugaboopathi. (2013). Various Attacks in Wireless Sensor Network: Survey. *IJSCE, 3*(1).

Wang, N., & Li, J. (2019). Shortest Path Routing With Risk Control for Compromised WSN. *IEEE Access: Practical Innovations, Open Solutions, 7*, 19303–19311. doi:10.1109/ACCESS.2019.2897339

Wang, Y., Attebury, G., & Ramamurthy, B. (2006). *A Survey of Security Issues in Wireless Sensor Network*. IEEE Communication Surveys.

Weber, R. H. (2010, January). Internet of Things-New security and privacy challenges. *Computer Law & Security Review, 26*(1), 23–30. doi:10.1016/j.clsr.2009.11.008

Xie, H. (2018). *Data Collection for Security Measurement in WSN: A Survey. IEEE IoT Journal*.

Xie, H., Yan, Z., Yao, Z., & Atiquzzaman, M. (2018). Data Collection for Security Measurement in Wireless Sensor Networks: A Survey. *IEEE Internet of Things Journal*.

Xie, M., Han, S., Tian, B., & Parvin, S. (2011, July). Anomaly detection in wireless sensor networks: A survey. *Journal of Network and Computer Applications, 34*(4), 1302–1325. doi:10.1016/j.jnca.2011.03.004

Ying, B., Makrakis, D., & Mouftah, H. T. (2013). Privacy preserving broadcast message authentication protocol for VANETs. *Journal of Network and Computer Applications*, *36*(5), 1352–1364. doi:10.1016/j.jnca.2012.05.013

Zaki, H. (2018). Analysis of cross-layer design of quality-of-service forward geographic wireless sensor network routing strategies in green internet of things. *IEEE Access: Practical Innovations, Open Solutions*, *6*, 20371–20389. doi:10.1109/ACCESS.2018.2822551

Zhang, C., Lin, X., Lu, R., & Ho, P.-H. (2008). RAISEan ficientRS SU-aided message authentication scheme in vehicular communication networks. *Proceedings of the IEEE ICC '08*, 1451–1457.

Zhang, C., Lu, R., Lin, X., Ho, P.-H., & Shen, X. (2008). An efficient identity-based batch verification scheme for vehicular sensor networks. *Proceedings of the 27th INFOCOM '08*, 246–250. 10.1109/INFOCOM.2008.58

Zhou, Fang, & Zhang. (2008). Security Wireless Sensor Networks: A Survety. *IEEE Communication Surveys*.

Zhou, D. H., Yan, Z., Fu, Y. L., & Yao, Z. (2018, August). A Survey on NetworkData Collection. *Journal of Network and Computer Applications*, *116*, 9–23. doi:10.1016/j.jnca.2018.05.004

Zhou, Q., Yang, G., & He, L. (2014). A secure enhance data aggregation based on ecc in wireless sensor network. *Sensors Journal*, *14*(4), 6701–6721. doi:10.3390140406701 PMID:24732099

Zhou, X., & Tang, X. (2011). Research and implementation of RSA algorithm for encryption and decryption. In *Proceedings of 2011 6th International Forum on ST* (vol. 2, pp. 1118-1121). IEEE. 10.1109/IFOST.2011.6021216

Zhu, X., Xu, F., Novak, E., Tan, C. C., Li, Q., & Chen, G. (2017). Using wireless link dynamics to extract a secret key in vehicular scenarios. *IEEE Transactions on MC*, *16*(7), 2065–2078. doi:10.1109/TMC.2016.2557784

Chapter 11
Real–Time Face Authentication Using Denoised Autoencoder (DAE) for Mobile Devices

Showkat Ahmad Dar
Annamalai University, India

Palanivel S.
Annamalai University, India

ABSTRACT

FBA (facial-based authentication), a non-contact biometric technology, has been evolving since its inception.. FBA can be used to unlock devices by showing their faces in front of devices. DLTs (deep learning techniques) have been receiving increased interest in FBA applications. Many proposals have used DLTs in this area. This chapter proposes DAEs (denoise auto encoders) for real-time classification of human faces. The proposed scheme balances accuracy with constraints of resource and time. The proposed DAE technique uses MDCs (mobile device cameras) for FBAs as they can address spoof or Windows-based attacks. The proposed DAE technique eliminates possible attacks on windows by immediately recognizing impostors. Moreover, feature extraction in DAE is dynamic and thus authenticates humans based on their facial images. Facial videos collected from MDCs results in realistic assessments. Spoof attacks using MDCs for bypassing security mechanisms are identified by DLTs in authentication.

INTRODUCTION

The current evolutional growth in technology has made it possible to embed heavy computational power in HHDs (Hand Held Devices) like PDAs (Personal Digital Assistants), SPs (Smart Phones), tablets and mobiles where HHDs are a part of daily life activities. HHDs have multi-touch displays with user friendly interfaces and easy operational procedures. Current mobiles are used for voice calls, sending and receiving messages, taking photographs and playing games. Additionally many financial and personal transactions can be done with these gadgets. HHDs store user's personal information and use them during financial

DOI: 10.4018/978-1-7998-9795-8.ch011

transactions like money transfers, handling multiple bank accounts, online payments, indulge in stock trading and many other useful applications which can be executed at anytime and from anywhere. This has resulted in complications of authenticating HHDs (Ortiz-Yepes et al., 2014).

Authentication of users is confirming their usage using their personal identities where their known identities are verified. Users can be authenticated using different mechanisms namely password based identifications or using User IDs, security tokens, device IDs or using their biometric identifiers like fingerprints. These user identifications authenticate them and grant access to transactions or digitally signed documents. Thus, many systems incorporate multitude of afore said security mechanisms including PINs (Personal Identification Numbers). But these mechanisms are prone to various forms of attacks like smudge attacks (Aviv et al., 2010). Moreover, such authentications are limited intrinsically as they provide one time authentications for entire device's access. This one time authentications leave devices open to attacks when users fail lock their resources.

Current studies on mobile security have proposed usage of biometric authentications for overcoming issues in traditional security mechanisms (Frank et al., 2012). Human biometrics is individualistic and distinguishable making its exploitation in authentications a justifiable area of approach. The approaches can be based on behavioral or physiological biometrics characteristics where physiological approaches use measurements of human body parts like face or retina or fingerprints or hands.

Physiological biometrics usage yield better results as they are less susceptible to changes. Further, biometric authentications based on physiological factors using mobile devices are stronger as it can combine a human being's past and present. Many applications in the areas of telecom, banking, and security use biometric authentications making FBAs an active area of research. Google has incorporated FBA in mobile Android (Smart Lock) while Apple has done the same in iPhone (FaceID). However, these applications have one-time authentication FBAs. Hence, this work focuses on authentications using classifiers for mobiles.

DLTs have established their significance in FBAs (Chaudhuri, 2020) ;(Singh et al., 2020). Facial recognitions need to leverage on a hierarchical architecture for discriminating instances (Mehdipour Ghazi & Kemal Ekenel, 2016); (Prasad et al., 2020). DLTs, with the use of multiple layers, learning data representations for efficient feature extractions and thus improve any system's performance appreciably when applied on discriminative tasks or in learning data. This chapter introduces TSFAS (Two-Step Face Authentication Scheme) by combining physiological and patterns with PINs, a system that can be applied on modern mobile device based banking Systems. The proposed scheme uses dual authentication based on different studies (Ortiz-Yepes et al., 2014).

BACKGROUND

The study by Eldefrawy et al., (2012) proposed a 2FA (2-Factor Authentication) scheme using many OTPs (One Time Passwords). Their scheme two different nested hash chains and used an initial seed. The first chain updated seeds while the second produced OTPs. Other techniques were used to constrain applications. Their analysis showed better results in terms of security and performances when compared with other techniques.

Physiological and behavioral factors were used by Koong et al., (2014) in their study. Their proposed scheme used Multiple biometrics in user authentications. The scheme called pbLogon (physiological and behavioral user authentications) combined biometric factors from two sources namely physiological and behavioral received as input from multi-touch panel of mobiles. pbLogon used user's finger rotations on mobiles for enhanced security. The scheme also allowed user credentials to be replaced for tight security of privacy.

Biometric framework was formulated by Verma et al., (2019) in their study. The study's optical transformations were used in security authentications. The FBAs transformed faces using a phase retrieval algorithm. The framework used sparse mask subsequently for retrieving optimal features and making the process non-invertible. The extracted features were pooled into a chaotic strategy for storage. The study's chaotic parameters were linked to passwords and used in enrolments. The study's authentication scheme used two factors where user's face provided the initial knowledge on biometrics while chaotic parameters substantiated verifications. The proposed framework's security was evaluated in terms of collision resistance, non-invertible capability and sensitivity. Their simulation results showed high recognition rates by discriminating original and imposter faces in samples.

FBAs were clubbed by with voices by Kasban (2017) in their study's multi-modal biometric scheme. The scheme recognized voices of users using voice timbre and statistical/cepstral coefficients for comparisons. Voice recognitions were executed by GMM (Gaussian Mixture Model) while three techniques were used for facial recognitions namely LDAs (Linear Discriminate Analysis), Eigen faces and GFs (Gabor Filters). Their FBA scheme combined voice and biometric factors as a single multi-modal biometrics system which fused and assigned scores for features. Their experimental results showed good performances in terms of facial recognitions using obtained features.

OTPs were also used by Song et al., (2016) in their study. The proposed scheme used 3 factors for authenticating mobile banking procedures. The user's facial image was captured using MCDs and the face's brightness and background were stored as points (X, Y). The scheme computed distances between eyes, nose and mouth in the acquired image along with contours of the face which were then compared with previously stored facial features. Only when matches were found in the facial recognition database, the user was authenticated.

Behavioral features were exploited by Sitová et al., (2015) in their study. The scheme used HMOG (Hand Movement, Orientation, and Grasp) sets for continuous authentications of smart phone users. The study used HMOG for capturing minute movements and orientations of the user's face while grasping or holding or tapping the smart phone. The study's proposed authentication scheme was evaluated for in terms of BKGs (Biometric Key Generations) based on HMOG features of a dataset collected from virtual keyboard typing of 100 subjects. The study collected this data with subject's sitting and walking positions. Their experimental results showed that HMOG features had the capability to capture distinct bodily movements and specifically with subjects walking and taps on smart phones. The study's HMOG features, extracted at a sensor sampling rate 16 Hz with minimal overheads of 7.9% enhanced facial recognition accuracy.

Active user authentications were investigated by Fathy et al., (2015) in their study. The proposed scheme of FBAs was aimed at smart phones and examined videos recording of the user's face for authentications. The user videos were acquired under varying ambient conditions i.e. while performing different tasks for assessment of device mobility.

Their investigations of the acquired videos revealed unique favourable/challenging facial properties of smart phone videos. Additional challenges included partial faces, facial poses, facial blurs and facial fiducial point's localization errors from facial datasets. The study evaluated still images and image sets with facial intensity features around fiducial points using FBA algorithms. The study found that recognition rates dropped drastically when the test videos and enrolment videos belonged to different sessions.

Active authentications were reviewed by Mahfouz et al., (2017). The study highlighted components used by operational procedures of active authentications while giving an overview of behavioral biometric traits useful for development of such systems. The review's evaluations on smart phones projected each behavioral biometric trait's issues and limitations along with their strengths. The study concluded by discussing open research problems in the reviewed area.

A framework for reliability of authentications was proposed by Meng et al., (2014) in their study. The study's multimodal biometric proposal for user authentications was found to be appropriate. Their experimental validations of the proposed framework on touch enabled phones showed that by deploying the scheme false rates of single biometric systems reduced drastically. The study also identified challenges and issues in making user touchs the main aspect of future mobile based user authentications.

The study by Abuhamad et al., (2020) used DLTs for FBAs. The proposal called AUToSen used embedded sensors for identifying distinct behaviours of users with and without their smart phone interactions. The study also explored sensed data sufficiency for authenticating users accurately. AUToSen's experimental results showed expected accuracy levels in the readings of gyroscope, accelerometer, and magnetometer sensors.

FBAs using ROIs (Regions Of Interests) were used by Hu et al., (2015) in their study. Their proposal included eye based detections. The study pre-processed images with ROIs followed by LBPs (Local Binary Patterns) for feature extractions. The extracted features were reduced in terms of dimensionality using PCAs (Principal Component Analysis) and LDAs (Linear Discriminant Analysis) which were classified using minimum distances. The study implemented using Open CV (Open Source Computer Vision) SDKs. The study's experimental results on Android mobile facial samples demonstrated the scheme's effectiveness. The study proposed use of DLTs with XFace system as their future scope.

Tsai et al., (2012) used OTPs for authenticating M-banking transactions. The proposal combined OTP with personal biometrics. The procedure followed in the study starts from a client side request to a bank's server for M-banking service. The server then generates and transmits an OTP valid for a specific time period in M-banking systems. The transmitted OTP is verified at the client side before getting registered on the server for M-banking system services. ON registration, the server captures user's personal biometrics like fingerprints or iris image or facial image on the first service request from the registered client. This procedure not only adds strength to the authentication procedure but also prevents fraudulent requests. These biometrics are compared with older copies and if found the process is terminated by the M-banking server. Once the credentials are verified the client and server co-operate for M-banking transactions. The study proved that their proposal was a secure scheme with defined process stages allowing M-banking customers to secure their transactions from hackers and disallowing execution of transactions from stolen mobiles thus preventing client rights and personal information.

Risks in using smart phones were detailed by Alzubaidi & Kalita, (2016) in their study. The study projected potential risks for users when their smart phones were stolen or seized while detailing on continuous authentications. The study also analyzed existing approaches using behavioural biometrics in terms of methodology, datasets and evaluation metrics.

Hierarchical Correlations were used by Xi et al., (2012) in their study. The proposed scheme called HCFA (Hierarchical Correlation Based Face Authentication) aimed resource-constrained HHDs including mobiles and PDAs. The HCFA scheme generated partial correlation output peaks from selected facial regions which were then analyzed for relationships between cross correlation output peaks in conjunction with direct cross-correlation approaches. The study experimented their proposed scheme on public databases where their scheme achieved better performances when compared to direct correlation based approaches. Further, HCFA implementations on Nokia S60 CLDC emulator using Java ME to test the scheme's applicability showed it was implementable on most mobiles.

Sensor assisted FBAs were used by Chen et al., (2014) in their study with the aim of overcoming FBA shortcomings. Their proposal used motion/light sensors as defence against 2D media and virtual camera attacks without compromising authentication speeds. Their experimental results indicated enhanced levels of security obtained by their scheme while being 10 times quicker in operations (3, 30) when compared to existing 3D FBAs.

MAIN FOCUS OF THE CHAPTER

Mobile based e-commerce, specifically; banking from home (M-banking) has gained popularity. M-banking, a result of growths in technology and communications, have versatile and convenient functions built for HHDs. Trusted M-banking services are also an indispensable part of these applications.

Recent studies have projected the possibilities of using biometric authentications with physiological attributes in HHDs. FBAs can be used in locking HHDs or websites or any equipment with front cameras. Applications The major constraints in using FBAs in HHDs are ease of use and trusted security. Hence, these shortcomings have propelled researchers into the area of enhanced security for HHDs using FBAs.

Hence, this chapter focuses on FBAs for HHDs in the case of M-banking applications. A major objective of this work is systematically detail about the vulnerability of generic biometric authentications in HHDs. This work proposes TSFAS scheme for reliable user authentications on HHDs which are better than single biometric based authentications. The proposed work's framework characterizes and details FBA elements for reliable authentication mechanisms in HHDs.

SOLUTIONS AND RECOMMENDATIONS

This study introduces TSFAS scheme for authenticating users on HHDs based on their facial characteristics. This work attempts to solve security concerns identified and reported by previous studies. The proposed TSFAS scheme monitors user videos captured using MDCs. The proposed scheme's observations begin the moment a user unlocks a device and continues to use the device until end of user's session and relocks the device. This proposal is an active authentication system and similar to biometric recognitions which encompass two main stages namely enrolment and recognition stages as depicted in figure 1.

Figure 1. Architecture of the proposed TSFAS scheme

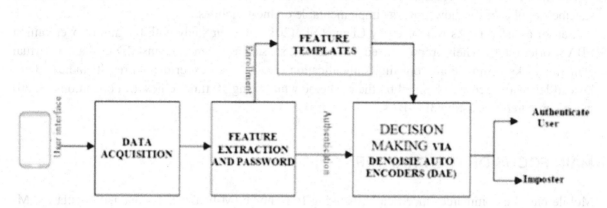

During enrolments, the proposed system gathers biometric data for extraction of distinctive features after analyzing them. These features are used to build a feature template similar to classifier training process. Enrolments are followed by recognitions where biometric details of the user are acquired freshly.

These details are compared with previously stored information for verification of the user's identity. The basic procedures followed in this study can be included in active authentications are detailed below:

1. Data acquisition Procedure: This is the preliminary step where user's raw biometric data is collected using smart phones where the quality of acquisition is significant recognitions and subsequent authentication procedures. MFSD (Mobile Face Spoofing Database) is a popular dataset which includes genuine and spoofed faces using MCDs (Wen et al., 2015). MFSD dataset includes 280 video clips from 35 users along with photo/video attack attempts. The collection includes captured genuine facial information using two types of cameras: MacBook Air's built-in camera and Google Nexus 5 Android phone's front camera. Spoofing attack videos were generated during acquisition of genuine facial video captures. Spoofing attacks encompass three types: iPad Air screen sourced high resolution replay video attacks while capturing videos from MacBook and Nexus devices; iPhone 5S screen based mobile replay video attacks while capturing videos from MacBook and Nexus devices and printed photo attacks on user facial images while capturing facial images from MacBook and Nexus devices

2. Feature extraction Procedure: The acquired raw biometric data is pre-processed for extracting distinctive features. The pre-processing part detects and eliminates outliers resulting in an improved quality of data. This is mainly done as data collected includes un-cooperative users in uncontrolled environments. This cleaning of data is followed by identification of discriminative features for extractions. This work extracts relevant features automatically using DAEs.

3. Generation of Feature templates: Feature templates of this work are repository databases generated by concatenating user's (device owner) extracted feature vectors. The templates are built built in the enrolment stage and subsequently used in the recognition stage for verifying matches between feature samples and claimed identities.

4. Authentication Procedure: This final procedure is a recognition process where user's extracted features are compared against feature templates. This work generates a matching score to take de-

cisions on user identities. Thus, the proposed procedure identifies original and pseudo users using DAEs.

Biometric Modes

Biometric based systems can be operated based on recognition contexts or verifications and identifications.

Verifications

Verifications involve 1-1 matches where claimed identities are comparing with stored identities. These matches generate a matching score based on a predefined threshold (th$\hat{I}$(0,1). When the score is greater than th, the claimed identity is legitimate. When it is lower than th, the claimed identity is not accepted as it may belong to an imposter. These authentications based on verifications when treated as binary classifications, the decision rules can be computed using Equation (1):

$$p(us_i) = \begin{cases} authenticate \; if p(us_i) > th \\ imposter \; if p(us_i) < th \end{cases} \tag{1}$$

Where, p(us$_i$) - user's (us$_i$) authentication score as computed using DAEs and pre-defined threshold th whose value lies in the interval [0,1].

Identifications

Identifications involve a 1-n relationship in matches where the system recognizes presented FBA with stored FBA templates of users. The algorithms used for identifications identity samples based on their matching scores and pre-defined thresholds. The matching scores generated for users is examined for the highest score for selections.

Figure 2. Overall process of the proposed TSFAS framework in M-banking application

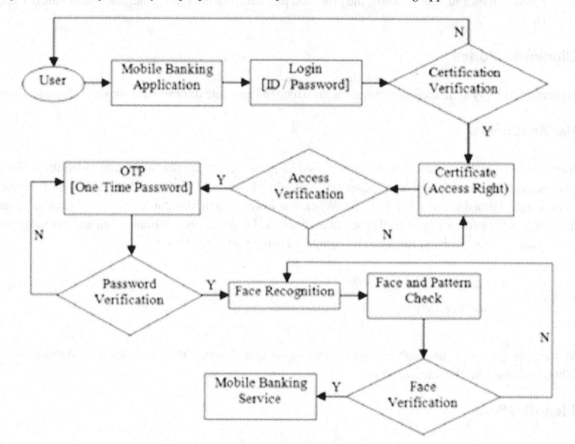

The overall process of authentication through face verification is implemented as follows: an image of the user is acquired using MCDs and when the extracted results correspond to the data saved in a facial recognition DB (database), the user is authenticated. The authentication system operates by image acquisition, feature extraction, face standardization and face verification. Figure 2 depicts the flow of face authentication technology; in the preprocessing, a user registers one's face to the DB; the first step is the extraction of face features via the deep learning model. The recognition part matches the face with the registered data on the DB and the service is executed after the user authenticates by matching (face and PIN/pattern of the user).

Facial matches using DAEs are executed by training the network with AEs (Auto Encoders) where outputs are constrained by equating them to inputs and thus making input and output nodes equivalent (Chen et al., 2014). The weights in layers are adjusted based on the reconstruction errors that get generated between network's inputs and outputs. This results in better learning if features by AEs from inputs. Also, AEs being an unsupervised technique do not need labelling. Though DAEs are based on AEs, they are more robust as they assume inputs have noises making them an ideal technique for learning of noisy images. Moreover, DAEs generalisation capabilities are far superior to AEs generalisation capabilities.

DAEs encompass three layers (Input, Hidden, Output) where the hidden and output layers are encoding and decoding layers. Assuming $\hat{I}\hat{I}R^d$ is a facial image where the data dimension is represented by d, and then DAE initially outputs a feature vector $\tilde{I}$ by assigning certain elements a value of 0 or by introducing Gaussian noises. DAEs use this generated image $\tilde{I}$ as an input image with where input layer units are d and equal in dimension to the input image. DAE encoding are non-linear transformations using Equation (2),

$$y = f_e\left(W\tilde{I} + b\right) \tag{2}$$

Where, $y\hat{I}R^h$- hidden layer outputs (Feature representations), h - hidden layer count, W- input-to-hidden weights, b - bias, f - hidden layer inputs (activation function). This work uses ReLU function (Meng et al., 2014) as the activation function and depicted in Equation (3),

$$f_e\left(W\tilde{I} + b\right) = \max\left(0, W\tilde{I} + b\right) \tag{3}$$

When the value of $\left(W\tilde{I} + b\right) < 0$, then the hidden layer's outputs will also be 0. Hence, ReLU activation produces sparse feature representations of input facial images. Further, ReLUs can train NNs (Neural Networks) faster on voluminous data effectively when compared to other activation functions. Decoding or reconstruction of DAE can be obtained by a mapping function given as Equation (4),

$$z = f_d\left(W'y + b'\right) \tag{4}$$

Where, $z\hat{I}R^d$– DAE output and also reconstructed facial image of original input image . Since, the output layer nodes equal in number to input nodes, $W' = W^T$ is called tied weights. When in the interval between 0 and 1, softplus function is chosen as the decoding function else the image is pre-processed by ZCA (Zero-Phase Component Analysis) whiteners and a linear function decodes values using Equation (5),

$$f_d(a) = \begin{cases} \log\left(1 + e^a\right), I \in [0,1] \\ \quad a, else \end{cases} \tag{5}$$

Where $= W'y + b'$. DAEs use reconstruction oriented training to train the network by output authentication of images to reconstruct input face images. Hence, reconstruction errors defined by Equation (6) is used as the objective or cost function. (6),

$$Cost = \begin{cases} -\dfrac{1}{m}\sum_{i=1}^{m}\sum_{j=1}^{d}\left[I_j^{(i)}\log\left(z_j^{(i)}\right) + \left(1 - z_j^{(i)}\right)\log\left(1 - z_j^{(i)}\right)\right] + \dfrac{\lambda}{2}\|w\|^2, I \in [0,1] \\ \qquad\qquad \dfrac{1}{m}\sum_{i=1}^{m}I^{(i)} - z^{(i)2} + \dfrac{\lambda}{2}\|w\|^2, else \end{cases} \tag{6}$$

Where cross-entropy function is used when the value of input face image is ranged from 0 to 1; the square error function is used otherwise. $I_j^{(i)}$ denotes j th element of the i th sample and $\|w\|^2$ is L2-regularization term, which is also called weight decay term. Parameter λ controls the regularization term. The MSGD (Minibatch Stochastic Gradient Descent) algorithm (Abuhamad et al., 2020) solves the optimization problem, and m in equation (6) denoting the size of the mini-batch.

EXPERIMENTAL RESULTS

Experiments with the proposed work's facial authentication system are detailed in this section. The scheme's success is assessed for its robustness as well as facial recognition accuracy. Figure 3 depicts real-world accesses and attacks from the MFSD database.

Figure 3. MSU MFSD Database samples. images in the top row are attack images while the bottom row displays true access images

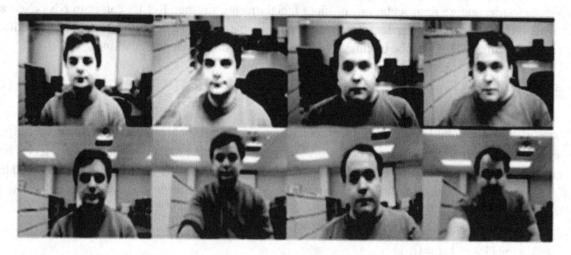

Evaluation Metrics

This work's proposed TSFAS scheme was tested for its effectiveness using performance metrics detailed below:

1. 1. FARs (False Acceptance Rates): This metric shows the rate of impostors wrongly classified as genuine users and computed using Equation (7).

$$FAR = \frac{\text{Imposter Samples Accepted}}{\text{Number of imposter samples}} \tag{7}$$

2.   2. FRRs (False Rejection Rates): This is the metric which specifies the ratio between genuine samples that were rejected assuming them as imposters to the total genuine samples and depicted in Equation (8).

$$FRR = \frac{Genuine\ Samples\ Rejected}{Number\ of\ Genuine\ samples} \tag{8}$$

3.   3. TRRs (True Rejection Rates): This rate specifies impostors identified and rejected against total imposter samples and computed using Equation (9).

$$TRR = \frac{Imposter\ Samples\ Rejected}{Number\ of\ Imposter\ samples} \tag{9}$$

4.   4. TARs (True Acceptance Rates): This metric is defined as genuine samples exactly identified against the total genuine samples and computed using Equation (10).

$$TAR = \frac{Genuine\ Samples\ Accepted}{Number\ of\ Genuine\ samples} \tag{10}$$

5.   5. EERs (Equal Error Rates): This is a joined metric with equal FARs and FRRs obtained based on adjusted acceptance threshold value. FARs and FRRs are correlated and one vale increases the other decreases correspondingly. EERs thus define smallest difference between FARs and FRRs and depicted as Equation (11).

$$EER = \frac{FAR + FRR}{2} \tag{11}$$

Table 1. Evaluation metrics for MFSD detection when classifiers on MSU datasets

METHODS	TRR (%)	faR (%)	taR (%)	frR (%)	ERR (%)
2FA	75.18	30.15	77.56	27.18	28.665
HCFA	84.25	25.41	87.71	23.67	24.541
TSFAS	92.58	18.43	93.47	15.46	16.945

Table 1 details on metrics computed from the MSU dataset. Results show the TRR, FAR, TAR and FRR for each authentication method. Notice that the proposed TSFAS system appears to be superior at identifying spoofed facial images than the 2FA and HCFA. Best performing TRRs exceed 92.58%, whereas other methods such as 2FA and HCFA give only 75.18% and 84.25% respectively.

CONCLUSION

As biometrics offer greater security than traditional methods of personal recognition, a great deal of effort has been made on making mobile banking more efficient with less imposter attacks by utilizing biometric authentication systems. In this chapter, a deep learning based automated facial authentication system(Two-Step Face Authentication Scheme (TSFAS) framework) that employs face authentication to initially perceive the presence of an authorized person, in order to grant the individual access to secure banking environments.

The key benefit of physiologically based biometric authentication is its ability to provide continuity in authentications using FBAs and PINs in M-banking applications where users communicate from their mobiles. The proposed scheme has also been evaluated for its accuracy, robustness for deducing genuine faces on the MSU dataset.

FUTURE RESEARCH DIRECTIONS

Future analysis will concentrate on improving the system by fixing its existing flaws. First, look into the possibility of using CNNs (Convolutional Neural Networks) and other deep learning classifiers to improve the facial recognition of the proposed scheme.

Examining procedures for addressing facial authentications for partially visible faces. Current methods are implemented for accessing the banking services such as ATM access, internet banking, passport verification, and online exam for reducing the fraudulent and crime activities with a multi-biometrics such as face, finger, and eye.

REFERENCES

Abuhamad, M., Abuhmed, T., Mohaisen, D., & Nyang, D. (2020). AUToSen: Deep-learning-based implicit continuous authentication using smartphone sensors. *IEEE Internet of Things Journal*, 7(6), 5008–5020. doi:10.1109/JIOT.2020.2975779

Alzubaidi, A., & Kalita, J. (2016). Authentication of smartphone users using behavioral biometrics. *IEEE Communications Surveys and Tutorials*, 18(3), 1998–2026. doi:10.1109/COMST.2016.2537748

Aviv, A. J., Gibson, K. L., Mossop, E., Blaze, M., & Smith, J. M. (2010). Smudge attacks on smartphone touch screens. *Woot*, 10, 1–7.

Chaudhuri, A. (2020). Deep Learning Models for Face Recognition: A Comparative Analysis. Deep Biometrics, 99-140. doi:10.1007/978-3-030-32583-1_6

Chen, S., Pande, A., & Mohapatra, P. (2014). Sensor-assisted facial recognition: an enhanced biometric authentication system for smartphones. *Proceedings of the 12th annual international conference on Mobile systems, applications, and services*, 109-122. 10.1145/2594368.2594373

Chen, Y., Lin, Z., Zhao, X., Wang, G., & Gu, Y. (2014). Deep learning-based classification of hyperspectral data. *IEEE Journal of Selected Topics in Applied Earth Observations and Remote Sensing*, 7(6), 2094–2107. doi:10.1109/JSTARS.2014.2329330

Eldefrawy, M. H., Khan, M. K., Alghathbar, K., Kim, T. H., & Elkamchouchi, H. (2012). Mobile one-time passwords: Two-factor authentication using mobile phones. *Security and Communication Networks*, 5(5), 508–516. doi:10.1002ec.340

Fathy, M. E., Patel, V. M., & Chellappa, R. (2015). *Face-based active authentication on mobile devices. In IEEE international conference on acoustics, speech and signal processing.* ICASSP.

Frank, M., Biedert, R., Ma, E., Martinovic, I., & Song, D. (2012). Touchalytics: On the applicability of touchscreen input as a behavioral biometric for continuous authentication. *IEEE Transactions on Information Forensics and Security*, 8(1), 136–148. doi:10.1109/TIFS.2012.2225048

Hu, J., Peng, L., & Zheng, L. (2015). XFace: A face recognition system for android mobile phones. *IEEE 3rd International Conference on Cyber-Physical Systems, Networks, and Applications*, 13-18.

Kasban, H. (2017). A robust multimodal biometric authentication scheme with voice and face recognition. *Arab Journal of Nuclear Sciences and Applications*, 50(3), 120–130.

Koong, C. S., Yang, T. I., & Tseng, C. C. (2014). A user authentication scheme using physiological and behavioral biometrics for multitouch devices. *TheScientificWorldJournal*, 2014(781234), 1–12. doi:10.1155/2014/781234 PMID:25147864

Mahfouz, A., Mahmoud, T. M., & Eldin, A. S. (2017). A survey on behavioral biometric authentication on smartphones. *Journal of Information Security and Applications*, 37, 28-37.

Mehdipour Ghazi, M., & Kemal Ekenel, H. (2016). A comprehensive analysis of deep learning based representation for face recognition. *Proceedings of the IEEE conference on computer vision and pattern recognition workshops*, 34-41.

Meng, W., Wong, D. S., Furnell, S., & Zhou, J. (2014). Surveying the development of biometric user authentication on mobile phones. *IEEE Communications Surveys and Tutorials*, 17(3), 1268–1293. doi:10.1109/COMST.2014.2386915

Ortiz-Yepes, D. A., Hermann, R. J., Steinauer, H., & Buhler, P. (2014). Bringing strong authentication and transaction security to the realm of mobile devices. *IBM Journal of Research and Development*, 58(1), 4–1. doi:10.1147/JRD.2013.2287810

Prasad, P. S., Pathak, R., Gunjan, V. K., & Rao, H. R. (2020). Deep learning based representation for face recognition. ICCCE 2019, 419-424. doi:10.1007/978-981-13-8715-9_50

Singh, N. S., Hariharan, S., & Gupta, M. (2020). Facial recognition using deep learning. In *Advances in Data Sciences* (pp. 375–382). Security and Applications. doi:10.1007/978-981-15-6634-9

Sitová, Z., Šeděnka, J., Yang, Q., Peng, G., Zhou, G., Gasti, P., & Balagani, K. S. (2015). HMOG: New behavioral biometric features for continuous authentication of smartphone users. *IEEE Transactions on Information Forensics and Security*, 11(5), 877–892. doi:10.1109/TIFS.2015.2506542

Song, J., Lee, Y. S., Jang, W., Lee, H., & Kim, T. (2016). Face Recognition Authentication Scheme for Mobile Banking System. *International Journal of Internet, Broadcasting and Communication*, 8(2), 38–42.

Tsai, C. L., Chen, C. J., & Zhuang, D. J. (2012). Trusted M-banking Verification Scheme based on a combination of OTP and Biometrics. *JoC*, *3*(3), 23–30.

Verma, G., Liao, M., Lu, D., He, W., & Peng, X. (2019). A novel optical two-factor face authentication scheme. *Optics and Lasers in Engineering*, *123*, 28–36. doi:10.1016/j.optlaseng.2019.06.028

Wen, D., Han, H., & Jain, A. K. (2015). Face spoof detection with image distortion analysis. *IEEE Transactions on Information Forensics and Security*, *10*(4), 746–761. doi:10.1109/TIFS.2015.2400395

Xi, K., Hu, J., & Han, F. (2012). Mobile device access control: An improved correlation based face authentication scheme and its java me application. *Concurrency and Computation*, *24*(10), 1066–1085. doi:10.1002/cpe.1797

Chapter 12
Recent Advancement on Dye–Sensitized Solar Cell (DSSC):
A Review

Biswajit Mandal

https://orcid.org/0000-0002-6582-0638

National Institute of Technology, Durgapur, India

Partha Sarathee Bhowmik

National Institute of Technology, Durgapur, India

Tapas Chakrabarti

Heritage Institute of Technology, India

ABSTRACT

Irrespective of the photo incident angle and lighting condition of a day, DSSC is a kind of photovoltaic device consistent to generate power. Power extracted in diffuse light condition from DSSC is greater than the generated power from a conventional existing photovoltaic cell. This lucrative feature drives many to improve the device performance. To fill the gap between theoretical and practical performance of the device, more study is required on this topic. This study reviews the various methods to prepare DSS cell in each step, working principle, different measuring systems for characterization of the cell, and how those characters affect the final product to achieve its goal.

INTRODUCTION

The dye-sensitized solar cell as a third-generation solar cell became a new trend of research. Globally forty percent of the total energy consumption is produced by thermal power plants. In a result of the combustion of coal, environment gifted by smoke and fumes. Greenhouse gases from those plant inherently affecting the atmosphere. Revolution was made by a French scientist in the year of 1839. Alexandre Edmond Becquerel studied the solar spectrum and discovered the photovoltaic effect. Onwards researchers

DOI: 10.4018/978-1-7998-9795-8.ch012

carried out their study on the same. The fruitful study on PV cell make it advance day by day. Advancement of solar cells reached to such an extent that it categorized in different generations shown in Figure 1 where data source is national renewable energy laboratory website. Now a day's silicon-based solar cells are commercially and extensively available all over the world. Solar energy to electrical energy conversion reduces the carbon foot print.

A considerable amount of capital is invested to maintain all the power generating station whether it is a coal-fired power plant or hydro-electrical power plant or energy from nuclear fusion or wind energy to electrical energy converter station to provide an uninterrupted power to the industry requirement as well as domestic purpose. The efficiency of a thermal power plant is a big issue. Low efficiency of such plants leads to more combustion of coal. The environmental impact of a hydro-electrical power plant, availability of uninterrupted wind power and nuclear accident, radioactive waste disposal, nuclear weapon proliferation from a nuclear power plant play an important role to inclined towards solar energy harvesting. Plenty of solar power urges the scientist to grab it for utilization more efficiently. A continuous effort made to achieve higher efficiency for existing solar cell. Various type of solar cell made by researchers using different semiconductor material to enhance the efficiency, availability of raw material, and moreover the easiness of commercialization. There are few types of solar cells named crystalline silicon solar cells, non-crystalline silicon solar cell known as thin-film solar cells, tandem solar cells, and dye-sensitized solar cells. Crystalline silicon solar cells divided as crystalline silicon concentrator cells, bifacial solar cells, buried contact solar cells, MIS solar cells, polycrystalline silicon solar cells, crystalline silicon solar cells. Thin film solar cells made from different type of materials, namely gallium-arsenide (GaAs), cadmium telluride (CdTe), copper-indium-Selenium ($CuInSe_2$), Titanium di-Oxide (TiO_2), copper indium sulfide ($CuInS_2$), copper aluminum selenide ($CuAlSe_2$), copper gallium selenide ($CuGaSe_2$)(Haloui et al., 2015; Parida et al., 2011). The silicon-based solar cells are popular enough nowadays due to their high efficiency compare to a solar cell made with other materials. Solar cell made of silicon operate with high efficiency in direct sunlight, but the shading and diffuse solar light condition make the FF very less and accordingly lower the performance of it. The DSSC perform very well in diffuse day light for its unique feature. FF remains above 0.7, even at a light intensity of less than 5 W/m² (O'regan & Grätzel, 1991). Under the above-mentioned light intensity, FF of the conventional silicon-based solar cell is less than 0.5 (O'regan & Grätzel, 1991). Low FF cause to poor energy outcomes. PCE of DSSC in direct sunlight is less as shown in Figure 1 compare to available solar cell in market. DSSC gets a keen interest of researchers to improve the performance of the device in direct solar radiation. An attempt has been taken to explain the methods in each step to fabricate the DSSC, working principle, scaling quantities, systems to evaluate those quantities and characterizing qualities towards achieving better performance, in different sections accordingly.

DYE-SENSITIZED SOLAR CELL

A new era with 7.1-7.9% of photo conversion efficiency in simulated light condition of DSSC make a niche in solar power industry and attract researcher's attention towards development of this solar cell (O'regan & Grätzel, 1991).

Fabrication

DSSC has two electrodes as shown in Figure 2. One is the photoanode or photoelectrode and another one is counter electrode (CE). Both are made of glass. Glasses are coated with fluorine doped tin-oxide $(SnO_2/F)/(TCO)$ with sheet resistance of 8 $\Omega/\ddot{y}$ (Berginc et al., 2014). The surfaces of those purchased glass are clean for 10 minutes in a detergent solution with the help of ultrasonication bath, followed by rinsing of double distilled water, acetone and ethanol (Gurung et al., 2016). Rinsing does help to avoid the resistance loss of the substrate (Armendariz-Mireles et al., 2017). The wet substrate dried under nitrogen atmosphere discussed in (Sharma et al., 2015). TiO_2 paste consist of 3 g of TiO_2 powder(P25), 3.5 ml of DI water, 0.1 ml of AcAc and 0.3 ml of triton X-100 in (Kang et al., 2011). Raw materials are stimulated for 24 hours to make TiO_2 paste by a magnetic stirrer (J. C. Chou, Wu, et al., 2018). TiO_2 paste can be adsorbed on photo anode by spin coating (Chakrabarti et al., 2018; J. C. Chou, Kuo, et al., 2018; Gurung et al., 2016), doctor blading (Gurung et al., 2016), spray coating (H.-T. Chou et al., 2017), liquid phase deposition technique (Rahman et al., 2018). Active area taken by individual researchers as 0.23 cm^2 (Rahman et al., 2018), 0.57 cm^2 (J. C. Chou et al., 2015), 1.00 cm^2 (Kadachi et al., 2016), 0.16 cm^2

Figure 1. Categorization of solar cell

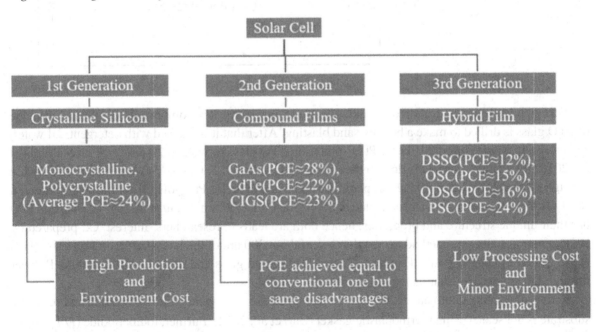

(Armendariz-Mireles et al., 2017), hence affect the PCE. Area of the TiO_2 layer is depending on the size of TiO_2 particles and thickness of the layer (O'regan & Grätzel, 1991). On an average the thickness of this layer is 10 µm (Mehmood, Hussein, et al., 2016). Further that layer sintered for 3 hours at 250° C, as it could keep away the organic blender as well as make it solid (Kadachi et al., 2016). Dye solution prepared with N-719 mixes with tert-butyl alcohol and acetonitrile (V: V=1:1). Photoanode is made after deposition in 0.3 mM of dye solution in dark for 24 hours (Kang et al., 2011). Further, photoanode rinses in acetonitrile for 2 hours and dried in air (Thapa et al., 2013).

Figure 2. Schematic diagram of DSSC working principle

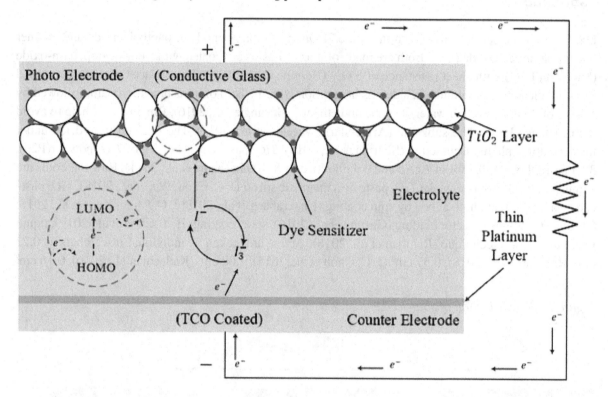

Next step leads to preparation of counter electrode, one of the key components of DSSC. CE made of FTO glass is drilled to make a hole by sand blasting. After that it is washed with detergent, DI water, acetone and isopropyl alcohol. Then, Pt is sputter on FTO glass to make a 20 nm thick layer (Tedla et al., 2016). Pt coating on TCO is done by a sputtering system (H. T. Chou, Liu, et al., 2018). CE made through spin coating with 5 mM chloroplatinic acid hexahydrate [$H_2PtC_{16}\cdot6H_2O$] solution in 2-propanol [C_3H_8O] at 3000 rpm for 30 s and annealed at 300°C for 1 hour (Sönmezoğlu et al., 2014). FTO and ITO has their unique structure and properties, hence both are leads to researchers' interest. CE prepared by RF magnetron sputtering method to coat thin layer (about 300 nm of thickness) of Pt on ITO glass (Han et al., 2013). In another case CE prepared using ITO coated glass and deposited 40 nm thick Pt layer through DC sputtering (Shanmugam et al., 2009).

Active area facing photo anode and Pt layer faced CE are sandwiched like in Figure 2 and resulting substrate is hot sealed using thermoplastic gasket (Bari et al., 2012). Further, iodine/iodide (I/I_3^-) electrolyte is injected through the pin hole from the back of CE by vacuum backfilling technique. Composition of electrolyte are 0.3 M 1,2-dimethyl-3-propylimidazolium iodide (DMPII), 0.5 M LiI, 0.05 M I_2 and 0.5 M 4-tert-butyl-pyridine in 3-methoxypropionitrile in (Yang et al., 2011). The diameter of the hole to inject electrolyte inside the device is 1 mm used in (Peng et al., 2013). Sealant used in (Bari et al., 2012) is thermoplastic used to seal the pin hole and made the final product. Surlyn film used as sealant and spacer but pin hole is sealed by a thin glass slide using UV-gel (Tedla et al., 2016).

Working Principle

M. Grätzel, the pioneer of DSSC, summarized it's working in a convenient way in (Grätzel, 2005). Photosensitizing dye after exposed to light got excited and electron goes to lowest unoccupied molecular orbital (LUMO) from highest occupied molecular orbital (HOMO). The electron from the LUMO injected to the conduction band of TiO_2 (the semiconducting material) layer. In a result dye become oxidized.

Dye regenerated after getting electron from electrolyte possess iodide/triiodide redox. Iodide become triiodide as a result of electron donation to the dye layer. Later, injected electron in photoanode is collected by CE through external load circuit. Collected electron is penetrated by CE to the electrolyte. In a result triiodide or oxidized electrolyte is regenerated and become iodide. Pt layer on CE, work as a catalyst to supply electron from external circuit to electrolyte (Han et al., 2013). Electrolyte inside the DSSC work as a bridge to carry the charge between the photoanode and CE. Working of DSSC can be easily understood with the help of equations (1) – (4). S, used in equations (1) – (4), stands for dye adsorbed TiO_2 attached to TCO coated glass associated with photoanode.

Photo Excitation of Dye: $S + h\nu \rightarrow S^*$ (1)

Reduction of Dye: $S + h\nu \rightarrow S^*$ (2)

Regeneration of Dye: $S^+ + \dfrac{3}{2}I^- \rightarrow S + \dfrac{1}{2}I_3^-$ (3)

Regeneration of iodine: $I_3^- + 2e \rightarrow 3I^-$ (4)

MEASURING PARAMETERS

Parameters describe the device performance are calculated on the basis on few measurable quantities like open circuit voltage (v_{oc}), incident light power (P_{in}), current density (J_{sc}), maximum voltage (V_m) and maximum current (J_m) at maximum power point. FF, PCE (η) are such kind of parameters contribute to distinguish the device. The device distinguishable properties are calculated with the help of equations (5) and (6). FF and PCE are derived for each successful experiment made by researcher and few of them are tabulated in Table 1. Modification of semiconducting material, variation in electrolyte, transformation of electrocatalytic material inherently change the device performance, are shown as major changes in Table 1.

Table 1. Parameter with major changes

Ref.	Major Changes		η (%)		η (%) Rise	J_{sc} (mA/cm^2)		F.F.		Lighting Condition
	Earlier	Introduced	Earlier	Now		Earlier	Now	Earlier	Now	
(J. C. Chou, Wu, et al., 2018)	PE with TiO_2	PE with IGZO/TiO_2	2.64	3.38	28.03	6.74	8.33	0.62	0.63	100 mW/cm²
(J. C. Chou, Kuo, et al., 2018)	TP (without sputtering IGZO)	TiO_2- IGZO Composite Photoanode (TIP)	3.34	5.47	63.77	8.35	12.40	0.63	0.64	100 mW/cm²
(Mehmood, Hussein, et al., 2016)	Pure TiO_2	0.06% CNT+TiO_2	3.59	5.25	46.23	13.80	18.02	0.34	0.40	AM1.5G, 100 mW/cm²
(Thapa et al., 2013)	CE with (ECN: CNP:: 30:70)	CE with neat CNP	6.64	7.30	9.94	13.37	13.76	0.63	0.65	AM1.5, Light intensity 100 mW/ cm²
(H. T. Chou, Liu, et al., 2018)	DTA	DMP	4.60	5.34	16.09	11.40	11.85	0.54	0.64	AM1.5G, 100 mW/cm²
(Mehmood et al., 2018)	FTO/TiO_2/N719	N719 co-sensitized with (22 mM of Pb(S_2COEt)$_2$ in $CHCl_3$)	6.11	7.90	29.29	15.14	17.98	0.55	0.57	-
(J.-C. Chou et al., 2016)	TiO_2	Fe_3O_4-TiO_2	2.34	3.54	51.28	4.82	9.15	0.65	0.56	100 mW/cm²
(C. Y. Hsu et al., 2013)	Without pre-treatment	H_2O_2 & NaOH pre-treatment (5M)	4.42	5.38	21.72	8.77	10.03	0.72	0.77	100 mW/cm²
(Sigdel et al., 2015)	$TiCl_4$ treated SnO_2 fibre	$TiCl_4$ treated SnO_2/P25-TiO_2	4.06	5.72	40.88	10.75	11.97	0.50	0.60	AM1.5 illumination, 100 mW/cm²
(Lee et al., 2014)	Porous TiO_2	Porous TiO_2 with ZnO nanotip	6.29	7.34	16.69	13.12	19.31	0.63	0.55	Simulated sunlight of AM 1.5
(Jia et al., 2016)	CE with Pt sprayed	CE with $MoSe_2$ sprayed	8.76	9.60	9.59	18.16	19.45	0.64	0.65	AM1.5, 100 mW/cm²
(Mehmood, Zaheer Aslam, et al., 2016)	TiO_2	0.05% AC+TiO_2	3.38	5.45	61.24	12.33	16.54	0.37	0.44	AM1.5G, 100 mW/cm²
(Tas et al., 2017)	Pt CE	PAni:Al in P@6	5.75	5.97	3.83	13.01	13.59	0.63	0.58	AM1.5G, 1000 W/m²
(Hu et al., 2012)	Double stripped shaped FDSSC	Triple stripped shaped FDSSC	0.22	0.25	13.64	0.86	1.11	36.19	31.67	AM1.5G, 100 mW/cm²
(Kasaudhan et al., 2014)	SnO_2 (only)	SnO_2:TiO_2 (1:1)	4.63	6.17	33.26	12.87	13.47	0.55	0.63	AM1.5, 100 mW/cm²
(Kyaw et al., 2012)	0.25 cm^2 of active area	0.10 cm^2 of active area	2.41	4.60	90.87	7.98	9.76	0.48	0.70	AM1.5G, 100 mW/cm²

Measurement System

This section illustrated the measuring systems corresponding to DSSC. In previous section it was already discussed that overall performance regarding the decision making of third generation solar cell is depend on PCE as well as on FF. Parameters are determined by solar simulator system to get PCE, FF related to DSSC. Concern to get energy from DSSC in a feasible way via reconfiguration of internal structure of the device using the data taken from different measurement system which are documented in Table 2. For example, data available in Table 2 is showing 7-SCSpec system, is used to measure incident photon to current conversion efficiency (IPCE). Complete information about light harvesting of DSSC can be obtain from the IPCE spectra (Xu et al., 2012). All other tabulated systems in Table 2 are useful to extract characterizing properties. The characterizing properties obtained from the measuring systems are listed in top row, under that name of the systems and below the system name are the information related to the measuring system in Table 2. Other than tabulated systems, electron spectroscopy (XPS) is used to measures elemental composition, chemical state and electronic state of substrate (J. C. Chou et al., 2014).

$$FF = \frac{\left(V_m \times J_m\right)}{\left(V_{oc} \times J_{sc}\right)} \tag{5}$$

$$\eta\left(\%\right) = \frac{V_{oc} \times J_{sc} \times FF}{P_{in}} \times 100 \tag{6}$$

CHARACTERIZING QUALITIES

The ejected electron from dye due to the reduction of the dye may be combined with tri-iodide instead of injected in photoanode is addressed dark current. Reduction of dark current (0.107 mA/cm^2 to 0.036 mA/cm^2) improve the J_{sc} profile (8.35 mA/cm^2 to 12.40 mA/cm^2) leads to enhance of PCE (3.34% to 5.47%) (J. C. Chou, Kuo, et al., 2018).

Interfacial contact area is one of the key factors for charge transfer resistance in between electrolyte and CE. With increase in surface roughness (4.34 nm (for Pt) to 8.43 nm (for Pt/AZO)) make larger interfacial contact area (Gurung et al., 2016). Image obtained from TEM shows the particle size of Fe_3O_4 is about 223.55 nm in (J.-C. Chou et al., 2016). Such nanoparticle material used to increase the surface area of TiO_2 film. J-V curve recorder shows that lower resistance and higher catalytic effect are responsible for higher J_{sc} and V_{oc} (Pt > Pt + C) (Sakai et al., 2018). The crystallinity of a sample (TiO_2) makes hassle-free to decide its purity. The XRD patterns in (Xu et al., 2012) shows that the shape of diffraction peaks concludes to crystallinity. The crystalline size calculated in (Kumari et al., 2018) using the equation (7) known as Scherrer equation, where k is a constant, λ is x-ray wavelength, β is full width of diffraction line and θ is the Bragg angle.

The study of EIS with the operating condition of 10 mV ac input signal with a frequency range of 10 mHz to 1 MHz is used to observe the charge transfer resistance of the cell from resultant Nyquist plot in (Mehmood et al., 2018). Three arcs (semicircles) are the derived from the Nyquist plot. The first arc represents the charge transport resistance (CTR) at CE and electrolyte interface (R_2), the second one represents CTR at electrolyte and photoanode interface (R_3) and the third one represents Warburg resistance

$$D = \frac{k\lambda}{\beta cos\theta} \tag{7}$$

(Z_w). The Z_w does exist inside the device due to the diffusion process of redox couple in the electrolyte. It may consider in series with R_3. R_1 is the resistance in between conductor and FTO (H.-T. Chou et al., 2015; J. C. Chou, You, et al., 2017). C_1 and C_2 are the capacitance associated with interfaces as R_2 and R_3 are accordingly, shown in Figure 3. Sample B ($R_3 = 288\ \Omega$) with higher CTR compare to sample A ($R_3 = 76\ \Omega$) have better cell efficiency shows that charge recombination is inversely proportional to the value of R_3 (Mehmood et al., 2018). Higher the value of R_3 slower the charge recombination and better the cell performance and lifetime of the electron (Mehmood et al., 2017).

Annealing temperature and time make a big difference in photoconversion efficiency shown by different literature. Sheet resistivity becomes less ($1{:}25 \times 10^{-3}\ \Omega{\cdot}cm$ at 250°C) after increasing the annealing temperature up to a certain level ($7.8 \times 10^{-3}\ \Omega{\cdot}cm$ before annealing) (Heo et al., 2009). Experimented with gold doped reduced Graphene Oxide in CE at different annealing times at 120°C. For a shorter period of annealing (15,30,45,60 min.) initiate less dark current compare to long time annealing (75,90 min.) (Rahman et al., 2018).

Table 2. Measuring Systems associated with characterization of DSSC

Photovoltaic Parameters	Surface Morphology	Crystallinity	J-V Curve Recorder	Compositional Analysis	Nanoparticle Characterization (morphology, particle size)	Surface roughness & Structure	Electrochemical Impedance Analysis & Nyquist Plot	Absorption Spectra of Dye	Film Thickness & Cross Section	Functional Group of Material
Solar Simulator	Scanning Electron Microscope (SEM)	X-ray diffraction (XRD)/ Diffractometer	Computer controlled digital source meter	Energy Dispersive X-ray Spectro-meter (C.-Y. Hsu et al., 2013)	Transmission Electron Microscope (TEM)	Atomic Force Microscopy (AFM)	Electrochemical Impedance Spectroscopy (EIS)	UV-Vis Spectrophotometer	Profilometer	Profilometer Fourier Transform Infrared (FTIR) Spectrometer
MFS-PV-Basic-HMT-Taiwan (J.-C. Chou et al., 2016; J. C. Chou, Chu, et al., 2016; J. C. Chou, Kuo, et al., 2018)	Hitachi S4800-I (J. C. Chou, Kuo, et al., 2018), FEI Serion 200 (Zhang et al., 2016)	Bruker AXS Gmbh, Karlsruhe, Germany (J. C. Chou, Kuo, et al., 2018)	Keithley 2400 (C.-Y. Hsu et al., 2013; Kim et al., 2010), Keithley 2420 (Lai et al., 2010)	Incident photon to current conversion efficiency	JEM-1400, Japan (J.-C. Chou et al., 2016), JEOL, JEM-2100F (Mehmood et al., 2015)	Bruker Dimension ICON, U. S. A. (J.-C. Chou et al., 2016)	Eco-Chemie Autolab PGSTAT 302N Electrochemical Workstation (Irannejad et al., 2018)	JASCO V-600, Taiwan (J.-C. Chou et al., 2016)	DEKTAK 150, Veeco Instruments, Inc. (De Rossi et al., 2014; Vesce et al., 2013)	JASCO MFT 2000 (Tarini et al., 2017)
YSS-E40, Yamashita Denso, Japan (C.-Y. Hsu et al., 2013)	JSM-6390LV (Sharma et al., 2015), JEOL JSM-6700F (Zhou et al., 2016)	Rigaku D/MAX2500 Diffractometer (J.-C. Chou et al., 2016; J. C. Chou, Hsu, et al., 2017; J. C. Chou, Lin, et al., 2016)	Keithley Electro-meter, 6517 (Kadachi et al., 2016), Keithley 2401 (Ciani et al., 2014)	7-SCSpec system, Saifan Beijing (Yang et al., 2011)	Philips CM200 TEM (Tsekouras et al., 2010)	Topometrix TMX 2000 (Kadachi et al., 2016)	CHI 660C Instruments, China (Xu et al., 2012), Compactstat, IVIUM Technology (Choi et al., 2011)	UV-Cecil CE 3041(Kadachi et al., 2016), Shimadzu UV-1800 (Loryuenyong et al., 2016)	ACCRETECH SURFCOM 1500 (Hossain & Takahashi, 2014)	JASCO FTIR 680-Plus (Irannejad et al., 2018)

The gap between HOMO and LUMO plays a crucial role to modify the efficiency of the cell. Smaller the band gap higher the PCE. The intensity of diffusion of dye on the semiconductor layer as well as the electron injection method impacted by solvent treatment. Treatment of acetone solvent over ethanol level up the J_{sc} from 0.68 to 1.35 mA/cm^2 with an around equal amount of V_{oc} (Sreekala et al., 2012). It happens due to the reduction of the band gap, enhancement of dye diffusion, and an extensive coverage range of light wavelength.

Figure 3. Equivalent circuit diagram of DSSC

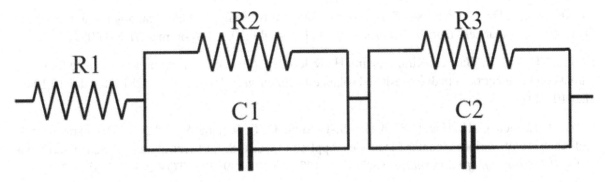

CONCLUSION

This paper summarizes the characterizing qualities like the dark current, charge transfer resistance, the particle size of substances, surface area, annealing time, etc. are used to characterize the DSSC. Manipulation of these values by alteration of material in use, modification in the process of fabricating make a difference in the performance of the device. Many have tried and are trying to enhance efficiency but till date, its value is around 12% whereas theoretically, it could be 32%. Reviewing of the ample amount of literature, Pt highlighted as an expensive material used to prepare the counter electrode of DSSC. Over the decade, the effort put to replace the Pt material for cost-effectiveness beside PCE. Operating life span of DSSC degrades when it is exposed under ultraviolet light. Research is going on to achieve the expected operating life of 25 years of the solar cell. It's become an emerging technology for green building for its transparency to use as a power generating window.

ACKNOWLEDGMENT

This research received no known specific grant from any funding agency in the public, commercial, or not-for-profit sectors.

REFERENCES

Armendáriz-Mireles, E. N., Rocha-Rangel, E., Caballero-Rico, F., Ramirez-De-Leon, J. A., & Vázquez, M. (2017). Effect of. *IEEE Journal of Photovoltaics*, 7(5), 1329–1337. doi:10.1109/JPHOTOV.2017.2720260

Bari, D., Cester, A., Wrachien, N., Ciammaruchi, L., Brown, T. M., Reale, A., Di Carlo, A., & Meneghesso, G. (2012). Reliability study of ruthenium-based dye-sensitized solar cells (DSCs). *IEEE Journal of Photovoltaics*, *2*(1), 27–34. doi:10.1109/JPHOTOV.2011.2180702

Berginc, M., Krašovec, U. O., & Topič, M. (2014). Outdoor ageing of the dye-sensitized solar cell under different operation regimes. *Solar Energy Materials and Solar Cells, 120*(B), 491–499. doi:10.1016/j.solmat.2013.09.029

Chakrabarti, T., Dey, A., & Sarkar, S. K. (2018). Comparative analysis of physical organic and inorganic Dyesensitized solar cell. *Optical Materials*, *82*, 141–146. doi:10.1016/j.optmat.2018.05.009

Choi, H., Hwang, S., Bae, H., Kim, S., Kim, H., & Jeon, M. (2011). Electrophoretic graphene for transparent counter electrodes in dye-sensitised solar cells. *Electronics Letters*, *47*(4), 281–283. doi:10.1049/el.2010.2897

Chou, H.-T., Lien, C.-H., Hsu, H.-C., Chen, S.-T., Sung, C.-T., & Jiang, S.-C. F. (2017). Characteristics and Analyses of Various Counter Electrodes Applied in Quasi-Solid Electrolyte Dye-Sensitized Solar Cells. *IEEE Journal of Photovoltaics*, *8*(1), 137–143. doi:10.1109/JPHOTOV.2017.2766530

Chou, H. T., Liu, H. C., Hsu, H. C., Chen, C. Y., & Lai, C. H. (2018). Investigation of Deformed. *IEEE Journal of Photovoltaics*, *8*(3), 763–768. doi:10.1109/JPHOTOV.2018.2806307

Chou, H.-T., Tseng, K.-C., & Hsu, H.-C. (2015). Fabrication of deformed. *IEEE Journal of Photovoltaics*, *6*(1), 211–216. doi:10.1109/JPHOTOV.2015.2487819

Chou, J. C., Chu, C. M., Liao, Y. H., Huang, C. H., Lin, Y. J., Wu, H., & Nien, Y. H. (2016). The incorporation of graphene and magnetic beads into dye-sensitized solar cells and application with electrochemical capacitor. *IEEE Journal of Photovoltaics*, *6*(1), 223–229. doi:10.1109/JPHOTOV.2015.2501730

Chou, J.-C., Chu, C.-M., Liao, Y.-H., Lai, C.-H., Lin, Y.-J., You, P.-H., Hsu, W.-Y., Lu, C.-C., & Nien, Y.-H. (2016). An investigation on the photovoltaic properties of dye-sensitized solar cells based on. *IEEE Journal of the Electron Devices Society*, *5*(1), 32–39. doi:10.1109/JEDS.2016.2618839

Chou, J. C., Hsu, W. Y., Liao, Y. H., Lai, C. H., Lin, Y. J., You, P. H., Chu, C. M., Lu, C. C., & Nien, Y. H. (2017). Photovoltaic Analysis of Platinum Counter Electrode Modified by Graphene Oxide and Magnetic Beads for Dye-Sensitized Solar Cell. *IEEE Transactions on Semiconductor Manufacturing*, *30*(3), 270–275. doi:10.1109/TSM.2017.2725385

Chou, J. C., Huang, C. H., Liao, Y. H., Chuang, S. W., Tai, L. H., & Nien, Y. H. (2015). Effect of Different Graphene Oxide Contents on Dye-Sensitized Solar Cells. *IEEE Journal of Photovoltaics*, *5*(4), 1106–1112. doi:10.1109/JPHOTOV.2015.2419137

Chou, J. C., Kuo, C. H., Liao, Y. H., Lai, C. H., You, P. H., Ko, C. C., Yang, Z. M., & Wu, C. Y. (2018). A Barrier Structure for Photoelectrode of Dye-Sensitized Solar Cell for Enhancing Efficiency. *IEEE Photonics Technology Letters*, *30*(6), 521–524. doi:10.1109/LPT.2018.2800771

Chou, J. C., Lin, Y. J., Liao, Y. H., Lai, C. H., Chu, C. M., You, P. H., & Nien, Y. H. (2016). Photovoltaic Performance Analysis of Dye-Sensitized Solar Cell with ZnO Compact Layer and. *IEEE Journal of the Electron Devices Society*, *4*(6), 402–409. doi:10.1109/JEDS.2016.2614940

Chou, J. C., Shih, P. H., Hu, J. E., Liao, Y. H., Chuang, S. W., & Huang, C. H. (2014). Electrochemical Analysis of Photoelectrochromic Device Combined Dye-Sensitized Solar Cell. *IEEE Transactions on Nanotechnology, 13*(5), 954–962. doi:10.1109/TNANO.2014.2333013

Chou, J. C., Wu, C. Y., Liao, Y. H., Lai, C. H., Yang, C. M., You, P. H., Kuo, C. H., & Ko, C. C. (2018). IGZO/. *IEEE Journal of Photovoltaics, 8*(3), 769–776. doi:10.1109/JPHOTOV.2018.2815711

Chou, J. C., You, P. H., Liao, Y. H., Lai, C. H., Chu, C. M., Lin, Y. J., Hsu, W. Y., Lu, C. C., & Nien, Y. H. (2017). Fabrication and Photovoltaic Properties of Dye-Sensitized Solar Cells Based on Graphene-. *IEEE Transactions on Semiconductor Manufacturing, 30*(4), 531–538. doi:10.1109/TSM.2017.2747121

Ciani, L., Catelani, M., Carnevale, E. A., Donati, L., & Bruzzi, M. (2014). Evaluation of the aging process of dye-sensitized solar cells under different stress conditions. *IEEE Transactions on Instrumentation and Measurement, 64*(5), 1179–1187. doi:10.1109/TIM.2014.2381352

De Rossi, F., Brown, T. M., Reale, A., & Di Carlo, A. (2014). Large-area electrodeposition of counterelectrodes utilizing the same integrated conductive grid for fabrication of parallel flexible dye solar cell modules. *IEEE Journal of Photovoltaics, 4*(6), 1552–1559. doi:10.1109/JPHOTOV.2014.2354255

Grätzel, M. (2005). Solar energy conversion by dye-sensitized photovoltaic cells. *Inorganic Chemistry, 44*(20), 6841–6851. doi:10.1021/ic0508371 PMID:16180840

Gurung, A., Elbohy, H., Khatiwada, D., Mitul, A. F., & Qiao, Q. (2016). A Simple Cost-Effective Approach to Enhance Performance of Bifacial Dye-Sensitized Solar Cells. *IEEE Journal of Photovoltaics, 6*(4), 912–917. doi:10.1109/JPHOTOV.2016.2551462

Haloui, H., Touafek, K., Zaabat, M., El Hocine, H. B. C., & Khelifa, A. (2015). The Copper Indium Selenium (. *Energy Procedia, 74*, 1213–1219. doi:10.1016/j.egypro.2015.07.765

Han, Q., Yu, M., & Liu, J. (2013). Nanocrystalline titanium dioxide prepared by hydrothermal method and its application in dye-sensitised solar cells. *Micro & Nano Letters, 8*(5), 238–242. doi:10.1049/mnl.2012.0941

Heo, J. H., Jung, K. Y., Kwak, D. J., Lee, D. K., & Sung, Y. M. (2009). Fabrication of titanium-doped indium oxide films for dye-sensitized solar cell application using reactive RF magnetron sputter method. *IEEE Transactions on Plasma Science, 37*(8), 1586–1592. doi:10.1109/TPS.2009.2023477

Hossain, M. F., & Takahashi, T. (2014). Hydrothermal synthesis of novel ZnO nanomushrooms for improving the solar cells performance. *IEEE Transactions on Nanotechnology, 13*(4), 755–759. doi:10.1109/TNANO.2014.2319097

Hsu, C. Y., Cherng, S. J., Lin, Y. J., & Chen, C. M. (2013). A compact nano-. *IEEE Electron Device Letters, 34*(11), 1415–1417. doi:10.1109/LED.2013.2282401

Hu, J. E., Yang, S. Y., Chou, J. C., & Shih, P. H. (2012). Fabrication of flexible dye-sensitised solar cells with titanium dioxide thin films based on screen-printing technique. *Micro & Nano Letters, 7*(12), 1162–1165. doi:10.1049/mnl.2012.0529

Irannejad, N., Rezaei, B., Ensafi, A. A., & Zandi-Atashbar, N. (2018). Photovoltaic performance analysis of dye-sensitized solar cell based on the Ag(4,4¢-dicyanamidobiphenyl) complex as a light-scattering layer agent and linker molecule on. *IEEE Journal of Photovoltaics*, *8*(5), 1230–1236. doi:10.1109/JPHOTOV.2018.2829779

Jia, J., Wu, J., Dong, J., Tu, Y., Lan, Z., Fan, L., & Wei, Y. (2016). High-Performance Molybdenum Diselenide Electrodes Used in Dye-Sensitized Solar Cells and Supercapacitors. *IEEE Journal of Photovoltaics*, *6*(5), 1196–1202. doi:10.1109/JPHOTOV.2016.2585021

Kadachi, Z., Ben Karoui, M., Azizi, T., & Gharbi, R. (2016). Effect of. *Micro & Nano Letters*, *11*(2), 94–98. doi:10.1049/mnl.2015.0154

Kang, C., Zhang, Z., Zhang, Y., He, Y., Xie, Y., & Xie, E. (2011). Enhanced efficiency in dye-sensitised solar cells using a. *Micro & Nano Letters*, *6*(8), 579–581. doi:10.1049/mnl.2011.0225

Kasaudhan, R., Elbohy, H., Sigdel, S., Qiao, H., Wei, Q., & Qiao, Q. (2014). Incorporation of. *IEEE Electron Device Letters*, *35*(5), 578–580. doi:10.1109/LED.2014.2312355

Kim, S., Lim, H., Kim, K., Kim, C., Kang, T. Y., Ko, M. J., Kim, K., & Park, N. G. (2010). Synthetic strategy of low-bandgap organic sensitizers and their photoelectron injection characteristics. *IEEE Journal of Selected Topics in Quantum Electronics*, *16*(6), 1627–1634. doi:10.1109/JSTQE.2010.2042683

Kumari, K., Chakrabarti, T., Jana, A., Bhattachartjee, D., Gupta, B., & Sarkar, S. K. (2018). Comparative Study on Perovskite Solar Cells based on Titanium, Nickel and Cadmium doped. *Optical Materials*, *84*, 681–688. doi:10.1016/j.optmat.2018.07.071

Kyaw, H. H., Bora, T., & Dutta, J. (2012). One-diode model equivalent circuit analysis for ZnO nanorod-based dye-sensitized solar cells: Effects of annealing and active area. *IEEE Transactions on Nanotechnology*, *11*(4), 763–768. doi:10.1109/TNANO.2012.2196286

Lai, S. C., Yang, M. F., Dolmanan, S., Ke, L., & Sun, X. W. (2010). Efficiency optimization on dye-sensitized solar cells with low-frequency noise analysis. *IEEE Transactions on Electron Devices*, *57*(9), 2306–2309. doi:10.1109/TED.2010.2053490

Lee, M. K., Yen, H., & Cheng, N. R. (2014). Efficiency enhancement of DSSC with aqueous solution deposited ZnO nanotip array. *IEEE Photonics Technology Letters*, *26*(5), 454–456. doi:10.1109/LPT.2013.2296098

Loryuenyong, V., Yaotrakool, S., Prathumted, P., Lertsiri, J., & Buasri, A. (2016). Synergistic effects of graphene-polyaniline counter electrode in dye-sensitised solar cells. *Micro & Nano Letters*, *11*(2), 77–80. doi:10.1049/mnl.2015.0363

Mehmood, U., Afzaal, M., Al-Ahmed, A., Yates, H. M., Hakeem, A. S., Ali, H., & Al-Sulaiman, F. A. (2017). Transparent Conductive Oxide Films for High-Performance Dye-Sensitized Solar Cells. *IEEE Journal of Photovoltaics*, *7*(2), 518–524. doi:10.1109/JPHOTOV.2016.2641303

Mehmood, U., Al-Ahmed, A., Afzaal, M., Hakeem, A. S., Abdullahi Haladu, S., & Al-Sulaiman, F. A. (2018). Enhancement of the Photovoltaic Performance of Dye-Sensitized Solar Cells by Cosensitizing. *IEEE Journal of Photovoltaics*, *8*(2), 512–516. doi:10.1109/JPHOTOV.2018.2790699

Mehmood, U., Harrabi, K., Hussein, I. A., & Ahmed, S. (2015). Enhanced photovoltaic performance of dye-sensitized solar cells using. *IEEE Journal of Photovoltaics, 6*(1), 196–201. doi:10.1109/JPHOTOV.2015.2479468

Mehmood, U., Hussein, I. A., Al-Ahmed, A., & Ahmed, S. (2016). Enhancing Power Conversion Efficiency of Dye-Sensitized Solar Cell Using. *IEEE Journal of Photovoltaics, 6*(2), 486–490. doi:10.1109/JPHOTOV.2016.2514703

Mehmood, U., Zaheer Aslam, M., Shawabkeh, R. A., Hussein, I. A., Ahmad, W., & Ghaffar Rana, A. (2016). Improvement in Photovoltaic Performance of Dye Sensitized Solar Cell Using Activated Carbon-. *IEEE Journal of Photovoltaics, 6*(5), 1191–1195. doi:10.1109/JPHOTOV.2016.2574127

O'regan, B., & Grätzel, M. (1991). A low-cost, high-efficiency solar cell based on dye-sensitized colloidal TiO 2 films. *Nature, 353*(6346), 737–740. doi:10.1038/353737a0

Parida, B., Iniyan, S., & Goic, R. (2011). A review of solar photovoltaic technologies. *Renewable & Sustainable Energy Reviews, 15*(3), 1625–1636. doi:10.1016/j.rser.2010.11.032

Peng, W., Zeng, Y., Gong, H., Leng, Y. Q., Yan, Y. H., & Hu, W. (2013). Evolutionary algorithm and parameters extraction for dye-sensitised solar cells one-diode equivalent circuit model. *Micro & Nano Letters, 8*(2), 86–89. doi:10.1049/mnl.2012.0806

Rahman, M. Y. A., Sulaiman, A. S., & Ali Umar, A. (2018). Dye-sensitised solar cell utilising gold doped reduced graphene oxide counter electrode: Influence of annealing time. *Micro & Nano Letters, 13*(8), 1224–1226. doi:10.1049/mnl.2018.0054

Sakai, K., Kizu, T., Kiwa, T., & Tsukada, K. (2018). Analysis of AC Impedance in Localized Region Using Magnetic Field Distribution Measured by HTS-SQUID. *IEEE Transactions on Applied Superconductivity, 28*(4), 1–5. doi:10.1109/TASC.2018.2796609

Shanmugam, M., Farrokh Baroughi, M., & Galipeau, D. (2009). High. *Electronics Letters, 45*(12), 648–649. doi:10.1049/el.2009.3527

Sharma, S., Khannam, M., Boruah, M., Nath, B. C., & Dolui, S. K. (2015). Development of Dye-Sensitized Solar Cells Based on Gold/Gelatin Gel Electrolyte: Effect of Different Aspect Ratio of Gold Nanocrystals. *IEEE Journal of Photovoltaics, 5*(6), 1665–1673. doi:10.1109/JPHOTOV.2015.2478031

Sigdel, S., Elbohy, H., Gong, J., Adhikari, N., Sumathy, K., Qiao, H., Wei, Q., Sayyad, M. H., Zai, J., Qian, X., & Qiao, Q. (2015). Dye-sensitized solar cells based on porous hollow tin oxide nanofibers. *IEEE Transactions on Electron Devices, 62*(6), 2027–2032. doi:10.1109/TED.2015.2421475

Sönmezoğlu, S., Akyürek, C., & Akiş, H. (2014). Modification of juglon dye as a sensitiser in dye-sensitised solar cells. *IET Optoelectronics, 8*(6), 270–276. doi:10.1049/iet-opt.2013.0048

Sreekala, C. O., Jinchu, I., Sreelatha, K. S., Janu, Y., Prasad, N., Kumar, M., Sadh, A. K., & Roy, M. S. (2012). Influence of solvents and surface treatment on photovoltaic response of dssc based on natural curcumin dye. *IEEE Journal of Photovoltaics, 2*(3), 312–319. doi:10.1109/JPHOTOV.2012.2185782

Tarini, M., Prakash, N., Mohamed Mathar Sahib, I. K., & Hayakawa, Y. (2017). Novel Sugar Apple-Shaped. *IEEE Journal of Photovoltaics, 7*(4), 1050–1057. doi:10.1109/JPHOTOV.2017.2698500

Tas, R., Can, M., & Sonmezoglu, S. (2017). Exploring on Photovoltaic Performance of Dye-Sensitized Solar Cells Using Polyaniline as a Counter Electrode: Role of Aluminum-Solvent Interactions. *IEEE Journal of Photovoltaics*, 7(3), 792–801. doi:10.1109/JPHOTOV.2017.2669643

Tedla, A., Mu, Y.-T., Sharma, J., & Tai, Y. (2016). Shelf-life studies on an ionic-liquid-stabilized dye-sensitized solar cell. *IEEE Journal of Photovoltaics*, 7(1), 177–183. doi:10.1109/JPHOTOV.2016.2614125

Thapa, A., Zhao, Y., Poudel, P., Elbohy, H., Vaagensmith, B., Zhang, Z., Fong, H., & Qiao, Q. (2013). Evaluation of counter electrodes composed by carbon nanofibers and nanoparticles in dye-sensitized solar cells. *IEEE Transactions on Electron Devices*, 60(11), 3883–3887. doi:10.1109/TED.2013.2279518

Tsekouras, G., Miyashita, M., Kho, Y. K., Teoh, W. Y., Mozer, A. J., Amal, R., Mori, S., & Wallace, G. G. (2010). Charge transport in dye-sensitized solar cells based on flame-made. *IEEE Journal of Selected Topics in Quantum Electronics*, 16(6), 1641–1648. doi:10.1109/JSTQE.2010.2049734

Vesce, L., Riccitelli, R., Mincuzzi, G., Orabona, A., Soscia, G., Brown, T. M., Di Carlo, A., & Reale, A. (2013). Fabrication of spacer and catalytic layers in monolithic dye-sensitized solar cells. *IEEE Journal of Photovoltaics*, 3(3), 1004–1011. doi:10.1109/JPHOTOV.2013.2262374

Xu, F., Wu, Y., Zhang, X., Gao, Z., & Jiang, K. (2012). Controllable synthesis of rutile. *Micro & Nano Letters*, 7(8), 826–830. doi:10.1049/mnl.2012.0398

Yang, J., Gao, Z., Tian, L., Ma, P., Wu, D., & Yang, L. (2011). Spindle-like. *Micro & Nano Letters*, 6(8), 737–740. doi:10.1049/mnl.2011.0317

Zhang, Y., Qi, T., Wang, Q., Zhang, Y., Wang, D., & Zheng, W. (2016). Preparation of. *IEEE Journal of Photovoltaics*, 7(1), 399–403. doi:10.1109/JPHOTOV.2016.2627620

Zhou, Y., Yang, L., Lu, J., Wu, Y., Li, C., Liu, Y., & Li, M. (2016). Photoelectric properties of three-dimensional urchin-like zinc oxide/titanium dioxide composite micronanostructures. *Micro & Nano Letters*, 11(5), 277–280. doi:10.1049/mnl.2015.0394

KEY TERMS AND DEFINITIONS

Characterizing Qualities: The measurable parameters determine the character or the performance of the cell.

Charge Transport Resistance: The resistance to transfer electron between the one layer (electrolyte) to another layer (CE).

Photosensitizing Dye: The dye inside DSSC is capable to absorb solar energy.

Sheet Resistance: It is known as surface resistance or surface resistivity of the thin film on photoanode.

Warburg Resistance: The resistance of redox diffusion at electrolyte/CE.

Chapter 13
A Linguistic Perspective of Assamese Language as Used on Facebook

Seuji Sharma
Gauhati University, India

ABSTRACT

The chapter attempts to look at different themes and issues relating to the use of Assamese language on Facebook. This study examines the changes observed at different levels of linguistic analysis. The users have been seen making some changes at phonological level which is associated with the phonemes or sounds in Assamese. Modifications have also been observed regarding the use of sentence structure as well as phrase structure, and the matters related to these areas have been dealt with at a grammatical level. Since linguistic analysis covers a vast area, some specific domains are being dealt with in this chapter, especially from the areas of phonology, morphology, and syntax.

INTRODUCTION

Assamese, the easternmost member of the Indo-Aryan family of language (Kakati, 1941, p 1), has widely been used by the users, belonging to Assam, on Facebook, one of the most popular social networking sites in the World. Assam represents one of the highest ethnically and linguistically diverse areas of the North-east India and hence Assamese, as a major language, spoken in Assam, plays the role of lingua-franca among the different speech communities in eastern India. (Goswami& Tamuli, 2003, pp 391-443). The earliest specimen of Assamese language and literature, available in the Charyas and Dohas, is supposed to have flourished between the 8th and 12th centuries A.D. (Das, 2010, p19). From fourteenth century onwards, the Assamese language can be divided into three periods on the basis of the literary style, early period (14th century-16th century), middle period (17th century- beginning of the 19th century) and modern period (early 19th –present times). Different types of prose are seen to have developed in a specific manner which has contributed a lot in the emergence and enhancement of the clear, stable and pure literary form and style of modern Assamese which reflects the uniqueness

DOI: 10.4018/978-1-7998-9795-8.ch013

of the language in its use. Though as a well-established language Assamese has a glorious tradition of elucidating and representing new thoughts and ideas, but the Assamese-speaking population is decreasing precariously. The total population of Assamese speaker in Assam is nearby 13 million which makes up 48.38% of the population of the state according to the Language Census of 2011, whereas in 1971, the Assamese-speaking populace was 60.89% of the total population of Assam. (://www.time8. in/new-decline-trend-only-1-26-per-cent-of-indias-). In spite of the fact that the Assamese-speaking population is dwindling alarmingly, a large group of people is still working for the language, nourishing and reflecting their ideas, hopes, aspirations towards social as well as other life- related problems with the help of the language itself. In this era of globalization, like the users of other languages, the users of Assamese language too, have tried to share their views and to participate in different discussions by using their mother tongue. On Facebook, several groups are seen representing the ideas and thoughts of their members in Assamese, both orthographically and linguistically. Some remarkable features are observed which have brought few changes to the grammar of the language and thus a glimpse of newness in the style and form is seen. These types of changes are being observed at all levels of linguistic analysis, i.e. at the levels of phonology, morphology, syntax and semantics. Before going into details, it should be made clear that no drastic change is observed in the use of Assamese in the groups. But still, some widespread usages of some particular features are typical to a large number of Facebook users following Assamese. The striking patterns which seem to be generic for a large group of users of Assamese are discussed under two headings in this paper, first, changes occurring at phonological level are examined, and, secondly, the discussion on the change occurring at grammatical level is taken up in two stages. The first stage focuses on the modification observed at the morphological level, whereas the discussion at the second stage includes different aspects under syntax where changes are being made. Semantic change, i.e. the change in meaning, can also be observed in some contexts but this is not a common type of change noticed on Facebook. For example, the youths in Assam frequently produce a word *kamʊr*, which means 'to bite'/ 'to harm'. But now-a-days, people are using the same term in two senses: 'to bite/ harm' and 'of an irritating nature', where the vowel phoneme *ʊ* has been replaced with *u*. But words indicating such type of extension in meaning is very few in number and also not available on Facebook. This study, therefore, has been delimited focusing only on the changes observed at the phonological and grammatical levels.

LITERATURE REVIEW

Most of the Assamese linguists and grammarians have discussed about the structure of Assamese language at different levels in detail. Dr. Banikanta Kakati's Assamese, Its Formation and Development (1941) is the first research work on the grammar of Assamese language with a modern perspective. This work has attempted to analyze linguistic materials under different grammatical and historical categories which leads to the recording of systematized informations about the formation and growth of Assamese language. (Kakati, p. x-xi). Dr. U. N. Goswami (Asamiya Bhashar Byakaran, 1991) and Dr. G. C. Goswami (Asamiya Byakaranar Moulik Bichar, 2004) have also focused on various morphological and syntactic elements of Assamese grammar with detailed analysis. Dr. G.C Goswami and Dr. Jyotiprakash Tamuli (Asamiya, 2003) have identified and discussed the key issues relating to the grammarical analysis of Assamese within the perspective of descriptive linguistics. Again, Dr. Runima Chowdhary (1995) has treated the structure of Assamese verbs in detail. Though there is no significant work on this area of language, i,e., the use of Assamese language on social media, the foregoing references indicate the nature of linguistic resources on the Assamese language that are currently available. These resources provide a helpful support to any researcher working on any aspects of the structure of Assamese language including the area that has been taken up for this study. This is because since the language of social media represents a relatively recent emerging area of the language, it is not surprising that no such research focusing on this aspect of the language in use is available. Even then, to the extent that Assamese language used in social media falls within and conforms to the broader framework of the Assamese language dealt with in the previous literature, such literature is relevant to the present study. Though there is no previous significant work on this area of Assamese language, the study on similar areas are available in other languages worldwide. Several writers, such as Sudesh Sharma (2014), Andrea Hollington and Nico Nassenstein (2018), have discussed how media and social networking have influenced the transition of different languages. Social media channels are offering such a type of platform which is contributing to the evolution of language very rapidly. In every level of linguistic analysis this change can be observed in the language and this is true in case of Assamese language too.

DATA COLLECTION AND METHODOLOGY

The data is based on the written source of formal and informal kinds. The data has been collected from a wide range of natural contexts found on Facebook and generalized statements have been made on the basis of patterns inherent in the data itself. An attempt is made here to analyze and describe the language as used by the users on Facebook who are the native speakers of Assamese. While examining the objective or physical data the empirical approach in methodology is supplemented with the introspective method. For this language-centric study, data are analysed through the process of interlinearisation. First, morpheme-to-morpheme break-up is provided, followed by the interlinearised glossed text and finally the meaning of the sentence is provided.

CHANGES OBSERVED AT THE PHONOLOGICAL LEVEL

Language change is an inevitable phenomenon. The change in languages can be observed at different levels of linguistic analysis. The phonological level is concerned with the phonemes or sound-system of a language and in Assamese, sound change has been observed occurring at this level on Facebook. The changes observed influencing the phonological pattern of the language are examined in this section. These changes can be observed occurring with both vowels and consonant phonemes in the language. The most common types of changes relating to the sound or phonemes are substitution, insertion and deletion which are observed below:

ʊ Becomes *u*

In the majority of writings, it is observed that ʊ, the phoneme used to represent the back half-close rounded vowel in Assamese, has been replaced by *u*, the phoneme used to represent the back close rounded vowel. This type of change is seen in the vowels occurring in the initial, medial and final positions in words. A few words which will illustrate this type of change at sound level are presented in Table 1:

Table 1. Words showing the replacement of ʊ by u

Position of the vowel	Standard Assamese	Form used on Facebook
word-final	*hɔjtʊ* 'perhaps'	*hɔjtu*
word-middle	*dekʰʊn* 'an expression to reflect contrary to expectation'	*dekʰun*
word-middle	*ɔnɯɹʊɖ* 'request'	*ɔnɯɹuɖ*
word-middle	*tulɔni bija* 'a ceremony organized when a girl attains puberty'	*tulɔni bija*
word-middle	*apʊnaɹ* 'your (honorific)'	*apunaɹ*
word-middle	*dʊbag niħa* ' midnight'	*dubag niħa*
word-initial	*ʊmɔla* 'to be observing closely'	*umɔla*

The Table presented above clearly shows the change of phoneme ʊ in word-initial, word-middle and word-final positions.

u Becomes ʊ

Some users on Facebook are observed to replace u by ʊ, as in :

tʰup kʰa > tʰʊp kʰa 'to assemble'
aguwai gol > agʊwai gol '(Someone) proceeded.'
enekuwa > enekʊwa 'of such type'

In intergenerational transfer, the distinction between these two distinctive sounds has become obliterated when younger speakers tend to interchange one of the sound to the other. Over time, this may lead to the phonemic merger as the clear evidence of this change happening is the tendency to use spelling *u* into the spelling ʊ and vice versa.

e Becomes *i*

In case of the indeclinable word *neki*, used for making an interrogative sentence, it is observed that the vowel *e, the* phoneme representing the front half-open unrounded vowel in Assamese, is produced as *i*, the phoneme representing the front close unrounded vowel, by some users, resulting in *niki*, and in some cases the term has been seen using as contracted form *ni*. For example,

1. *moi za-m niki?*
    1SG go-FUT+1 INDCLN
    'Should I go?
2. *tʰijɔ di-e ni baɹu?*
    stand give-PRES+3 INDCLN well
    'Does he stand?'
3. *kɔtʰa as-il ni?*

matter be-pst+3 INDCLN

'Do you have something to say?'

4. tʊɹ-ʊ enekuwa

2sg(NON.HON) +EMP such typesuch type

hɔ-j ni?

become-PRES+3 INDCLN

'Does it happen to you also?

In example (1), it is observed that the interrogative term *neki* has been replaced by the term '*niki*'. This phenomenon can be analyzed under the process of distant assimilation where one sound becomes more similar, a change in a sound brought about by the influence of a neighboring sound. Here, the front close unrounded vowel phoneme/sound *i* has influenced the front half-open unrounded vowel *e* and hence, *e* is being replaced by *i*. Again, sentences (2)-(4) shows that the term *neki* has taken the contracted form *ni* which can frequently be observed in the varieties spoken in Upper Assam primarily.

Insertion of ɹ

Some users insert ɹ, the phoneme representing the alveolar voiced approximant in Assamese, in the middle position, especially before *z*, the phoneme representing the voiced palatal fricative, as observed in:

5. *ɦahazjɔ > ɦahaɹzjɔ* 'help'

 ɦɔzja > ɦɔɹzja 'bed'
 pʰulɔɦɔzja >pʰulɔɦɔɹzja 'a bridal bed'

In Standard Assamese, such words do not take ɹ before z, but in social media this type of occurrence is common.

Replacement of b by w

In Assamese the finite verb in future as well as in the non-finite form of verb, the sound *b*, the phoneme representing the voiced unaspirated bilabial stop in Assamese, is used with verb root, which is observed being replaced by *w*, the phoneme indicating the voiced bilabial semi-vowel. The following instances will prove the finding:

6. teʊ kɔtʰa-kʰini

3sg(HON) matter-CL.PL

kɔ-wɔ kʰʊz-il-e

speak-NON.FIN want-PST-3

'He wanted to speak about the matter.'

7. *manuh-zɔn g ɔɹ-ɔloi za-wɔ*

man-CL.SG homeDAT go-FUT+3

'The man will go home.'

8. apuni kailoi lɔ-wɔ

2SG(HON) tomorrow take-NON.FIN
paɹ-e
can-PRES+2(HON)
'You can take tomorrow.'

The words *kɔbɔ* (5), *zawɔ* (6) and *lɔwɔ* (7) are used as *kɔbɔ*, *zabɔ* and *lɔbɔ* in Standard Assamese and thus it is seen that the phoneme *w* has replaced *b* on Facebook.

Findings

Sample 1 and Sample 2, presented in Table 2, exhibit how the users have replaced *i* by *e* and *w* by *b* respectively.

Table 2. Data related to phonological change

Sample	Word limit	Changes	Number
Sample 1	7	ʊ > u	
		u > ʊ	
		e > i	1
		b > w	
		Insertion of ɹ	
Sample 2	8	ʊ > u	
		u > ʊ	
		e > i	
		b > w	1
		Insertion of ɹ	

CHANGES OBSERVED AT THE GRAMMATICAL LEVEL

This section looks at the changes that the users have made in the sentence structure. The typical changes seen in the expressions are not only associated with the processes of insertion, deletion and substitution, but also with the addition of some loan words in the sentences which have partially affected the grammar of this language. The changes are observed occurring at both morphological and syntactic levels which cover two important aspects in analyzing and describing a language. The following is a brief discussion of the areas where transformations occur.

At Morphological Level

The changes at morphological level can be noticed in the word-formation process in Assamese. The uses of nominative case marker, the adverbial marker and the dative case-marker are the three main areas which are observed being affected by the changes on Facebook at the morphological level.

Changes Observed in Using the Nominative Case-Marker

The use of nominative case-marker primarily depends on the adjacent word in Assamese. Assamese permits two forms to function as nominative case-markers: *i* and *e*, and the use of these forms depend on a condition whether the root/stem is consonant-ending or vowel- ending and accordingly the resultant words exhibit morphophonemic changes after suffixing the nominative marker to the roots or the stems. But this type of agreement between the root word /stem and the case- marker is not observed in many words on Facebook. For example,

Table 3. Morphophonemic changes after suffixing nominative case-markers

Roo t word	Root/stem with nominative case-marker	Morphophonemic change	Standa rd As.	Form used on Facebook
bɔhɔntɔ 'a name'	*bɔhɔntɔ+ i*	*i = i*	*bɔhɔntɔi*	*bɔhɔntɔje*
saɹisɔku 'two pairs of eyes'	*saɹisɔku+e*	*e > we*	*saɹisɔk uwe*	*saɹisɔkuje*
edmi n tim 'the admi n team'	*edmin tim+e*	*e = e*	*edmin time*	*edmin timje*
ɔnɯaɖa 'a name'	*ɔnɯaɖa+i*	*i = i*	*ɔnɯaɖ ai*	*ɔnɯaɖaje*
zeneɹesj ɔntʊ 'the generation'	*zeneɹesjɔntʊ +e*	*e > we*	*zeneɹes jɔn tʊwe*	*zeneɹesjɔntʊje*

The examples presented in Table 3 illustrate that the forms signaling the nominative case-marker turn to *je* after suffixation in the writings on Facebook. It can be observed here that *e, we* and *i* all the allomorphs of the nominative case marker have been treated as *e, we* and *i* in Standard Assamese, while the users on Facebook have used only *je* form. It should be mentioned here that when the root morpheme ends with the vowel -*i*, then, after adding nominative case marker it turns to *je* in Standard Assamese, as in:

maɖuɹi + e = maɖuɹije
Madhuri+ nom. = 'Madhuri'
pɔllɔbi + e = pɔllabije
Pallabi + nom. = Pallabi and so on.

But recent writings on Facebook exhibit the fact that the users have suffixed je without considering the consonant-ending and vowel-ending status of the root word.

Changes Observed in Using the Adverbializer

Assamese allows a particular marker –*koi* which can be suffixed to the root/stem to convert adjectives or adverb to another adverb. But on facebook, it is observed that –*ke* has been used alternatively in the place of –*koi*. The application of this form is presented with example in Table 4:

Table 4. The use of the adverbializer

Root	Root with adverbializer	Standard Assamese	Form used on Facebook
b̪al 'good'	b̪al+koi	b̪alkoi 'in a good manner'	b̪alke
gʊpa '(of eyes) sunken'	g ʊpa+koi	g ʊpakoi 'angrilly with contracted or wrinked eyelids'	g ʊpake
kiba 'unusual, something else'	kiba+koi	kibakoi 'somehow'	kibake

Another change, which has been observed only in one word, can also be mentioned here. A very limited number of users, specially from the areas belonging to Upper Assam use an allomorph of the instrumental case marker in Assamese, i.e. ɹe as adverbializer. For example:

9.   b̪al-eɹe tʰak-a

      good-ADVLZR stay-IMP
      'Stay well'

This may be considered a case of syncretism, the merging of different inflectional varieties of a word during the development of a language. But this use is very restricted and spoken only in some specific regions, and also there is no supportive evidence to observe whether this is an adverbializer or the users are using the instrumental marker to express the adverb of manner here.

Change Observed in Using the Dative Case-Marker

The dative case-marker in Assamese –*loi* is seen replaced by –*le* by a group of users of the Facebook. It can be illustrated with the help of the examples presented in Table 4:

Table 5. The use of the dative case-marker

Root/stem	Root/stem with dative case-marker	Standard Assamese	Form found in Facebook
gaʊbuɹ 'the villages'	gaʊbuɹ+loi	gaʊbuɹɔloi 'to the villages'	gaʊbuɹle
mul kɔtʰa 'the main issue'	mul kɔtʰa+loi	mul kɔtʰaloi 'to the main issue'	mul kɔtʰale
ebaɹ 'once'	ebaɹ+loi	ebaɹɔloi 'for once'	ebaɹle

The examples provided in the Table clearly show that the users apply –*le* in place of –*loi* which signals the function of the dative case-marker. It has been observed that people belonging to almost all parts of Assam frequently use the suffix -*le* in conversation and so the use might have the impact on the Assamese youth and unconsciously they are reflecting it through their writings. Some people also write the word without using the dative case-marker, as observed in:

10. mɔi guwahati za-m
     1SG Guwahati go- FUT+1
     'I'll go to Guwahati.'
11. ɦi gɔɹ gol
     3SG (NON.HON) home go+PST+3
     'He went home.'

The dative case-marker *-loi* should be added to the terms *guwahati* and *g ɔɹ* in sentences (8) and (9) respectively and the correct forms are: *guwahatiloi and g ɔɹɔloi.*

Another important point noticed in the use of the dative case-marker is that a group of users apply the locative case- marker *–t/-ɔt* in place of dative case marker. The following examples will prove the findings:

12. manuh-zɔn daktɔɹ-ɔɹ tat gol
     man-CL.SG doctor-GEN there go+PST+3
     'The man went to visit the doctor.'
13. ɔŋkita g ɔɹ-ɔt za-b-ɔ
     Ankita home-LOC go-FUT-3
     'Ankita will go home.'

The word *tat* in sentence (11) can also be analysed as 'that+loc' and thus in standard Assamese the words should contain the suffix *-loi* instead of *-t/-ɔt*. The proper forms are as follows:

daktɔɹɔɹ taloi 'to the doctor'
gɔɹɔloi 'to the house'

This type of usage is very common for the people of Central and Lower Assam which has now prominently been observed on Facebook.

The Use of Shortening

The adverb *ekebare* 'completely' is observed to have been used in a reduced form *eke* in some expressions but in the same sense that the term *ekebare* carries in Standard Assamese. For example,

14. *bɔliud mubi eke gʊtei-kʰɔn*
     Bollywood movie completely all-CL.SG
     'This is all a Bollywood movie.'
15. gɔɹ eke bɔɹai di-se
     home completely full+CAUS give- IMPV+ PRES+3
     'The house is fully filled up.'

The term eke, in Assamese, is used in words which are identical or similar in nature. There is a possibility that a group of users on Facebook might use eke as a contracted form of ekebare as there is a scope of comparing the things when eke is used in certain contexts.

Change Observed in the Use of Non-Finite Form -bɔloi

Assamese permits the suffix bɔloi to function as a non-finite form, that cannot perform action as the root of an independent clause, in the language. This form has widely been used as *bɔle* by a large group of users, as observed in:

16. *tak ɦʊwa-bɔle sesta kɔɹ-il-e*
    3SG+ACC sleep-CAUS-NON.FIN try do-PST-3SG
    'She has tried to make him sleep.
17. *ɹam ḅat kʰa-bɔle gɔɹ-ɔle gol*
    Ram rice eat-NON.FIN home-DAT go + PST
    'Ram went home to have his meal.'

   It should be mentioned here that for the speakers from Upper Assam, the term *-bɔle* is a frequently occurring form and instead of using bɔloi, they use bɔle in their conversation.

At Syntactic Level

A limited number of common types of changes are observed at sentence level, especially in the formation of the verb phrase. These changes can be analyzed from two perspectives at the sentence level, first, when the users apply loan words in a native context; and second, when they try to reform the subject-verb agreement.

   The youth flawlessly practice code-mixing, an intrasentential phenomenon, that refers to the mixing of various linguistic units from two participatory grammatical system in the same utterance. The data elicited also leads to the striking change seen in the relative clause structure. The following discussion deals with various types of reformations observed at verb phrase as well as in relative clause structures:

Insertion of Copula hɔ 'to be'

In Assamese, the finite form of the copula *hɔ* occurs in some specific conditions, such as, in negative form of the verb, or in Tag questions, or in declarative sentences only in some limited context. In other situations, it remains in covert position. But some users on facebook apply *hɔ* in finite verb form carrying the marker of the simple present tense overtly in the contexts where it is not supposed to be used. For example:

18. *a. kʊn, kʊn?*
    who, who
    'Who is there?'
    [Standard Assamese]
       b.   *kʊn, kʊn hɔj?*
    who, who be +PRES+3
    'Who is there?'
    [Facebook use]
19. *a. tai mʊr spesijel frend*

3SG(NON.HON) 1SG+GEN spesijel frend

'She is my special friend.'

[Standard Assamese]

      b.   tai mʊr spesijel frend hɔj

3SG(NON.HON) 1SG +GEN special friend be+PRES+3

'She is my special friend.'

[Facebook use]

The sentences above exhibit that *hɔj* has been used in the written form on Facebook. Most of the Assamese youths use *hɔj* while they interact with one another and their informal use of *hɔj* might influence their writings. This might also be due to the fact that Assamese youths are exposed to English and Hindi language more and both the languages permit a linking verb to occur in that position.

Insertion of e in the Verb Form in Final Position

Assamese is a language that exhibits subject-verb agreement which is actually a consequence of introducing the concept of transitivity through the verb when the nominative case-marker is applied to the word functioning as subject. If the finite verb is a transitive one, in Assamese, it takes the suffix e in final position in the verb forms in Simple past, as in:

20.   *ɹam-e bag̣ -tʊ maɹ-il-e*

      Ram-NOM tiger-CL.SG kill-PST-3

      'Ram killed the tiger.'

21.   *ɹaḍa-i ḅat kʰa-l-e*

      Radha-NOM rice eat-PST-3

      'Radha took her meal.'

Again, with intransitive verbs, *e* is not used, as observed in the examples below:

22.   *ɹam ah-il*

      Ram come-PST+3

      'Ram came.'

23.   *ɹaḍa bɔh-il*

      Radha sit down-PST+3

      'Radha sat down.'

But this rule has not been followed by some users on Facebook as they have been observed applying e in final position irrespective of the fact that in Assamese it can be suffixed to the transitive verbs only, with the exception in case of the verb root *ħʊ* 'to sleep.' The analysis of the verbal constituents given below will indicate this:

24.   *teʊ baḍa de-is-ile*

      3 SG(HON) protest give-IMPV-PST+3

      'He protested.'

(Correct form :*disil*)

25. *pɹita-ɹ sɔɹdi lag-ile*
    Prita-GEN cold get-PST+3
    'Prita got a cold.'
    (Correct form : *lagil*)

26. *ɦi hɔtʰat utʰ-ile*
    3SG(NON.HON) suddenly get up-PST+3
    'He got up suddenly.'
    (Correct form: *utʰil*)

Use of Loan Words in Verb Phrase

It has become a common trait to use English terms frequently in Assamese sentence even if most of those loan words have their equivalent terms in Assamese. For example:

27. *gilti fil kɔɹ-i as-ʊ*
    guilty feel do-CONJT IMPV-PRES +1
    'I am feeling guilty.'
    (St. As. *dʊɦi anubɔb kɔɹi asʊ*, where guilty feel = *dʊɦi anubɔb*)

28. *inzeksɔn-tʊ pus kɔɹ-a*
    injection-CL.SG push do-PRES+2(fam)
    'Push the injection.'
    (St. As. : *inzeksɔn/bezitʊ ɦumuwai dija*, where 'to push' = *ɦumuwai de*)

29. *lait pʰud kʰa-bɔ di-bɔ*
    light food eat-NON.FIN give-FUT+2(hon)
    'Offer (him) some light food.'
    (St. As. : *patɔlija ahaɹ kʰabɔ diba*, where 'light food' = *patɔlija ahaɹ*)

30. *ɹest kɔɹ-i lɔ-a*
    rest do-CONJT take-PRES+2(fam)
    'Take some rest.'
    (St. As. : *ziɹɔni lʊwa*, 'to take rest' = *ziɹɔni lɔ*)

31. *signel di-s-e*
    signal give-IMPV-PRES+3
    '(Someone) has given a signal.'
    (St. As. : *ɦɔŋket dise*, where 'to give a signal' = *ɦɔŋket de*)

32. *dɹes ɹedi kɔɹ-il-ʊ*
    dress ready do-PST-1
    'I made my dress ready.'
    (St. As. : *kapɔɹ ɦazu kɔrilʊ*, where 'to make a dress ready' = *kapɔɹ ɦazu kɔr*)

The verbal constituents in the examples given above show that though the users apply the loan words, they somehow try to relate the words in some particular contexts where the verb in Assamese can convey the proper meaning. It has been noticed that the users, while trying to apply loan items in native construction, especially in verb phrase, have used a particular verb root *kɔɹ* 'to do' in Assamese. Example (30) also has another structure which is more common in day-today use and also on social media:

33. *ɹest lɔ-a*

rest take-PRES+2(FAM)
'Take some rest.'

   The examples given above also reveal the fact that the language shift is a very common and natural phenomenon in using any language.

The Use of Loan Words in Native Context

It has been observed that a very limited number of users are applying English verbs by using those as verb roots and making them causative and in doing so, they are suffixing some forms used in Assamese to the borrowed items which can make the loan words causative. The examples provided below illustrate the smooth blending of English and Assamese observed in informal kind of conversation found specially in youth language practices:

34. pʰɔtʊ-kʰɔn aplʊd-abɔ mɔn gol
    photo-CL.SG upload-CAUS mind *go*+PST+*3*
    'I felt like uploading the photo.'
35. *mʊk iman teg-a-i na-tʰak-ib-i*
    1SG+ACC so much tag-CAUS-NON.FIN NEG-stay-FUT2(NON.HON)
    'Don't tag me so much.'

   The sentences (34) and (35) above two non-finite verb forms: *aplʊdabɔ* and *tegai* The root morphemes are the English terms: upload and tag. These forms have been tried to give a native structure by adding two non-finite suffixes to them- *bɔ* and *i*. Again, in case of *aplʊdabɔ* it has been observed that it is not possible to use the non-finite form *bɔ* to a non-native root morpheme and hence a causative suffix a has been added to the root form first and then only the non-finite form has been suffixed to the base form *aplʊda*. In case of tag also, the same phonemic situation can be observed. But if the root word is an Assamese verb, then only the non-finite form can be added to the verb form, as in:

kɔɹ $_+$ *ibɔ =kɔɹibɔ* 'to do'
do+ non.fin
kʰa + *bɔ* = *kʰabɔ* 'to eat'
eat + non.fin

The youth use linguistic resources not only from English, but also from Hindi, as observed in:

36. *fesbuk hila-i de-l-i*
    Facebook shake-NON.FIN give-PST-2NON.HON
    '(You) shook the Facebook.'
37. *skuti-kʰɔn-ɔɹ kɔmi as-e*

scooty-CL.SG-GEN lack be-3PRES
'Only scooty is not available here.'

It has been observed here that in (36), the non-finite form *i* is suffixed to the Hindi verb root *hila* whereas, *kɔmi* in (37) has been used as the original Hindi version without any modification to it and it is functioning as an important part of the predicate which contains a pure Assamese verb form *ase*.

Replacement of Standard Form by Dialectal Variation

As far as the dialectal variation in Assam is concerned, all the dialects of Assamese can be broadly divided into two groups, Eastern Assamese and Western Assamese.(Kakati, p.16) . The phonological and morphological features of the dialects reveal that the Eastern Assamese dialect may also be divided into two groups, the Eastern and the Central dialects, and thus the dialect of Assamese may be regrouped as three major dialect groups, namely, Eastern, Central and Western. (Goswami & Tamuli, p.399-400). But each of these dialect groups is an assimilation of several varieties and on Facebook, it is observed that the speakers of many of those varieties are sharing their ideas and views through the language varieties they use at home. Examples of such groups are : *'ami bozeiɹa'*, *'ami nɔlbeiɹa'*, *'kʰati dɔɹɔŋɔɹ zija likiɹa'* etc. Though they select their local varieties to communicate with their ideas in these groups, some users have been observed applying some non-standard forms while writing something in Standard Assamese. This is illustrated below:

38. bɔɹɔhun-e biz-ai-s-e
     rain-NOM wet-CAUS-IMPV-PRES+3
     'The rain has wetted (someone).'
     (St. As. *tijaise*)
39. bɔɹɔhun-ɔt biz-i gol
     rain-LOC wet-CONJT go+PST+3
     'It got wet in the rain.'
     (St. As. *titi gol)*
40. bɔɹi-kʰɔn laɹ-ile-i bih-aj
     leg-CL.SG touch-NON.FIN-EMP pain-PRES+3
     'My leg hurts the moment I touch it.'
     (St As. *sulei*)

In the instances cited above it is clearly observed how the forms used in different dialects are being applied to the markers and the resultant words are being used in formal contexts. It is worth mentioning here that the Standard Assamese language emerged from the Sibsagar variety of Assam (i.e. *hibɔxagɔɹija upɔbaħa*) and hence the varieties of Upper Assam region are nearer to Standard Assamese. A vast difference can be observed between Upper Assam and Lower Assam varieties not only in their vocabulary, but also in their use of the language. The writings of Facebook reflect this difference and though most of the users are aware of the fact that they are using an open platform for delivering their thoughts and ideas, still due to the influence of their varieties, they, sometimes use the words from their varieties. Another observation can be noted here that the users do not use their words as they use it in informal talking, but unconsciously they replace the word with their local form keeping the whole structure just like the same that should be in Standard Assamese. In the words *ḅiz-ai-s-e*, *ḅiz-i gol* and *laɹ-ile-i* in (38), (39) and (40), only the root morphemes *ḅiz* and *laɹ* are words used in lower Assam varieties, but the words are structured grammatically based on the patterns observed in Standard Assamese. These forms in dialectal variations would be something like : *ḅizɔlak* (*ḅizaise*), *ḅizi gel* (*ḅizi gol*) and *lalli* (*laɹilei*).

It has been perceived that basically in dialect groups, available on Facebook, the primary aim of the users is to preserve their own forms at phonological and syntactic levels. So they try to maintain the distinct forms to reflect the uniqueness of their particular varieties through their writings. But, though they are aware of the fact that when they express something in an open forum, that should represent the Standard Assamese version, still sometimes they use some of the words from their own varities. This may be due to their spontaneous response and also sometimes, due to the lack of proper grammatical knowledge of the language.

Use of -ha :

Assamese permits the use of *-ha*, an interjection denoting surprise, in spoken form as it is an expression used more in informal situation. But it is observed that *-ha* is used in the written form formally on Facebook, as in :

41. kijɔ gɔ-is-il-i,
    why go-IMPV-PST-2(NON.HON),
    sɔr kʰa-bɔloi ha ?
    slap eat-NON.FIN is it?
    'Why did you go there, to get slapped, is it?'
42. *tɔi tai-k nɔ-kɔ-bi ha*
    2SG(NON.HON) 3SG(NON.HON)-ACC NEG speak-FUT-2 ok
    'Don't disclose the matter to her, okay?'

Though basically ha as an expression of astonishment, when used in casual conversation, it simply can be treated as a vocative term, as observed in sentences (41) and (42).

Change in Relative Clause Structure

A relative clause is a subordinate clause introduced by a relative pronoun or adverb that gives further information about someone or something in the main clause. In Assamese, relative clauses begin with relative pronouns such as *zi* 'who', *zot* 'where', *zak* 'whom', *zaɹ* 'whose' etc. But it is observed that some users on Facebook use a term neki which is an indeclinable word used for making interrogative question just after the relative pronoun and it is clearly illustrated in the given examples:

43. ħei-ħɔkɔl loɹa-loi zi neki
    that-CL.PL boy-DAT who INDCL
    ɡ ɔɹ-ɔɹ pɔɹa duɹoit tʰak-e
    home-GEN POSTP far+ LOC stay-PRES+3
    '(It is) to all those boys who stay away from their homes.'
44. pʰesbuk etija ene eta madjɔm

facebook now such one medium

hoi go-is-e

become+NON.FIN go-IMPV-PRES+3

zot neki misa kotʰa ɦɔsa aɹu

where INDCL false matter true and

ɦɔsa kotʰa misa kɔr-ibɔ paɹ-e

true matter false do-NON.FIN can-PRES+3

'Facebook has become such a medium now through which one can make false matters true and vice versa.'

45. *ɦei loɹa-buɹ-ɔloi zi-je*

that boy-CL.PL-DAT who-NOM

neki g ɔɹ-ɔt pani e-gilas-ʊ

INDCL home-LOC water one-glass-EMP

nize loi na-kʰa-j

own take+ NON.FIN NEG-eat-PRES+3

'(It is) to all those boys who don't even take a glass of water on their own.'

The examples (43-45) make it clear that the relative pronouns *zi, zot* and *zije* take *neki* after the term which is not acceptable in Standard Assamese. Examples also would be found on Facebook with other types of relative constructions such as, *zoɹpɹa neki* 'from where' (St. Ass. *zoɹpɹa*), *zoloi neki* 'to where' (St. Ass. *zoloi*) and so on.

Findings

In Table 6, we see that from Sample 3, there are significant numbers of adverbializer and dative case markers present.

Similarly, from Sample 7 and Sample 8, presented in Table 7, we see that there are several loan words in native context and loan words in verb phrase.

Table 6. Data related to morphological change

Sample	Word count	Changes (observed in the use of)	Number
Sample3	110	nominative case marker	0
		adverbializer	1
		dative case marker	4
		shortening	0
		non-finite-*bɔloi*	2
Sample 4	202	nominative case marker	0
		adverbializer	1
		dative case marker	6
		shortening	0
		non-finite-*bɔloi*	2
Sample 5	4	nominative case marker	0
		adverbializer	0
		dative case marker	0
		shortening	1

Table 7. Data related to syntactic change

Sample	Word count	Changes	Number
Sample 6	12	using copula	0
		Insertion of *e*	1
		Loan words in VP	0
		Loan words in native context	0
		Replacement by dialectal variation	0
		Use of *ha*	0
		Relative clause structure	0
Sample 7	23	Loan words in native context	2
Sample 8	35	Loan words in VP	3

CONCLUSION

The change in Assamese on Facebook, in this study, has been considered in different sections and sub-sections in terms of its occurrence at the various levels of the language, with special attention to its occurrence at the levels of phonology, morphology and syntax. The elements associated with the use of Assamese on Facebook are found to occur frequently both in the formal style as well as in the informal style of the language. It is seen that an increasing number of changes has been occurred in the literary activities among the online Assamese youth communities. It may be because of the fact that the users find it convenient to express them in simple language which they are used to. The use of local as well as spoken varieties in sentence level may be due to the unawareness of the users or the lack of proper grammatical knowledge about the language. As languages change over time and changes are the reflections of the user's performance of a language in use, both grammatical and linguistic performances play great roles in bringing novelty to a language. A large group of Assamese people, especially the Assamese youths are well-exposed to social media for whom social media is a key to learn and improve their skills. It is used by individual speakers who wish to communicate in the target language in a natural environment. Besides functioning as a medium of communication, social media such as Twitter, Facebook, You Tube etc. have been used by generations to gain knowledge. Social media is having an impact on language and it is true in case of Assamese language also. The words that surround the users every day influence them and its impact can be observed in the words which the users use to express their feelings, thoughts and ideas. The situation is something which can lead the users, mainly the young generation to communicate with each other in a more informal way rather than express their ideas through formal writing. This results in a form which might be the combination of informal, personal communication and formal style already exists in the grammatical rule of the language. This type of change in the use of language can be observed not only in Facebook, it can be observed in other tools also which are a part of digital communication. Acronyms, abbreviations and neologisms has grown up and they are influencing the use of Assamese language day by day. Though this study primarily focuses on the changes observed in the grammatical patterns of the language, two important areas relating to language change has also been observed while dealing with the data found on Facebook. These are : code-switching and code-mixing. Code-mixing is observed when someone uses one word or phrase from one language to another language, as already observed in sentence (37), arranging the Hindi word *kɔmi* with the Assamese verb *ase*. Again code-switching is a linguistic phenomenon that occurs when a speaker alternates between two or more languages in the context of a single conversation or situation. In some writings on Facebook code-switching occurs and it has been observed that in novels or short stories this type of situation arises. But as this alternation does not affect the grammatical structure of Assamese language, so this type of language behavior has not been treated in this study. Whatever be the reason behind the changes observed on Facebook regarding Assamese language, the changes are being observed to bring newness to the formal and well-established style of writings in Assamese language.

Abbreviation

1-first person ; 2- second person ; 3- third person; ACC- accusative ; CAUS- causative ; CL- classifier ; CONJT- conjunctive ; DAT- dative ; EMP- emphatic ; FAM -familiar ; FUT- future ; GEN- genitive ; HON- honorific ; IMP- imperative IMPV- imperfective ; INDCL- indeclinable ; LOC- locative ; NOM- nominative ; NON.FIN- non. finite ; NON.HON- non.honorific ; PL- plural; POSTP- post position PRES- present ; PST- past ; SG- singular

Symbols and Notational Conventions

The list of the IPA symbols of Assamese segmental phonemes used to examine data:

a.   Vowels:
  1.   i Front close unrounded vowel
  2.   e Front half-open unrounded vowel

3. a Front open unrounded vowel
4. ɔ Back open rounded vowel
5. o Back half-open rounded vowel
6. ʊ Back half-close rounded vowel
7. u Back close rounded vowel

b. Consonants:

1. p Voiceless unaspirated bilabial stop
2. Pʰ Voiceless aspirated bilabial stop
3. b Voiced unaspirated bilabial stop
4. b̤ Voiced breathy bilabial stop
5. t Voiceless unaspirated alveolar stop
6. tʰ Voiceless aspirated alveolar stop
7. d Voiced unaspirated alveolar stop
8. d̤ Voiced breathy alveolar stop
9. k Voiceless unaspirated velar stop
10. kʰ Voiceless aspirated velar stop
11. g Voiced unaspirated velar stop
12. g̤ Voiced breathy velar stop
13. m Voiced bilabial stop
14. n Voiced alveolar nasal
15. ŋ Voiced velar nasal
16. s Voiceless palatal fricative
17. z Voiced palatal fricative
18. h Voiced glottal fricative
19. ɹ Voiced alveolar approximant
20. l Voiced alveolar lateral
21. w Voiced bilabial semi-vowel
22. j Voiced alveolar semi-vowel
23. ħ Voiceless pharyngeal fricative

Notational conventions:

1. The data has been represented by following the standard procedure of interlinearization. This is done in the form of a three-line presentation, i.e, the data line shown by using IPA symbols, the morpheme-by-morpheme gloss line and the free translation line. In some places where morpheme-by-morpheme gloss line is considered to be redundant, the data is accompanied only by the free translation.
2. In-text examples of Assamese words are given in italics.
3. English translations of Assamese constructions are given within single inverted comma.(' ')
4. There are certain cases where some particular words are not divided into smaller constituent parts, i.e, the base or root form has not been indicated. In such cases the sequence has been treated as words, not morphemes, and those words are indicated with a '+' sign while glossing.

ACKNOWLEDGMENT

I am very much indebted to Professor Jyotiprakash Tamuli, the Head of the Department of Linguistics, Gauhati University for suggesting me the topic and offering invaluable guidance and support. I would like to thank Dr. Naba K. Sarma, Assistant Professor, Kanya Mahavidyalaya, Guwahati, for his constant help and encouragement.

REFERENCES

Chowdhary, R. (1995). *Assamese Verbs: A Study in the Structural Paradigm.* ABILAC.

Das, B. (2010). Axamiya Bhasha. In Axamiya Aru Axamar Bhasha. Aank-Baak.

Goswami, G. C. (2004). *Asamiya Byakaranar Moulik bichar.* Bina Library.

Goswami, G. C., & Tamuli, J. (2003). Asamiya. In The Indo-Aryan Languages. Routledge.

Goswami, U. N. (1991). *Asamiya Bhashar Byakaran* (1st ed.). Baruah Agency.

Heruntergeladen, K. (1941). *Assamese its Formation and Development.* Department of Historical and Antiquarian Studies, Government of Assam.

Hollington & Nassenstein. (2018). *African Youth language practices and social media.* De Gruyter.

Sharma, S. (2014) Transition of English Language through Media and Social Networking. *Scholarly Research Journal of Interdisciplinary Studies*, 2(14). https://www.time8.in/new-decline-trend-only-1-26-per-cent-of-indias-population-speak-assamese/

Chapter 14
"Serendipity Engineering for Seductive Hypermedia" and "User Analysis Using Socialnomics":
Enhancing Understanding Using Ecological Cognition

Jonathan Bishop
https://orcid.org/0000-0002-9919-7602
Crocels Community Media Group, UK

Mark M. H. Goode
Cardiff University, UK

ABSTRACT

This chapter expends the application of the ecological cognition framework to serendipity engineering, seductive hypermedia, user analysis, and socialnomics. It updates the theory to better account for the advances in computational science computational intelligence. In terms of 'serendipity engineering for seductive hypermedia', the chapter looks at how to design information systems to account for the pleasant occurrences that happen in offline environments studied by those in sales and marketing where beneficial outcomes often occur by chance encounters. In terms of 'user analysis using socialnomics', it looks at how a parametric user model based on the ecological framework can be used to understand users of information systems. To do this, a number of socialnomics equations based on the parametric user model are explored, including to calculate probability of seduction and probability of serendipity in an information system. The parametric model presented has great applicability for information and communications technology solution providers.

DOI: 10.4018/978-1-7998-9795-8.ch014

INTRODUCTION

It has been argued that one of the greatest challenges in intelligent systems design is to harness "technologies to verify and apply longstanding theories from distributed AI, agent systems, and other areas of networked intelligent systems research" (Willmott, 2004). It has been argued that intelligent systems research is required to "prevent users being overwhelmed by the complexity of the systems with which they will be asked to interact" (Steventon & Wright, 2010). One approach to intelligent systems research is to designing intelligent systems that think and act like humans (de Lope, 2007) is ecological cognition (Bishop & Goode, 2021).

Ecological Cognition

An essential premise of ecological cognition is that the world which we observe is socially constructed from how we perceive it and we then construct an alternative reality, whether it be called our uncon-

Figure 1. The 8-Base ecological cognition framework

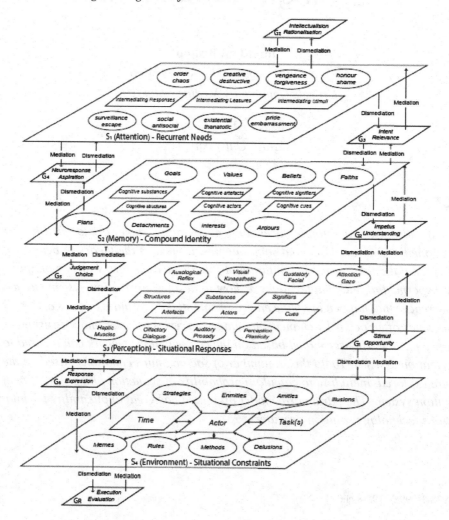

scious or sub-conscious, that is more consistent with the reality we would prefer to perceive (Bishop, 2007; Hutchins, 2000; Jensen, Thomas W., 2017; Jensen, Thomas Wiben & Greve, 2019; Johansson Falck, 2018). Through using these, how our reality is constructed can be described, including by drawing on the dedicated multimedia studies literature, such as that recommended elsewhere (Cunliffe & Elliott, 2005). The most recent ecological cognition framework is presented in Figure 1 is associated with a parametric user model in Equation 1 (Bishop & Goode, 2021; Bishop, Kommers, & Bechkoum, In Press), which provides an exemplary means to create intelligent systems even compared to earlier embodiments (Bishop, 2013).

Serendipity Engineering

It has been argued that Serendipity Engineering *"builds upon randomness, interaction, chaos and complexity for innovative aspects and directions to be identified and taken advantage in favour of the user. In this way, serendipity and unintended outcomes can be manipulated to orchestrate pleasant surprises"* (Lambropoulos, Fardoun, & Alghazzawi, 2016). Serendipity Engineering builds upon randomness, interaction, chaos and complexity (Lambropoulos et al., 2016).

BACKGROUND

The discipline of ecological cognition (EC) can be applied through serendipity engineering for seductive hypermedia and user analysis using socialnomics (SESH-UAUS). This can be done by making use of the parametric user model, including to produce k-scores for use with statistical packages like SPSS (Field, 2005) in order to advance computational science and computational intelligence. The parametric user model in Equation 1 below places phantasy construction as an esteem need and fantasy construction as a deficit need. The equation assumes that psychological nutritional intake (n) is half that (0.5) of what is needed for an optimal cognitive state with consonance reflected as a joinder (j) of 1. Therefore, for an optimal state, where Ob is 48 and knol is 1, nutritional intake needs to be multiplied by two to balance the two parts of the equation reflecting interval. Equation 1 therefore shows all aspects of the parametric user model as one equation for the calculation of knol (k), which is the speed of memory access. This it could be argued, along with the ecological cognition frameworks, is one of the main conceptual frameworks contributed by this paper. This can be seen as a progression of the earlier equations, where x1 has been replaced with ca_{eS}, y1 has been replaced with cb_{eS}, ž has been replaced with cc_{eS}, and c with c_{1eS}.

Equation 1 provides an easy way to turn questionnaire-based scales, or observational device-based scales into a parametric user model for analysing and influencing human behaviour (Bishop & Goode, 2021). The construction of information systems that impact on intervention (i), joinder (j) and nutrition (n) so as to influence the neurotransmitters resulting behavioural consequences of doing so could be an important part of situation ecological cognition in a digital economy. This could happen in online communities, where users' behaviour can be analysed and influenced using log data or other ways of attributing the values of the parametric user model. Equally, it could happen in organic communities, where actors sharing the same physical space could have their different levels of wakefulness accounted for by using physical sensors, including those based on the Internet of Things, to analyse and influence their behaviour. In order for this to be done, it is necessary to understand how the parametric user model might operate in large-scale virtual environments.

$$k_a = \left\{ \begin{array}{l} C_{min} \\ E_S \\ C_{max} \end{array} \left[\frac{\displaystyle\sum_{e=0}^{M} \left(\frac{\left(\left(x_{GS2} + c\breve{a}_{eS} \right) * \left(y_{GS2} + c\breve{b}_{eS} \right) - c\breve{c}_{eS} \right) / \left(i_S + j_S \right))_e}{c_{eS}} \right)}{5} + F \\ \frac{\displaystyle\sum_{d=0}^{D} \left(\frac{\left(\left(x_{GS2} + c\breve{a}_{dS} \right) + \left(z_{GS4} + c\breve{b}_{dS} \right) - c\breve{c}_{dS} \right) * 2n_S)_d}{2c_{dS}} \right)}{2.5} + Ob \right] \right\}$$

Equation 1. A parametric user model for calculating 'knol' for a given actor (k_a) using the ecological cognition framework (a theory of ordinary memory)

USING THE PARAMETRIC USER MODEL TO UNDERSTAND SERENDIPITY AND SEDUCTION AMONG USERS OF LARGE-SCALE VIRTUAL ENVIRONMENTS

A LSVE based on the parametric user model be used to determine whether the group of users are likely to form part of a successful online community where opportunities for genuine serendipity could occur due to them being around fewer disagreeable actors. This could be done by measuring the standard deviation (SD) between the k-scores for each group (M_C) so that the lower the SD, the greater the chance that all the actors within that community (N_C) will have positive relationships. This is the principle of empathism (Bishop, May 19 2013). People with empathism have a common way of thinking towards other actors like them and often in opposition to actors unlike them (Bishop, May 19 2013; Bolognini, 1997) and so using Equation 1 with Equation 2 could allow for the selection of actors so that they form online communities of like-minded people, regardless of whether those communities are toxic (Leavitt, 2017).

Equation 2 shows how one might compute the mean knol for a specific online community of actors (M_{Ce}) within a community (N_C) (Bishop & Goode, 2021). In this context the N_C could refer to an online community being analysed using a management information system (MIS) with the purpose of seeing whether there is a difference in k-scores between the six different communities. The k-score would be calculated by applying the TIWWCHNT-20 Scale (Bishop, 2014) to a sample of actors and then assigning as y-values all the statements in the factor they score highest in, which would determine the community they belong to (N_C). The x value would be asking their position on the actor taking on the role of PUA in a given situation (S) in terms of their interest in them or detachment from them.

$$M_{Ce} = \sum_{S=1}^{N_C} \frac{k_S}{N_C}$$

Equation 2. Mean knol for an optimised (e) community (M_C) based on k-scores (k_s) for that community (N_C) in a given situation (S)

$$\hat{S}k = \frac{M_{Ck}}{0.98}$$

Equation 3. Probability of Serendipity ($\hat{S}k$) based on Mean knol for group ($k=M_{Ck}$) and serendipity threshold ($k=0.98$)

Equation 3 shows an alternative to standard deviation, namely the probability of serendipity ($\hat{S}k$) occurring based on dividing the Mean k-score for a given group by the serendipity threshold of 0.98 (Bishop & Goode, 2021). The further the Mean from the serendipity threshold, the less likely serendipity is to occur. This is based on the principle that on the one hand the more alike a community is the lower their individual k-scores need to be as a result of groupthink, meaning serendipity is less likely. On the other hand the more different a community is the less likely there are to be opportunities for serendipity to occur.

The serendipity threshold ($k=0.98$) in Equation 3 could be replaced with the intellectualisation threshold of 1.118 or the rationalisation threshold of 1.21, which in the case of the former would mean if M_c was at the serendipity threshold ($k=0.98$) the community would have a collective score of an average actor ($k=0.81$) or in the case of the latter would mean they would be exceeding their collective limits ($k=1.14$) as the optimal k-score for the human race would be 1 if the human brain had evolved to meet homomagnus equilibrium, but it is presently 0.81 in most people because it usually meets the Nash equilibrium where the remaining 0.19 accounts for factors like distrust and inability to resolve competing interests.

Achieving a k-score of 1 would mean a person would in effect be on auto-pilot and providing their cognitions are configured to act in their own interests at the same time as considering those of others then the homomagnus equilibrium could be maintained. However, in most cases where an actor experiences the homomagnus equilibrium of a knol of 1 it will be short lived, such as being briefly experienced after a moment of serendipity, where knol is 0.98.

$$`k = \left(\frac{\hat{S}k}{k_{Sa}} \right)$$

Equation 4. Probability of Seduction ($\check{S}k$) for an actor (k_{Sa}) based on probability of Serendipity ($\hat{S}k$)

Equation 4 presents an formula for measuring the probability of seduction ($\check{S}k$) in a given situation for a given actor (k_{Sa}) based on their k-score in that situation within the community of which they are part, which is computed in Equation 2 and Equation 3 (Bishop & Goode, 2021). The difference between seduction and serendipity is that the former tried to generate the same experiences as the latter, but the latter occurs by chance whereas the former occurs intentionally, usually by a party other than the one experiencing serendipity.

$$`k = \left(\left(\frac{\left(\sum_{S=1}^{N_C} \frac{k_S}{N_C} \right)}{\hat{S}t} \right) \bigg/ k_{Sa} \right)$$

Equation 5. A model for supporting 'serendipity engineering for seductive hypermedia' and 'user analysis using socialnomics'

Equation 5 combines Equation 2 to Equation 4 for calculating seduction (Šk) and introduces a new variable of serendipity threshold (Ŝt), which can be either 0.98 or another value as required, such as the intellectualisation threshold of 1.118 or the rationalisation threshold of 1.21 (Bishop & Goode, 2021). It can be seen that the k-score value produced by the parametric user model (Equation 1) is included twice. In the first instance as k_S it is included as part of the computation of the Mean k-scores for a given community (N_c) and on the second occasion as k_{Sa} it is included to refer to a specific actor being studied, such as a specific online community member being investigated by a clinical psychologist. Equation 5 therefore computes the probability of a specific actor being seduced into experiencing a feeling of serendipity, which is intentional and not by chance and thus is not actual serendipity even if it feels the same. However, it has been argued that linking serendipity to chance is only part of understanding it as a "plot" (De Rond, 2014). Such information can assist in assessing the risk of a given actor being drawn into situations that might feel desirable but would cause them harm, including the development of compulsive behaviours leading to digital addiction. To detect digital addiction a clinical psychologist could use the TIWWCHNT-20 scale (Bishop, 2014; Bishop, 2017) for determining phantasies and the digital addiction checklist (Bishop, 2015) for determining fantasies. By assisting with a diagnosis, a clinical psychologist can be of great assistance to an actor in managing their health (Fan, Lin, & Lin, 2015).

$$` k_{ag} = \left( \frac{100}{\left( median\left( \hat{Sk}_C \right) \right)} \right) *` k_o$$

Equation 6. Computing an actor's (a) higher order (g) Serendipity (Šk) probability (Škag) towards an artefact (o) based on median of organic Serendipity (Šk) responses to an object ($_o$) within a group ($_c$)

$$median(a) = \frac{a_{\lfloor (\#x+1)\div 2 \rfloor} + a_{\lceil (\#x+1)\div 2 \rceil}}{2}$$

Equation 7 Equation for calculating median (Courtesy: Wikimedia Foundation)

Equation 6 (Bishop & Goode, 2021) is used along with Equation 7 (Bishop & Goode, 2021) to compute the higher order thinking required to determine how able someone is to take advantage of a serendipitous event.

IMPLICATIONS AND FUTURE RESEARCH DIRECTIONS

Discussion

This chapter expends the application of the ecological cognition framework to serendipity engineering, seductive hypermedia, user analysis and socialnomics. It updates the theory to better account for the advances in computational science computational intelligence. In terms of 'serendipity engineering for seductive hypermedia,' the chapter looks at how to design information systems to account for the pleasant occurrences that happen in offline environments studied by those in sales and marketing where beneficial outcomes often occur by chance encounters. In terms of 'user analysis using socialnomics,' it looks at how a parametric user model based on the ecological framework can be used to understand users of information systems. To do this number of socialnomics equations based on the parametric user model are explored, including to calculate probability of seduction and probability of serendipity in an information system. The parametric model presented has great applicability for information and communications technology solution providers.

REFERENCES

Bishop, J. (2007). Ecological cognition: A new dynamic for human-computer interaction. In B. Wallace, A. Ross, J. Davies, & T. Anderson (Eds.), The mind, the body and the world: Psychology after cognitivism (pp. 327-345). Imprint Academic.

Bishop, J. (2013). Assisting human interaction (US/20130095460 ed.). US: PCT/GB2011/050814/A1.

Bishop, J. (2013). The empathic psychopathy in public life: Towards an understanding of 'autism' and 'empathism' and 'dopaminergic-serotonergic asynchronicity.' *Conference on the Implications of Research on the Neuroscience of Affect, Attachment, and Social Cognition.*

Bishop, J. (2014). Dealing with internet trolling in political online communities: Towards the this is why we can't have nice things scale. *International Journal of E-Politics, 5*(4), 1–20. doi:10.4018/ijep.2014100101

Bishop, J. (2015). Determining the risk of digital addiction to adolescent targets of internet trolling: Implications for the UK legal system. In J. Bishop (Ed.), *Psychological and social implications surrounding internet and gaming addiction* (pp. 31–42). IGI Global. doi:10.4018/978-1-4666-8595-6.ch003

Bishop, J. (2017). Developing and validating the "This is why we can't have nice things scale": Optimising political online communities for internet trolling. In Y. Ibrahim (Ed.), *Politics, protest, and empowerment in digital spaces* (pp. 153–177). IGI Global. doi:10.4018/978-1-5225-1862-4.ch010

Bishop, J., & Goode, M. M. H. (2021). Towards 'serendipity engineering for seductive hypermedia' and 'user analysis using socialnomics': The role of ecological cognition. *The 8th International Conference on Computational Science & Computational Intelligence (CSCI'21).*

Bishop, J., Kommers, P. A. M., & Bechkoum, K. (in press). Ecological cognition for measuring psi-hit and psi-miss online: Using K-scores to understand anomalistic psychology in project management teams. *International Journal of Innovation, Management and Technology.*

Bolognini, S. (1997). Empathy and 'empathism'. *The International Journal of Psycho-Analysis, 78*(2), 279–293.

Cunliffe, D., & Elliott, G. (2005). Multimedia computing. Lexden Publishing Ltd.

de Lope, J. (2007). Concepts and models for the future generation of emotional and intelligent systems. *International Work-Conference on the Interplay between Natural and Artificial Computation,* 41-50.

De Rond, M. (2014). The structure of serendipity. *Culture and Organization, 20*(5), 342–358. doi:10.1 080/14759551.2014.967451

Fan, S., Lin, W., & Lin, I. (2015). Psychosocial care and the role of clinical psychologists in palliative care. *The American Journal of Hospice & Palliative Care, 32*(8), 861–868. doi:10.1177/1049909114543492 PMID:25024459

Field, A. (2005). *Discovering statistics using SPSS (introducing statistical methods series)* (2nd ed.). Sage Publications Ltd.

Hutchins, E. (2000). Ecological cognition and cognitive ecology. *Proceedings of the Human Factors and Ergonomics Society Annual Meeting, 44*(22), 566-569.

Jensen, T. W. (2017). Doing metaphor: An ecological perspective on metaphoricity in discourse. *Metaphor: Embodied Cognition and Discourse,* 257.

Jensen, T. W., & Greve, L. (2019). Ecological cognition and metaphor. *Metaphor and Symbol, 34*(1), 1–16. doi:10.1080/10926488.2019.1591720

Johansson Falck, M. (2018). From ecological cognition to language: When and why do speakers use words metaphorically? *Metaphor and Symbol, 33*(2), 61–84. doi:10.1080/10926488.2018.1434937

Lambropoulos, N., Fardoun, H. M., & Alghazzawi, D. M. (2016). Chrono-spatial intelligence in global systems science and social media: Predictions for proactive political decision making. *International Conference on Social Computing and Social Media,* 201-208. 10.1007/978-3-319-39910-2_19

Leavitt, A. J. (2017). *Combatting toxic online communities* (1st ed.). The Rosen Publishing Group, Inc.

Steventon, A., & Wright, S. (2010). *Intelligent spaces: The application of pervasive ICT.* Springer Science & Business Media.

Willmott, S. (2004). Deploying intelligent systems on a global scale. *IEEE Intelligent Systems, 19*(5), 71–73. doi:10.1109/MIS.2004.39

APPENDIX

Tables for Calculating the Conversion of Cognitions Into Phantasies

This annex presents tables for calculating phantasies (p_i), which are a core part of the parametric user model (Bishop & Goode, 2021).

Table 1 is for converting goals and other cognitions into phantasies and fantasies (Bishop & Goode, 2021). Goals run from 1 to 9, phantasies from -5 to +5 and fantasies from -2.5 to 2.5, meaning the conversion variable for a phantasy is half that for a fantasy. A goal that is perceived as external to an actor is called a strategy.

Table 1. Compound identity – Converting goals and other cognitions into phantasies

Signifier Representation	Reducer	Signification Internal Representation	Reducer	Signified External Representation	Reducer	Shifter	Transformer
x / x_{4S}	$x_1 / C\breve{a}_{eS}$	y / y_{2a}	$y_1 / C\breve{b}_{eS}$	z / z_{3S}	$z_2 / C\breve{b}_{dS}$	$\breve{z} / C\breve{c}_{eS}$	$c / c_{1eS} / 2c_{1dS}$
Goal	0	Goal	0	Strategy	0	41	8
Goal	0	Plan	3	Method	3	23	4.4
Goal	0	Value	0	Rule	0	18.5	3.5
Goal	0	Belief	4	Meme	4	32	6.2
Goal	0	Interest	0	Amity	0	45.5	8.9
Goal	0	Detachment	1	Enmity	1	27.5	5.3

Table 2 is for converting plans and other cognitions into phantasies and fantasies (Bishop & Goode, 2021). Plans run from -2 to 2, phantasies from -5 to +5 and fantasies from -2.5 to 2.5, meaning the conversion variable for a phantasy is half that for a fantasy. A plan that is perceived as external to an actor is called a method.

Table 2. Compound identity – Converting plans and other cognitions into phantasies

Signifier Representation	Reducer	Signification Internal Representation	Reducer	Signified External Representation	Reducer	Shifter	Transformer
x / x_{4S}	$x_1 / C\breve{a}_{eS}$	y / y_{2a}	$y_1 / C\breve{b}_{eS}$	z / z_{3S}	$z_2 / C\breve{b}_{dS}$	$\breve{z} / C\breve{c}_{eS}$	$c / c_{1eS} / 2c_{1dS}$
Plan	3	Goal	0	Strategy	0	23	4.4
Plan	3	Plan	3	Method	3	13	2.4
Plan	3	Value	0	Rule	0	10.5	1.9
Plan	3	Belief	4	Meme	4	18	3.4
Plan	3	Interest	0	Amity	0	25.5	4.9
Plan	3	Detachment	1	Enmity	1	18	3.4

Table 3 is for converting values and other cognitions into phantasies and fantasies (Bishop & Goode, 2021). Values run from 1 to 4, phantasies from -5 to +5 and fantasies from -2.5 to 2.5, meaning the conversion variable for a phantasy is half that for a fantasy. A value that is perceived as external to an actor is called a rule.

Table 3. Compound identity – Converting values and other cognitions into phantasies

Signifier Representation	Reducer	Signification Internal Representation	Reducer	Signified External Representation	Reducer	Shifter	Transformer
x / x_{4S}	$x_1 / C\breve{a}_{eS}$	y / y_{2a}	$y_1 / C\breve{b}_{eS}$	z / z_{3S}	$z_2 / C\breve{b}_{dS}$	$\breve{z} / C\breve{c}_{eS}$	$c / c_{1eS} / 2c_{1dS}$
Value	0	Goal	0	Strategy	0	18.5	3.5
Value	0	Plan	3	Method	3	10.5	1.9
Value	0	Value	0	Rule	0	8.5	1.5
Value	0	Belief	4	Meme	4	14.5	2.7
Value	0	Interest	0	Amity	0	20.5	3.9
Value	0	Detachment	1	Enmity	1	14.5	2.7
Value	0	Faith	1	Illusion	1	4.5	0.7
Value	0	Ardour	2	Delusion	2	4.5	0.7

Table 4 is for converting beliefs and other cognitions into phantasies and fantasies (Bishop & Goode, 2021). Beliefs run from -3 to +3, phantasies from -5 to +5 and fantasies from -2.5 to 2.5, meaning the conversion variable for a phantasy is half that for a fantasy. A belief that is perceived as external to an actor is called a meme.

Table 4. Compound identity – Converting beliefs and other cognitions into phantasies

Signifier Representation	Reducer	Signification Internal Representation	Reducer	Signified External Representation	Reducer	Shifter	Transformer
x / x_{4S}	$x_1 / C\breve{a}_{eS}$	y / y_{2a}	$y_1 / C\breve{b}_{eS}$	z / z_{3S}	$z_2 / C\breve{b}_{dS}$	$\breve{z} / C\breve{c}_{eS}$	$c / c_{1eS} / 2c_{1dS}$
Belief	4	Goal	0	Strategy	0	32	6.2
Belief	4	Plan	3	Method	3	18	3.4
Belief	4	Value	0	Rule	0	14.5	2.7
Belief	4	Belief	4	Meme	4	25	4.8
Belief	4	Interest	0	Amity	0	35.5	6.9
Belief	4	Detachment	1	Enmity	1	21.5	4.1
Belief	4	Faith	1	Illusion	1	7.5	1.3
Belief	4	Ardour	2	Delusion	2	7.5	1.3

Table 5 is for converting interests and other cognitions into phantasies and fantasies (Bishop & Goode, 2021). Interests run from 1 to 10, phantasies from -5 to +5 and fantasies from -2.5 to 2.5, meaning the conversion variable for a phantasy is half that for a fantasy. An interest that is perceived as external to an actor is called an amity.

Table 5. Compound identity – Converting interests and other cognitions into phantasies

Signifier Representation	Reducer	Signification Internal Representation	Reducer	Signified External Representation	Reducer	Shifter	Transformer
x / x_{4S}	$x_1 / C\breve{a}_{eS}$	y / y_{2a}	$y_1 / C\breve{b}_{eS}$	z / z_{3S}	$z_2 / C\breve{b}_{dS}$	$\breve{z} / C\breve{c}_{eS}$	$c / c_{1eS} / 2c_{1dS}$
Interest	0	Goal	0	Strategy	0	45.5	8.9
Interest	0	Plan	3	Method	3	25.5	4.9
Interest	0	Value	0	Rule	0	20.5	3.9
Interest	0	Belief	4	Meme	4	35.5	6.
Interest	0	Interest	0	Amity	0	50.5	9.9
Interest	0	Detachment	1	Enmity	1	35.5	6.9
Interest	0	Faith	1	Illusion	1	10.5	1.9
Interest	0	Ardour	2	Delusion	2	10.5	1.9

Table 6 is for converting detachments and other cognitions into phantasies and fantasies (Bishop & Goode, 2021). Detachments run from 0 to 6, phantasies from -5 to +5 and fantasies from -2.5 to 2.5, meaning the conversion variable for a phantasy is half that for a fantasy. A detachment that is perceived as external to an actor is called a enmity.

Table 6. Compound identity – Converting detachments and other cognitions into phantasies

Signifier Representation	Reducer	Signification Internal Representation	Reducer	Signified External Representation	Reducer	Shifter	Transformer
x / x_{4S}	$x_1 / C\breve{a}_{eS}$	y / y_{2a}	$y_1 / C\breve{b}_{eS}$	z / z_{3S}	$z_2 / C\breve{b}_{dS}$	$\breve{z} / C\breve{c}_{eS}$	$c / c_{1eS} / 2c_{1dS}$
Detachment	1	Goal	0	Strategy	0	32	6.2
Detachment	1	Plan	3	Method	3	18	3.4
Detachment	1	Value	0	Rule	0	14.5	2.7
Detachment	1	Belief	4	Meme	4	25	4.8
Detachment	1	Interest	0	Amity	0	35.5	6.9
Detachment	1	Detachment	1	Enmity	1	25	4.8
Detachment	1	Faith	1	Illusion	1	7.5	1.3
Detachment	1	Ardour	2	Delusion	2	7.5	1.3

Table 7 is for converting faiths and other cognitions into phantasies and fantasies (Bishop & Goode, 2021). Faiths run from Null (0) to 5, phantasies from -5 to +5 and fantasies from -2.5 to 2.5, meaning the conversion variable for a phantasy is half that for a fantasy. A faith that is perceived as external to an actor is called an illusion.

Table 7. Compound identity – Converting faiths and other cognitions into phantasies

Signifier Representation	Reducer	Signification Internal Representation	Reducer	Signified External Representation	Reducer	Shifter	Transformer
x/x_{4S}	$x_1/C\breve{a}_{eS}$	y/y_{2a}	$y_1/C\breve{b}_{eS}$	z/z_{3S}	$z_2/C\breve{b}_{dS}$	$\breve{z}/C\breve{c}_{eS}$	$c/c_{1eS}/2c_{1dS}$
Faith	1	Goal	0	Strategy	0	9.5	3.4
Faith	1	Plan	3.	Method	3	5.5	1.8
Faith	1	Value	0	Rule	0	4.5	1.4
Faith	1	Belief	4	Meme	4	7.5	2.6
Faith	1	Interest	0	Amity	0	10.5	3.8
Faith	1	Detachment	1	Enmity	1	7.5	2.6
Faith	1	Faith	1	Illusion	1	2.5	0.6
Faith	1	Ardour	2	Delusion	2	4.5	1

Table 8 is for converting ardours and other cognitions into phantasies and fantasies (Bishop & Goode, 2021). Ardours run from -1 to Null (0), phantasies from -5 to +5 and fantasies from -2.5 to 2.5, meaning the conversion variable for a phantasy is half that for a fantasy. An ardour that is perceived as external to an actor is called a delusion. A faith phantasy, however, runs from 0 to 5, and a faith fantasy from 0 to 2.5. A ardour phantasy runs from 0 to -5 and a ardour fantasy from 0 to -2.5.

Table 8. Compound identity – Converting ardours and other cognitions into phantasies

Signifier Representation	Reducer	Signification Internal Representation	Reducer	Signified External Representation	Reducer	Shifter	Transformer
x/x_{4S}	$x_1/C\breve{a}_{eS}$	y/y_{2a}	$y_1/C\breve{b}_{eS}$	z/z_{3S}	$z_2/C\breve{b}_{dS}$	$\breve{z}/C\breve{c}_{eS}$	$c/c_{1eS}/2c_{1dS}$
Ardour	2	Goal	0	Strategy	0	1	-3.4
Ardour	2	Plan	3	Method	3	1	-1.8
Ardour	2	Value	0	Rule	0	1	-1.4
Ardour		Belief	4	Meme	4	1	-2.6
Ardour	2	Interest	0	Amity	0	1	-3.8
Ardour	2	Detachment	1	Enmity	1	1	-2.6
Ardour	2	Faith	1	Illusion	1	1	-0.6
Ardour	2	Ardour	2	Delusion	2	1	-1

Chapter 15
Smart Textile Materials for Fashion

Merve Küçükali Öztürk
Istanbul Bilgi University, Turkey

ABSTRACT

High-tech textiles play ever-increasing roles as technology becomes increasingly integrated into our everyday lives. Smart textiles are materials that sense and react to environmental conditions or stimuli. Examples include chromatic materials that change color in response to environmental changes, phase change materials for thermoregulation, and shape-memory polymers that change shape in response to temperature changes. The main technical components used to create fashionable wearables are interfaces, microprocessors, inputs (sensors), outputs (actuators), software, energy (batteries and solar panels), and materials (electronic textiles and enhanced materials). Moreover, the role of 3D printing in fashion has grown substantially, with remarkable increases in awareness and interest in the technology from designers. This is because 3D printing allows fashion designers to remove traditional design limits and produce fascinating designs. Detailed information on "smart fashion," as well as its functions and performance characteristics, is given in this chapter.

HISTORY OF WEARABLE TECHNOLOGY

Studies of wearable sensors and computing applications started prior to 2000. In 1998, the Georgia Tech Wearable Motherboard utilized optical fibers, special sensors, and interconnects to both screen and detect bullet injuries. A data bus integrated with monitoring devices that was similar to an electrocardiogram (ECG) was used to transmit data to the sensors. In 1997, the "Cyber jacket" was developed by scientists at the University of Bristol, Department of Computer Science. It contained a wearable mobile computer system and included a mobile computing software architecture with a natural communication model. In 1999, a collaboration between Levi's fashion and Philips Electronics began the ICD+ jacket Project. It was to be the first wearable electronics garment on the market (Henock, 2011). The first ECG bio-physical display jackets with light emitting diode (LED)/optic displays were developed in 2005 by Wainwright and

DOI: 10.4018/978-1-7998-9795-8.ch015

David Bychkov, the CEO of Exmovere. Watch-based galvanic skin response (GSR) sensors were connected to embedded, machine-washable displays in the denim jacket via Bluetooth (Syduzzaman, 2015).

Wearable Technology Brands

CuteCircuit

CuteCircuit is the world's first wearable technology fashion brand and was created in 2004. CuteCircuit's co-founders, Francesca Rosella and Ryan Genz, come from a heritage of fashion design couture, and interactive design and anthropology, respectively (CuteCircuit). The world's first wearable, sharable, programmable T-shirt was designed and patented by CuteCircuit (Patent number: US10356356).

MakeFashion

MakeFashion, which was launched in June 2012 by a trio of Calgarians, has grown into the world's largest fashion technology community. More than 250 wearable tech garments have been created and introduced at over 60 international events. They present fashion designers and artists to the exciting world of wearables through a series of informative, hands-on, designer-led workshops (MakeFashion).

THE SECOND SKIN

Pailes-Friedman of the Pratt Institute states that "What makes smart fabrics revolutionary is that they have the ability to do many things that traditional fabrics cannot, including communicate, transform, conduct energy, and even grow" (Paul, 2019). Our five senses are our input and output devices and the means by which we give and receive data about the states of our bodies and the world around us. Our garments interact with all of our senses; they are seen, heard, felt, smelled, touched, and sometimes even tasted (Rupini, 2015). Smart textiles utilize our senses as a way of collecting information from and about us via pressure, temperature, light, low-voltage current, moisture, and other means (Barnes, 2016). Some smart materials can accumulate information from our bodies and convert it into data, which can then be communicated via various methods (Stoppa, 2014). A fabric might convey low-voltage electric pulses via software, or a fiber or yarn can convert a physical measurement into data (Seyedin, 2019). This capacity to react to external stimuli gives 'smart' or 'intelligent' textiles their name (Stoppa, 2014). Smart textiles can gather information from our bodies and environments, and then respond (Cheng, 2010).

There are two types of smart textile reactions: extroverted and introverted. Extroverted reactions produce obvious external changes that are experienced by someone other than the wearer. For instance, clothing can light up, change shape or color, create sound, or produce an aroma. Embedded fabrics with digital devices 'E-textiles' are one example of this. In an introverted reaction, the textile responds to a stimulus but does not produce a noticeable physical change. Rather, the fabric changes in order to stimulate at least one of the wearer's own senses. For instance, technical textiles produced for sportspeople seek to provide comfort, heat control, and moisture management. The vast majority of these textiles achieve this via a mechanical response that is defined during construction of the yarn and fabric and inclusion of a coating or finishing process (Barnes, 2016). Smart materials fall into three main categories based on their functions.

Passive Smart Materials

Passive smart materials act as sensors that sense the environment or stimuli. They assemble data and can provide information about their surroundings via methods such as color and thermal or electrical resistivity changes (Soh, 2012; Stoppa, 2014; Zhang, 2001). One example is a fabric that changes color when your body temperature changes. Photochromatic inks are pre-programmed to change color at particular temperatures (Ferrara, 2014).

Active Smart Materials

Active smart materials have the capacity to both sense and react to external stimuli. When they are exposed to an environment, they can act as both sensors and actuators. They have ability to modify their geometric or material properties in response to electrical, thermal, or magnetic fields. For instance, piezoelectric and magneto-strictive materials are active smart materials. They can be used as sensors and actuators. Piezoelectric materials can generate electric charges in response to applied mechanical stress (Kamila, 2013).

Very Smart Materials

Very smart materials act as sensors and receive stimuli. They can respond to data and can reshape themselves and adapt to environmental conditions (Abdullah, 2019). Shape-memory alloys, smart polymers, and smart fluids are examples of this material category (Callister, 2012).

KEY SMART TEXTILE-INTEGRATED FUNCTIONAL DEVICES

Major types of textile-integrated functional devices used to create fashionable wearables include sensors, actuators, connectors, wires, antennas, batteries and supercapacitors, and memory devices (Shi, 2020).

Sensors

Mechanical, chemical, pressure, optical, humidity, and temperature sensors have been developed (Sohraby, 2007). Fiber sensors, which can measure temperature; strain and stress; gases; biological species; and smell are typical smart fibers that can be attached directly to textiles. Using textile sensors, the physical and emotional states of the wearer can be changed via the ever-changing properties of the wearer's epidermis (Boczkowska, 2006). Textile-based motion sensors are also used in smart textiles due to their non-irritating properties and the potential for integration into clothes. Textile-based motion sensors enhance wearer comfort and the clothes that they are integrated into can be reused. Textile-based sensors can be used to measure and analyze the movement of every part of the human body. First, smart clothes can remind office workers to stretch and exercise or provide posture corrections when the sensing textiles are embedded to the neck, shoulders, spine, etc. Second, textile sensors may assume a significant role in informing users of physical exercise requirements. Third, sensing textiles might be utilized for posture correction in sports education via integration into posture correction programs. They can provide the wearer with knowledge about whether joints in various parts of the body are at the correct angles (Cho,

2011). Sensors can detect blushing, sweating, and tension and temperature variations. The actuators respond by producing specific outputs (McGrath, 2013).

Currently, many fashionable wearables use conventional sensors to collect data (Bansal, 2017). These sensors are added to the fashionable wearable and their proper placement on the clothing is important to collection of essential data. Common embedded sensors measure changes in information sources that range from proximity to smell. They can gather data from the human body, as well as environmental data such as light, humidity, temperature, sound, or smoke data (Khan, 2019; Seymour, 2008). The data is collected from inputs and computed using an inter-processor communication (Nicolescu, 2018). A piezoresistive sensor was built up in the form of a removable insole. When integrated with read-out electronics, this piezoresistive sensor could be used to estimate the step rate during training. The data could be displayed on the screen of a smart watch (Capineri, 2014).

Actuators

Textile-integrated actuators can be utilized for two purposes. The first application category collects data and the second transfers energy. In textile applications, light, sound, heat, and motion are the primary modalities of actuation. Motion actuation can be based on electrostatic attraction, electromagnetic effects, thermal actuation, electrochemical principles, or piezoelectricity. Of these, electromagnetic effects (motors) and thermal effects (shape-memory alloys) are the most common (Langereis, 2013). The first thermally actuated materials were shape-memory alloys that could remember and return to their original shapes after being damaged (Kongahage, 2019). Actuators can stimulate the senses of the wearer or his or her audience (Hwan-Kwon, 2013). For instance, shape-memory alloys can change shape inside a garment. This provides a visual change for an audience and a tactile change for the wearer (Stead, 2005). Electric-field actuation is a consequence of electrostatic interactions between electrodes or molecular reorganization within the actuator material structure. Electronic artificial muscles and electroactive polymers are used as actuators. Electric fields can be created by dielectric elastomers (Kongahage, 2019). Dielectric elastomer actuators are "stretchable capacitors" that can offer muscle-like strain and force responses to an applied voltage. As generators, dielectric elastomers perform energy harvesting with few moving parts. Power can be delivered by stretching and contracting a relatively low-cost, rubbery material. Dielectric elastomers have been demonstrated to harvest energy from walking, pushing buttons, and heat engines (Kornbluh, 2012).

Photochromic inks can stimulate the visual sense of the wearer. In one study, photochromic silica nanoparticles were coated onto knitted cotton fabrics via screen-printing. All coated fabrics exhibited photochromism under UV and solar irradiation. These smart materials can be used in specific application areas such as brand protection, camouflage, and security printing (Pinto, 2016). In another study, LEDs were utilized as actuators on a jacket intended for firefighters. Thermal sensors connected to LED displays on the sleeve and back were embedded into the interior and exterior layers of the coat to control the temperature near the firefighter and inside of the coat (Das, 2014).

Connectors

Fabric sensors should be connected to other fabric circuit elements or other sensors. The sensing element must be solidly and flexibly joined to data connectors and interconnection lines. There are three basic types of connectors and interconnect bonds: mechanical, physical, and chemical. Mechanical connections involve joining of components to conduction lines. Physical connections incorporate microwelding, thermoplastic adhesion, or mixed conductive polymer adhesion. Chemical connections include covalent chemical bonding, acid oxidation, hydrogen bonding, and plasma pre-treatment (Castano, 2014).

Conductive yarns are typical e-textile interconnect materials (Castano, 2014). Data can be distributed across the body via textile-based conductive wires or transmitted via textile antennas (Roh, 2010). Textile-based antennas can be applied easily to fabric. Basic textile antennas are conductive yarns of specific lengths that can be stitched or woven into non-conducting fabrics (Stoppa, 2014).

Wireless connectivity allows communication between different wearable components, such as wireless input and output interfaces or storage devices, via Bluetooth. Moreover, wireless connectivity can establish communication with surrounding information technology (IT) infrastructure and provide access to external data and information via global system for mobile communication (GSM) or third-generation (3G) (Carrelli, 2005). Wireless communication enables data transmission without the use of wires. The most common wireless communication and navigation systems used in the fashionable wearable design are wireless fidelity (WIFI), Bluetooth, Infrared (IR), global positioning system (GPS), etc (Seneviratne, 2017).

Energy

Energy is needed to perform calculations on the captured data via microchips on the body. Energy is delivered primarily by batteries. Flexible fiber batteries are preferred for use in smart textiles due to their ease of fabrication and flexibility. In addition, non-hazardous battery chemicals and cheap, easily available materials are used in the battery designs (Qu, 2014). Because a battery has a limited lifetime and can have negative effects on the human body, there is a need for alternative energy sources. Organic photovoltaics that can be worn on the human body and produce enough electricity to charge a battery are desired because of their potential as an affordable energy technology (Su, 2012). Solar energy has been utilized as a power source. It relies on solar panels applied onto the surface of a fashionable wearable (Satharasinghe, 2019a). Solar fiber is a flexible photovoltaic fiber that transforms sunlight into electrical energy via a yarn that can be incorporated into many types of fabrics (Varma, 2018). One study developed a novel energy source in the form of photovoltaic fabrics. The solar fabric was woven with electronic yarns made by embedding miniature crystalline silicon solar cells within the textile yarn fibers and connecting them via fine copper wires. These solar fabrics were washable (Satharasinghe, 2019a). The human body is an alternative energy source for smart textiles, which can produce power derived via human kinetics and body heat exchange (Chermahini, 2012). Wearable nanogenerators are used in wearable devices and portable electronic devices. One study detailed the development of a flexible hybrid piezoelectric fiber-based two-dimensional fabric nanogenerator. This nanogenerator is easily applied to clothing and can transfer or convert human mechanical energy into electrical energy. A 1.9 V output voltage and 24 nA output current, which is large enough to power an LCD, can be generated by placing the fabric nanogenerator on an elbow pad on a human arm (Zhang, 2015).

Electronic Textiles (E-Textiles)

An electronic textile is a fabric that can conduct electricity. E-textiles can be inserted into a textile structure alongside sensors, batteries, and LEDs. Conductive materials can be added to the fabric to create an e-textile (Stoppa, 2014). E-textiles provide advanced functions such as color change; energy storage and conversion; and conductivity (Wang, 2020).

Smart fabric transducers (SFTs) are supplemented by completely flexible macro-electronic technologies: flexible displays; organic light-emitting diodes (OLEDS); micro-electromechanical systems (MEMS); fabric photovoltaic and energy harvesting devices; etc. These provide soft-computing wearable fabric-based sensing platforms. Two different types of sensing elements, intrinsic and extrinsic, have been developed. Intrinsic sensing elements can be developed from conductive polymers and doped polymer composites. Extrinsic sensing elements can be developed by modifying fabrics. Soft fabrics are produced for flexibility (Castano, 2014). Electrical conductivity can be provided by using conductive polymers or by coating conventional fibers with conductive materials. Various materials such as conducting polymer composites, metals, and carbon-based materials, such as carbon nanotubes, carbon nanopowders, and graphene have been used to provide conductivity. Fiber-based sensing devices can be embedded into the fabric. Such sensors can be woven or knitted into various textile structures due to their flexible, lightweight, conformable forms (Chatterjee, 2019). Designer Zane Berzina developed E-Static Shadows, a woven electronic textile membrane that responds to electrostatic energy. The final product was created from hundreds of hand-fastened LED lights, transistors, and woven electronic circuits (Berzina, 2009).

To provide conductivity, metal fibers are twisted into yarns. To avoid the use of separate wires, these yarns are commonly sewn directly onto non-conductive fabrics to connect electronic components. Woven or knitted fabrics from these yarns can assemble data directly from electrical impulses collected from the client when the fabric is worn directly on the skin. Data accumulated from the environment can be transmitted directly to implanted sensors, avoiding the need for wires (Agcayazi, 2018; Stoppa, 2014).

E-textiles can be used to harvest, store, and generate energy from the environment and our bodies (Yılmaz, 2018; Zhi, 2018). Wake Forest University researcher Corey Hewitt developed a power felt that generated electricity from body heat. The material comprises carbon nanotubes contained inside flexible plastic filaments and feels like normal felt. The temperature of an uncovered fingertip is sufficient to produce a quantifiable current. This material can be applied to flashlight housings, pipe insulation, sports equipment, and wound wrappings. Moreover, it can be utilized in automotive seat upholstery that uses warmth from the driver's buttocks to support the vehicle's battery or help power its electronics (Hewitt, 2012).

A novel, adaptable, wearable e-textile triboelectric energy harvesting system (WearETE) was developed to store energy from daily human motion. The proposed energy harvester is versatile, stretchable, and wearable. The proposed WearETE system relies on triboelectric energy harvesting, which is a developing kinetic energy change technology. Foam and e-textile are used as the tribomaterials because they are inexpensive and rely on inexpensive fabrication techniques. An apparatus for measuring and calculating power efficiency is used to measure and calibrate random human motion. The proposed WearETE system may be used to control wearable electronics during human motion via a wearable energy harvester (Li, 2017).

In another study, a solar E-yarn was produced by soldering ten miniature crystalline silicon solar cells, in parallel, onto two multi-strand copper wires. The solar cells were individually encapsulated along with a supporting yarn. The cells were covered by four packing fibers and a polyester, knitted, tubular sheath. These solar E-yarns are woven into fabrics and used as weft yarns. As warp yarns polyester yarns are used. Fabric charging performance was tested and solar energy harvesting fabric field tests were performed. The results indicated that the solar energy harvesting fabric and commercial solar panels have comparable power densities. The study demonstrated that solar energy harvesting fabrics can be used to generate power under natural sunlight (Satharasinghe, 2019b).

E-textiles can also be used to develop color changing materials. In one study, stainless steel wires (SSWs) were used as substrates for development of red, green, blue (RGB) electrochromic fibers. Three types of electrochromic materials were placed on the SSWs. A polymer gel electrolyte was coated onto the electrochromic layer and another fine stainless steel wire was wound on. The RGB colors are seen by the naked eye other than color changes from oxidized to reduced states. Moreover, these electrochromic fibers have exceptionally short reaction times, brilliant flexibility, and excellent structural stability despite being exposed to bending and folding. Furthermore, they can be embedded into fabrics to produce additional color combinations by regulating voltages and parallel connections between different circuits (Li, 2014). In the "Body Electric AW15" collection by Clara Daguin, the outer garments contain hand-embroidered electronic circuits that show a combination of human and computer anatomies (Daguin, 2015). Ying Gao created a collection of robotic dresses that contained twisted and curled fibrous panels. The dress movements are activated using a fingerprint scanner incorporated in a wooden frame placed around the wearer's neck. The device sends data to a microprocessor that activates the motors embedded in each of the panels. All of the dresses were made from gauzy nylon mesh, while translucent thermoplastic was used for the threads in the kinetic panels (Gao, 2017).

HEAT STORING, THERMO-REGULATED TEXTILES, AND CLOTHING

Phase change materials (PCMs) can absorb, store, and release energy in the form of heat. These materials change phases and absorb energy during heating, and release the equivalent energy to their surroundings during the converse cooling process (Hayes, 2016; Westbroek, 2005). Thermal energy transfer occurs when a material changes from a solid to a liquid or from a liquid to a solid (Delgado, 2018). Ice is an example of a phase change material that changes phase when heated at 0°C. Its conversion to water during this process causes it to absorb a large amount of heat, thus cooling its surroundings (Pan, 2011). Some PCMs change states at a temperature slightly above or below human skin temperature and thus can be used to make protective clothing for changing climatic conditions (Arjun, 2014; Williams, 2009). Every material absorbs heat and stores it during heating. The stored heat is released to the environment during cooling (Arjun, 2014). However, PCM materials absorb more heat than conventional materials. The heat storage limit of a textile material can be considerably improved by incorporating PCMs. The impact of a phase change material on thermally comfortable, protective clothes increases rapidly when the wearer experiences temperature changes or irregular contact with cold materials (Mondal, 2008).

Several techniques can be used to incorporate PCMs into textile fabrics. These include fiber technology, coating, lamination, and microencapsulation (Babu, 2018). In the fiber technology method, PCMs are directly added to the polymer solution, which is then spun using conventional methods (Arjun, 2014). The microencapsulated PCM fibers can store heat over long periods (Aguilar, 2019). In the coating method, microspheres that contain PCMs are wetted and dispersed in a water dispersion that contains a surfactant, a dispersant, an anti-foaming agent, and a polymer mixture. The coating can then be applied to a textile substrate. Several different coating techniques such as knife-over-roll, knife-over-airpad-drycure, gravure, dip coating, and transfer coating can be applied (Singha, 2012). In the lamination method, microcapsules are blended into a water-blown polyurethane foam blend, which is laminated onto a fabric. At the end of the process, water is removed from the system via drying (Pause,

2000). PCM-incorporated textiles can be used in space; sportswear; bedding and accessories; shoes and accessories; and medical applications (Arjun, 2014).

SELF-HEALING FABRICS

Self-healing materials include polymers, metals, ceramics, and their composites that can renew themselves to recover their unique arrangements of properties when harmed via thermal, mechanical, ballistic, or other means. Improving product lifetimes can save substantial costs for users and is useful in any sector (Wool, 2008). Self-healing materials have been applied to textiles and garments because their self-repair capabilities provide functional properties for smart textiles (Cheung, 2018; Gaddes, 2016).

Polyurethanes (PUs) are probably the most versatile group of plastics. They exhibit a wide range of densities, hardnesses, and stiffnesses, which make them applicable to various types of PU stretchable fibers; stiff elastomers; and flexible, rigid, lightweight foams. PU materials are applied as coatings, adhesives, furniture, textile fibers, artificial leather, etc. Effective self-healing systems can be created using microcapsules with PU shells (Szmechtyk, 2015). In one study, a reactive isophorone diisocyanate was enclosed inside a PU shell via interfacial polymerization and used as a catalyst-free healing agent (Yang, 2008). In an another similar study, double-walled polyurethane/poly(urea-formaldehyde) microcapsules (PU/UF) were prepared for use in self-healing materials. A modified encapsulation method based on interfacial polymerization was utilized to create liquid-filled microcapsules with two distinct shell walls. The second, inner shell improved the mechanical properties and thermal stabilities of UF microcapsules (Caruso, 2010). Researchers at SINTEF (The Foundation for Scientific and Industrial Research at the Norwegian Institute of Technology) added microcapsules that contained a glue-like substance to the plastic polyurethane that is applied to the surface of an underlayment in a professional raincoat. The capsules released a sealant when there was a tear in the coating. The sealant hardens when it comes in contact with air or water, and the coating seals itself (Sharma, 2013).

Moreover, reversible polymers can be used as self-repairing materials. A new linear polyurethane synthesized via a Diels-Alder (DA) reaction can exhibit self-healing properties under heat treatment. The self-healing efficiency is controlled by the recuperation of breaking tensile strength after being harmed and healed. The healed sample retains 66% of the mechanical properties of PU-DA. Therefore, PU-DA can be used in self-healing coatings and thermo-reversible adhesives (Du, 2013).

Another self-repairing textile technology exhibits rubber-like behavior. The rubber-like substance recovers its original structure after being stretched. Due to its elastic molecular properties, the material can be repaired automatically (D'Ambrosio, 2008). There are studies on the self-healing performances of zinc dimethacrylate (ZDMA)-reinforced thermoplastics (Liu, 2019). A study in which ZDMA was used to introduce strong ionic interactions that convert natural rubber into a self-healing material shows 95% recovery of mechanical properties after damage and healing when ZDMA-infused material was used (Xu, 2016). In another study, carbon-black-filled self-healing natural rubber was developed. Addition of carbon black to a self-healing natural rubber compound improved the rubber performance. The tensile healing efficiency of the carbon black-filled self-healing natural rubber was approximately 40–70% and the elongation healing efficiency reached approximately 80–95% (Khimi, 2019).

3D PRINTED FASHION

In 3D printing, one makes 3D solid objects from a digital file. The production of a 3D printed object is achieved using additive processes. In such processes, an object is made by depositing progressive layers of material until the object is complete. One can use 3D printing to produce complex shapes utilizing less material than traditional manufacturing methods (Al-Maliki, 2015).

The first step in 3D printing is 3D modeling. Computer-aided design (CAD) fashion design software can help fashion designers to perform rendering and visualization. This is quite helpful for fashion designers. Moreover, perfect patterns can be created by using CAD software (Meng, 2012; Sayem, 2010). The most commonly used fashion design software programs are CLO3D, TUKA 3D, MarvelousDesigner, and Browzwear (Absher, 2020). CLO3D can generate renderings from 2D patterns and provides good visualization of final products. In addition, it can show how clothing fits and visualize silhouettes (Wang, 2020). Using TUKA 3D software, one can experience a virtual fitting session using an animated model that can move, dance, run, etc (Sareen, 2011). MarvelousDesigner is software that allows one to create 3D virtual clothing and observe garment fit (Hoch, 2014). The Browzwear VStitcher software program lets designers stitch pattern pieces, places the stitched patterns around a 3D symbol, and performs simulations to create 3D virtual models. Naturally, 3D CAD programs are valuable to fashion designers, as they encourage designers to imagine how a garment could appear in reality without making a sample. The V-Stitcher program has a user-friendly interface (Min, 2018). After 3D modeling, a 3D printer can be used to read the design from the CAD software and print a sample. Thus, 3D printing provides many advantages to the fashion industry. One example is that it allows designers to create intricate details at low cost. Another benefit is that 3D printing lets designers practice with different materials (Kuhn, 2015). Furthermore, 3D-printed clothes minimize solid waste while saving fuel and packaging in the clothing industry (Vanderploeg, 2017). Danit Peleg is a fashion designer known for her 3D printed fashion work. Danit Peleg's latest collection of wearable 3D-printed fashion is 'Liberty Leading the People' (Peleg, 2015). Sylvia Heisel is another innovative designer who works with 3D-printed garments that are wearable, practical, and beautiful. She designed a 3D-printed coat (Heisel, 2015). Julia Daviy is a 3D-printed clothing designer. The Pangolin 3D-printed dress was produced from a printable, nano-enhanced elastomer that provides the garment with both flexibility and durability (Threeasfour, 2016).

CONCLUSION

Clothing plays important roles in helping people to define and discover themselves. It is a fundamental part of many lives and has aesthetic functions. Hi-tech clothing is a growing area of fashion. The rate of wearable technology development is accelerating rapidly. Beyond aesthetics, hi-tech clothing can meet the physiological, biomechanical, ergonomic, and psychological requirements of consumers. Clothing is often referred to as our second skin. Smart garments interact with all of our senses; they are seen, heard, felt, smelled, touched, and may even be tasted. They get information from the human body and convert it into data that can then be communicated in various ways, and sometimes even react to such information. Smart materials can be categorized into passive, active, and very smart materials based on their functions.

In this chapter, the importance of smart textile materials to fashion has been highlighted. After taking a historical look at wearable technology development, smart materials were described. The major types of textile-integrated functional devices used to create fashionable wearables were also explained in detail. Moreover, smart textile types have been classified and explained, and technical information has been provided regarding designs and alternative usage. Furthermore, information regarding 3D-printed fashion, which helps fashion designers by producing fascinating designs, has been provided alongside design examples. This review describes the development and importance of smart fashion by collecting and organizing previous and recent studies. Therefore, the comprehensive content of this chapter may help readers to understand the term "wearable technology" correctly.

REFERENCES

Abdullah, Y. S., & Al-Alwan, H. A. (2019). Smart material systems and adaptiveness in architecture. *Ain Shams Engineering Journal, 10*(3), 623–638. doi:10.1016/j.asej.2019.02.002

Absher, K. A. (2020). *Exploring the use of 3D apparel visualization software to fit garments for people with disabilities* [Master's thesis]. North Carolina State University, Raleigh, NC, United States.

Agcayazi, T., Chatterjee, K., Bozkurt, A., & Ghosh, T. K. (2018). Flexible interconnects for electronic textiles. *Advanced Materials Technologies, 3*(10), 1700277. doi:10.1002/admt.201700277

Aguilar, M. R., & San Román, J. (Eds.). (2019). *Smart polymers and their applications*. Woodhead Publishing. doi:10.1016/B978-0-08-102416-4.00001-6

Al-Maliki, J. Q., & Al-Maliki, A. J. Q. (2015). The processes and technologies of 3D printing. *International Journal of Advances in Computer Science and Technology, 4*(10), 161–165.

Arjun, D., & Hayavadana, J. (2014). Thermal energy storage materials (PCMs) for textile applications. *Journal of Textile and Apparel, Technology and Management, 8*(4).

Babu, V. R., & Arunraj, A. (2018). Thermo regulated clothing with phase change materials. *Journal of Textile Engineering & Fashion Technology, 4*(5), 344–347. doi:10.15406/jteft.2018.04.00162

Bansal, S., & Sud, S. (2017). Advancement and history of techno fashion. *International Journal of Arts, 7*(2), 33–37.

Barnes, N. (2016). *Smart textiles for designers–inventing the future of fabrics*. Academic Press.

Berzina, Z. (2009). *E-Static Shadows*. http://www.zaneberzina.com/

Boczkowska, A., & Leonowicz, M. (2006). Intelligent materials for intelligent textiles. *Fibres & Textiles in Eastern Europe, 59*(5), 13–17.

Callister, W. D. Jr, & Rethwisch, D. G. (2012). *Fundamentals of materials science and engineering: An integrated approach*. John Wiley & Sons.

Capineri, L. (2014). Resistive sensors with smart textiles for wearable technology: From fabrication processes to integration with electronics. *Procedia Engineering, 87*, 724–727. doi:10.1016/j.proeng.2014.11.748

Carrelli, C. (Ed.). (2005). Ubiquitous services and applications: Exploiting the potential; 27–29 April 2005, Marriott Hotel, Heidelberg, Germany; Incl. CD-ROM. Margret Schneider.

Caruso, M. M., Blaiszik, B. J., Jin, H., Schelkopf, S. R., Stradley, D. S., Sottos, N. R., & Moore, J. S. (2010). Robust, double-walled microcapsules for self-healing polymeric materials. *ACS Applied Materials & Interfaces*, *2*(4), 1195–1199. doi:10.1021/am100084k PMID:20423139

Castano, L. M., & Flatau, A. B. (2014). Smart fabric sensors and e-textile technologies: A review. *Smart Materials and Structures*, *23*(5), 053001. doi:10.1088/0964-1726/23/5/053001

Chatterjee, K., Tabor, J., & Ghosh, T. K. (2019). Electrically conductive coatings for fiber-based e-textiles. *Fibers (Basel, Switzerland)*, *7*(6), 51. doi:10.3390/fib7060051

Cheng, T. E., & Choi, T. M. (Eds.). (2010). *Innovative quick response programs in logistics and supply chain management*. Springer Science & Business Media. doi:10.1007/978-3-642-04313-0

Cheung, T. W., & Li, L. (2018). Sustainable development of smart textiles: A review of 'self-functioning' abilities which makes textiles alive. *Journal of Textile Engineering & Fashion. Technology*, *4*, 152–127.

Cho, G., Jeong, K., Paik, M. J., Kwun, Y., & Sung, M. (2011). Performance evaluation of textile-based electrodes and motion sensors for smart clothing. *IEEE Sensors Journal*, *11*(12), 3183–3193. doi:10.1109/JSEN.2011.2167508

CuteCircuit. (n.d.). https://cutecircuit.com/

D'Ambrosio, P., De Tommasi, D., Ferri, D., & Puglisi, G. (2008). A phenomenological model for healing and hysteresis in rubber-like materials. *International Journal of Engineering Science*, *46*(4), 293–305. doi:10.1016/j.ijengsci.2007.12.002

Daguin, C. (2015). *Body Electric AW15*. https://www.claradaguin.com/bodyelectric

Das, S. C., & Chowdhury, N. (2014). Smart textiles: New possibilities in textile engineering. *Journal of Polymer and Textile Engineering*, *1*(1), 1–4.

Delgado, J. M., Martinho, J. C., Sá, A. V., Guimarães, A. S., & Abrantes, V. (2018). *Thermal energy storage with phase change materials: A literature review of applications for buildings materials*. Springer.

Du, P., Liu, X., Zheng, Z., Wang, X., Joncheray, T., & Zhang, Y. (2013). Synthesis and characterization of linear self-healing polyurethane based on thermally reversible Diels–Alder reaction. *RSC Advances*, *3*(35), 15475–15482. doi:10.1039/c3ra42278j

Ferrara, M., & Bengisu, M. (2014). Materials that change color for intelligent design. In M. Rossi (Ed.), *Materials that change color* (pp. 81–100). Springer. doi:10.1007/978-3-319-00290-3_4

Gaddes, D., Jung, H., Pena-Francesch, A., Dion, G., Tadigadapa, S., Dressick, W. J., & Demirel, M. C. (2016). Self-healing textile: Enzyme encapsulated layer-by-layer structural proteins. *ACS Applied Materials & Interfaces*, *8*(31), 20371–20378. doi:10.1021/acsami.6b05232 PMID:27419265

Gao, Y. (2017). *Possible Tomorrows*. http://yinggao.ca/

Hayes, S. G., & Venkatraman, P. (Eds.). (2016). *Materials and technology for sportswear and performance apparel.* CRC Press.

HeiselS. (2015). https://heisel.co/

Henock, D. (2011). *Literature over view of smart textiles* [Master's thesis]. University of Boras, Borås, Sweden.

Hewitt, C. A., Kaiser, A. B., Roth, S., Craps, M., Czerw, R., & Carroll, D. L. (2012). Multilayered carbon nanotube/polymer composite based thermoelectric fabrics. *Nano Letters, 12*(3), 1307–1310. doi:10.1021/nl203806q PMID:22316286

Hoch, H. (2014, April). *3D virtual prototyping in apparel design* [Paper presentation]. Symposium on Undergraduate Research & Creative Expression, Iowa City, IA.

Hwan Kwon, Y. (2013). *Pattern changing clothing: Interactive, customizable, and original wearables* [Unpublished master's thesis]. Rochester Institute of Technology, Rochester, NY.

Kamila, S. (2013). Introduction, classification and applications of smart materials: An overview. *American Journal of Applied Sciences, 10*(8), 876–880. doi:10.3844/ajassp.2013.876.880

Khan, S., Ali, S., & Bermak, A. (2019). Recent developments in printing flexible and wearable sensing electronics for healthcare applications. *Sensors (Basel), 19*(5), 1230. doi:10.339019051230 PMID:30862062

Khimi, S. R., Syamsinar, S. N., & Najwa, T. N. L. (2019). Effect of carbon black on self-healing efficiency of natural rubber. *Materials Today: Proceedings, 17*, 1064–1071. doi:10.1016/j.matpr.2019.06.513

Kongahage, D., & Foroughi, J. (2019). Actuator materials: Review on recent advances and future outlook for smart textiles. *Fibers (Basel, Switzerland), 7*(3), 21. doi:10.3390/fib7030021

Kornbluh, R. D., Pelrine, R., Prahlad, H., Wong-Foy, A., McCoy, B., Kim, S., Eckerle, J., & Low, T. (2012). Dielectric elastomers: Stretching the capabilities of energy harvesting. *MRS Bulletin, 37*(3), 246–253. doi:10.1557/mrs.2012.41

Kuhn, R., & Minuzzi, R. F. B. (2015). The 3D printing's panorama in fashion design. *Moda Documenta: Museu. Memoria e Design, 11*(1), 1–12.

Langereis, G. R., Bouwstra, S., & Chen, W. (2013). Sensors, actuators and computing systems for smart textiles for protection. In R. A. Chapman (Ed.), *Smart textiles for protection* (pp. 190–213). Woodhead Publishing. doi:10.1533/9780857097620.1.190

Li, K., Zhang, Q., Wang, H., & Li, Y. (2014). Red, green, blue (RGB) electrochromic fibers for the new smart color change fabrics. *ACS Applied Materials & Interfaces, 6*(15), 13043–13050. doi:10.1021/am502929p PMID:25057906

Li, X., & Sun, Y. (2017). WearETE: A scalable wearable e-textile triboelectric energy harvesting system for human motion scavenging. *Sensors (Basel), 17*(11), 2649. doi:10.339017112649 PMID:29149035

Liu, Y., Li, Z., Liu, R., Liang, Z., Yang, J., Zhang, R., Zhou, Z., & Nie, Y. (2019). Design of self-healing rubber by introducing ionic interaction to construct a network composed of ionic and covalent cross-linking. *Industrial & Engineering Chemistry Research, 58*(32), 14848–14858. doi:10.1021/acs.iecr.9b02972

MakeFashion. (n.d.). http://www.makefashion.ca/

McGrath, M. J., Ni Scanaill, C., & Nafus, D. (2013). *Sensor technologies: Healthcare, wellness, and environmental applications.* Springer Nature. doi:10.1007/978-1-4302-6014-1

Meng, Y., Mok, P. Y., & Jin, X. (2012). Computer aided clothing pattern design with 3D editing and pattern alteration. *Computer Aided Design, 44*(8), 721–734. doi:10.1016/j.cad.2012.03.006

Min, S., & Carrico, M. (2018, January). *Exploration of students' design process with Browzwear V-Stitcher, 3D CAD program* [Paper presentation]. International Textile and Apparel Association (ITAA) Annual Conference, Iowa City, IA.

Mondal, S. (2008). Phase change materials for smart textiles–An overview. *Applied Thermal Engineering, 28*(11–12), 1536–1550. doi:10.1016/j.applthermaleng.2007.08.009

Nebati Chermahini, A. N. (2012, January). *Smart clothes that express your mood* [Conference presentation]. IWBE workshop of bionic engineering conference: International Society of Bionic Engineering (ISBE), Zhangjiajie, China.

Nicolescu, G., & Mosterman, P. J. (2018). *Model-based design for embedded systems.* CRC Press. doi:10.1201/9781315218823

Pan, N., & Sun, G. (Eds.). (2011). *Functional textiles for improved performance, protection and health.* Elsevier. doi:10.1533/9780857092878

Paul, R. (2019). *High performance technical textiles.* John Wiley & Sons, Incorporated. doi:10.1002/9781119325062

Pause, B. (2000). Measuring the thermal barrier function of phase change materials in textiles. *Technical Textiles International, 9*(3), 20–21.

Peleg, D. (2015). *Fashion designer.* https://danitpeleg.com/

Pinto, T., Costa, P., Sousa, C. M., Sousa, C. A., Pereira, C., Silva, C. J., Pereira, M. F. R., Coelho, P. J., & Freire, C. (2016). Screen-printed photochromic textiles through new inks based on SiO2@ naphthopyran nanoparticles. *ACS Applied Materials & Interfaces, 8*(42), 28935–28945. doi:10.1021/acsami.6b06686 PMID:27704753

Qu, H., Semenikhin, O., & Skorobogatiy, M. (2014). Flexible fiber batteries for applications in smart textiles. *Smart Materials and Structures, 24*(2), 025012. doi:10.1088/0964-1726/24/2/025012

Roh, J. S., Chi, Y. S., & Kang, T. J. (2010). Wearable textile antennas. *International Journal of Fashion Design. Technology and Education, 3*(3), 135–153.

Rupini, R. V., & Nandagopal, R. (2015). A study on the influence of senses and the effectiveness of sensory branding. *Journal of Psychiatry, 18*(2), 236.

Sareen, R., Sareen, I., Delevan, J. B., & Vishnevsky, B. (2011). *U.S. Patent Application No. 13/008,906.* US Patent Office.

Satharasinghe, A., Hughes-Riley, T., & Dias, T. (2019). Solar energy-harvesting e-textiles to power wearable devices. *Multidisciplinary Digital Publishing Institute Proceedings*, *32*(1), 1. doi:10.3390/proceedings2019032001

Satharasinghe, A., Hughes-Riley, T., & Dias, T. (2019). An investigation of a wash-durable solar energy harvesting textile. *Progress in Photovoltaics: Research and Applications*, *28*(6), 578–592. doi:10.1002/pip.3229

Sayem, A. S. M., Kennon, R., & Clarke, N. (2010). 3D CAD systems for the clothing industry. *International Journal of Fashion Design, Technology and Education*, *3*(2), 45–53.

Seneviratne, S., Hu, Y., Nguyen, T., Lan, G., Khalifa, S., Thilakarathna, K., Hassan, M., & Seneviratne, A. (2017). A survey of wearable devices and challenges. *IEEE Communications Surveys and Tutorials*, *19*(4), 2573–2620. doi:10.1109/COMST.2017.2731979

Seyedin, S., Zhang, P., Naebe, M., Qin, S., Chen, J., Wang, X., & Razal, J. M. (2019). Textile strain sensors: A review of the fabrication technologies, performance evaluation and applications. *Materials Horizons*, *6*(2), 219–249. doi:10.1039/C8MH01062E

Seymour, S. (2008). *Fashionable technology: The intersection of design, fashion, science, and technology*. Springer. doi:10.1007/978-3-211-74500-7

Sharma, A. (2013). Eco-friendly textiles: A boost to sustainability. *Asian Journal of Home Science*, *8*(2), 768–771.

Shi, J., Liu, S., Zhang, L., Yang, B., Shu, L., Yang, Y., Ren, M., Wang, Y., Chen, J., Chen, W., Chai, Y., & Tao, X. (2020). Smart textile-integrated microelectronic systems for wearable applications. *Advanced Materials*, *32*(5), 1901958. doi:10.1002/adma.201901958 PMID:31273850

Singha, K. (2012). A review on coating & lamination in textiles: Processes and applications. *American Journal of Political Science*, *2*(3), 39–49.

Soh, C. K., Yang, Y., & Bhalla, S. (Eds.). (2012). *Smart materials in structural health monitoring, control and biomechanics*. Springer Science & Business Media. doi:10.1007/978-3-642-24463-6

Sohraby, K., Minoli, D., & Znati, T. (2007). *Wireless sensor networks: Technology, protocols, and applications*. John Wiley & Sons. doi:10.1002/047011276X

Stead, L. J. (2005). *'The emotional wardrobe': A fashion perspective on the integration of technology and clothing* [Unpublished doctoral dissertation]. University of the Arts London.

Stoppa, M., & Chiolerio, A. (2014). Wearable electronics and smart textiles: A critical review. *Sensors (Basel)*, *14*(7), 11957–11992. doi:10.3390140711957 PMID:25004153

Su, Y. W., Lan, S. C., & Wei, K. H. (2012). Organic photovoltaics. *Materials Today*, *15*(12), 554–562. doi:10.1016/S1369-7021(13)70013-0

Syduzzaman, M. D., Patwary, S. U., Farhana, K., & Ahmed, S. (2015). Smart textiles and nano-technology: A general overview. *Journal of Textile Science & Engineering*, *5*, 1000181.

Szmechtyk, T., Sienkiewicz, N., Woźniak, J., & Strzelec, K. (2015). Polyurethanes as self-healing materials. *Current Chemistry Letters*, *4*(2), 61–66. doi:10.5267/j.ccl.2015.3.001

Threeasfour. (2016). https://threeasfour.com/ /

Vanderploeg, A., Lee, S. E., & Mamp, M. (2017). The application of 3D printing technology in the fashion industry. *International Journal of Fashion Design, Technology and Education*, *10*(2), 170–179.

Varma, S. J., Sambath Kumar, K., Seal, S., Rajaraman, S., & Thomas, J. (2018). Fiber-type solar cells, nanogenerators, batteries, and supercapacitors for wearable applications. *Advancement of Science*, *5*(9), 1800340. doi:10.1002/advs.201800340 PMID:30250788

Wang, G., Hou, C., & Wang, H. (Eds.). (2020). *Flexible and wearable electronics for smart clothing*. John Wiley & Sons. doi:10.1002/9783527818556

Wang, Y. X., & Liu, Z. D. (2020). Virtual clothing display platform based on CLO3D and evaluation of fit. *Journal of Fiber Bioengineering and Informatics*, *13*(1), 37–49. doi:10.3993/jfbim00338

Westbroek, P., Priniotakis, G., & Kiekens, P. (2005). *Analytical electrochemistry in textiles*. Elsevier.

Williams, J. T. (Ed.). (2009). *Textiles for cold weather apparel*. Elsevier. doi:10.1533/9781845697174

Wool, R. P. (2008). Self-healing materials: A review. *Soft Matter*, *4*(3), 400–418. doi:10.1039/b711716g PMID:32907199

Xu, C., Cao, L., Lin, B., Liang, X., & Chen, Y. (2016). Design of self-healing supramolecular rubbers by introducing ionic cross-links into natural rubber via a controlled vulcanization. *ACS Applied Materials & Interfaces*, *8*(27), 17728–17737. doi:10.1021/acsami.6b05941 PMID:27337545

Yang, J., Keller, M. W., Moore, J. S., White, S. R., & Sottos, N. R. (2008). Microencapsulation of isocyanates for self-healing polymers. *Macromolecules*, *41*(24), 9650–9655. doi:10.1021/ma801718v

Yilmaz, N. D. (Ed.). (2018). *Smart textiles: Wearable nanotechnology*. John Wiley & Sons. doi:10.1002/9781119460367

Zhang, M., Gao, T., Wang, J., Liao, J., Qiu, Y., Yang, Q., Xue, H., Shi, Z., Zhao, Y., Xiong, Z., & Chen, L. (2015). A hybrid fibers based wearable fabric piezoelectric nanogenerator for energy harvesting application. *Nano Energy*, *13*, 298–305. doi:10.1016/j.nanoen.2015.02.034

Zhang, X., & Tao, X. (2001). Smart textiles: Passive smart. *Textile Asia*, *32*(6), 45–49.

Zhi, C., & Dai, L. (Eds.). (2018). *Flexible energy conversion and storage devices*. John Wiley & Sons. doi:10.1002/9783527342631

Chapter 16
WDM Systems:
An Insight

Neeraj Sharma

https://orcid.org/0000-0002-6168-9118

Panjab University, Chandigarh, India

ABSTRACT

A communication system transmits and receives information from one place to another, where the separation between transmitter and receiver may be of few kilometers or transoceanic distances. Fiber-optic communication is one of such communication systems where optical fibers are deployed for information transmission. The capacity of a fiber-optic communication system is very high since it has large carrier frequency (Capacity~100 THz) in the visible or near-infrared region of the electromagnetic spectrum. The transmission of multiple optical channels over the same fiber has provided a simple way to extend the system capacity. Channel multiplexing can be achieved through time-division multiplexing (TDM) or frequency division multiplexing (FDM). In optical communication, FDM is known as wavelength division multiplexing (WDM). This chapter includes the discussion about the working principle of the WDM system, WDM components, classification of WDM system, and other supporting technologies.

WDM SYSTEMS: AN INTRODUCTION

WDM is a multiplexing technology where N different modulated channels at different carrier wavelengths are combined and transmitted simultaneously over the same fiber. The optical signal at the receiver is demultiplexed into separate channels. This helps in the efficient utilization of huge available bandwidth of optical fibers and the sharing of various optical components. WDM helps in capacity up-gradation of existing point to point fiber optic transmission links, whereby a number of individual high data rate channels are multiplexed. It also provides multiplexing varied types of signals on different wavelengths like synchronous and asynchronous, digital, and analog information can be sent simultaneously, and independently, over the same fiber, without the need for any common signal structure. The link capacity and flexibility can further be increased by the use of wavelength-sensitive optical routing devices. WDM also provides features like wavelength switching which allows reconfigurations of the optical

DOI: 10.4018/978-1-7998-9795-8.ch016

layer. Optical devices like OADMs, OXCs, and wavelength converters help in implementing wavelength switching. Figure 1 shows the block diagram of a WDM system.

Figure 1. Block diagram of a WDM system

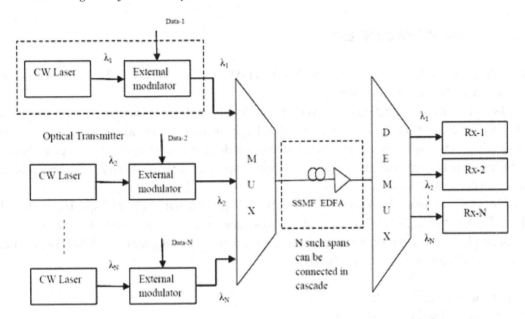

It can be seen in Figure 1 that N different optical transmitters are transmitting information on N different optical carriers (λ_N) which are multiplexed to transmit on a single fiber optic link. The fiber-optic link or transmission line consists of a number of spans of SSMF and EDFA, where EDFA is used to compensate for the fiber attenuation. At the end of the fiber-optic link, the channels are demultiplexed using a demultiplexer and provided to the respective optical receiver, where demodulation is performed to recover the information signal. If every transmitter works at a data rate of B b/s, then the total data rate will be NB. Typically the optical carrier frequencies (wavelengths) are equally spaced and frequency difference between two consecutive channels is known as a frequency or channel spacing Δf. The channel spacing is there to prevent co-channel interference and does not contribute to any data transmission. This causes wastage of optical spectrum thereby reducing the efficient use of spectrum i.e. spectral efficiency (SE). SE is one of the important parameters of a WDM system which is a measure of efficient utilization of resources and sometimes also related to the cost of transmission per bit. SE is defined as the ratio of bit rate per channel (B) to channel spacing (Δf).

$$SE = \frac{B}{\Delta f} \tag{1.1}$$

In 2002, the international telecommunication union (ITU) has standardized the channel frequencies of a WDM system on a 100 GHz (» 0.8 nm) grid and it is defined as ITU.T G.692 standards (ITU-T G.692, 2002). The ITU-T recommendation G.692 specifies selecting the channel frequencies from a grid of frequencies referenced to 193.1 THz (1552.524 nm). However, for coherent communication which generally operates at a symbol rate of 28 GBd and with advanced modulation formats like QPSK or QAM, such large channel spacing leads to poor SE and poor utilization of resources. Recently, ITU standardized the WDM channel spacing ranging from 12.5 GHz to 100 GHz and wider (ITU-T G.694.1, 2012).

TYPES OF THE WDM SYSTEM

WDM systems are categorized as coarse WDM (CWDM) or dense WDM (DWDM) depending on the channel spacing (Δf) between consecutive channels.

CWDM: ITU recommendations on CWDM are for city and access networks, with large channel spacing equal to 20 nm (ITU-T G.694.2, 2003). The large channel spacing allows the use of cheap components such as low-cost laser sources. But at the same time, it results in huge wastage of bandwidth and requires more transceivers due to lack of optical amplification over shorter reach and economical nature of the network or system.

DWDM: ITU recommendations (ITU G.694.1) on DWDM are with a channel spacing of 100 GHz or 50 GHz (ITU-T G.694.1, 2012). The transmission distance is easily greater than 1000 km with the help of optical amplifiers. Small channel spacing leads to higher SE and higher costs. DWDM transmission may be assigned the following optical bands.

1. Short band (S-band): 1400 – 1530 nm
2. Conventional band (C-band): 1530 - 1565 nm
3. Long band (L-band): 1565 – 1625 nm

WDM SYSTEM COMPONENTS

The implementation of the WDM system requires a variety of passive and/or active devices to combine, distribute, isolate, and amplify optical power at different wavelengths. Passive devices require no external control for their operation and usually applied to split or combine optical signals and have limited applications in the long-haul WDM system. Active devices like optical amplifiers process the optical signal and provide a large degree of network flexibility in long-haul WDM systems. Figure 1 shows the involvement of various components in the designing of a WDM system. The functions of these components are being explained in subsequent sections.

Optical Transmitter

An optical transmitter consists of two basic components: laser and external modulator. Optical transmitters act as a source of the light carrier, the characteristics of which are modulated by the digital data sequence. WDM being predominantly a digital communication technology uses digital data as an information sequence to modulate any one of the characteristics of the optical carrier. This digital data sequence may, in turn, be able to be seen as a digital version of an analog signal which may be a voice or video signal. The laser source is operated in continuous wave (CW) mode which generates a carrier frequency. Direct modulation of the optical source is possible but it is generally suitable for low data rate communication systems (B< 10 Gb/s) and that too over a short reach (< 100 km). For high data rate over a long distance, it is required to apply an external modulator. The phase modulator, Mach-Zehnder (MZ) interferometer modulator, and electro-absorption (EA) modulator are the most frequently applied external modulators. Figure 2 shows the diagram of an optical transmitter with an external modulator.

The digital data sequence is usually encoded to enhance the system capability against channel impairments. The output of this optical transmitter can be an intensity modulated signal or a phase modulated signal, according to the characteristic (amplitude/phase) of the optical carrier which is being modulated

Figure 2. Optical transmitter

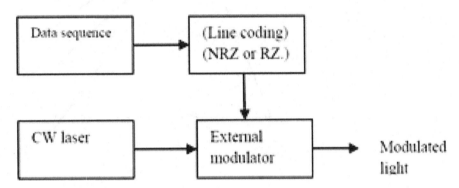

There are various types of modulation formats e.g. intensity modulation formats or phase modulation formats. The detailed discussion on modulation formats is presented in section 1.5.

WDM Multiplexer and Demultiplexer

In a WDM system, multiple wavelengths are combined using a multiplexer and inverse operation of separation at the receiver end is done by a demultiplexer (Kumar and Deen, 2014). These photonic devices are the main components of a WDM system which are used as a multiplexer and can also be used as a demultiplexer. The simplest example for a mux/demux is a prism that separates (or combine) different colors of light as shown in Figure 3.

Figure 3. Demultiplexing characteristics of a prism

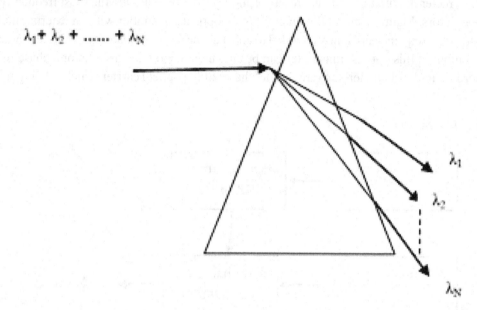

The multiplexers used in telecommunication applications are classified into two categories (i) interference-based multiplexer (use MZ or other types of the interferometer); (ii) diffraction-based multiplexer makes use of diffraction to spatially separate the wavelengths. MZ interferometer can be cascaded to form *1* x *N* demultiplexer (Verbeek et al. 1988) whereas diffraction-based mux/demux makes use of Bragg diffraction to combine or isolate the wavelength components (Agrawal, 2010). Diffraction-based mux/demux is of further two types (i) Array-wave guide gratings; (ii) phase-array demultiplexers.

Transmission Channel or Fiber-Optic Link

The transmission path consists of a number of spans where every single span has an SSMF of certain length and an EDFA amplifier to compensate for the attenuation losses. The propagation equation of an optical signal with a slowly varying envelope of electric field E at time T and the position z along the fiber is given by non-linear Schrodinger equation (NLSE) (Agrawal, 2010).

$$\frac{\partial E}{\partial z} + \alpha E + i\frac{\beta_2(\omega_0)}{2}\frac{\partial^2 E}{\partial T^2} - \frac{\beta_3(\omega_0)}{6}\frac{\partial^3 E}{\partial T^3} = i\gamma\left(\left|E\right|^2 E + \frac{i}{\omega_0}\frac{\partial}{\partial T}\left(\left|E^2\right|E\right) - \rho\tau_{R_1}E\frac{\partial\left|E\right|^2}{\partial T}\right) \quad (1.2)$$

Where α is fiber attenuation, β_2 and β_3 are first and second-order GVD parameters respectively and $\omega0$ is reference frequency of the signal. The parameter γ is given by:

$$\gamma = \frac{\omega_0 n_2}{cA_{eff}} \tag{1.3}$$

Where n_2 is the nonlinear refractive index coefficient and A_{eff} is the effective area of fiber. This takes into account various linear and nonlinear effects. The parameter ρ is the fractional contribution of delayed response of a material to the total nonlinearity and τ_{R_1} is parallel Raman shift time. EDFA amplifier compensates for the attenuation losses taking place in each span.

Optical Receiver

The main function of the optical receiver is to convert incoming optical signal into an electrical signal and then to retrieve the information signal with as less BER as possible. The achievement of minimum BER is not only dependent on the receiver design but also depends on the transmitter design and characteristics of the transmission channel. There are different types of optical receivers which are applied depending on the type of modulation format used at the transmitter side. Direct detection receiver and a coherent receiver are two main optical receivers. Direct detection is used for the intensity modulation formats and a coherent receiver is used for phase modulation formats. The direct detection receiver is a simple receiver and such a system uses inline compensation for the channel impairments like dispersion in the optical domain and no receiver-side processing is generally used in it. The coherent receiver, on the other hand, is a complex receiver; it does have processing circuitry at the receiver side.

LINE CODING AND PULSE SHAPING

The representation of digital data in electrical waveforms is known as line coding. In the case of binary coding, bit '1' is sent by transmitting at pulse *p(t)* and for '0' bit no pulse is transmitted. This line code is known as *unipolar* or *on-off* line code, as shown in Figure 4. Beside unipolar, polar and bipolar are the other line codes.

Figure 4. Unipolar line codes

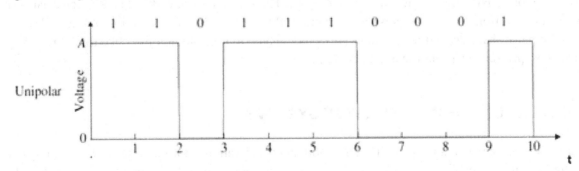

The message signal in digital fiber optic link can be the internet data, voice data (after ADC), or any other form of digital data in electrical form, where the electrical waveform is assigned through line coding. *The next step is to select pulse shape p(t) for electrical form, the widely used pulse shapes are non-return-to-zero (NRZ) and return-to-zero (RZ).* In case of NRZ, the signal does not return to zero levels if there are two consecutive '1's in a bit stream, whereas in the case of RZ, the signal returns to zero at the end of each bit slot as shown in Figure 5.

The *message* signal may be expressed as

$$m(t) = A_0 \sum_{n=-\infty}^{\infty} a_n P(t - nT_b) \tag{1.4}$$

Where a_n is the binary data in the bit slot, $p(t)$ represents the pulse shape, T_b is the bit interval and A_0 is a constant.

Figure 5. Pulse shapes (a) NRZ, and (b) RZ

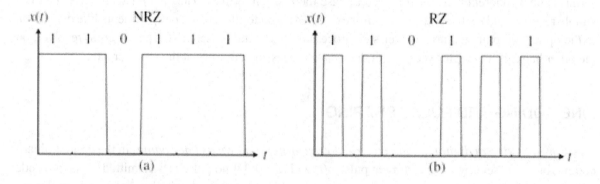

The advantage of NRZ is that it requires fewer transitions between '0' and '1' compared with RZ since the signal amplitude remains the same if consecutive bits are '1' or '0'. Therefore the bandwidth consumption by NRZ signal is less than an RZ signal. The wider spectral width of an RZ signal can also be understood from the shorter pulse width compared to NRZ pulse. The selection of line codes and specific pulse shape depend on a number of factors related to transmission link, like timing recovery, available spectrum, efficient use of bandwidth, ISI etc.

MODULATION FORMATS FOR WDM SYSTEMS

During the designing of an optical link, an important consideration is format of the transmitted optical signal. *The modulation format decides how the electrical signal would be converted into an optical bit stream.* This is of great importance because, in any digital optical link, decision circuitry in the receiver must be able to extract precise timing information from the optical signal. The three main aims of timing are; (i) To allow the signal to be sampled by a receiver at the time when SNR is maximum, (ii) to maintain the proper pulse spacing (iii) to indicate the beginning and end of each timing interval. In addition, the modulation format provides inherent error detection capability against the errors introduced by channel noise. These features can be incorporated into the digital data stream by using an appropriate modulation format. The purpose of this section is to examine the different types of modulation formats that are well suited for digital transmission on an optical link.

There are different types of modulation formats available according to the characteristic (amplitude/phase) of the optical carrier which is being modulated. In an SSMF, the optical field has three physical attributes that can be used to carry information: intensity, phase, and polarization. Depending on which of these three quantities is used for information transport, we create differentiation between intensity, phase, and polarization modulation formats. In this section, intensity and phase modulation formats are being discussed in detail and polarization modulation formats are discussed in a separate section 1.6. The auxiliary modulation formats like chirped modulation formats or partial response duobinary or pseudo-multilevel formats like carrier suppressed RZ formats are not discussed here as it is not the area of interest and more detail discussion about these formats can be found in Ref. (Winzer & Essiambre, 2006). Figure 6 shows the classification of intensity (amplitude) and phase modulation formats.

Figure 6. Classification of modulation formats

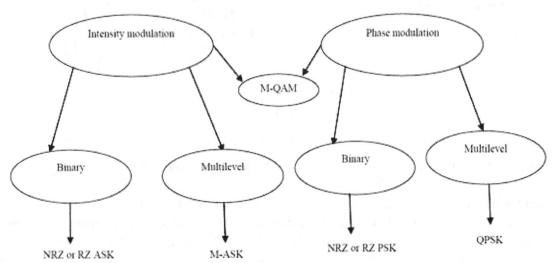

Intensity Modulation Formats

A laser is an optical source that generates a carrier frequency (f_c) whose amplitude or phase can be varied in accordance with the message signal by means of an optical modulator. The laser signal can be described as

$$c(t) = A \sin(2\pi f c_t + \theta) \tag{1.5}$$

If amplitude A is varied in accordance with a digital message m*(t)* while fc and θ remain constant, the resulting signal is known as amplitude shift keying (ASK) or on-off-keying (OOK). Then the modulated signal can be represented mathematically as

$$s(t) = K_a m(t) \sin(2\pi fc_t + \theta) \qquad (1.6)$$

Where K*a* is amplitude sensitivity.

The optical ASK can be generated using the MZ modulator as depicted in Figure 7. As shown in Figure 7 the digital message signal (data sequence) is needed to be encoded with the help of a line code, we can use NRZ or RZ electrical signal. The electrical NRZ signal is provided as an input to an MZ modulator, which modulates the intensity of the optical carrier from a CW laser and thus resulting in an ASK signal as represented in Figure 7.

Figure 7. Generation of optical NRZ-ASK signal

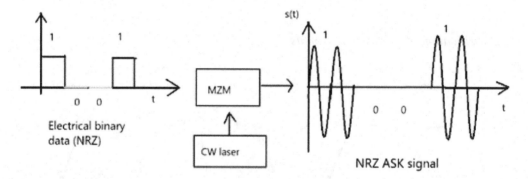

Similarly, RZ data sequence can be provided to the MZ modulator and an RZ ASK signal can be generated.

Besides the binary level modulation format, we also have a multilevel intensity modulation format. M-ASK is an example of a multilevel modulation format. Here *M* stands for the number of levels or symbols. *For example, there could be four levels with voltages -3 V, -1 V, + 1 V and + 3 V. These four levels can be assigned to by four different symbols, '00', '01', '10' and '11'. It can be mapped to four voltages as - 3 V to '00', - 1 V to '01', + 1 V to '11' and + 3 V to '10'.* A multilevel modulation format provides an opportunity to encode multiple bits in a single symbol compared to the binary level where only one bit per symbol is encoded. Therefore if we transmit B_s symbols per second, then the number of bits per second (B) can be calculated for M-ASK as

$$B = B_s \log_2 M \qquad (1.7)$$

Hence data rate (B) gets enhanced by $\log_2 M$ compared to binary modulation format. For example, if M = 4, then we can encode 2 bits per symbol which means double data rate can be supported. Fig. 1.8 represents the M-ASK signal and also compares it with binary modulation format.

Figure 8. Comparison of NRZ (binary level) and M-ASK (multilevel)

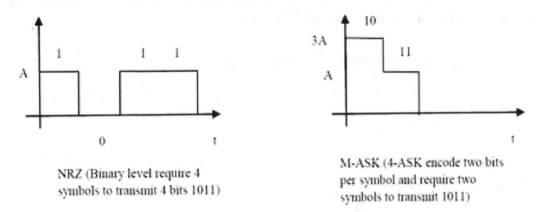

NRZ (Binary level require 4
symbols to transmit 4 bits 1011)

M-ASK (4-ASK encode two bits
per symbol and require two
symbols to transmit 1011)

The M-ASK signal which encodes a higher number of bits per symbol than binary NRZ also requires a complex transmitter and receiver circuitry to obtain desired performance in terms of BER.

Phase Modulation Formats

When phase angle θ of Eq. 1.5 is varied in accordance with the message signal $m(t)$ while keeping the amplitude A and frequency f_c constant, the resulting scheme is known as phase modulation. The modulated signal $s(t)$ can be represented as

$$s(t) = A \sin[2\pi f c_t + K p_m(t)] \tag{1.8}$$

Where K_p is called phase sensitivity.

When $m(t)$ is a digital signal then modulation is known as phase-shift keying (PSK) or binary PSK. Similar to the case of intensity modulation the output of the MZ modulator will be a PSK signal and the data sequence can be NRZ or RZ and the resulting format will be an NRZ or RZ PSK. Table 1 relates the binary data and output optical phase.

Table 1. Binary data and output optical phase (PSK)

Binary	1	0	1	1
Optical phase	0	π	0	0

Further NRZ signal can be encoded with differential encoding and a Differential phase-shift keying (DPSK) signal can be obtained.

Again similar to M-ASK we have M-PSK which is a multilevel phase modulation scheme. For example when M = 2, it is BPSK with two-phase levels 0 or π. When M = 4, the signal is known as quadrature phase-shift keying (QPSK). The phase of the carrier takes any one of the four levels 0, π/2, π, 3π/2. Figure 9 represents the BPSK and QPSK signals.

Figure 9. Constellation diagram of BPSK and 4-PSK/QPSK

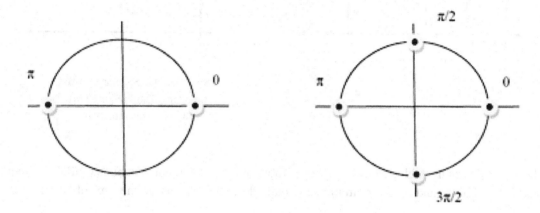

In BPSK we can encode one bit per symbol whereas in QPSK we can encode 2 bits per symbol. Hence QPSK provides more bits per second compare to BPSK. Figure 10 gives the timing diagram of BPSK and QPSK which makes a clear distinction between binary level BPSK and multilevel M-PSK or QPSK in this case.

Figure 10. Timing diagrams of multilevel QPSK and binary level BPSK

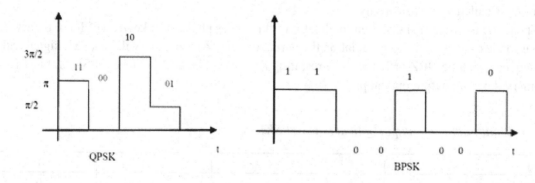

To increase the bit rate further, multi-level ASK and PSK can be combined to obtain quadrature amplitude modulation (QAM).

Quadrature Amplitude Modulation (QAM)

In M-ary ASK, the amplitude of the carrier is modulated with constant f_c and θ. In M-ary PSK, the phase of the carrier is varied with constant A and f_c. If we combine M-ASK and M-PSK in such a way that both amplitude and phase is varied simultaneously, we get M-ary amplitude and phase-shift keying (APSK) or QAM. The signal waveform is represented as

$$s(t) = m_I(t) \cos(2\pi fc_t) + mQ_t) \sin(2\pi fct,) \tag{1.9}$$

Where

$$m_I(t) = p(t)A_j \cos(\theta j,) \tag{1.10}$$

$$m_Q(t) = -p(t) A_j \sin(\theta j,) \tag{1.11}$$

$$and \; A_j = \frac{\sqrt{m_I^2 + m_Q^2}}{p(t)} \tag{1.12}$$

The amplitude of the in-phase carrier $\cos(2\pi fc_t)$ is modulated by $mI_t)$ and quadrature carrier $\sin(2\pi fct,)$ is modulated by $mQ(_t)$. Figure 11 represents the constellation diagram of 4-QAM signal, where $A1 = A3, A2 = A4, \theta1 = 0, \theta2 = \pi/2, \theta3 = \pi$ and $\theta4 = 3\pi/2$. A QAM signal hence has simultaneous amplitude modulation of in-phase and quadrature carrier.

Figure 11. Constellation diagram of a 4-QAM signal

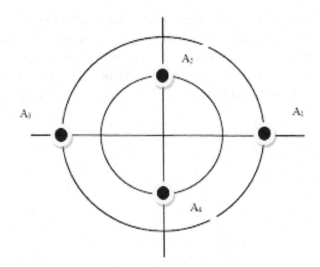

In this way, we can encode more bits per symbol by using M-QAM compared to BPSK or QPSK. However, it has denser constellation which requires complex processing at the receiver.

Brief Review of Modulation Formats

Optical modulation formats are studied intensively in the literature related to WDM systems and findings of this literature helped in improving the performance of the WDM system significantly. Winzer and Essiambrein 2006, compared the various modulation formats to highlight their resilience to key impairments found in an optical network such as amplified spontaneous emission (ASE), chromatic dispersion (CD), polarization mode dispersion (PMD), WDM crosstalk and fiber nonlinearity. *They defined the term advanced modulation formats as those formats that go beyond OOK such as DPSK, QPSK, and QAM.* Lach and Idler 2011, discussed the OOK technology for channel rate 10 Gb/s or higher. They highlighted that distributed feedback (DFB) laser in CW mode with MZ modulator or EA modulator can be used for 10 Gb/s applications. It also had concluded that OOK can achieve a SE of 0.5 b/s/Hz and for higher SE one has to switch to DQPSK modulation format. Further higher SE can only be obtained with the help of polarization mode multiplexed modulation formats. Agallin and Lucki 2014, discussed the benefits and limits of intensity and phase modulation formats. They exhibited the benefits of phase modulation formats over intensity modulation formats using numerical simulations. Agrell et al. 2016, discussed how OOK modulation formats dominated the WDM system up to 2006, and still for 10 Gb/s per wavelength it is a dominating modulation format because of simplest implementation of IM-DD. In recent times (since 2008) another category of optical modulation format has gained huge popularity known as polarization division multiplexed (PDM) or dual-polarization (DP) QPSK and QAM (DP-QPSK or PDM-QPSK/DP-QAM or PDM-QAM). DP-QPSK and DP-QAM provide very high SE. These modulation formats are discussed in section 1.6.

Polarization-Division Multiplexing (PDM)

PDM is employed to further enhance the capacity of existing WDM systems. It helps to double the capacity of a WDM system. The digital coherent receiver makes use of PDM and WDM to enhance the capacity. An SSMF supports two polarization modes one with electric field align to X-axis and other align to Y-axis. Hence, it is possible to explore the polarization as an extra dimension and to transmit information using each of the polarization modes. The block diagram of the PDM system is shown in Figure 12.

Figure 12. Description of a PDM system at transmitter side

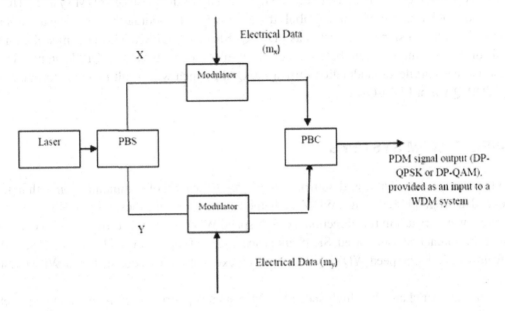

Figure 12 shows that the laser beam is made to split into two X and Y polarization components, which are then modulated by two independent data streams. These components are combined using a polarization beam combiner (PBC) and then transmitted as one of the channels of a WDM system over the fiber channel. At the receiver, the input signal is split by polarization beam splitter (PBS) into two separate beams consisting of X and Y polarization components and from which the original data streams m_x and m_y can be retrieved by two separate receivers as shown in Figure 13.

Figure 13. Description of polarization demultiplexing at the receiver side

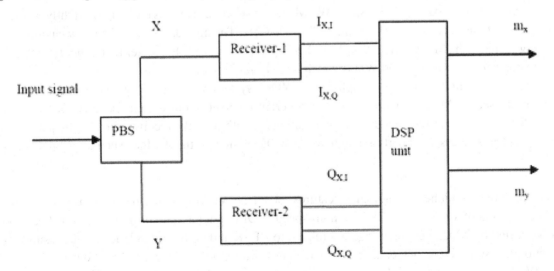

In this way, PDM can be employed to double the capacity of the existing WDM system. The QPSK modulation format has an SE of 2 bits/symbol. If we apply QPSK modulation format to a PDM system then it would result in a signal designated as PDM-QPSK or DP-QPSK. This new modulation format has an SE of 4 bits/symbol, where both the polarization components carry a QPSK signal. The same is true for another multilevel modulation format i.e. QAM which will result in a new format that is be termed as DP-QAM or PDM-QAM.

HIGH-SPEED WDM SYSTEMS

The past two decades have witnessed tremendous growth in the field of communication both in terms of data rates and in geographic coverage. WDM has helped a lot in achieving these targets. High-speed WDM systems are a way forward in this direction. A high-speed WDM system is different from conventional WDM in terms of data rate supported, SE, channel spacing, and supporting technologies. The following are the features of a high-speed WDM system which make it ahead of a conventional WDM system.

1. High bit rate per channel: A high-speed WDM system supports a very high data rate per channel ($B \geq 40$ Gb/s).
2. Advanced Modulation format: A high-speed WDM system uses advanced modulation formats such as QPSK and QAM. These advanced modulation formats encode more bits per symbol compared to OOK. Thus it helps to achieve a higher bit rate per wavelength or channel.
3. Polarization division multiplexing: High-speed WDM systems use PDM to further enhance the capacity of WDM systems. PDM helps in doubling the bit rate supported by advanced modulation formats.
4. Digital coherent receiver: A digital coherent receiver integrates the advanced modulation format based WDM system with PDM. It also enables the compensation of various linear and nonlinear fiber impairments in the electrical domain at the receiver side with the help of DSP circuits.
5. Narrow channel spacing: High-speed WDM has consecutive channels packed very tightly. Typically such systems have a channel spacing (Δf) £ 100 GHz. The high data rate and narrow channel spacing increase the SE significantly. SE of these systems is generally greater than 2 b/s/Hz compared to conventional OOK based WDM which has SE of 0.5 b/s/Hz.
6. High-speed digital circuitry: High-speed WDM system which employs advanced modulation format and PDM along with the digital coherent receiver, require high-speed ADCs/DACs and DSP circuitry to implement digital equalization algorithms at the receiver side. High-speed digital circuitry is an essential part of a high-speed WDM system without which such a system could not be realized.

All the above mentioned technological features helped the WDM system to move from its conventional application area of 10 Gb/s and OOK to high-speed WDM systems. The progress towards high-speed WDM started by 2002, when investigation related to BPSK and QPSK modulation format using direct detection had started (Gnauck et al. 2002; Griffin & Carter, 2002). The commercial deployment of 40 Gb/s WDM started in 2006 (Fishman et al. 2006; Atsunobu et al. 2008). It is the PDM technology particularly DP-QPSK which allowed the reduction of symbol rate by a factor of 4 compared to OOK and BPSK. This drastic fall in symbol rate to support the same bit rate revolutionized the WDM technology and brought 40 Gb/s or even 100 Gb/s data rate to 10 GBd and 25 GBd respectively and thereby converging it within the range of 10 and 25 GBd ADCs. This, in turn, enabled the digital coherent receiver to use DSP to perform digital equalization to channel impairments.

Commercial coherent systems were introduced in 2008 and 2010 which were using DP-QPSK at 11.5 and 28 GBd based customized CMOS ASICs to handle complex DSP functionality (Sun et al. 2008 ; Winzer 2010). The analog electric signal (two-phase and two polarization dimensions) needed to be converted to a digital signal by ADCs so that it can be processed by the DSP unit. Agile Engine's 20-million gate CMOS ASIC was used for this purpose (Roberts et al. 2009). Agile Engine's CMOS ASICs can execute 12 trillion integer operations per second to implement linear and nonlinear filtering as required to equalize the fiber impairments in the electrical domain (Roberts et al. 2009). This ASIC is implemented in 90 nm commercial CMOS technology.

A high-speed WDM system can work at a data rate as high as 224 Gb/s (Xu. et al. 2018). Channel spacing as low as 20 GHz has been reported [18] and SE in excess of 10 b/s/Hz. When channel spacing becomes equal to the baud rate then the system is known as the Nyquist WDM system (Zhang et al. 2015). However, with a decrease in channel spacing the transmission distance becomes quite limited (< 1000 km) and a long-haul WDM transmission is difficult to achieve.

When a signal is transmitted over a distance, it is subjected to a number of adverse situations like attenuation, distortion, overlapping of symbols, etc. thereby making faithful recovery of signal difficult at the receiver side. In the upcoming section, various factors adversely affecting signal transmission will be investigated.

FACTORS CAUSING SIGNAL DISTORTION IN A HIGH-SPEED WDM SYSTEM

Transmission of an optical signal in a high-speed WDM system is mostly through an already deployed legacy SSMF. The structure of an SSMF is shown in Fig. 1.14. It has an outside layer called cladding and an inner layer called core. The refractive index of the core is kept greater than cladding to facilitate total internal reflection (TIR), through which signal propagates mainly in the core. The propagation equation which governs the transmission of light through an optical fiber could be obtained by a nonlinear Schrödinger equation (Eq.1.2).

Figure 14. Structure of an optical fiber (for an SSMF, core diameter = 8-10 μm)

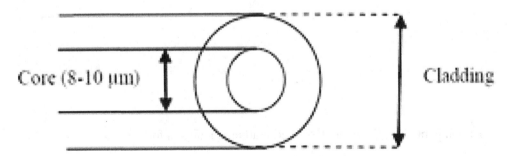

The different types of signal impairments which affect the performance of a WDM system are being described as follows.

Fiber Losses

The optical signal when propagated through a fiber experiences fall in magnitude. This fall in magnitude is known as fiber losses or fiber attenuation the mathematical representation of which is given as

$$\alpha(z) = -\frac{10}{z} log_{10}\left(\frac{P_{out}}{P_{in}}\right)$$

(1.13)

where z is the length of the fiber transmission distance, P_{out} and P_{in} are output and input power levels respectively at the receiver and transmitter end. Fiber losses are mainly caused by material absorption and Rayleigh scattering. The fiber attenuation is minimum in the third wavelength window (C and L band) thereby making it more suitable for long-haul WDM transmission (Keiser G. 2000).

Chromatic Dispersion

Chromatic dispersion in an SSMF is induced by carrier wavelength-dependent refractive index. This causes different spectral components to propagate with different velocities (Keiser G. 2000). It results in the broadening of the optical pulses in the time domain as the signal propagates through the fiber as shown in Figure 15. The fall in magnitude shown in the figure is because of fiber attenuation. The intersymbol interference (ISI) which happens because of chromatic dispersion, is shown by the hatched region. After a certain amount of ISI, adjacent pulses can no longer be individually distinguished at the receiver end and errors will occur. The main source of fiber dispersion is the group velocity dispersion (GVD) or intra-modal dispersion.

Figure 15. Effect of dispersion on the signal propagation

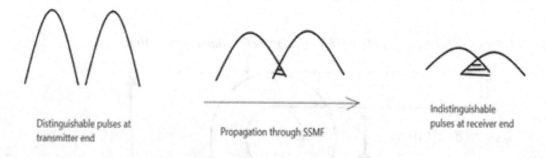

Distinguishable pulses at transmitter end

Propagation through SSMF

Indistinguishable pulses at receiver end

The dispersion parameter D can be described mathematically as follows.

$$D = -\frac{2\pi c}{\lambda^2}\beta_2$$

(1.14)

where $\beta_2 = \dfrac{d\beta_1}{d\lambda}$ and $\beta_1 = \dfrac{d\beta}{d\lambda}$, β is the propagation constant and β_2 is known as GVD parameter. The D has units of ps/nm/km and its approximate value is 17 ps/nm/km at 1550 nm.

Polarization Mode Dispersion (PMD)

An SSMF has a single mode of propagation and two orthogonal polarization states. In a perfectly symmetrical fiber, these two modes (X and Y) are identical and have the same propagation characteristics. However, due to imperfections in the waveguide geometry combined with mechanical stress, these polarization states get degenerated and start propagating at different velocities, giving rise to differential group delay (DGD). PMD can be represented mathematically as

$$D_{PMD} = \frac{\Delta\tau}{\sqrt{L}} \tag{1.15}$$

Where $\Delta\tau$ is DGD and L is the transmission distance. The unit of PMD is ps/km^{-2}.

In contrast to chromatic dispersion, which is a relatively stable phenomenon along with fiber, PMD varies randomly along with a fiber. PMD depends on the way in which fiber is deployed and also on the operating temperature conditions. PMD does not create a significant problem for low bit rates (B £ 10 Gb/s) but needs to be compensated for high data rate systems.

Nonlinear Fiber Impairments

An SSMF has a very small core area ($A_{eff} = 80$ μm^2), this results in strong nonlinearity effects in it. From nonlinear Schrödinger Eq. 1.2, nonlinearity coefficient γ is given as

$$\gamma = \frac{n_2\omega_0}{cA_{eff}} \tag{1.16}$$

Where n_2 is the nonlinear refractive index, ω_0 is the center frequency. These nonlinear effects based on Kerr nonlinearity mainly SPM, XPM, and FWM are described as follows.

1.   Self-phase modulation (SPM)

SPM is the phase modulation that a pulse develops itself. SPM is developed due to the intensity dependence refractive index that results in the conversion of the intensity fluctuations to phase variations [20]. For silica fiber, refractive index n is given as

$$n = n_0 + n_2I(t) \tag{1.17}$$

Where n_0 is the refractive index of the material; n_2 is the nonlinear index and $I(t)$ is the intensity of the optical signal. The induced phase variations result in a frequency chirp in the carrier wave. The SPM induced phase shift is given as

$$\varphi S_{PM} = \gamma Pin_{L_e}f_f \tag{1.18}$$

Where $Le_{ff=}[1-\exp(-\alpha L)]/\alpha$ is the effective length of the fiber path.

In the case of the intensity-modulated signal, the SPM can be ignored as no information is carried by the phase of the carrier wave. However, in phase-modulated systems, SPM induced chirp will cause the pulse broadening, which will degrade the system performance. In a digital coherent receiver, AE can be used to compensate for residual dispersion.

2.   Cross phase modulation (XPM)

In a WDM system, the nonlinear phase shift depends not only on the optical power in a single channel but also on the optical power in all the channels. The contribution to the nonlinear phase shift of channel j from the other channels is called XPM and is given as

$$\varphi_{j,XPM} = 2\gamma L_{eff}\sum_{m\neq j}P_m \tag{1.19}$$

Eq. 1.15 shows that the power of the adjacent channels leads to phase changes in channel j. In general, XPM increases with a decrease in channel spacing. DSP algorithm can be used to compensate for the inter-channel interference (ICI) introduced by XPM.

3.   Four-wave mixing (FWM)

FWM is a third-order nonlinear effect resulting from the dependence of refractive index on the intensity of the light signal. FWM can be viewed as the scattering process in which two photons of energy $h\nu_1$ and $h\nu_2$ create two new photons of energies $h\nu_3$ and $h\nu_4$. Figure 1.16 shows an example where ν_1 combines with ν_2 to generate sidebands $2\nu_1 - \nu_2$ and $2\nu_2 - \nu_1$.

Figure 16. Effect of FWM (generation of sidebands)

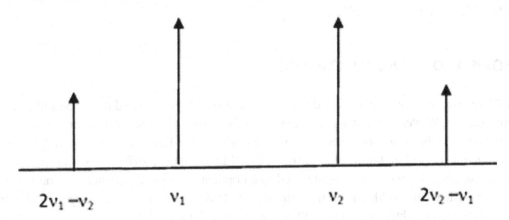

In a WDM system, non-uniform channel spacing can be used to suppress the FWM but for uniform channel spacing, FWM can also lead to ICI (Sharma et al. 2015).

Other nonlinear effects also occur in optical fiber, such as Raman and Brillouin scattering. These effects are due to the nonlinear interaction between photons and phonons. While Raman and Brillouin scattering are important in some optical fiber applications such as Raman amplification (Thakur et al. 2022), they are generally insignificant for coherent systems in 1550 nm band, compared to Kerr nonlinearity.

Besides the above-mentioned fiber impairments, some other system phenomena also contribute to the degradation of performance in a WDM system and should also be taken into consideration while designing a high-speed WDM system. A brief introduction of these phenomena is being presented in the subsequent sub-sections.

Laser Phase Noise

The output of the single-frequency laser is not strictly monochromatic but rather has frequency deviations that change randomly. The laser phase noise is characterized by its linewidth ($\Delta\nu$). Laser phase noise is quantified as phase variance (σ^2), which is proportional to an observation time (T) and the linewidth, given as

$$\sigma2 = 2\pi(\Delta\upsilon)T \qquad (1.20)$$

The total phase noise consists of linewidth contribution from transmitter and receiver, as well as nonlinear phase noise and amplified spontaneous emission (ASE). Laser phase noise is important because a phase-modulated system phase carries the information and hence phase noise can affect the performance of the system (Sharma et al. 2020, 2021).

Amplified Spontaneous Emission

ASE is the noise introduced by inline amplifiers and in a long-haul WDM system ASE builds up in the system. The ASE noise has a constant (white) signal spectrum. When compared with CD and fiber nonlinearity, which are deterministic, the impact of ASE noise is random. ASE is also described as additive white Gaussian noise (AWGN).

NARROWBAND OPTICAL FILTERING

In a WDM system, there are numbers of devices which are either filter-based or behaves like an optical filter. For example, WDM mux and demux are the filter-based devices that combine or separate different wavelengths. Similarly in an optical network, there are many filter-based devices required at intermediate nodes such as optical add-drop multiplexers (OADMs) or optical switches/optical cross-connects (OXCs). These optical devices are concatenated in an optical network; this concatenation narrows the overall optical filter bandwidth and distorts the signal. This distortion becomes significant when the number of channels is tightly packed in a WDM system to enhance the SE.

SUMMARY

In this chapter, we have discussed the working principle of a WDM system, its components, and the possible choice of modulation formats available. The structure of the transmitter and receiver has also been discussed. The chapter also defined a high-speed WDM system, its features, and various types of signal impairments that could affect the performance.

REFERENCES

Agalliu, R., & Lucki, M. (2014). *Benefits and limits of modulation formats for optical communications.* Advances in Electrical and Electronic Engineering. doi:10.15598/aeee.v12i2.992

Agrawal, G. P. (2010). *Fiber optic communication system* (4th ed.). John Wiley & Sons. doi:10.1002/9780470918524

Agrell, E., Karlsson, M., Chraplyvy, A. R., Richardson, D. J., Krummrich, P. M., Winzer, P., Roberts, K., Fischer, J. K., Savory, S. J., Eggleton, B. J., Secondini, M., Kschischang, F. R., Lord, A., Prat, J., Tomkos, I., Bowers, J. E., Srinivasan, S., & Brandt, P. (2016). Road map of optical communications. *Journal of Optics*, *18*(6), 2016. doi:10.1088/2040-8978/18/6/063002

Atsunobu, O., Daisuke, T., Tomohiko, K., & Shinji, I. (2008). *43-Gbps RZ-DQPSK transponder for long-haul optical transmission system.* https://www.yokogawa.com/in/library/resources/yokogawa-technical-reports/43-gbps-RZ-DQPSK-transponder-for-long-haul-optical-transmission-system/(accesed: April 2020)

Fishman, A. D., Thompson, A. W., & Vallone, L. (2006). LambdaXtreme® transport system: R&D of a high capacity system for low cost, ultra long haul DWDM transport. *Bell Labs Technical Journal*, *11*(2), 27–53. doi:10.1002/bltj.20160

Gnauck, A. H. (2002). *2.5 Tb/s (64/spl times/42.7 Gb/s) transmission over 40/spl times/100 km NZDSF using RZ-DPSK format and all-Raman-amplified spans.* Optical Fiber Communication Conference and Exhibit.

Griffin, A. R., & Carter, C. A. (2002). *Optical differential quadrature phase-shift key (ODQPSK) for high capacity optical transmission.* Optical Fiber Communication Conference and Exhibit. doi:10.1109/OFC.2002.1036420

ITU-T G.692 (2002). *Optical interfaces for multi-channel systems with optical amplifiers, Corrigendum 2.* https://www.itu.int/rec/T-REC-G.692-200206-I!Cor2/en

ITU-T G.694.1 (2012). *Special grid for WDM applications: DWDM frequency grid.* https://www.itu.int/rec/T-REC-G.694.1-201202-I/en

ITU-T G.694.2 (2003). *Spectral grid for WDM applications: CWDM wavelength grid.* https://www.itu.int/rec/T-REC-G.694.2-200312-I

Keiser, G. (2000). Optical fiber communications (3rd ed.). McGraw-Hill International Editions.

Kumar & Deen. (2014). *Fiber optic communications* (1st ed.). Wiley & sons.

Lach, E., & Idler, W. (2011). Modulation formats for 100G and beyond. *Optical Fiber Technology, 17*(5), 377–386. doi:10.1016/j.yofte.2011.07.012

Roberts, K., O'Sullivan, M., Kuang-Tsan Wu, Han Sun, Awadalla, A., Krause, D. J., & Laperle, C. (2009). Performance of dual-polarization QPSK for optical transport systems. *Journal of Lightwave Technology, 27*(16), 3546–3559. doi:10.1109/JLT.2009.2022484

Sharma, N., Agrawal, S., & Kapoor, V. (2020). Estimation of frequency offset prior to adaptive equalization for improved performance of DP-QPSK DWDM system. *Optical Fiber Technology, 55.*

Sharma, N., Agrawal, S., & Kapoor, V. (2021). Performance optimization of OADM based DP-QPSK DWDM optical network with 37.5 GHz channel spacing. *Optical Switching and Networking, 40.*

Sharma, N., Vij, R., & Badhan, N. (2015, March). Enhanced spectral efficiency for intensity modulated DWDM systems. *2015 Twenty First National Conference on Communications (NCC)*, 1-6. 10.1109/NCC.2015.7084818

Sun, H., Wu, T.-K., & Roberts, K. (2008). Real-time measurements of a 40 Gb/s coherent system. *Optics Express, 16*(2), 873–879. doi:10.1364/OE.16.000873 PMID:18542161

Thakur, K., Sharma, N., & Singh, J. (2020, June). Performance Analysis of Backward Pumped Raman Amplifier based DWDM System at 40Gb/s. *2020 5th International Conference on Communication and Electronics Systems (ICCES)*, 47-51. 10.1109/ICCES48766.2020.9138017

Verbeek, H. B., Henry, C. H., Olsson, N. A., Orlowsky, K. J., Kazarinov, R. F., & Johnson, B. H. (1988). Integrated four-channel Mach-Zehnder multi/demultiplexer fabricated with phosphorous doped SiO/sub 2/ waveguides on Si. *Journal of Lightwave Technology, 6*(6), 1011–1015. doi:10.1109/50.4092

Winzer, J. P. (2010, July). Beyond 100G ethernet. *Comm. Mag, 48*(7), 26–30. doi:10.1109/MCOM.2010.5496875

Winzer, J. P., & Essiambre, J.-R. (2006). Advanced Modulation Formats for High-Capacity Optical Transport Networks. *Journal of Lightwave Technology*, *24*(12), 4711–4728. doi:10.1109/JLT.2006.885260

Xu, C., Gao, G., Chen, S., & Zhang, J. (2018). Pulse-overlapping super-Nyquist WDM system. *Journal of Lightwave Technology*, *36*(18), 3941–3948. doi:10.1109/JLT.2018.2833120

Zhang, S., Huang, Y., Yaman, F., & Inada, Y. (2015). Performance study of 100-Gb/s super-Nyquist QPSK and Nyquist 8QAM over 25-GHz spacing. *IEEE Photonics Technology Letters*, *27*(13), 1445–144. doi:10.1109/LPT.2015.2425352

Chapter 17
Water–Level Prediction Utilizing Datamining Techniques in Watershed Management

Umamaheswari P.

 https://orcid.org/0000-0003-2007-697X

SASTRA University (Deemed), India

ABSTRACT

The massive wastage of water occurs due to irregular heavy rainfall and water released from dams. Many statistical methods are of the previous techniques used to predict water level, which give approximate results. To overcome this disadvantage, gradient descent algorithm has been used. This gives more accurate results and provides higher performance. K-means algorithm is used for clustering, which iteratively assigns each data point to one of the k groups according to the given attribute. The clustered output will be refined for further processing in such a way that the data will be extracted as ordered datasets of year-wise and month-wise data. Clustering accuracy has been improved to 90.22%. Gradient descent algorithm is applied for reducing the error. It also helps in predicting the amount of water to be stored in watershed for future usage. Watershed development appears to be helpful in terms of groundwater recharge, which benefits the farmers. It can also be used for domestic purposes.

1. INTRODUCTION

Water scarcity is the major issue in today's world. Massive wastage (J.Nittin Johnson et al, 2013; Yun Hwan Kima et al, 2013; Parneet Kaur et al, 2015) of water occurs due to uneven rainfall which results in water being released from dams. Because of this, districts, towns and villages suffer from water scarcity. Over 95 thousand million cubic feet (TMC) to 110 TMC water is released from dams but not even 4 TMC water is reaching surrounding towns as per research carried out We are pushed to a situation where we have to save water in every possible way. To save water and to avoid wastage of water we propose to develop a watershed in Kumbakonam town situated in Thanjavur district. The town has three water resources such as Vennar, Vettar, and Kaveri. We would like to predict the water level measurement in

DOI: 10.4018/978-1-7998-9795-8.ch017

watershed. A watershed is an area of land that stores rain water into one location such as a stream, lake or wetland. These watersheds supply the water, which can be used for drinking purposes, irrigation besides providing habitation to various plants and animals. To make weather pattern recognition efficiently many artificial neural network and Machine learning model had been used in extreme rainfall conditions (N. Q. Hung et al, 2009; V. K. Somvanshi et al, 2006; Teegavarapu, R.S.V, 2014). The development of physically based models of frequently needs in-depth knowledge and capability regarding hydrological constraints, reported to be highly inspiring as stated in reference (c. Liu et al, 2006), heavy association of sea surface temperature (SST) anomalies with regional and global climate has also been well documented in several studies (Maria C et al, 2005; Sahai AK et al 2000; French et al, 1992).

Spatial interpolation methods as observations from different sites are used in local or global variants of these methods for assessment of missing data and it suggested bias-correction methods related to those used in climate change studies for correcting missing precipitation estimates provided by the best spatial interpolation method (Hall *et al.* 1993, N.Q. Hung et al 2009) and (Hsu *et al.* 1995; Zhan Y, Shen D, 2005; Box, G.E.P. and Jenkins, 1970) have recognized artificial neural network for rainfall-runoff modeling. (Goswami et al 2009) has used ANNs with three layers, namely, input layer, hidden layer and output layer for experimental forecasts of all India Summer Monsoon Rainfall. (French et al, 1992) discussed on rainfall forecasting using neural networks. Here an attempt to represent the rainfall process in terms of a single–hidden layer feed forward Neural Network is made (Kulshrestha et al, 2006)

The Box-Jenkins method(Young PC, 2002) is also widely used time series forecasting methods in practice. It is one of the most popular models in traditional time series forecasting (A. Altunkaynak et al, 2011; Nayak, M.A et al, 2013) and is often used as a benchmark model for association with any other forecasting method. It is often difficult to identify a forecasting model because the underlying laws may not be clearly unstated. In addition, hydrological (Zubair, L et al, 2006; Kim, B et al, 2015), time series may display signs of seasonality and nonlinearity which traditional linear forecasting techniques are hard equipped to handle, often producing unsatisfactory results.

2. Method Applied

2.1 Standardization and Normalization

In data mining applications, data preprocessing plays a key role. It concerns the normalization of the data. This initial step is important when dealing with parameters of different units and scales. For example, some data mining techniques (Sudhir B et al, 2013) use the Euclidean distance and some are using Manhattan distance. When two input data sets are in different standards, a common unit must be used for both. This process of conversion to a common unit is called standardization. Z-score normalization technique is used for normalizing values within a particular range.

2.2 Classification

Bayesian network classification (Punithavathi.J, Baskaran,R, 2011) is used for representing the conditional dependencies of a set of data. It is a probabilistic graphical model which can be represented using a directed acyclic graph. It is used for finding the probabilistic relationship between data where events are represented using nodes and edges represent probabilistic relations between events. Nodes which are not connected represents conditional independency of variables. Since we propose a prediction model, Bayesian network is the most suitable.

2.3 Clustering

In order group similar object, data mining technique uses K-means algorithm to cluster data. Since our data sets are large, in order to process them quickly and efficiently, fast algorithm such as k-means is used. Observations are partitioned in to k-clusters in such way that in each cluster contains a particular observation.

2.4 Gradient Descent

Gradient descent is used for optimization. It is computationally efficient, generates stable convergence and stable error gradient. There are types of gradient Descent existing for updating parameter. Here we used Mini Batch gradient descent It reduces prediction error and improves prediction accuracy. Another name of gradient descent is steepest descent (Khalil Jouili et al, 2016; Patil C. Y et al, 2010). Machine learning challenges such as linear regression can be solved using Gradient descent. The relationship between two or more independent variables and one continuous variable can be explained using multiple linear regression which can forecast values for future years.

2.5 Posterior Probability

Posterior probability can be obtained by updating prior probability using Bayes theorem. Posterior probability of a random event is captured after the evidence or background is taken into consideration. Posterior probability is the probability that event B occurs assuming that which the event A had already occurred. Posterior probability is directly proportional to the product of likelihood and prior probability. By using these techniques, more accurate and optimized results can be obtained.

3. PROPOSED MODEL

In Artificial neural networks (Sioul Line Kong A et al, 2011; N. Q. Hung et al, 2009; Rogers, J.C., Coleman, J.S.M., 2003), back propagation method is one of the previous techniques used to predict the water level. It gives less accurate and approximate results. To overcome this disadvantage and to increase the accuracy, this proposal uses machine learning techniques such as Bayesian network classification, k mean clustering, gradient descent and posterior probability to find the monthly quantity of water that can be stored in the watershed which benefits the 106 taluks in Kumbakonam town. The overall process has three major components such as representation, evaluation and optimization. The water level prediction model of proposed approach is shown Fig.1.

Figure 1.

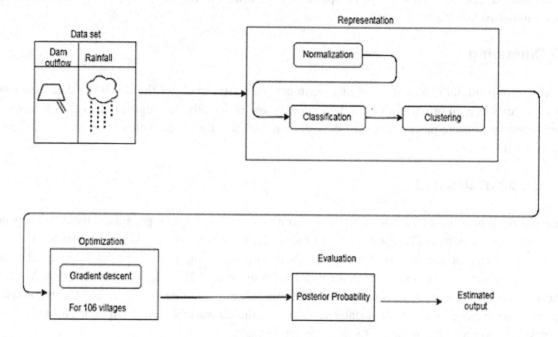

3.1 Data Set and Preprocessing

Input data set consists of past 15 years dam outlet readings and rainfall readings of Thanjavur district. Standardization as an initial preprocessing step to make data into appropriate format. Hence rainfall data is collected in millimeter (mm) (Table 1) and dam water level is measured in Thousand Million Cubic feet (TMC). Finally readings in mm and TMC should be converted to cm³ as shown in Table 3 & 4.

3.1.1. Dam Data Conversion (TMC to cm³)

$TMC \rightarrow m^3 \rightarrow l \rightarrow cm^3$

1 TMC = 28316846.592*1000*1000 cm³   (1)

Where

1TMC = 28316846.592 m³

1m3 = 1000l

1l = 1000 cm³

3.1.2 Rain Data Conversion (mm to cm³):

$$mm \rightarrow cm \rightarrow cm^3 \tag{2}$$

$1 \text{ mm} = 0.1*(cm)^3$

Where

$1 \text{ mm} = 0.1 \text{ cm}$

$0.1 \text{ cm} = (0.1)^3 \text{ cm}^3$

Table 1. Rainfall data in mm

Year	Jan	Feb	Mar	Apr	May	June	July	Aug	Sep	Oct	Nov	Dec
2001	17.67	0.701	0.548	88.282	12.697	143.49	83.147	47.735	52.15	216.92	151.14	132.93
2002	8.858	1.381	0.089	3.606	59.708	23.442	9.96	31.14	99.65	290.02	243.75	93.794
2004	3.9	0.1	2.1	8.7	301.1	16.1	46.4	57.2	234.7	394.7	223.7	20.9
2005	0.6	2	9.7	93.4	102.2	7.5	52.6	92.1	150.9	242.3	508.5	202.4
2006	11	0	39	28.8	65	30.2	1.8	70.5	150.3	222.1	185.2	37.8
2007	0.5	9	0	57.7	46	29.1	41.4	152.6	68.7	278.6	62.5	326.3
2008	6.1	17.3	140	3.6	11.1	23.4	58	129.8	39.1	191.9	723.8	107.4
2009	19.4	0	18.6	55.4	23.2	20.1	9.3	125.9	114.4	40.1	449.8	320.6
2010	29.8	0	0	10.4	96.6	44.6	39.9	144.2	162.3	209.3	398.7	229.1
2012	2.1	0.8	7.3	9.6	13	12.6	31.6	80.5	88.6	334	86.4	19
2013	14.5	14.8	53.5	0.8	20.7	24.6	11.5	146.5	117	94.2	131.4	86.2
2014	4.2	10.5	0	0.1	131	7.5	51.7	115.9	40.6	233	175.6	140.5
2015	1.8	0	6.9	91.9	99.2	28.7	47.1	78.4	55.4	153.1	328.7	212.6

Table 2. Rainfall data in cm³

Year	Jan	Feb	Mar	Apr	May	June	July	Aug	Sep	Oct	Nov	Dec
2001	5.52	0.00	0.00	688.04	2.05	2954.43	574.83	108.77	141.84	10206.31	3452.26	2348.71
2002	0.70	0.00	0.00	0.05	212.86	12.88	0.99	30.20	989.57	24395.06	14481.46	825.14
2004	0.06	0.00	0.01	0.66	27298.09	4.17	99.90	187.15	12928.24	61489.56	11194.33	9.13
2005	0.00	0.01	0.91	814.78	1067.46	0.42	145.53	781.23	3436.12	14225.26	131483.99	8291.47
2006	1.33	0.00	59.32	23.89	274.63	27.54	0.01	350.40	3395.29	10955.84	6352.18	54.01
2007	0.00	0.73	0.00	192.10	97.34	24.64	70.96	3553.56	324.24	21624.36	244.14	34741.71
2008	0.23	5.18	2744.00	0.05	1.37	12.81	195.11	2186.88	59.78	7066.83	379189.01	1238.83
2009	7.30	0.00	6.43	170.03	12.49	8.12	0.80	1995.62	1497.19	64.48	91003.55	32952.67
2010	26.46	0.00	0.00	1.12	901.43	88.72	63.52	2998.44	4275.19	9168.70	63378.03	12024.73
2012	0.01	0.00	0.39	0.88	2.20	2.00	31.55	521.66	695.51	37259.70	644.97	6.86
2013	3.05	3.24	153.13	0.00	8.87	14.89	1.52	3144.22	1601.61	835.90	2268.75	640.50
2014	0.07	1.16	0.00	0.00	2248.09	0.42	138.19	1556.86	66.92	12649.34	5414.69	2773.51
2015	0.01	0.00	0.33	776.15	976.19	23.64	104.49	481.89	170.03	3588.60	35513.96	9609.26

After standardization we will have data sets in common unit and after normalization, we will obtain values on a given range. Fig.1 shows input data set containing rainfall data and dam outflow data. Classification and labelling as

H (high) and L (low). In clustering classified data is further labelled as HH (high), HL (medium) and L(low). Gradient descent is used for forecasting using multiple linear regression. Posterior Probability computed using J48 algorithm and the forecasted values are classified according to clusters HH, HL and L.

3.2 Normalization

Here Z-score normalization has been used to get values in range as shown in Table 3 & 4.

$$z = (x - \mu) / (\tilde{A} / \sqrt{n})$$ (3)

Here the dataset has multiple samples and so it needs to describe the standard deviation of those sample mean using above formula. To identify capacity of water shed, rain data readings have been added to dam outflow. Since two different timings have been taken in to consideration, this task is done for following timings in every day. 8.00 a.m and 4.00 p.m. So that the classified output will not be biased.

Table 3. Normalized rainfall data

Year	Jan	Feb	Mar	Apr	May	June	July	Aug	Sep	Oct	Nov	Dec
2001	0.28	-0.49	-0.30	1.49	-0.34	3.33	3.03	-1.00	-0.61	-0.37	-0.51	-0.48
2002	-0.38	-0.49	-0.30	-0.63	-0.31	-0.28	-0.71	-1.06	-0.37	0.47	-0.41	-0.60
2004	-0.46	-0.49	-0.30	-0.63	3.32	-0.29	-0.06	-0.94	3.03	2.65	-0.44	-0.67
2005	-0.47	-0.49	-0.30	1.88	-0.20	-0.30	0.23	-0.47	0.33	-0.13	0.71	0.01
2006	-0.29	-0.49	-0.22	-0.56	-0.30	-0.27	-0.71	-0.81	0.32	-0.32	-0.48	-0.67
2007	-0.47	-0.04	-0.30	-0.04	-0.33	-0.27	-0.25	1.71	-0.56	0.31	-0.54	2.20
2008	-0.44	2.73	3.32	-0.63	-0.34	-0.28	0.56	0.64	-0.63	-0.55	3.06	-0.57
2009	0.53	-0.49	-0.29	-0.11	-0.34	-0.29	-0.71	0.49	-0.22	-0.96	0.32	2.05
2010	3.15	-0.49	-0.30	-0.63	-0.22	-0.19	-0.30	1.28	0.57	-0.43	0.06	0.32
2012	-0.47	-0.49	-0.30	-0.63	-0.34	-0.30	-0.51	-0.67	-0.45	1.23	-0.54	-0.67
2013	-0.05	1.52	-0.10	-0.63	-0.34	-0.28	-0.71	1.39	-0.19	-0.92	-0.52	-0.62
2014	-0.46	0.23	-0.30	-0.63	-0.04	-0.30	0.18	0.14	-0.63	-0.22	-0.49	-0.44
2015	-0.47	-0.49	-0.30	1.76	-0.21	-0.27	-0.03	-0.70	-0.60	-0.76	-0.21	0.12

Table 4. Normalized dam readings

DATE	OUTFLOW	
	8.00.AM	4.00 PM
1/2/2001	-0.9847007	-2.012249
2/2/2001	-1.0949545	-0.000527
3/2/2001	-1.168457	-0.000527
4/2/2001	-1.1562066	-0.000527
5/2/2001	-1.1643735	-2.012249
6/2/2001	-1.2133752	-2.012249
7/2/2001	-1.1562066	-0.000527
8/2/2001	-1.1602901	-0.000527
9/2/2001	-1.1562066	-0.000527
10/2/2001	-0.0618355	0.670494
11/2/2001	0.91003143	0.670494
12/2/2001	0.88144711	0.670494
13/2/2001	0.89369753	0.670494
14/2/2001	0.89369753	0.670494
15/2/2001	0.91819838	0.670494

3.3 Classification and Clustering

Based on Water storing capacity of a watershed [1-3], the minimum Min: 2.19 TMC, Max: 95.66 TMC average value is taken for that Z-score is calculated. If sum value (outflow+ rainfall) is greater than or equal to -0.70711 means label it as H for each data. If sum value is less than -0.70711 means label it as L for both timings. Labelling is done to identify which month has higher storage. There are 365 total instances. Out of them 324 instances are correctly classified and 41 instances are incorrectly classified. In confusion matrix, 241 samples are correctly classified as H label. 20 samples are incorrectly classified H label as L label. 83 samples are correctly classified L label. 21 samples incorrectly classified L label as H label. Here Capacity is parent node. Outflow, rain and sum are the child nodes. Based on the capacity of other three nodes namely Outflow, rain, sum are classified. Then the probability distribution is calculated by using Bayes Theorem.

$$P (V|C) = (P(C|V) * P(V)) /P(C) \tag{5}$$

Where V is the values. C is the capacity ie. H or L. After classification, data in excel must be changed as follows. In order to find different ranges, the following values have been observed.

Capacity 1: Min of "H": 6.816772, Max of "H": -2.77594, Avg : 2.020414
Capacity 2: Min of "H": 6.997528, Max of "H": -0.70674, Avg : 3.145394

Here observation of timing-1 is concerned, If the sum value greater than or equal to 2.020414 is referred to HH else HL. Similarly, data is clustered for each month and as for as timing-2 is concerned, If the sum value greater than or equal to 3.145394 is referred to HH otherwise it is stated as HL. Hence 3 groups of data such as HH (High), HL (Medium), L(Low) is used in the clustering process. This proposed work is concerned, simple K-Means algorithm is used for clustering and three number of clusters are created. Here class label is ignored in attributes list and number of iterations will be 8. Here initially 3 clusters are formed. In final cluster 0 indicates 2102 instances (both correct and incorrect data). Similarly for cluster 1 and 2. Cluster 0, 1, 2 represents L, HH and HL respectively. Hence out of 4748 instances 1739 instances (i.e.37%) are incorrectly clustered.

Figure 2.

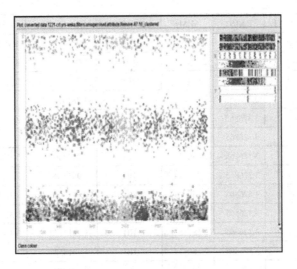

Figure 3.

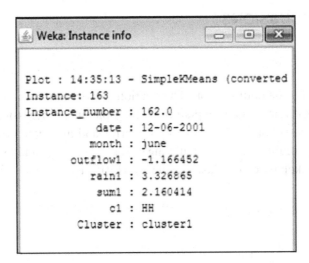

Instance information window (*Fig.3*) shows the calculated outflow value and sum value will be clustered for June month as it is shown in the cluster visualization window (*Fig.2*). Here cluster 0 labeled as L and indicated in Red dots. Similarly cluster 1, 2 are labelled HH, HL and plotted in green and blue color. Here months are placed on the horizontal axis then capacity and predicted cluster placed in the cluster visualization. In table .5, the clustered values have been calculated and shown for June month.

Table 5. Clustered table

DATE	MONTH	OUTFLOW1	RAIN1	SUM1	CLUSTER1	OUTFLOW2	RAIN2	SUM2	CLUSTER2
1/6/2001	JUNE	-1.1992319	3.326865	2.127633	HH	-1.2907287	3.326865	2.036137	HL
2/6/2001	JUNE	-1.2057879	3.326865	2.121077	HH	-1.2936073	3.326865	2.033258	HL
3/6/2001	JUNE	-1.2358364	3.326865	2.091029	HH	-1.3713288	3.326865	1.955536	HL
4/6/2001	JUNE	-1.2567793	3.326865	2.070086	HH	-1.2810135	3.326865	2.045852	HL
5/6/2001	JUNE	-1.1846629	3.326865	2.142202	HH	-1.1786442	3.326865	2.148221	HL
6/6/2001	JUNE	-1.1626273	3.326865	2.164238	HH	-1.1800835	3.326865	2.146782	HL
7/6/2001	JUNE	-1.1564355	3.326865	2.17043	HH	-1.215346	3.326865	2.111519	HL
8/6/2001	JUNE	-1.0586414	3.326865	2.268224	HH	-0.9053596	3.326865	2.421506	HL
9/6/2001	JUNE	-0.6769346	3.326865	2.649931	HH	-0.5790012	3.326865	2.747864	HL
10/6/2001	JUNE	-0.6976954	3.326865	2.62917	HH	-1.0960651	3.326865	2.2308	HL
11/6/2001	JUNE	-1.1396812	3.326865	2.187184	HH	-1.1917777	3.326865	2.135088	HL
12/6/2001	JUNE	-1.1664517	3.326865	2.160414	HH	-1.2018527	3.326865	2.125013	HL
13/6/2001	JUNE	-0.8300908	3.326865	2.496774	HH	0.26765943	3.326865	3.594525	HH
14/6/2001	JUNE	0.29153704	3.326865	3.618402	HH	0.23383618	3.326865	3.560701	HH
15/6/2001	JUNE	0.32850578	3.326865	3.655371	HH	1.13465001	3.326865	4.461515	HH

4. RESULT AND DISCUSSIONS

4.1. Optimization

Gradient descent is used for the optimization. The relationship between two or more independent variables and one continuous variable can be explained by multiple linear regression. For the extracted data gradient descent algorithm is applied for reducing the error and also predicting the amount of water stored in watershed for upcoming years by calculating the actual and predicted value. So for each month, average of sum value is taken based on cluster values (HH, HL, L).

Figure 4.

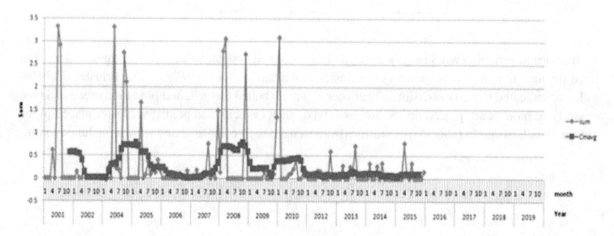

4.2 The T-Test and ANOVA

The optimized results can be examined by the t-test and ANOVA (Table 6&7a,7b) and to verify whether group means differ from one another. The t-test is used to compare two clusters, while ANOVA is possibly do more than two clusters. The t-test ANOVA includes three assumptions: independence assumption (the elements of one sample are not related to those of the other sample), normality assumption (samples are randomly drawn from the normally distributed populations with unknown population means; otherwise the means are no longer best measures of central tendency, thus test will not be valid), and equal variance assumption (the population variances of the two groups are equal).It is carried out for the class L,HH,HL in this proposed approach.

Table 6. Detailed Accuracy by class

TP RATE	FP RATE	PRECISION	RECALL	F-MEASURE	MCC	ROC AREA	PRC AREA	CLASS
1.0000	0.000	1.000	1.000	1.000	1.000	1.000	1.000	L
0.735	0.020	0.949	0.735	0.829	0.771	0.938	0.883	HH
0.961	0.132	0.784	0.961	0.863	0.794	0.934	0.855	HL
0.899	0.051	0.911	0.899	0.897	0.855	0.957	0.912	HH

Table 7a. The study of linear regression

Regression Statistics	
Multiple R	0.0549516
R Square	0.003019678
Adjusted R Square	-0.00345422
Standard Error	0.275993487
Observations	156

Table 7b. Anova test

	DF	SS	MS		F	Significance F
Regression	1	1.062117	1.062117		1.704769	0.193613
Residual	154	95.94613	0.623027			
Total	155	97.00824				

4.3 Posterior Probability

In this module, already calculated forecast values are classified based on cluster label (HH, HL,L) using J48 algorithm for each month. It is referred to c4.5 algorithm and used to generate a decision tree. It is often known as extension of Quinlan's earlier ID3 algorithm. The decision trees formed by J48 can be used for classification, and for this reason, it is often referred to as a statistical classifier. The following table describes the accuracy for clustering and classification process in percentage.

Table 8. Clustering accuracy prediction

Capacity	Incorrect clustering in percentage				Accuracy in percentage		
C1	36				90		
C2	37				90.22		

Table 9. Classification Accuracy for two time periods

Year	capacity1	capacity2
2001	88.7671	100
2002	100	99.726
2004	99.7268	100
2005	99.1098	99.7
2006	100	94.24
2007	100	100
2008	100	100
2009	99.726	100
2010	100	99.726
2012	100	100
2013	100	99.671
2014	99.726	100
2015	100	100

Here the number of instances for leaf node is identified as two and the confidence Factor is 0.5(for more accuracy). So the total no. of instances are 612 as per the classification result. By applying the above specified data techniques, the accuracy of system increases compared to existing techniques .Therefore in this proposed method data mining techniques enable forecasting of values which will prove to be useful for predictive analysis

5. CONCLUSION AND FUTURE ENHANCEMENT

This model can be implemented in any place and small villages, taluks or metropolitan cities where water needs to be saved, utilized for domestic purposes and prevent water from mixing with ocean. The prototype will ensure good storage of water in watershed. Alternatively, addition of attributes such as evaporation and soil erosion may also give appropriate result. Any month having higher evaporation rate or soil erosion rate then that will result in variation in the amount of water outflow. Attributes such as evaporation and soil erosions are taken into account and undergo classification and clustering process, so that we will be able to get the most accurate result

Our future work in this direction, building on these outcomes, will involve using the rainfall extreme fields in conjunction with concurrent synoptic-scale atmospheric circulation patterns to develop spatially distributed stochastic based case for urban flood risk estimation and producing coherent flood exceedance maps at the urban scale. In order to address some notable gaps in understanding how rainfall processes are manifested in space and time and change with climate can be taken as further research.

REFERENCES

Altunkaynak, A., & Şen, Z. (n.d.). Steady state flow with hydraulic conductivity change around large diameter wells, hydrological processes, Wiley publisherTony Hall, Precipitation Forecasting Using A Neural Network. *Weather and Forecasting, 14.*

Anindita, L., & Nugraha. (2016). Dam Water Level Prediction System Utilizing Artificial Neural Network Back Propagation, Case Study: Ciliwung Watershed, Katulampa Dam. *Proceedings of 2016 International Conference on ICT For Smart Society.*

Box, G. E. P., & Jenkins, G. M. (1970). *Time Series Analysis: Forecasting and Control.* Holden-Da y.

Cleary, J. G., & Trigg, L. E. (1995). K*: An Instance-based learner using an entropic distance measure. *Proceedings of the 12th Int. Conf. on Machine Learning*, 108-114.

Farmani, R., Kakoudakis, K., Behzadian, K., & Butler, D. (2017). Pipe Failure Prediction in Water Distribution Systems Considering Static and Dynamic Factors. *Proceedings of International Conference in "Emerging Trends in Science, Technology and Management-2013.*

French, Krajewski, & Cuykendall. (1992). Rainfall forecasting in space and time using a neural network. *Journal of Hydrology (Amsterdam), 137*(1), 1–31.

Goswami, Venugopal, & Sengupta, Madhusoodanan, & Xavier. (2006). Increasing Trend of Extreme Rain Events Over India in a Warming Environment. *Science,* 1.

Hsu, Moncrieff, Tung, & Liu. (2006a). Temporal variability of warm-season precipitation over North America: Statistical analysis of radar measurement. *J. Atmos. Sci.*

Hung, N. Q., Babel, M. S., Weesakul, S., & Tripathi, N. K. (2009). An artificial neural network model for rainfall forecasting in Bangkok, Thailand. *Hydrology and Earth System Sciences, 13,* 1413–1425.

Hung, N. Q., Babel, M. S., Weesakul, S., & Tripathi, N. K. (2009). An artificial neural network model for rainfall forecasting in Bangkok, Thailand. *Hydrology and Earth System Sciences, 13*, 1413–1425.

Jouili & Braiek. (2016). A gradient descent control for output tracking of a class of non-minimum phase nonlinear systems. *Journal of Applied Research and Technology.* doi:10.1016/j.proeng.2017.03.217

Kaur, P., Singh, M., & Josan, G. S. (2015). Classification and prediction based data mining algorithms to predict slow learners in education sector. *Proceedings of XVIII International Conference on Water Distribution Systems Analysis.* 10.1016/j.procs.2015.07.372

Kim, B., Sanders, B. F., Famiglietti, J. S., & Guinot, V. (2015). Urban flood modeling with porous shallow- water equations: A case study of model errors in the presence of anisotropic porosity. *Journal of Hydrology (Amsterdam), 523*, 680–692.

Kima, Y. H., Yoo, S. J., Gu, Y. H., Lim, J. H., Han, D., & Baik, S. W. (2013). Crop Pests Prediction Method using Regression and Machine Learning Technology: Survey. *Proceedings of 2013 International Conference on Future Software Engineering and Multimedia Engineering.*

Meganathan, S., Bala Krishnan, R., Sumathi, A., Sheik Mohideen Shah, S., & Senthilkumar, J. (2019). An Experiment in Weather Prediction for North East and South West Monsoon Over Chennai. *International Journal of Recent Technology and Engineering, 8*, 4460–4465.

Nayak, M. A., & Ghosh, S. (2013). Prediction of extreme rainfall event using weather pattern recognition and support vector machine classifier. *Theoretical and Applied Climatology, 114*, 583–603.

Neural Networks in Forecasting Minimum Temperature. (n.d.). International Journal of Electronics & *Tongxin Jishu, 2*(3), 101–105.

Nittin Johnson, Govindaradjane, & Sundararajan. (2013). Impact of Watershed Management on the Groundwater and Irrigation Potential: A Case Study. *International Journal of Engineering and Innovative Technology, 2*(8).

Patil, C. Y., & Ghatol, A. A. (2010). Rainfall forecasting using local parameters over a meteorological station: An artificial neural network approach. *International J. of Engg. Research & Indu. Appls, 3*(2), 341–356.

Punithavathi, J., & Baskaran, R. (2011). Land use and land cover using remote sensing and GIS techniques - A case study of Thanjavur District, Tamil Nadu, India. *Proceedings of International Journal of Current Research, 3*(10), 237–244.

Raj, Y. E. A. (1996). Inter and intra-seasonal variation of thermodynamic parameters of the atmosphere over coastal Tamil Nadu during northeast monsoon. *Mausam (New Delhi), 47*(3), 259–268.

Rogers, J. C., & Coleman, J. S. M. (2003). Interactions between the Atlantic multidecadal oscillation, El Nino/La Nina, and the PNA in winter Mississippi Valley stream flow. *Geophys. Res. Lett., 30*(10), 1518. 2003GL017216 doi:10.1029/

Sahai, A. K., Somann, M. K., & Satyan, V. (2000). All India Summer Monsoon Rainfall Prediction Using an Artificial Neural Netw. *Climate Dynamics, 16*(4), 291–302.

Siou, Kong, Johannet, Borrell, & Pistre. (2011). Complexity selection of a neural network model for karst flood forecasting: The case of the Lez Basin (Southern France). *Journal of Hydrology, 403*, 367-380.

Somvanshi, V. K. (2006). Modeling and prediction of rainfall using artificial neural network and ARIMA techniques. *J. Ind. Geophys. Union, 10*(2), 141–151.

Somvanshi, V. K. (2006). Modeling and prediction of rainfall using artificial neural network and ARIMA techniques. *J. Ind. Geophys. Union, 10*(2), 141–151.

Teegavarapu, R. S. V. (2014). Statistical corrections of spatially interpolated precipitation estimates. *Hydrological Processes, 28*(11), 3789–3808. http://dx.doi. org/10.1002/hyp.9906

Valverde, Campos, & Nelson. (2005). Artificial Neural Network Technique for Rainfall Forecasting Applied to the Sao Paulo Region. *Journal of Hydrology (Amsterdam), 301*, 146–162.

Young, P. C. (2002). Advances in real-time flood forecasting. Philos Trans R Soc London. *Ser A, 360*, 1433–1450.

Zhan, Y., & Shen, D. (2005). Design efficient support vector machine for fast classification. *Pattern Recognition, 38*, 157–161. doi:10.1016/j.patcog

Zubair, L., & Ropelewski. (2006). The strengthening relationship of ENSO and the North East Monsoon rainfall over Sri Lanka and Southern India. *Journal of Climate, 19*(8), 1567–1575.

Compilation of References

Abdullah, Y. S., & Al-Alwan, H. A. (2019). Smart material systems and adaptiveness in architecture. *Ain Shams Engineering Journal, 10*(3), 623–638. doi:10.1016/j.asej.2019.02.002

Absher, K. A. (2020). *Exploring the use of 3D apparel visualization software to fit garments for people with disabilities* [Master's thesis]. North Carolina State University, Raleigh, NC, United States.

Abuhamad, M., Abuhmed, T., Mohaisen, D., & Nyang, D. (2020). AUToSen: Deep-learning-based implicit continuous authentication using smartphone sensors. *IEEE Internet of Things Journal, 7*(6), 5008–5020. doi:10.1109/JIOT.2020.2975779

Adewoyin, A. D., Olopade, M. A., Oyebola, O. O., & Chendo, M. A. (2019). Development of CZTGS/CZTS tandem thin film solar cell using SCAPS-1D. *Optik (Elsevier), 176*, 132–142. doi:10.1016/j.ijleo.2018.09.033

Agalliu, R., & Lucki, M. (2014). *Benefits and limits of modulation formats for optical communications.* Advances in Electrical and Electronic Engineering. doi:10.15598/aeee.v12i2.992

Agcayazi, T., Chatterjee, K., Bozkurt, A., & Ghosh, T. K. (2018). Flexible interconnects for electronic textiles. *Advanced Materials Technologies, 3*(10), 1700277. doi:10.1002/admt.201700277

Agrawal, G. P. (2010). *Fiber optic communication system* (4th ed.). John Wiley & Sons. doi:10.1002/9780470918524

Agrell, E., Karlsson, M., Chraplyvy, A. R., Richardson, D. J., Krummrich, P. M., Winzer, P., Roberts, K., Fischer, J. K., Savory, S. J., Eggleton, B. J., Secondini, M., Kschischang, F. R., Lord, A., Prat, J., Tomkos, I., Bowers, J. E., Srinivasan, S., & Brandt, P. (2016). Road map of optical communications. *Journal of Optics, 18*(6), 2016. doi:10.1088/2040-8978/18/6/063002

Aguilar, M. R., & San Román, J. (Eds.). (2019). *Smart polymers and their applications.* Woodhead Publishing. doi:10.1016/B978-0-08-102416-4.00001-6

Alam, M. R., Reaz, M. B. I., & Ali, M. A. M. (2012). A Review of Smart Homes—Past, Present, and Future. *IEEE Transactions on Systems, Man and Cybernetics. Part C, Applications and Reviews, 42*(6), 1190–1203. doi:10.1109/TSMCC.2012.2189204

Aliu, O., Imran, A., Imran, M., & Evans, B. (2013, February). A survey of self organisation in future cellular networks. *IEEE Communications Surveys and Tutorials, 15*(1), 336–361. doi:10.1109/SURV.2012.021312.00116

Al-Karaki, J. N., & Kamal, A. E. (2004, December). Routing techniques in wireless sensor networks: A survey. *IEEE Wireless Communications, 11*(6), 6–28. doi:10.1109/MWC.2004.1368893

Al-Maliki, J. Q., & Al-Maliki, A. J. Q. (2015). The processes and technologies of 3D printing. *International Journal of Advances in Computer Science and Technology, 4*(10), 161–165.

Altunkaynak, A., & Şen, Z. (n.d.). Steady state flow with hydraulic conductivity change around large diameter wells, hydrological processes, Wiley publisherTony Hall, Precipitation Forecasting Using A Neural Network. *Weather and Forecasting, 14.*

Alyani, N. (2012). The Improvement of Key management Based OnLogical Key Hierarchy by Implementing Diffie Hellman Algorithm. *Journal of ETCIS, 3,* 3.

Alzubaidi, A., & Kalita, J. (2016). Authentication of smartphone users using behavioral biometrics. *IEEE Communications Surveys and Tutorials, 18*(3), 1998–2026. doi:10.1109/COMST.2016.2537748

Anand, R., Singh, J., Pandey, D., Pandey, B. K., Nassa, V. K., & Pramanik, S. (2022). Modern Technique for Interactive Communication in LEACH-Based Ad Hoc Wireless Sensor Network. In M. M. Ghonge, S. Pramanik, & A. D. Potgantwar (Eds.), *Software Defined Networking for Ad Hoc Networks.* Springer. doi:10.1007/978-3-030-91149-2_3

Andrae, A. S., & Edler, T. (2015). On global electricity usage of communication technology: Trends to 2030. *Challenges., 6*(1), 1–41. doi:10.3390/challe6010117

Anindita, L., & Nugraha. (2016). Dam Water Level Prediction System Utilizing Artificial Neural Network Back Propagation, Case Study: Ciliwung Watershed, Katulampa Dam. *Proceedings of 2016 International Conference on ICT For Smart Society.*

An, J., & Chung, W. (2016). A novel indoor healthcare with time hopping-based visible light communication. In *Proceedings of IEEE 3rd World Forum on Internet of Things (WF-IoT)* (pp. 19-23). 10.1109/WF-IoT.2016.7845438

An, J., Pham, Q. N., & Chung, W. Y. (2017). Single cell three channel wavelength division multiplexing in visible light communication. *Optics Express, 25*(21), 25477–25485. doi:10.1364/OE.25.025477 PMID:29041214

Arjun, D., & Hayavadana, J. (2014). Thermal energy storage materials (PCMs) for textile applications. *Journal of Textile and Apparel, Technology and Management, 8*(4).

Armendáriz-Mireles, E. N., Rocha-Rangel, E., Caballero-Rico, F., Ramirez-De-Leon, J. A., & Vázquez, M. (2017). Effect of. *IEEE Journal of Photovoltaics, 7*(5), 1329–1337. doi:10.1109/JPHOTOV.2017.2720260

Armstrong-Hélouvry, B., Dupont, P., & Canudas De Wit, C. (1994). A survey of models, analysis tools and compensation methods for the control of machines with friction. *Automatica, 30*(7), 1083–1138. doi:10.1016/0005-1098(94)90209-7

Aslan, J., Mayers, K., Koomey, J. G., & France, C. (2018). Electricity intensity of Internet data transmission: Untangling the estimates. *Journal of Industrial Ecology, 22*(4), 785–798. doi:10.1111/jiec.12630

Åström, K. J., & Murray, R. M. (2008). *Feedback systems: An introduction for scientists and engineers.* Princeton University Press.

Atsunobu, O., Daisuke, T., Tomohiko, K., & Shinji, I. (2008). *43-Gbps RZ-DQPSK transponder for long-haul optical transmission system.* https://www.yokogawa.com/in/library/resources/yokogawa-technical-reports/43-gbps-RZ-DQPSK-transponder-for-long-haul-optical-transmission-system/(accesed: April 2020)

Atzori, L., Iera, A., & Morabito, G. (2010, October). The Internet of Things: A survey. *Computer Networks, 54*(15), 2787–2805. doi:10.1016/j.comnet.2010.05.010

Aviv, A. J., Gibson, K. L., Mossop, E., Blaze, M., & Smith, J. M. (2010). Smudge attacks on smartphone touch screens. *Woot, 10,* 1–7.

Ayana, A. G., & University, H. (2015). *Towards improving Brill's tagger lexical and transformation rule for Afaan Oromo language.* Hawassa University.

Babu, V. R., & Arunraj, A. (2018). Thermo regulated clothing with phase change materials. *Journal of Textile Engineering & Fashion Technology, 4*(5), 344–347. doi:10.15406/jteft.2018.04.00162

Bagul, P., Mishra, A., Mahajan, P., Kulkarni, M., & Dhopavkar, G. (2014). Rule based POS tagger for Marathi text. *The Proceedings of International Journal of Computer Science and Information Technologies, 5*(2), 1322–1326.

Baker, H. K., Kumar, S., & Pandey, N. (2021). Thirty years of *Small Business Economics*: A bibliometric overview. *Small Business Economics, 56*(1), 487–517. doi:10.100711187-020-00342-y

Bandyopadhyay, S., Goyal, V., Dutta, S., Pramanik, S., & Sherazi, H. H. R. (2021). Unseen to Seen by Digital Steganography. In S. Pramanik, M. M. Ghonge, R. Ravi, & K. Cengiz (Eds.), *Multidisciplinary Approach to Modern Digital Steganography*. IGI Global. doi:10.4018/978-1-7998-7160-6.ch001

Bansal, R., Jenipher, B., Nisha, V., Makhan, R., Pramanik, S., Roy, S., & Gupta, A. (2022). Big Data Architecture for Network Security. In Cyber Security and Network Security. Wiley. doi:10.1002/9781119812555.ch11

Bansal, S., & Aryal, P. (2016). Evaluation of new materials for electron and hole transport layers in perovskite-based solar cells through SCAPS-1D simulations. *IEEE 43rd Photovoltaic Specialists Conf.*, 747–750.

Bansal, S., & Sud, S. (2017). Advancement and history of techno fashion. *International Journal of Arts, 7*(2), 33–37.

Bapu, B. R. (2017). Link Quality Based Opportunistic Routing Algorithm foQoSOS: Aware Wireless Sensor Networks Security. *WPC, 97*(1), 1563–1578.

Bari, D., Cester, A., Wrachien, N., Ciammaruchi, L., Brown, T. M., Reale, A., Di Carlo, A., & Meneghesso, G. (2012). Reliability study of ruthenium-based dye-sensitized solar cells (DSCs). *IEEE Journal of Photovoltaics, 2*(1), 27–34. doi:10.1109/JPHOTOV.2011.2180702

Barman, A. K., Sarmah, J., & Sarma, S. K. (2013, April). Pos tagging of Assamese language and performance analysis of CRF++ and FNTBL approaches. In *2013 UKSim 15th International Conference on Computer Modelling and Simulation* (pp. 476-479). IEEE.

Barnes, N. (2016). *Smart textiles for designers–inventing the future of fabrics*. Academic Press.

Barua, A. G., & Tiru, B. (2006). Variation of width of the hysteresis loop with temperature in an emitter-coupled Schmitt trigger. *Indian Journal of Pure and Applied Physics, 44*, 482–485.

Baruah, P.P., & Bhattacharya, P. (2012). *Status of Wetlands in Guwahati University Campus*. Gauhati University.

Basaran, C., & Kang, K.-D. (2009). *Quality of Service in Wireless Sensor Network s*. Springer London. doi:10.1007/978-1-84882-218-4_12

Becchi, M., & Crowley, P. (2007a). A Hybrid Finite Automaton for Practical Deep Packet Inspection. *Proceedings of the ACM Conference on Emerging Networking Experiments and Technologies*.

Becchi, M., & Crowley, P. (2007b). An Improved Algorithm to Accelerate Regular Expression Evaluation. *Proceedings of the 3rd ACM/IEEE Symposium on Architecture for Networking and Communications Systems*, 145-154.

Becchi, M., & Crowley, P. (2008). Extending Finite Automata to Efficiently Match Perl-Compatible Regular Expressions. *Proceedings of the ACM International Conference on Emerging Networking Experiments and Technologies*.

Berginc, M., Krašovec, U. O., & Topič, M. (2014). Outdoor ageing of the dye-sensitized solar cell under different operation regimes. *Solar Energy Materials and Solar Cells, 120*(B), 491–499. doi:10.1016/j.solmat.2013.09.029

Berzina, Z. (2009). *E-Static Shadows*. http://www.zaneberzina.com/

Bird, S., Klein, E., & Loper, E. (2009). *Natural language processing with Python: analyzing text with the natural language toolkit.* O'Reilly Media, Inc.

Bishnoi, S., & Pandey, S. K. (2018). Device performance analysis for lead-free perovskite solar cell optimization. *IET Optoelectronics, 124*(4), 185–190. doi:10.1049/iet-opt.2017.0135

Bishop, J. (2007). Ecological cognition: A new dynamic for human-computer interaction. In B. Wallace, A. Ross, J. Davies, & T. Anderson (Eds.), The mind, the body and the world: Psychology after cognitivism (pp. 327-345). Imprint Academic.

Bishop, J. (2013). Assisting human interaction (US/20130095460 ed.). US: PCT/GB2011/050814/A1.

Bishop, J., & Goode, M. M. H. (2021). Towards 'serendipity engineering for seductive hypermedia' and 'user analysis using socialnomics': The role of ecological cognition. *The 8th International Conference on Computational Science & Computational Intelligence (CSCI'21).*

Bishop, J. (2013). The empathic psychopathy in public life: Towards an understanding of 'autism' and 'empathism' and 'dopaminergic-serotonergic asynchronicity.' *Conference on the Implications of Research on the Neuroscience of Affect, Attachment, and Social Cognition.*

Bishop, J. (2014). Dealing with internet trolling in political online communities: Towards the this is why we can't have nice things scale. *International Journal of E-Politics, 5*(4), 1–20. doi:10.4018/ijep.2014100101

Bishop, J. (2015). Determining the risk of digital addiction to adolescent targets of internet trolling: Implications for the UK legal system. In J. Bishop (Ed.), *Psychological and social implications surrounding internet and gaming addiction* (pp. 31–42). IGI Global. doi:10.4018/978-1-4666-8595-6.ch003

Bishop, J. (2017). Developing and validating the "This is why we can't have nice things scale": Optimising political online communities for internet trolling. In Y. Ibrahim (Ed.), *Politics, protest, and empowerment in digital spaces* (pp. 153–177). IGI Global. doi:10.4018/978-1-5225-1862-4.ch010

Bishop, J., Kommers, P. A. M., & Bechkoum, K. (in press). Ecological cognition for measuring psi-hit and psi-miss online: Using K-scores to understand anomalistic psychology in project management teams. *International Journal of Innovation, Management and Technology.*

Biswas, S., & Misic, J. (2013). A cross-layer approach to privacypreserving authentication in WAVE-enabled VANETs. *IEEE Transactions on Vehicular Technology, 62*(5), 2182–2192. doi:10.1109/TVT.2013.2238566

Boczkowska, A., & Leonowicz, M. (2006). Intelligent materials for intelligent textiles. *Fibres & Textiles in Eastern Europe, 59*(5), 13–17.

Bodur, H., & Kara, R. (2017). Implementing Diffie-Hellman key exchange method on logical key hierarchy for secure broadcast transmission. In *2017 at CICN* (pp. 144–147). IEEE. doi:10.1109/CICN.2017.8319374

Bogdan. (2018). *Part of speech tagging using an lstm network.* https://nlpforhackers.io/lstm-pos-tagger-keras/

Bolognini, S. (1997). Empathy and 'empathism'. *The International Journal of Psycho-Analysis, 78*(2), 279–293.

Bonnet, M. (2020). *Status of lightning detection Performance and limitations of existing systems.* Academic Press.

Box, G. E. P., & Jenkins, G. M. (1970). *Time Series Analysis: Forecasting and Control.* Holden-Da y.

Brill, E. (1995). Transformation-based error-driven learning and natural language processing: A case study in part-of-speech tagging. *Computational Linguistics, 21*(4), 543–565.

Brown, M. (2000). PGP in Constrained Wireless Devices. *Proc.9th USENIX Security Symp.*

Bube, R. H., & Fahrenbruch, A. L. (1983). *Fundamentals of solar cells* (1st ed.). Academic Press.

Cahyadi, W. A., Jeong, T., Kim, Y., Chung, Y., & Adiono, T. (2015). Patient monitoring using Visible Light uplink data transmission. In *Proceedings of International Symposium on Intelligent Signal Processing and Communication Systems (ISPACS)* (pp. 431-434). 10.1109/ISPACS.2015.7432810

Callister, W. D. Jr, & Rethwisch, D. G. (2012). *Fundamentals of materials science and engineering: An integrated approach*. John Wiley & Sons.

Canudas De Wit, C., & Lischinsky, P. (1996). Adaptive friction compensation with partially known dynamic friction model. *IFAC Proceedings Volumes, 29*(1), 2078-2083. 10.1016/S1474-6670(17)57978-1

Capineri, L. (2014). Resistive sensors with smart textiles for wearable technology: From fabrication processes to integration with electronics. *Procedia Engineering, 87*, 724–727. doi:10.1016/j.proeng.2014.11.748

Carrelli, C. (Ed.). (2005). Ubiquitous services and applications: Exploiting the potential; 27–29 April 2005, Marriott Hotel, Heidelberg, Germany; Incl. CD-ROM. Margret Schneider.

Caruso, M. M., Blaiszik, B. J., Jin, H., Schelkopf, S. R., Stradley, D. S., Sottos, N. R., & Moore, J. S. (2010). Robust, double-walled microcapsules for self-healing polymeric materials. *ACS Applied Materials & Interfaces, 2*(4), 1195–1199. doi:10.1021/am100084k PMID:20423139

Castano, L. M., & Flatau, A. B. (2014). Smart fabric sensors and e-textile technologies: A review. *Smart Materials and Structures, 23*(5), 053001. doi:10.1088/0964-1726/23/5/053001

Chakrabarti, T., Dey, A., & Sarkar, S. K. (2018). Comparative analysis of physical organic and inorganic Dyesensitized solar cell. *Optical Materials, 82*, 141–146. doi:10.1016/j.optmat.2018.05.009

Chakraborty, K., Choudhury, M. G., & Paul, S. (2019). Numerical study of Cs_2TiX_6 (X=Br⁻, I⁻, F⁻ and Cl⁻) based perovskite solar cell using SCAPS-1D device simulation. *Solar Energy, 194*, 886–892. doi:10.1016/j.solener.2019.11.005

Chakraborty, K., Choudhury, M. G., & Paul, S. (2021). Study of Physical, Optical and Electrical Properties of Cesium Titanium (IV) Based Single Halide Perovskite Solar Cell. *IEEE J. of Photovoltaics, 11*(2), 386–390. doi:10.1109/JPHOTOV.2021.3050268

Chapman, S. (2003). *Electric Machinery Fundamentals*. McGraw-Hill.

Chatterjee, K., Tabor, J., & Ghosh, T. K. (2019). Electrically conductive coatings for fiber-based e-textiles. *Fibers (Basel, Switzerland), 7*(6), 51. doi:10.3390/fib7060051

Chatterjee, S., Baishya, R., & Tiru, B. (2020). Estimating the Characteristics of the Forward Voltage Gain Scattering Parameter of Indoor Power Line Channel Using Only Input Port Measurement. *Wuxiandian Gongcheng, 29*(4), 644–653. doi:10.13164/re.2020.0644

Chatterjee, S., & Tiru, B. (2018). Optimization of the components of a visible light communication system for efficient data transfer. In *Proceedings of IEEE EDKCON Conference* (pp.373-378). 10.1109/EDKCON.2018.8770450

Chatterjee, S., & Tiru, B. (2020). Development of a visible light communication system for reducing flicker in low data rate requirement. *Int. J. Nanoparticles, 12*(1/2), 59–72. doi:10.1504/IJNP.2020.106001

Chaudhuri, A. (2020). Deep Learning Models for Face Recognition: A Comparative Analysis. Deep Biometrics, 99-140. doi:10.1007/978-3-030-32583-1_6

Cheng, T. E., & Choi, T. M. (Eds.). (2010). *Innovative quick response programs in logistics and supply chain management*. Springer Science & Business Media. doi:10.1007/978-3-642-04313-0

Chen, S., Pande, A., & Mohapatra, P. (2014). Sensor-assisted facial recognition: an enhanced biometric authentication system for smartphones. *Proceedings of the 12th annual international conference on Mobile systems, applications, and services*, 109-122. 10.1145/2594368.2594373

Chen, T., Chang, C.-Y., Wang, C.-L., & Chen, Y.-S. (2011). Green technologies for wireless communications and mobile computing. *IET Communications*, 5(18), 2595–2597. doi:10.1049/iet-com.2011.0852

Chen, Y., Lin, Z., Zhao, X., Wang, G., & Gu, Y. (2014). Deep learning-based classification of hyperspectral data. *IEEE Journal of Selected Topics in Applied Earth Observations and Remote Sensing*, 7(6), 2094–2107. doi:10.1109/JSTARS.2014.2329330

Cheung, T. W., & Li, L. (2018). Sustainable development of smart textiles: A review of 'self-functioning' abilities which makes textiles alive. *Journal of Textile Engineering & Fashion. Technology*, 4, 152–127.

Cho, G., Jeong, K., Paik, M. J., Kwun, Y., & Sung, M. (2011). Performance evaluation of textile-based electrodes and motion sensors for smart clothing. *IEEE Sensors Journal*, 11(12), 3183–3193. doi:10.1109/JSEN.2011.2167508

Choi, H., Hwang, S., Bae, H., Kim, S., Kim, H., & Jeon, M. (2011). Electrophoretic graphene for transparent counter electrodes in dye-sensitised solar cells. *Electronics Letters*, 47(4), 281–283. doi:10.1049/el.2010.2897

Chou, H. T., Liu, H. C., Hsu, H. C., Chen, C. Y., & Lai, C. H. (2018). Investigation of Deformed. *IEEE Journal of Photovoltaics*, 8(3), 763–768. doi:10.1109/JPHOTOV.2018.2806307

Chou, H.-T., Lien, C.-H., Hsu, H.-C., Chen, S.-T., Sung, C.-T., & Jiang, S.-C. F. (2017). Characteristics and Analyses of Various Counter Electrodes Applied in Quasi-Solid Electrolyte Dye-Sensitized Solar Cells. *IEEE Journal of Photovoltaics*, 8(1), 137–143. doi:10.1109/JPHOTOV.2017.2766530

Chou, H.-T., Tseng, K.-C., & Hsu, H.-C. (2015). Fabrication of deformed. *IEEE Journal of Photovoltaics*, 6(1), 211–216. doi:10.1109/JPHOTOV.2015.2487819

Chou, J. C., Chu, C. M., Liao, Y. H., Huang, C. H., Lin, Y. J., Wu, H., & Nien, Y. H. (2016). The incorporation of graphene and magnetic beads into dye-sensitized solar cells and application with electrochemical capacitor. *IEEE Journal of Photovoltaics*, 6(1), 223–229. doi:10.1109/JPHOTOV.2015.2501730

Chou, J. C., Hsu, W. Y., Liao, Y. H., Lai, C. H., Lin, Y. J., You, P. H., Chu, C. M., Lu, C. C., & Nien, Y. H. (2017). Photovoltaic Analysis of Platinum Counter Electrode Modified by Graphene Oxide and Magnetic Beads for Dye-Sensitized Solar Cell. *IEEE Transactions on Semiconductor Manufacturing*, 30(3), 270–275. doi:10.1109/TSM.2017.2725385

Chou, J. C., Huang, C. H., Liao, Y. H., Chuang, S. W., Tai, L. H., & Nien, Y. H. (2015). Effect of Different Graphene Oxide Contents on Dye-Sensitized Solar Cells. *IEEE Journal of Photovoltaics*, 5(4), 1106–1112. doi:10.1109/JPHOTOV.2015.2419137

Chou, J. C., Kuo, C. H., Liao, Y. H., Lai, C. H., You, P. H., Ko, C. C., Yang, Z. M., & Wu, C. Y. (2018). A Barrier Structure for Photoelectrode of Dye-Sensitized Solar Cell for Enhancing Efficiency. *IEEE Photonics Technology Letters*, 30(6), 521–524. doi:10.1109/LPT.2018.2800771

Chou, J. C., Lin, Y. J., Liao, Y. H., Lai, C. H., Chu, C. M., You, P. H., & Nien, Y. H. (2016). Photovoltaic Performance Analysis of Dye-Sensitized Solar Cell with ZnO Compact Layer and. *IEEE Journal of the Electron Devices Society*, 4(6), 402–409. doi:10.1109/JEDS.2016.2614940

Chou, J. C., Shih, P. H., Hu, J. E., Liao, Y. H., Chuang, S. W., & Huang, C. H. (2014). Electrochemical Analysis of Photoelectrochromic Device Combined Dye-Sensitized Solar Cell. *IEEE Transactions on Nanotechnology*, 13(5), 954–962. doi:10.1109/TNANO.2014.2333013

Chou, J. C., Wu, C. Y., Liao, Y. H., Lai, C. H., Yang, C. M., You, P. H., Kuo, C. H., & Ko, C. C. (2018). IGZO/. *IEEE Journal of Photovoltaics*, *8*(3), 769–776. doi:10.1109/JPHOTOV.2018.2815711

Chou, J. C., You, P. H., Liao, Y. H., Lai, C. H., Chu, C. M., Lin, Y. J., Hsu, W. Y., Lu, C. C., & Nien, Y. H. (2017). Fabrication and Photovoltaic Properties of Dye-Sensitized Solar Cells Based on Graphene-. *IEEE Transactions on Semiconductor Manufacturing*, *30*(4), 531–538. doi:10.1109/TSM.2017.2747121

Chou, J.-C., Chu, C.-M., Liao, Y.-H., Lai, C.-H., Lin, Y.-J., You, P.-H., Hsu, W.-Y., Lu, C.-C., & Nien, Y.-H. (2016). An investigation on the photovoltaic properties of dye-sensitized solar cells based on. *IEEE Journal of the Electron Devices Society*, *5*(1), 32–39. doi:10.1109/JEDS.2016.2618839

Chow, C. W., Shiu, R. J., Liu, Y. C., Liao, X. L., Lin, K. H., Wang, Y. C., & Chen, Y. Y. (2018). Using advertisement light-panel and CMOS image sensor with frequency-shift-keying for visible light communication. *Optics Express*, *26*(10), 12530–12535. doi:10.1364/OE.26.012530 PMID:29801291

Chowdhary, R. (1995). *Assamese Verbs: A Study in the Structural Paradigm*. ABILAC.

Ciani, L., Catelani, M., Carnevale, E. A., Donati, L., & Bruzzi, M. (2014). Evaluation of the aging process of dye-sensitized solar cells under different stress conditions. *IEEE Transactions on Instrumentation and Measurement*, *64*(5), 1179–1187. doi:10.1109/TIM.2014.2381352

Cleary, J. G., & Trigg, L. E. (1995). K*: An Instance-based learner using an entropic distance measure. *Proceedings of the 12th Int. Conf. on Machine Learning*, 108-114.

Cummins, K., Krider, E., & Malone, M. (1998). The U.S. National Lightning Detection NetworkTM and Applications of Cloud-to-Ground Lightning Data by Electric Power Utilities. *IEEE Transactions on Electromagnetic Compatibility*, *40*(4), 465–480. doi:10.1109/15.736207

Cunliffe, D., & Elliott, G. (2005). Multimedia computing. Lexden Publishing Ltd.

CuteCircuit. (n.d.). https://cutecircuit.com/

D'Ambrosio, P., De Tommasi, D., Ferri, D., & Puglisi, G. (2008). A phenomenological model for healing and hysteresis in rubber-like materials. *International Journal of Engineering Science*, *46*(4), 293–305. doi:10.1016/j.ijengsci.2007.12.002

Daguin, C. (2015). *Body Electric AW15*. https://www.claradaguin.com/bodyelectric

Das, B. (2010). Axamiya Bhasha. In Axamiya Aru Axamar Bhasha. Aank-Baak.

Das, S. C., & Chowdhury, N. (2014). Smart textiles: New possibilities in textile engineering. *Journal of Polymer and Textile Engineering*, *1*(1), 1–4.

de Lope, J. (2007). Concepts and models for the future generation of emotional and intelligent systems. *International Work-Conference on the Interplay between Natural and Artificial Computation*, 41-50.

De Rond, M. (2014). The structure of serendipity. *Culture and Organization*, *20*(5), 342–358. doi:10.1080/14759551.2014.967451

De Rossi, F., Brown, T. M., Reale, A., & Di Carlo, A. (2014). Large-area electrodeposition of counterelectrodes utilizing the same integrated conductive grid for fabrication of parallel flexible dye solar cell modules. *IEEE Journal of Photovoltaics*, *4*(6), 1552–1559. doi:10.1109/JPHOTOV.2014.2354255

Deepa & Suguna. (2017). An optimized QoS-based clustering with multi-path routing protocol for Wireless Sensor Networks. *Journal of King Saud University-Computer and Information Sciences*.

Delgado, J. M., Martinho, J. C., Sá, A. V., Guimarães, A. S., & Abrantes, V. (2018). *Thermal energy storage with phase change materials: A literature review of applications for buildings materials.* Springer.

Dhatchayeny, D. R., Sewaiwar, A., Tiwari, S. V., & Chung, Y. H. (2015). Experimental Biomedical EEG Signal Transmission Using VLC. *IEEE Sensors Journal, 15*(10), 5386–5387. doi:10.1109/JSEN.2015.2453200

Douceur, J. R. (2002). The sybil attack. Lecture Notes in Computer Science, 2429, 251–260. doi:10.1007/3-540-45748-8_24

Du, P., Liu, X., Zheng, Z., Wang, X., Joncheray, T., & Zhang, Y. (2013). Synthesis and characterization of linear self-healing polyurethane based on thermally reversible Diels–Alder reaction. *RSC Advances, 3*(35), 15475–15482. doi:10.1039/c3ra42278j

Dutta, S., Pramanik, S., & Bandyopadhyay, S. K. (2021). Prediction of Weight Gain during COVID-19 for Avoiding Complication in Health. *International Journal of Medical Science and Current Research, 4*(3), 1042–1052.

Eldefrawy, M. H., Khan, M. K., Alghathbar, K., Kim, T. H., & Elkamchouchi, H. (2012). Mobile one-time passwords: Two-factor authentication using mobile phones. *Security and Communication Networks, 5*(5), 508–516. doi:10.1002ec.340

Elhoseny, Yuan, Yu, Mao, El-Minir, & Riad. (2014). Balancing energy consumption in heterogeneous wireless sensor network using genetic algorithm. *IEEE Communications Letters.*

Elhoseny, M., Elminir, H., Riad, A., & Yuan, X. (2016). A secure data routing schema for WSN using elliptic curve cryptography and homomorphic encryption. *Journal of King Saud University-Computer and Information Sciences, 28*(3), 262–275. doi:10.1016/j.jksuci.2015.11.001

Erdelj & Akyildiz. (n.d.). *Help from the Sky: Leveraging UAVs for Disaster Management.* Academic Press.

Fang, J., Che, Z., & Jiang, Z. L. (2017). An Efficient Flicker-Free FEC Coding Scheme for Dimmable Visible Light Communication Based on Polar Codes. *IEEE Photonics Journal, 9*, 1-10. Advance online publication. doi:10.1109/JPHOT.2017.2689744

Fan, S., Lin, W., & Lin, I. (2015). Psychosocial care and the role of clinical psychologists in palliative care. *The American Journal of Hospice & Palliative Care, 32*(8), 861–868. doi:10.1177/1049909114543492 PMID:25024459

Farmani, R., Kakoudakis, K., Behzadian, K., & Butler, D. (2017). Pipe Failure Prediction in Water Distribution Systems Considering Static and Dynamic Factors. *Proceedings of International Conference in "Emerging Trends in Science, Technology and Management-2013.*

Fathy, M. E., Patel, V. M., & Chellappa, R. (2015). *Face-based active authentication on mobile devices. In IEEE international conference on acoustics, speech and signal processing.* ICASSP.

Felemban, E., Lee, C. G., & Ekici, E. (2006, June). MMSPEED. *IEEE Transactions on Mobile Computing, 5*(6), 738–754. doi:10.1109/TMC.2006.79

Ferrara, M., & Bengisu, M. (2014). Materials that change color for intelligent design. In M. Rossi (Ed.), *Materials that change color* (pp. 81–100). Springer. doi:10.1007/978-3-319-00290-3_4

Ficara, D., Di Pietro, A., Giordano, S., Member, S., Procissi, G., Vitucci, F., & Antichi, G. (2011). Differential Encoding of DFAs for Fast Regular Expression Matching. *IEEE/ACM Transactions on Networking, 19*(3), 683–694.

Ficara, D., Giordano, S., Procissi, G., Vitucci, F., Antichi, G., & Pietro, A. D. (2008). An Improved DFA for Fast Regular Expression Matching. *Proceedings of the ACM SIGCOMM Computer Communication Review, 38*(5), 29-40.

Field, A. (2005). *Discovering statistics using SPSS (introducing statistical methods series)* (2nd ed.). Sage Publications Ltd.

Fishman, A. D., Thompson, A. W., & Vallone, L. (2006). LambdaXtreme® transport system: R&D of a high capacity system for low cost, ultra long haul DWDM transport. *Bell Labs Technical Journal*, *11*(2), 27–53. doi:10.1002/bltj.20160

Frank, M., Biedert, R., Ma, E., Martinovic, I., & Song, D. (2012). Touchalytics: On the applicability of touchscreen input as a behavioral biometric for continuous authentication. *IEEE Transactions on Information Forensics and Security*, *8*(1), 136–148. doi:10.1109/TIFS.2012.2225048

French, Krajewski, & Cuykendall. (1992). Rainfall forecasting in space and time using a neural network. *Journal of Hydrology (Amsterdam)*, *137*(1), 1–31.

Gaddes, D., Jung, H., Pena-Francesch, A., Dion, G., Tadigadapa, S., Dressick, W. J., & Demirel, M. C. (2016). Self-healing textile: Enzyme encapsulated layer-by-layer structural proteins. *ACS Applied Materials & Interfaces*, *8*(31), 20371–20378. doi:10.1021/acsami.6b05232 PMID:27419265

Gäfvert, M. (1998). *Modelling the Furuta Pendulum*. Lund Institute of Technology, Department of Automatic Control. Lund Institute of Technology.

Ganesh, S., & Amutha, R. (2013). Efficient and secure routing protocol for wireless sensor networks throug SNR based dynamic clustering mechanisms. *Journal of Communications and Networks (Seoul)*, *15*(4), 422–429. doi:10.1109/JCN.2013.000073

Gao, Y. (2017). *Possible Tomorrows*. http://yinggao.ca/

Gauhati University. (2008). *Plantation for Conservation of Biodiversity and Eco-restoration in Gauhati University Campus*. Project proposal prepared by Committee for Scientific Plantation of Trees in Gauhati University Campus.

Gelenbe, E., & Caseau, Y. (2015). The impact of information technology on energy consumption and carbon emissions. *Ubiquity*, *1*(June), 1–15. doi:10.1145/2755977

Gnauck, A. H. (2002). *2.5 Tb/s (64/spl times/42.7 Gb/s) transmission over 40/spl times/100 km NZDSF using RZ-DPSK format and all-Raman-amplified spans*. Optical Fiber Communication Conference and Exhibit.

Gohar, R., & Rahnejat, H. (2008). *Fundamentals of Tribology*. Imperial College Press. doi:10.1142/p553

Gonzo, R., & Pokraka, A. (2021). Light-ray operators, detectors and gravitational event shapes. *J. High Energ. Phys.*, *15*. doi:10.1007/JHEP05(2021)015

Goodfellow, I., Bengio, Y., & Courville, A. (2016). *Deep learning*. MIT Press.

Goswami, G. C., & Tamuli, J. (2003). Asamiya. In The Indo-Aryan Languages. Routledge.

Goswami, G. C. (2004). *Asamiya Byakaranar Moulik bichar*. Bina Library.

Goswami, U. N. (1991). *Asamiya Bhashar Byakaran* (1st ed.). Baruah Agency.

Goswami, Venugopal, & Sengupta, Madhusoodanan, & Xavier. (2006). Increasing Trend of Extreme Rain Events Over India in a Warming Environment. *Science*, ●●●, 1.

Grätzel, M. (2005). Solar energy conversion by dye-sensitized photovoltaic cells. *Inorganic Chemistry*, *44*(20), 6841–6851. doi:10.1021/ic0508371 PMID:16180840

Griffin, A. R., & Carter, C. A. (2002). *Optical differential quadrature phase-shift key (ODQPSK) for high capacity optical transmission*. Optical Fiber Communication Conference and Exhibit. doi:10.1109/OFC.2002.1036420

Gubbi, J., Buyya, R., Marusic, S., & Palaniswami, M. (2013). Internet of Things (IoT): A vision, architectural elements, and future directions. *Future Generation Computer Systems*, *29*(7), 1645–1660. doi:10.1016/j.future.2013.01.010

Gurung, A., Elbohy, H., Khatiwada, D., Mitul, A. F., & Qiao, Q. (2016). A Simple Cost-Effective Approach to Enhance Performance of Bifacial Dye-Sensitized Solar Cells. *IEEE Journal of Photovoltaics, 6*(4), 912–917. doi:10.1109/JPHOTOV.2016.2551462

Haloui, H., Touafek, K., Zaabat, M., El Hocine, H. B. C., & Khelifa, A. (2015). The Copper Indium Selenium (. *Energy Procedia, 74*, 1213–1219. doi:10.1016/j.egypro.2015.07.765

Han, Q., Yu, M., & Liu, J. (2013). Nanocrystalline titanium dioxide prepared by hydrothermal method and its application in dye-sensitised solar cells. *Micro & Nano Letters, 8*(5), 238–242. doi:10.1049/mnl.2012.0941

Hayes, S. G., & Venkatraman, P. (Eds.). (2016). *Materials and technology for sportswear and performance apparel.* CRC Press.

Hayouni, Hamdi, & Kim. (2014). A Survey on Encryption Schemes in Wireless Sensor Network. *ASEA.*

He, Zeadally, Xu, & Huang. (n.d.). An efficient identity based conditional privacy-preserving authentication scheme for vehicular ad hoc networks. *IEEE Transactions on IFS, 10*(12), 2681–2691.

HeiselS. (2015). https://heisel.co/

Henock, D. (2011). *Literature over view of smart textiles* [Master's thesis]. University of Boras, Borås, Sweden.

Heo, J. H., Jung, K. Y., Kwak, D. J., Lee, D. K., & Sung, Y. M. (2009). Fabrication of titanium-doped indium oxide films for dye-sensitized solar cell application using reactive RF magnetron sputter method. *IEEE Transactions on Plasma Science, 37*(8), 1586–1592. doi:10.1109/TPS.2009.2023477

Heriche, H., Rouabah, Z., & Bouarissa, N. (2017). New ultra thin CIGS structure solar cells using SCAPS simulation program. *Int. J. of Hydrogen Energy, 42*(15), 9524–9532. doi:10.1016/j.ijhydene.2017.02.099

Heruntergeladen, K. (1941). *Assamese its Formation and Development.* Department of Historical and Antiquarian Studies, Government of Assam.

Hewitt, C. A., Kaiser, A. B., Roth, S., Craps, M., Czerw, R., & Carroll, D. L. (2012). Multilayered carbon nanotube/polymer composite based thermoelectric fabrics. *Nano Letters, 12*(3), 1307–1310. doi:10.1021/nl203806q PMID:22316286

Heywood, I., Cornelius, S., & Carver, S. (2003). *Introduction to Geographical Information Systems.* Pearson Education.

Hoch, H. (2014, April). *3D virtual prototyping in apparel design* [Paper presentation]. Symposium on Undergraduate Research & Creative Expression, Iowa City, IA.

Hollington & Nassenstein. (2018). *African Youth language practices and social media.* De Gruyter.

Holmes, D. (2014). Lighting for the Built Environment: Places of Worship. CIBSE.

Hossain, M. F., & Takahashi, T. (2014). Hydrothermal synthesis of novel ZnO nanomushrooms for improving the solar cells performance. *IEEE Transactions on Nanotechnology, 13*(4), 755–759. doi:10.1109/TNANO.2014.2319097

Hsu, Moncrieff, Tung, & Liu. (2006a). Temporal variability of warm-season precipitation over North America: Statistical analysis of radar measurement. *J. Atmos. Sci.*

Hsu, C. Y., Cherng, S. J., Lin, Y. J., & Chen, C. M. (2013). A compact nano-. *IEEE Electron Device Letters, 34*(11), 1415–1417. doi:10.1109/LED.2013.2282401

Hu, J., Peng, L., & Zheng, L. (2015). XFace: A face recognition system for android mobile phones. *IEEE 3rd International Conference on Cyber-Physical Systems, Networks, and Applications*, 13-18.

Huang, L., Jie, L., & Guizani, M. (2014). Secure and efficient data transmission for cluster-based wireless sensor networks. *IEEE Transactions on Parallel and Distributed Systems, 25*(3), 750–761. doi:10.1109/TPDS.2013.43

Huang, X., & Fang, Y. (2008). *Multiconstrained QoS multi-path routing in wireless sensor networks. Academic Press.*

Hu, J. E., Yang, S. Y., Chou, J. C., & Shih, P. H. (2012). Fabrication of flexible dye-sensitised solar cells with titanium dioxide thin films based on screen-printing technique. *Micro & Nano Letters, 7*(12), 1162–1165. doi:10.1049/mnl.2012.0529

Hung, N. Q., Babel, M. S., Weesakul, S., & Tripathi, N. K. (2009). An artificial neural network model for rainfall forecasting in Bangkok, Thailand. *Hydrology and Earth System Sciences, 13*, 1413–1425.

Hussein, Barges, & Jameel. (2017). Security Issues in Wireless Sensor Network. *Journal of JMESS, 3*(6).

Hutchins, E. (2000). Ecological cognition and cognitive ecology. *Proceedings of the Human Factors and Ergonomics Society Annual Meeting, 44*(22), 566-569.

Hwan Kwon, Y. (2013). *Pattern changing clothing: Interactive, customizable, and original wearables* [Unpublished master's thesis]. Rochester Institute of Technology, Rochester, NY.

Hwang. (2018). *Part-of-Speech Tagging with Trigram Hidden Markov Models and the Viterbi Algorithm.* https://stath-wang.github.io/part-of-speech-tagging-with-trigram-hidden-markov-models-and-the-viterbi-algorithm.html

Irannejad, N., Rezaei, B., Ensafi, A. A., & Zandi-Atashbar, N. (2018). Photovoltaic performance analysis of dye-sensitized solar cell based on the Ag(4,4¢-dicyanamidobiphenyl) complex as a light-scattering layer agent and linker molecule on. *IEEE Journal of Photovoltaics, 8*(5), 1230–1236. doi:10.1109/JPHOTOV.2018.2829779

ITU-T G.692 (2002). *Optical interfaces for multi-channel systems with optical amplifiers, Corrigendum 2.* https://www.itu.int/rec/T-REC-G.692-200206-I!Cor2/en

ITU-T G.694.1 (2012). *Special grid for WDM applications: DWDM frequency grid.* https://www.itu.int/rec/T-REC-G.694.1-201202-I/en

ITU-T G.694.2 (2003). *Spectral grid for WDM applications: CWDM wavelength grid.* https://www.itu.int/rec/T-REC-G.694.2-200312-I

Jalalian, D., Ghadimi, A., & Kiani, A. (2019). Modeling of a high-performance bandgap graded Pb-free HTM-free perovskite solar cell. *The European Physical Journal Applied Physics, 87*(1), 1–8. doi:10.1051/epjap/2019190095

Jawandhiya, Ghonge, Ali, & Deshpande. (2010). A Survey of MANET Atacks. *IJEST, 2*(9), 4063- 4071.

Jensen, T. W. (2017). Doing metaphor: An ecological perspective on metaphoricity in discourse. *Metaphor: Embodied Cognition and Discourse, 257.*

Jensen, T. W., & Greve, L. (2019). Ecological cognition and metaphor. *Metaphor and Symbol, 34*(1), 1–16. doi:10.1080/10926488.2019.1591720

Jia, J., Wu, J., Dong, J., Tu, Y., Lan, Z., Fan, L., & Wei, Y. (2016). High-Performance Molybdenum Diselenide Electrodes Used in Dye-Sensitized Solar Cells and Supercapacitors. *IEEE Journal of Photovoltaics, 6*(5), 1196–1202. doi:10.1109/JPHOTOV.2016.2585021

Jiang, J. J., & Conrath, D. W. (1997). *Semantic similarity based on corpus statistics and lexical taxonomy.* arXiv preprint cmp-lg/9709008.

Jiang, Y., Shi, M., Shen, X., & Lin, C. (2009). BAT: A robust signature scheme for vehicular networks using Binary Authentication Tree. *IEEE Transactionon on WC, 8*(4), 1974–1983.

Jing, X. Y., Yan, Z., & Pedrycz, W. (2019, 1). Security Data Collectio and data Analytics in the Internet: A Survey. *IEEE Communications Surveys and Tutorials, 21*(1), 586–618. Advance online publication. doi:10.1109/COMST.2018.2863942

Johansson Falck, M. (2018). From ecological cognition to language: When and why do speakers use words metaphorically? *Metaphor and Symbol, 33*(2), 61–84. doi:10.1080/10926488.2018.1434937

Joshi, P., Verma, M., & Verma, P. R. (2015). Secure authentication approach using Diffie-Hellman key exchange algorithm for WSN. In *2015 ICCICCT* (pp. 527–532). IEEE. doi:10.1109/ICCICCT.2015.7475336

Jouili & Braiek. (2016). A gradient descent control for output tracking of a class of non-minimum phase nonlinear systems. *Journal of Applied Research and Technology.* doi:10.1016/j.proeng.2017.03.217

Kadachi, Z., Ben Karoui, M., Azizi, T., & Gharbi, R. (2016). Effect of. *Micro & Nano Letters, 11*(2), 94–98. doi:10.1049/mnl.2015.0154

Kamila, S. (2013). Introduction, classification and applications of smart materials: An overview. *American Journal of Applied Sciences, 10*(8), 876–880. doi:10.3844/ajassp.2013.876.880

Kang, C., Zhang, Z., Zhang, Y., He, Y., Xie, Y., & Xie, E. (2011). Enhanced efficiency in dye-sensitised solar cells using a. *Micro & Nano Letters, 6*(8), 579–581. doi:10.1049/mnl.2011.0225

Kasaudhan, R., Elbohy, H., Sigdel, S., Qiao, H., Wei, Q., & Qiao, Q. (2014). Incorporation of. *IEEE Electron Device Letters, 35*(5), 578–580. doi:10.1109/LED.2014.2312355

Kasban, H. (2017). A robust multimodal biometric authentication scheme with voice and face recognition. *Arab Journal of Nuclear Sciences and Applications, 50*(3), 120–130.

Kasthuribai, P. T., & Sundararajan, M. (2018). Secured and QoS Based Energy-Aware Multipath Routing in MANET. *WPC, 101*(4), 2349–2364. doi:10.100711277-018-5820-4

Kaur, P., Singh, M., & Josan, G. S. (2015). Classification and prediction based data mining algorithms to predict slow learners in education sector. *Proceedings of XVIII International Conference on Water Distribution Systems Analysis.* 10.1016/j.procs.2015.07.372

Kaushik, D., Garg, M., Annu, Gupta, A., & Pramanik, S. (2021). Application of Machine Learning and Deep Learning in Cyber security: An Innovative Approach. InGhonge, M., Pramanik, S., Mangrulkar, R., & Le, D. N. (Eds.), *Cybersecurity and Digital Forensics: Challenges and Future Trends.* Wiley.

Keiser, G. (2000). Optical fiber communications (3rd ed.). McGraw-Hill International Editions.

Khan, L. U. (2017). Visible Light Communication: Applications, Architecture, Standardization and Research Challenges. *Digital Communications and Networks, 3*(2), 78–88. doi:10.1016/j.dcan.2016.07.004

Khan, S., Ali, S., & Bermak, A. (2019). Recent developments in printing flexible and wearable sensing electronics for healthcare applications. *Sensors (Basel), 19*(5), 1230. doi:10.339019051230 PMID:30862062

Khan, W., Daud, A., Khan, K., Nasir, J. A., Basheri, M., Aljohani, N., & Alotaibi, F. S. (2019). Part of speech tagging in urdu: Comparison of machine and deep learning approaches. *IEEE Access: Practical Innovations, Open Solutions, 7,* 38918–38936. doi:10.1109/ACCESS.2019.2897327

Khimi, S. R., Syamsinar, S. N., & Najwa, T. N. L. (2019). Effect of carbon black on self-healing efficiency of natural rubber. *Materials Today: Proceedings, 17,* 1064–1071. doi:10.1016/j.matpr.2019.06.513

Khoshsirat, N., & Yunus, N. A. M. (2013). Numerical simulation of CIGS thin film solar cells using SCAPS-1D. *IEEE Conf. Sustainable Utilization and Development in Engineering and Technology,* 63–67. 10.1109/CSUDET.2013.6670987

Khoshsirat, N., Yunus, N. A. M., Hamidon, M. N., & Shafie, S. (2015). Analysis of absorber layer properties effect on CIGS solar cell performance using SCAPS. *Optik (Elsevier), 126*(7-8), 681–686. doi:10.1016/j.ijleo.2015.02.037

Kima, Y. H., Yoo, S. J., Gu, Y. H., Lim, J. H., Han, D., & Baik, S. W. (2013). Crop Pests Prediction Method using Regression and Machine Learning Technology: Survey. *Proceedings of 2013 International Conference on Future Software Engineering and Multimedia Engineering.*

Kim, B., Sanders, B. F., Famiglietti, J. S., & Guinot, V. (2015). Urban flood modeling with porous shallow-water equations: A case study of model errors in the presence of anisotropic porosity. *Journal of Hydrology (Amsterdam), 523*, 680–692.

Kim, S., Lim, H., Kim, K., Kim, C., Kang, T. Y., Ko, M. J., Kim, K., & Park, N. G. (2010). Synthetic strategy of low-bandgap organic sensitizers and their photoelectron injection characteristics. *IEEE Journal of Selected Topics in Quantum Electronics, 16*(6), 1627–1634. doi:10.1109/JSTQE.2010.2042683

Komine, T., & Nakagawa, M. (2004). Fundamental analysis for visible-light communication system using LED lights. *IEEE Transactions on Consumer Electronics, 50*(1), 100–107. doi:10.1109/TCE.2004.1277847

Kongahage, D., & Foroughi, J. (2019). Actuator materials: Review on recent advances and future outlook for smart textiles. *Fibers (Basel, Switzerland), 7*(3), 21. doi:10.3390/fib7030021

Koong, C. S., Yang, T. I., & Tseng, C. C. (2014). A user authentication scheme using physiological and behavioral biometrics for multitouch devices. *TheScientificWorldJournal, 2014*(781234), 1–12. doi:10.1155/2014/781234 PMID:25147864

Kornbluh, R. D., Pelrine, R., Prahlad, H., Wong-Foy, A., McCoy, B., Kim, S., Eckerle, J., & Low, T. (2012). Dielectric elastomers: Stretching the capabilities of energy harvesting. *MRS Bulletin, 37*(3), 246–253. doi:10.1557/mrs.2012.41

Kraak, M. J., & Ormeling, F. (2004). *Cartography: Visualization of Geospatial Data.* Pearson Education.

Kuhn, R., & Minuzzi, R. F. B. (2015). The 3D printing's panorama in fashion design. *Moda Documenta: Museu. Memoria e Design, 11*(1), 1–12.

Kumar & Deen. (2014). *Fiber optic communications* (1st ed.). Wiley & sons.

Kumari, K., Chakrabarti, T., Jana, A., Bhattachartjee, D., Gupta, B., & Sarkar, S. K. (2018). Comparative Study on Perovskite Solar Cells based on Titanium, Nickel and Cadmium doped. *Optical Materials, 84*, 681–688. doi:10.1016/j.optmat.2018.07.071

Kumar, S., Chandrasekaran, B., Turner, J., & Varghese, G. (2007). Curing Regular Expressions Matching Algorithms from Insomnia, Amnesia and Acalculia. *Proceedings of the ACM/IEEE Symposium Architecture for Networking and Communication Systems*, 155-164.

Kumar, S., Dharmapurikar, S., Yu, F., Crowley, P., & Turner, J. (2006) Algorithms to Accelerate Multiple Regular Expressions Matching for Deep Packet Inspection. *Proceedings of the Conference on Applications, Technologies, Architectures, and Protocols for Computer Communications, 36*, 339-350.

Kumar, S., Turner, J. S., Crowley, P., & Mitzenmacher, M. (2007) HEXA: Compact Data Structures for Faster Packet Processing. *Proceedings of the International Conference on Network Protocols*, 246-255.

Kumar, S., Turner, J., & Williams, J. (2006). Advanced Algorithms for Fast and Scalable Deep Packet Inspection. *Proceedings of the ACM/IEEE Symposium Architecture for Networking and Communication Systems*, 81-92.

Kyaw, H. H., Bora, T., & Dutta, J. (2012). One-diode model equivalent circuit analysis for ZnO nanorod-based dye-sensitized solar cells: Effects of annealing and active area. *IEEE Transactions on Nanotechnology, 11*(4), 763–768. doi:10.1109/TNANO.2012.2196286

Lach, E., & Idler, W. (2011). Modulation formats for 100G and beyond. *Optical Fiber Technology, 17*(5), 377–386. doi:10.1016/j.yofte.2011.07.012

Lai, S. C., Yang, M. F., Dolmanan, S., Ke, L., & Sun, X. W. (2010). Efficiency optimization on dye-sensitized solar cells with low-frequency noise analysis. *IEEE Transactions on Electron Devices, 57*(9), 2306–2309. doi:10.1109/TED.2010.2053490

Lambropoulos, N., Fardoun, H. M., & Alghazzawi, D. M. (2016). Chrono-spatial intelligence in global systems science and social media: Predictions for proactive political decision making. *International Conference on Social Computing and Social Media*, 201-208. 10.1007/978-3-319-39910-2_19

Langereis, G. R., Bouwstra, S., & Chen, W. (2013). Sensors, actuators and computing systems for smart textiles for protection. In R. A. Chapman (Ed.), *Smart textiles for protection* (pp. 190–213). Woodhead Publishing. doi:10.1533/9780857097620.1.190

Lavorgna, L., Iaffaldano, P., Abbadessa, G., Lanzillo, R., Esposito, S., Ippolito, D., Sparaco, M., Cepparulo, S., Lus, G., Viterbo, R., Clerico, M., Trojsi, F., Ragonese, P., Borriello, G., Signoriello, E., Palladino, R., Moccia, M., Brigo, F., Troiano, M., ... Bonavita, S. (2022). Disability assessment using Google Maps. *Neurological Sciences, 43*(2), 1007–1014. doi:10.100710072-021-05389-7 PMID:34142263

Leacock, C., & Chodorow, M. (1998). Combining local context and WordNet similarity for word sense identification. *WordNet: An Electronic Lexical Database, 49*(2), 265-283.

Leal, A., Filho, J., Rocha, B., & Sá, J. (2016). *A Multiband Lightning Detector, 2014 International Conference on Lightning Protection (ICLP)*. ChinaILPS 2016 - International Lightning Protection Symposium.

Leavitt, A. J. (2017). *Combatting toxic online communities* (1st ed.). The Rosen Publishing Group, Inc.

Lee, M. K., Yen, H., & Cheng, N. R. (2014). Efficiency enhancement of DSSC with aqueous solution deposited ZnO nanotip array. *IEEE Photonics Technology Letters, 26*(5), 454–456. doi:10.1109/LPT.2013.2296098

Li, G. Q., Yan, Z., Fu, Y. L., & Chen, H. L. (2018). Data Fusion for NetworkIntrusion Detection: A review. Security and Communication Networks, 1-16.

Li, Y., Qing, L., & Li, T. (2010). Design and implementation of an improved RSA algorithm. *2010 International Conference on EDT*, 390-393.

Li, K., Zhang, Q., Wang, H., & Li, Y. (2014). Red, green, blue (RGB) electrochromic fibers for the new smart color change fabrics. *ACS Applied Materials & Interfaces, 6*(15), 13043–13050. doi:10.1021/am502929p PMID:25057906

Lindner, L., Sergiyenko, O., Rivas-López, M., Ivanov, M., Rodríguez-Quiñonez, J. C., Hernández-Balbuena, D., ... Mercorelli, P. (2017). Machine vision system errors for unmanned aerial vehicle navigation. In *2017 IEEE 26th International Symposium on Industrial Electronics (ISIE)* (pp. 1615-1620). IEEE Xplore. 10.1109/ISIE.2017.8001488

Lindner, L., Sergiyenko, O., Rodríguez-Quiñonez, J. C., Rivas-Lopez, M., Hernandez-Balbuena, D., Flores-Fuentes, W., Natanael Murrieta-Rico, F., & Tyrsa, V. (2016). Mobile robot vision system using continuous laser scanning for industrial application. *Industrial Robot: An International Journal, 43*(4), 360–369. doi:10.1108/IR-01-2016-0048

Lin, H. Q., Yan, Z., Chen, Y., & Zhang, L. F. (2018, March). A Survey on Network Security-Related Data Collection Technologi. *IEEE Access: Practical Innovations, Open Solutions, 6*, 18345–18365. doi:10.1109/ACCESS.2018.2817921

Lin, Q., Yan, H., Huang, Z., Chen, W., Shen, J., & Tang, Y. (2018). An ID-based linearly homomorphic signature scheme and itsapplication in blockchain. *IEEE Access: Practical Innovations, Open Solutions, 6*, 20632–20640. doi:10.1109/ACCESS.2018.2809426

Lin, X., Sun, X., Wang, X., Zhang, C., Ho, P.-H., & Shen, X. (2008). TSVC: Timed efficient and secure vehicular communications the privacy-preservingng. *IEEE Transactions on WC*, 7(12), 4987–4998. doi:10.1109/T-WC.2008.070773

Li, S., Neelisetti, R. K., Liu, C., & Lim, A. (2010). Efficient multi-path protocol for wireless sensor networks. *International Journal of Wireless and Mobile Networks*, 2(1), 110–130.

Lischinsky, P., Canudas De Wit, C., & Morel, G. (1999). Friction compensation for an industrial hydraulic robot. *IEEE Control Systems Magazine*, 19(1), 25–32. doi:10.1109/37.745763

Liu, C., & Wu, J. (2013). Fast Deep Packet Inspection with a Dual Finite Automata. *IEEE Transactions on Computers*, 62(2), 310–321.

Liu, G., Yan, Z., & Pedryczc, W. (2018, March). Data Collection for Attack Detectionand Security Measurement in Mobile Ad Hoc Networks: A Survey. *Journal of NCA*, 10(5), 105–122.

Liu, P., Huda, M. N., Sun, L., & Yu, H. (2020). A survey on underactuated robotic systems: Bio-inspiration, trajectory planning and control. *Mechatronics*, 72, 102443. doi:10.1016/j.mechatronics.2020.102443

Liu, S., Liu, X., Wang, S., & Muhammad, K. (2021). Fuzzy-aided solution for out-of-view challenge in visual tracking under IoT-assisted complex environment. *Neural Computing & Applications*, 33(4), 1055–1065. doi:10.100700521-020-05021-3

Liu, W., Zhang, S., & Fan, J. (2012). *A diagnosis-based clustering and multi-path routing protocol for WSN.* IJDSR.

Liu, Y., Li, Z., Liu, R., Liang, Z., Yang, J., Zhang, R., Zhou, Z., & Nie, Y. (2019). Design of self-healing rubber by introducing ionic interaction to construct a network composed of ionic and covalent cross-linking. *Industrial & Engineering Chemistry Research*, 58(32), 14848–14858. doi:10.1021/acs.iecr.9b02972

Li, X., & Sun, Y. (2017). WearETE: A scalable wearable e-textile triboelectric energy harvesting system for human motion scavenging. *Sensors (Basel)*, 17(11), 2649. doi:10.339017112649 PMID:29149035

Li, Y., Bandar, Z. A., & McLean, D. (2003). An approach for measuring semantic similarity between words using multiple information sources. *IEEE Transactions on Knowledge and Data Engineering*, 15(4), 871–882.

Lo, N. W., & Liu, F.-L. (2013). A Secure Routing Protocol to Prevent Cooperative Black Hole Attack in MAN. *ITES, Springer New York*, 234, 59–65.

Lo, N.-W., & Tsai, J.-L. (2016). An efficient conditional privacypreserving authentication scheme for vehicular sensor networks without pairings. *IEEE Transactions on ITS*, 17(5), 1319–1328.

Loryuenyong, V., Yaotrakool, S., Prathumted, P., Lertsiri, J., & Buasri, A. (2016). Synergistic effects of graphene-polyaniline counter electrode in dye-sensitised solar cells. *Micro & Nano Letters*, 11(2), 77–80. doi:10.1049/mnl.2015.0363

Lu, Jie, & Guizani. (2014). Secure and Efficient Data Transmission for Cluster-Based WSN. *IEEE Transactions on Parallel and Distributed Systems, 25*(3).

Lu, R., Lin, X., & Zhu, H. (2008). ECPP: Efficient conditional privacy preservation protocol for secure vehicular communications. *Proceedings of the 27th IEEE INFOCOM '08*, 1229–1237. 10.1109/INFOCOM.2008.179

Lyshevski, S. E. (1999). Nonlinear control of mechatronic systems with permanent-magnet DC motors. *Mechatronics*, 9(5), 539–552. doi:10.1016/S0957-4158(99)00014-8

Lyu, C., Zhang, X., Liu, Z., & Chi, C.-H. (2019). Selective Authentication Based Geographic Opportunistic Routing WSN for IOT Against DoS Attacks. *IEEE Access: Practical Innovations, Open Solutions*, 7, 31068–31082. doi:10.1109/ACCESS.2019.2902843

Ma, H., Lampe, L., & Hranilovic, S. (2017). Hybrid visible light and power line communication for indoor multiuser downlink. *Journal of Optical Communications and Networking*, *9*(8), 635–647. doi:10.1364/JOCN.9.000635

Mahfouz, A., Mahmoud, T. M., & Eldin, A. S. (2017). A survey on behavioral biometric authentication on smartphones. *Journal of Information Security and Applications*, *37*, 28-37.

MakeFashion. (n.d.). http://www.makefashion.ca/

Ma, N., Zeng, Z., Wang, Y., & Xu, J. (2021). Balanced strategy based on environment and user benefit-oriented carpooling service mode for commuting trips. *Transportation*, *48*(3), 1241–1266. doi:10.100711116-020-10093-0

Marshall, K. P., Walker, M., Walton, R. I., & Hotton, R. A. (2016). Enhanced stability and efficiency in hole-transport-layer-free CsSnI$_3$ perovskite photovoltaics. *Nature Energy*, *1*(12), 1–9. doi:10.1038/nenergy.2016.178

Martin, J. H. (2009). *Speech and language processing: An introduction to natural language processing, computational linguistics, and speech recognition*. Pearson/Prentice Hall.

McGrath, M. J., Ni Scanaill, C., & Nafus, D. (2013). *Sensor technologies: Healthcare, wellness, and environmental applications*. Springer Nature. doi:10.1007/978-1-4302-6014-1

Meganathan, S., Bala Krishnan, R., Sumathi, A., Sheik Mohideen Shah, S., & Senthilkumar, J. (2019). An Experiment in Weather Prediction for North East and South West Monsoon Over Chennai. *International Journal of Recent Technology and Engineering*, *8*, 4460–4465.

Megyesi, B. (1998). *Brill's rule based part-of-speech tagger for Hungarian* [Master's thesis]. University of Stockholm.

Mehdipour Ghazi, M., & Kemal Ekenel, H. (2016). A comprehensive analysis of deep learning based representation for face recognition. *Proceedings of the IEEE conference on computer vision and pattern recognition workshops*, 34-41.

Mehmood, U., Afzaal, M., Al-Ahmed, A., Yates, H. M., Hakeem, A. S., Ali, H., & Al-Sulaiman, F. A. (2017). Transparent Conductive Oxide Films for High-Performance Dye-Sensitized Solar Cells. *IEEE Journal of Photovoltaics*, *7*(2), 518–524. doi:10.1109/JPHOTOV.2016.2641303

Mehmood, U., Al-Ahmed, A., Afzaal, M., Hakeem, A. S., Abdullahi Haladu, S., & Al-Sulaiman, F. A. (2018). Enhancement of the Photovoltaic Performance of Dye-Sensitized Solar Cells by Cosensitizing. *IEEE Journal of Photovoltaics*, *8*(2), 512–516. doi:10.1109/JPHOTOV.2018.2790699

Mehmood, U., Harrabi, K., Hussein, I. A., & Ahmed, S. (2015). Enhanced photovoltaic performance of dye-sensitized solar cells using. *IEEE Journal of Photovoltaics*, *6*(1), 196–201. doi:10.1109/JPHOTOV.2015.2479468

Mehmood, U., Hussein, I. A., Al-Ahmed, A., & Ahmed, S. (2016). Enhancing Power Conversion Efficiency of Dye-Sensitized Solar Cell Using. *IEEE Journal of Photovoltaics*, *6*(2), 486–490. doi:10.1109/JPHOTOV.2016.2514703

Mehmood, U., Zaheer Aslam, M., Shawabkeh, R. A., Hussein, I. A., Ahmad, W., & Ghaffar Rana, A. (2016). Improvement in Photovoltaic Performance of Dye Sensitized Solar Cell Using Activated Carbon-. *IEEE Journal of Photovoltaics*, *6*(5), 1191–1195. doi:10.1109/JPHOTOV.2016.2574127

Mejia, C. E., Georghiades, C. N., Abdallah, M. M., & Al-Badarneh, Y. H. (2017). Code design for flicker mitigation in visible light communications using finite state machines. *IEEE Transactions on Communications*, *65*(5), 2091–2100. doi:10.1109/TCOMM.2017.2657518

Meng, W., Wong, D. S., Furnell, S., & Zhou, J. (2014). Surveying the development of biometric user authentication on mobile phones. *IEEE Communications Surveys and Tutorials*, *17*(3), 1268–1293. doi:10.1109/COMST.2014.2386915

Meng, Y., Mok, P. Y., & Jin, X. (2012). Computer aided clothing pattern design with 3D editing and pattern alteration. *Computer Aided Design, 44*(8), 721–734. doi:10.1016/j.cad.2012.03.006

Mikolov, T., Chen, K., Corrado, G., & Dean, J. (2013). *Efficient estimation of word representations in vector space.* arXiv preprint arXiv:1301.3781.

Min, S., & Carrico, M. (2018, January). *Exploration of students' design process with Browzwear V-Stitcher, 3D CAD program* [Paper presentation]. International Textile and Apparel Association (ITAA) Annual Conference, Iowa City, IA.

Mishra, N., & Mishra, A. (2011, June). Part of speech tagging for Hindi corpus. In *2011 International Conference on Communication Systems and Network Technologies* (pp. 554-558). IEEE. 10.1109/CSNT.2011.118

Mohammadi & Jadidoleslamy. (2011). A Comparison olink-layerer attacks on WSN. *GRAPH-HOC, 3*(1).

Mondal, S. (2008). Phase change materials for smart textiles–An overview. *Applied Thermal Engineering, 28*(11–12), 1536–1550. doi:10.1016/j.applthermaleng.2007.08.009

Moreno-Valenzuela, J. C. A.-A.-G. (2016). Adaptive Neural Network Control for the Trajectory Tracking of the Furuta Pendulum. IEEE.

Moreno-Valenzuela, J., Aguilar-Avelar, C., Puga-Guzmán, S. A., & Santibáñez, V. (2016). Adaptive Neural Network Control for the Trajectory Tracking of the Furuta Pendulum. *IEEE Transactions on Cybernetics, 46*(12), 3439–3452. doi:10.1109/TCYB.2015.2509863 PMID:28113230

Morin, A. J. (1833). New friction experiments carried out at Metz in 1831–1833. *Proceedings of the French Royal Academy of Sciences, 4*(1), 128.

Mostefaoui, M., Mazar, H., & Khelifi, S. (2015). Simulation of high efficiency CIGS solar cells with SCAPS-1D software. *Energy Procedia (Elsevier), 74*, 736–744. doi:10.1016/j.egypro.2015.07.809

Musilová, M., Šmelko, M., & Lipovský, P. (2017). Cube Very-Low-Frequency Radio Waves Detector and Whistlers. *8th International Conference on Mechanical and Aerospace Engineering.*

Nath, A., Manohar, G., Dani, K., & Devara, P. (2009). A study of lightning activity over land and oceanic regions of India. *Journal of Earth System Science, 118*(5), 467–481. doi:10.100712040-009-0040-7

Nayak, M. A., & Ghosh, S. (2013). Prediction of extreme rainfall event using weather pattern recognition and support vector machine classifier. *Theoretical and Applied Climatology, 114*, 583–603.

Nebati Chermahini, A. N. (2012, January). *Smart clothes that express your mood* [Conference presentation]. IWBE workshop of bionic engineering conference: International Society of Bionic Engineering (ISBE), Zhangjiajie, China.

Neural Networks in Forecasting Minimum Temperature. (n.d.). International Journal of Electronics & *Tongxin Jishu, 2*(3), 101–105.

Nicolescu, G., & Mosterman, P. J. (2018). *Model-based design for embedded systems.* CRC Press. doi:10.1201/9781315218823

Nittin Johnson, Govindaradjane, & Sundararajan. (2013). Impact of Watershed Management on the Groundwater and Irrigation Potential: A Case Study. *International Journal of Engineering and Innovative Technology, 2*(8).

Nowicki, M., Górski, Ł., & Bała, P. (2021). PCJ Java library as a solution to integrate HPC, Big Data and Artificial Intelligence workloads. *Journal of Big Data, 8*(1), 62. doi:10.118640537-021-00454-6

O'regan, B., & Grätzel, M. (1991). A low-cost, high-efficiency solar cell based on dye-sensitized colloidal TiO 2 films. *Nature, 353*(6346), 737–740. doi:10.1038/353737a0

Olsson, H., Åström, K. J., Canudas de Wit, C., Gäfvert, M., & Lischinsky, P. (1998). Friction Models and Friction Compensation. *European Journal of Control*, *4*(3), 176–195. doi:10.1016/S0947-3580(98)70113-X

Orovic, I., Stanković, S., & Beko, M. (2021). Multi-base compressive sensing procedure with application to ECG signal reconstruction. *EURASIP Journal on Advances in Signal Processing*, *18*(1), 18. Advance online publication. doi:10.118613634-021-00728-4

Ortiz-Yepes, D. A., Hermann, R. J., Steinauer, H., & Buhler, P. (2014). Bringing strong authentication and transaction security to the realm of mobile devices. *IBM Journal of Research and Development*, *58*(1), 4–1. doi:10.1147/JRD.2013.2287810

Orville, R., Henderson, R., & Bosart, L. (1987). *An East Coast Lightning Detection Network*. IEEE.

Pakray, P., Pal, A., Majumder, G., & Gelbukh, A. (2015, October). Resource building and parts-of-speech (POS) tagging for the Mizo language. In *2015 Fourteenth Mexican International Conference on Artificial Intelligence (MICAI)* (pp. 3-7). IEEE. 10.1109/MICAI.2015.7

Paksuniemi, M., Sorvoja, H., Alasaarela, E., & Myllyla, R. (2005). Wireless sensor and data transmission needs and technologies for patient monitoring in the operating room and intensive care unit. In *Proceedings of IEEE Engineering in Medicine and Biology 27th Annual Conference* (pp. 5182-5185). 10.1109/IEMBS.2005.1615645

Pan, N., & Sun, G. (Eds.). (2011). *Functional textiles for improved performance, protection and health*. Elsevier. doi:10.1533/9780857092878

Parameter Estimation. (2021, September 11). Retrieved from https://la.mathworks.com/discovery/parameter-estimation.html

Parida, B., Iniyan, S., & Goic, R. (2011). A review of solar photovoltaic technologies. *Renewable & Sustainable Energy Reviews*, *15*(3), 1625–1636. doi:10.1016/j.rser.2010.11.032

Patil, C. Y., & Ghatol, A. A. (2010). Rainfall forecasting using local parameters over a meteorological station: An artificial neural network approach. *International J. of Engg. Research & Indu. Appls*, *3*(2), 341–356.

Paul, R. (2019). *High performance technical textiles*. John Wiley & Sons, Incorporated. doi:10.1002/9781119325062

Pause, B. (2000). Measuring the thermal barrier function of phase change materials in textiles. *Technical Textiles International*, *9*(3), 20–21.

Pedersen, T., Patwardhan, S., & Michelizzi, J. (2004, July). WordNet: Similarity-Measuring the Relatedness of Concepts. In AAAI (Vol. 4, pp. 25-29). AAAI.

Peleg, D. (2015). *Fashion designer*. https://danitpeleg.com/

Peng, W., Zeng, Y., Gong, H., Leng, Y. Q., Yan, Y. H., & Hu, W. (2013). Evolutionary algorithm and parameters extraction for dye-sensitised solar cells one-diode equivalent circuit model. *Micro & Nano Letters*, *8*(2), 86–89. doi:10.1049/mnl.2012.0806

Pinto, T., Costa, P., Sousa, C. M., Sousa, C. A., Pereira, C., Silva, C. J., Pereira, M. F. R., Coelho, P. J., & Freire, C. (2016). Screen-printed photochromic textiles through new inks based on SiO2@ naphthopyran nanoparticles. *ACS Applied Materials & Interfaces*, *8*(42), 28935–28945. doi:10.1021/acsami.6b06686 PMID:27704753

Popov, V. L. (2010). *Contact Mechanics and Friction: Physical Principles and Applications*. Springer-Verlag. doi:10.1007/978-3-642-10803-7

Prabha, G., Jyothsna, P. V., Shahina, K. K., Premjith, B., & Soman, K. P. (2018, September). A deep learning approach for part-of-speech tagging in nepali language. In *2018 International Conference on Advances in Computing, Communications and Informatics (ICACCI)* (pp. 1132-1136). IEEE. 10.1109/ICACCI.2018.8554812

Pramanik, S., & Bandyopadhyay, S. K. (2014). Image Steganography Using Wavelet Transform and Genetic /Algorithm. *International Journal of Innovative Research in Advanced Engineering, 1*, 1–4.

Pramanik, S., Ghosh, R., Ghonge, M., Narayan, V., Sinha, M., Pandey, D., & Samanta, D. (2020). A Novel Approach using Steganography and Cryptography in Business Intelligence. In A. Azevedo & M. F. Santos (Eds.), *Integration Challenges for Analytics, Business Intelligence and Data Mining* (pp. 192–217). IGI Global.

Pramanik, S., & Suresh Raja, S. (2020). A Secured Image Steganography using Genetic Algorithm. *Advances in Mathematics: Scientific Journal, 9*(7), 4533–4541.

Prasad, P. S., Pathak, R., Gunjan, V. K., & Rao, H. R. (2020). Deep learning based representation for face recognition. ICCCE 2019, 419-424. doi:10.1007/978-981-13-8715-9_50

Punithavathi, J., & Baskaran, R. (2011). Land use and land cover using remote sensing and GIS techniques - A case study of Thanjavur District, Tamil Nadu, India. *Proceedings of International Journal of Current Research, 3*(10), 237–244.

PVS, A., & Karthik, G. (2007). Part-of-speech tagging and chunking using conditional random fields and transformation based learning. *Shallow Parsing for South Asian Languages, 21*, 21–24.

Qu, H., Semenikhin, O., & Skorobogatiy, M. (2014). Flexible fiber batteries for applications in smart textiles. *Smart Materials and Structures, 24*(2), 025012. doi:10.1088/0964-1726/24/2/025012

Rada, R., Mili, H., Bicknell, E., & Blettner, M. (1989). Development and application of a metric on semantic nets. *IEEE Transactions on Systems, Man, and Cybernetics, 19*(1), 17–30.

Rahman, M. Y. A., Sulaiman, A. S., & Ali Umar, A. (2018). Dye-sensitised solar cell utilising gold doped reduced graphene oxide counter electrode: Influence of annealing time. *Micro & Nano Letters, 13*(8), 1224–1226. doi:10.1049/mnl.2018.0054

Rajagopal, S., Roberts, R. D., & Lim, S. K. (2012). IEEE 802.15.7 visible light communication: Modulation schemes and dimming support. *IEEE Communications Magazine, 50*(3), 72–82. doi:10.1109/MCOM.2012.6163585

Rajbhandari, S., McKendry, J. J. D., Herrnsdorf, J., Chun, H., Faulkner, G., Haas, H., Watson, I. M., O'Brien, D., & Dawson, M. D. (2017). A review of gallium nitride LEDs for multi-gigabit-per-second visible light data communications. *Semiconductor Science and Technology, 32*(2), 1–40. doi:10.1088/1361-6641/32/2/023001

Raj, Y. E. A. (1996). Inter and intra-seasonal variation of thermodynamic parameters of the atmosphere over coastal Tamil Nadu during northeast monsoon. *Mausam (New Delhi), 47*(3), 259–268.

Raya, M., & Hubaux, J.-P. (2007). Securing vehicular ad hoc networks. *Journal of Computer Security, 15*(1), 39–68. doi:10.3233/JCS-2007-15103

Rehman, S. U., Ullah, S., Chong, P. H. J., Yongchareon, S., & Komosny, D. (2019). Visible Light Communication: A System Perspective-Overview and Challenges. *Sensors (Basel), 19*(5), 1153. doi:10.339019051153 PMID:30866473

Resnik, P. (1995). *Using information content to evaluate semantic similarity in a taxonomy.* arXiv preprint cmp-lg/9511007.

Roberts, K., O'Sullivan, M., Kuang-Tsan Wu, Han Sun, Awadalla, A., Krause, D. J., & Laperle, C. (2009). Performance of dual-polarization QPSK for optical transport systems. *Journal of Lightwave Technology, 27*(16), 3546–3559. doi:10.1109/JLT.2009.2022484

Rogers, J. C., & Coleman, J. S. M. (2003). Interactions between the Atlantic multidecadal oscillation, El Nino/La Nina, and the PNA in winter Mississippi Valley stream flow. *Geophys. Res. Lett., 30*(10), 1518. 2003GL017216 doi:10.1029/

Roh, J. S., Chi, Y. S., & Kang, T. J. (2010). Wearable textile antennas. *International Journal of Fashion Design. Technology and Education, 3*(3), 135–153.

Roy, A., Guinaudeau, C., Bredin, H., & Barras, C. (2014, May). Tvd: a reproducible and multiply aligned tv series dataset. LREC 2014.

Rupini, R. V., & Nandagopal, R. (2015). A study on the influence of senses and the effectiveness of sensory branding. *Journal of Psychiatry, 18*(2), 236.

Sahai, A. K., Somann, M. K., & Satyan, V. (2000). All India Summer Monsoon Rainfall Prediction Using an Artificial Neural Netw. *Climate Dynamics, 16*(4), 291–302.

Sakai, K., Kizu, T., Kiwa, T., & Tsukada, K. (2018). Analysis of AC Impedance in Localized Region Using Magnetic Field Distribution Measured by HTS-SQUID. *IEEE Transactions on Applied Superconductivity, 28*(4), 1–5. doi:10.1109/TASC.2018.2796609

Samanta, D., Dutta, S., Galety, M. G., & Pramanik, S. (2021). A Novel Approach for Web Mining Taxonomy for High-Performance Computing. *The 4th International Conference of Computer Science and Renewable Energies (ICCSRE'2021).* 10.1051/e3sconf/202129701073

Sareen, R., Sareen, I., Delevan, J. B., & Vishnevsky, B. (2011). *U.S. Patent Application No. 13/008,906.* US Patent Office.

Sarkar, K., & Gayen, V. (2012). A practical part-of-speech tagger for Bengali. In *2012 Third International Conference on Emerging Applications of Information Technology* (pp. 36-40). IEEE. 10.1109/EAIT.2012.6407856

Satharasinghe, A., Hughes-Riley, T., & Dias, T. (2019). An investigation of a wash-durable solar energy harvesting textile. *Progress in Photovoltaics: Research and Applications, 28*(6), 578–592. doi:10.1002/pip.3229

Satharasinghe, A., Hughes-Riley, T., & Dias, T. (2019). Solar energy-harvesting e-textiles to power wearable devices. *Multidisciplinary Digital Publishing Institute Proceedings, 32*(1), 1. doi:10.3390/proceedings2019032001

Sayem, A. S. M., Kennon, R., & Clarke, N. (2010). 3D CAD systems for the clothing industry. *International Journal of Fashion Design, Technology and Education, 3*(2), 45–53.

Semchedine, F., Saidi, N. A., Belouzir, L., & Bouallouche-Medjkoune, L. (2017). QoS-Based Protocol for Routing in Wireless Sensor Networks. *WPC, 97*(3), 4413–4429. doi:10.100711277-017-4731-0

Seneviratne, S., Hu, Y., Nguyen, T., Lan, G., Khalifa, S., Thilakarathna, K., Hassan, M., & Seneviratne, A. (2017). A survey of wearable devices and challenges. *IEEE Communications Surveys and Tutorials, 19*(4), 2573–2620. doi:10.1109/COMST.2017.2731979

Seyedin, S., Zhang, P., Naebe, M., Qin, S., Chen, J., Wang, X., & Razal, J. M. (2019). Textile strain sensors: A review of the fabrication technologies, performance evaluation and applications. *Materials Horizons, 6*(2), 219–249. doi:10.1039/C8MH01062E

Seymour, S. (2008). *Fashionable technology: The intersection of design, fashion, science, and technology.* Springer. doi:10.1007/978-3-211-74500-7

Shanmugam, M., Farrokh Baroughi, M., & Galipeau, D. (2009). High. *Electronics Letters, 45*(12), 648–649. doi:10.1049/el.2009.3527

Sharma, N., Agrawal, S., & Kapoor, V. (2020). Estimation of frequency offset prior to adaptive equalization for improved performance of DP-QPSK DWDM system. *Optical Fiber Technology, 55.*

Sharma, N., Agrawal, S., & Kapoor, V. (2021). Performance optimization of OADM based DP-QPSK DWDM optical network with 37.5 GHz channel spacing. *Optical Switching and Networking, 40.*

Sharma, S. (2014) Transition of English Language through Media and Social Networking. *Scholarly Research Journal of Interdisciplinary Studies, 2*(14). https://www.time8.in/new-decline-trend-only-1-26-per-cent-of-indias-population-speak-assamese/

Sharma, A. (2013). Eco-friendly textiles: A boost to sustainability. *Asian Journal of Home Science, 8*(2), 768–771.

Sharma, K., & Ghose, M. K. (2010). *Wireless Sensor Networks: An Overview on its Security Threats.* IJCA.

Sharma, M., Tandon, A., Narayan, S., & Bhushan, B. (2017). *Classification and analysis of security attacks in WSNs and IEEE 802.15. 4 standards: A survey. In ICACCA.* IEEE.

Sharma, N., Vij, R., & Badhan, N. (2015, March). Enhanced spectral efficiency for intensity modulated DWDM systems. *2015 Twenty First National Conference on Communications (NCC)*, 1-6. 10.1109/NCC.2015.7084818

Sharma, S., Khannam, M., Boruah, M., Nath, B. C., & Dolui, S. K. (2015). Development of Dye-Sensitized Solar Cells Based on Gold/Gelatin Gel Electrolyte: Effect of Different Aspect Ratio of Gold Nanocrystals. *IEEE Journal of Photovoltaics, 5*(6), 1665–1673. doi:10.1109/JPHOTOV.2015.2478031

Sharon, T. (2021). Blind-sided by privacy? Digital contact tracing, the Apple/Google API and big tech's newfound role as global health policy makers. *Ethics and Information Technology, 23*(S1), 45–57. doi:10.100710676-020-09547-x PMID:32837287

Shi, J., Liu, S., Zhang, L., Yang, B., Shu, L., Yang, Y., Ren, M., Wang, Y., Chen, J., Chen, W., Chai, Y., & Tao, X. (2020). Smart textile-integrated microelectronic systems for wearable applications. *Advanced Materials, 32*(5), 1901958. doi:10.1002/adma.201901958 PMID:31273850

Shi, P., Gu, C., & Jing, Z. (2019). QoS Aware Routing Protocol Through Cross-layer Approach in Asynchronous Duty-Cycled WSNs. *IEEE Access: Practical Innovations, Open Solutions, 7*, 57574–57591. doi:10.1109/ACCESS.2019.2913679

Sidhu, R., & Prasanna, V. K. (2004). Fast Regular Expression Matching using FPGAs. *Proceedings of the 9th Annual IEEE Symposium on Field-Programmable Custom Computing Machines*, 227-238.

Sigdel, S., Elbohy, H., Gong, J., Adhikari, N., Sumathy, K., Qiao, H., Wei, Q., Sayyad, M. H., Zai, J., Qian, X., & Qiao, Q. (2015). Dye-sensitized solar cells based on porous hollow tin oxide nanofibers. *IEEE Transactions on Electron Devices, 62*(6), 2027–2032. doi:10.1109/TED.2015.2421475

Singh, J., Joshi, N., & Mathur, I. (2013). *Part of speech tagging of Marathi text using trigram method.* arXiv preprint arXiv:1307.4299.

Singha, K. (2012). A review on coating & lamination in textiles: Processes and applications. *American Journal of Political Science, 2*(3), 39–49.

Singha, K. R., Purkayastha, B. S., & Singha, K. D. (2012). Part of Speech Tagging in Manipuri with Hidden Markov Model. *International Journal of Computer Science Issues, 9*(6), 146.

Singha, K. R., Purkayastha, B. S., & Singha, K. D. (2012). Part of Speech Tagging in Manipuri: A Rule based Approach. *International Journal of Computers and Applications, 51*(14).

Singh, N. S., Hariharan, S., & Gupta, M. (2020). Facial recognition using deep learning. In *Advances in Data Sciences* (pp. 375–382). Security and Applications. doi:10.1007/978-981-15-6634-9

Singla, A., Sharma, D., & Vashisth, S. 2017. Data connectivity in flights using visible light communication. In *Proceeding of International Conference on Computing and Communication Technologies for Smart Nation (IC3TSN)* (pp. 71-74). 10.1109/IC3TSN.2017.8284453

Sinha, M., Chacko, E., Makhija, P., & Pramanik, S. (2021). Energy Efficient Smart Cities with Green IoT. In Green Technological Innovation for Sustainable Smart Societies: Post Pandemic Era. Springer.

Siou, Kong, Johannet, Borrell, & Pistre. (2011). Complexity selection of a neural network model for karst flood forecasting: The case of the Lez Basin (Southern France). *Journal of Hydrology, 403*, 367-380.

Sitová, Z., Šeděnka, J., Yang, Q., Peng, G., Zhou, G., Gasti, P., & Balagani, K. S. (2015). HMOG: New behavioral biometric features for continuous authentication of smartphone users. *IEEE Transactions on Information Forensics and Security, 11*(5), 877–892. doi:10.1109/TIFS.2015.2506542

Smith, R., Estan, C., Jha, S., & Kong, S. (2008a). Deflating the Big Bang: Fast and Scalable Deep Packet Inspection with Extended Finite Automata. *Proceedings of the ACM SIGCOMM 2008 Conference on Applications, Technologies, Architectures, and Protocols for Computer Communications*, 207-218.

Smith, R., Estan, C., & Jha, S. (2008b). Faster Signature Matching with Extended Automata. *IEEE Symposium on Security and Privacy*, 187-201.

Soh, C. K., Yang, Y., & Bhalla, S. (Eds.). (2012). *Smart materials in structural health monitoring, control and biomechanics*. Springer Science & Business Media. doi:10.1007/978-3-642-24463-6

Sohraby, K., Minoli, D., & Znati, T. (2007). *Wireless sensor networks: Technology, protocols, and applications*. John Wiley & Sons. doi:10.1002/047011276X

So, J., & Byun, H. (2017). Load-Balanced Opportunistic Routing for Duty-CycledWireless Sensor Networks. *IEEE Transactions on Mobile Computing, 16*(7), 1940–1955. doi:10.1109/TMC.2016.2606427

Somvanshi, V. K. (2006). Modeling and prediction of rainfall using artificial neural network and ARIMA techniques. *J. Ind. Geophys. Union, 10*(2), 141–151.

Song, J., Lee, Y. S., Jang, W., Lee, H., & Kim, T. (2016). Face Recognition Authentication Scheme for Mobile Banking System. *International Journal of Internet, Broadcasting and Communication, 8*(2), 38–42.

Sönmezoğlu, S., Akyürek, C., & Akiş, H. (2014). Modification of juglon dye as a sensitiser in dye-sensitised solar cells. *IET Optoelectronics, 8*(6), 270–276. doi:10.1049/iet-opt.2013.0048

Sreekala, C. O., Jinchu, I., Sreelatha, K. S., Janu, Y., Prasad, N., Kumar, M., Sadh, A. K., & Roy, M. S. (2012). Influence of solvents and surface treatment on photovoltaic response of dssc based on natural curcumin dye. *IEEE Journal of Photovoltaics, 2*(3), 312–319. doi:10.1109/JPHOTOV.2012.2185782

Stead, L. J. (2005). *'The emotional wardrobe': A fashion perspective on the integration of technology and clothing* [Unpublished doctoral dissertation]. University of the Arts London.

Steventon, A., & Wright, S. (2010). *Intelligent spaces: The application of pervasive ICT*. Springer Science & Business Media.

Stoppa, M., & Chiolerio, A. (2014). Wearable electronics and smart textiles: A critical review. *Sensors (Basel), 14*(7), 11957–11992. doi:10.3390140711957 PMID:25004153

Studer, A., Bai, F., Bellur, B., & Perrig, A. (2009). Flexible, extensible, and efficient VANET authentication. *Journal of Communications and Networks (Seoul), 11*(6), 574–588. doi:10.1109/JCN.2009.6388411

Sun, H., Wu, T.-K., & Roberts, K. (2008). Real-time measurements of a 40 Gb/s coherent system. *Optics Express, 16*(2), 873–879. doi:10.1364/OE.16.000873 PMID:18542161

Susanto, W., Babuška, R., Liefhebber, F., & van der Weiden, T. (2008). Adaptive Friction Compensation: Application to a Robotic Manipulator. *IFAC Proceedings Volumes, 41*(2), 2020–2024. 10.3182/20080706-5-KR-1001.00343

Su, Y. W., Lan, S. C., & Wei, K. H. (2012). Organic photovoltaics. *Materials Today, 15*(12), 554–562. doi:10.1016/S1369-7021(13)70013-0

Syduzzaman, M. D., Patwary, S. U., Farhana, K., & Ahmed, S. (2015). Smart textiles and nano-technology: A general overview. *Journal of Textile Science & Engineering, 5*, 1000181.

Szmechtyk, T., Sienkiewicz, N., Woźniak, J., & Strzelec, K. (2015). Polyurethanes as self-healing materials. *Current Chemistry Letters, 4*(2), 61–66. doi:10.5267/j.ccl.2015.3.001

Tang, C. K., Chan, K. H., Fung, L. C., & Leung, S. W. (2009). Electromagnetic Interference Immunity Testing of Medical Equipment to Second- and Third-Generation Mobile Phones. *IEEE Transactions on Electromagnetic Compatibility, 51*(3), 659–664. doi:10.1109/TEMC.2009.2021524

Tan, Y. Y., & Chung, W. Y. (2014). Mobile health-monitoring system through visible light communication. *Bio-Medical Materials and Engineering, 24*(6), 3529–3538. doi:10.3233/BME-141179 PMID:25227066

Tan, Y. Y., Jung, S. J., & Chung, W. Y. (2013). Real time biomedical signal transmission of mixed ECG Signal and patient information using visible light communication. In *Proceedings of 35th Annual International Conference of the IEEE Engineering in Medicine and Biology Society (EMBC)* (pp. 4791-4794). 10.1109/EMBC.2013.6610619

Tarini, M., Prakash, N., Mohamed Mathar Sahib, I. K., & Hayakawa, Y. (2017). Novel Sugar Apple-Shaped. *IEEE Journal of Photovoltaics, 7*(4), 1050–1057. doi:10.1109/JPHOTOV.2017.2698500

Tas, R., Can, M., & Sonmezoglu, S. (2017). Exploring on Photovoltaic Performance of Dye-Sensitized Solar Cells Using Polyaniline as a Counter Electrode: Role of Aluminum-Solvent Interactions. *IEEE Journal of Photovoltaics, 7*(3), 792–801. doi:10.1109/JPHOTOV.2017.2669643

Tedla, A., Mu, Y.-T., Sharma, J., & Tai, Y. (2016). Shelf-life studies on an ionic-liquid-stabilized dye-sensitized solar cell. *IEEE Journal of Photovoltaics, 7*(1), 177–183. doi:10.1109/JPHOTOV.2016.2614125

Teegavarapu, R. S. V. (2014). Statistical corrections of spatially interpolated precipitation estimates. *Hydrological Processes, 28*(11), 3789–3808. http://dx.doi. org/10.1002/hyp.9906

Thakur, K., Sharma, N., & Singh, J. (2020, June). Performance Analysis of Backward Pumped Raman Amplifier based DWDM System at 40Gb/s. *2020 5th International Conference on Communication and Electronics Systems (ICCES)*, 47-51. 10.1109/ICCES48766.2020.9138017

Tham, M. J. (2012, March). Design considerations for developing a parts-of-speech tagset for Khasi. In *2012 3rd National Conference on Emerging Trends and Applications in Computer Science* (pp. 277-280). IEEE. 10.1109/NCETACS.2012.6203274

Tham, M. J. (2013, September). Preliminary investigation of a morphological analyzer and generator for Khasi. In *2013 1st International Conference on Emerging Trends and Applications in Computer Science* (pp. 256-259). IEEE. 10.1109/ICETACS.2013.6691433

Tham, M. J. (2018, December). Challenges and issues in developing an annotated corpus and hmm pos tagger for Khasi. *The 15th international conference on natural language processing.*

Thapa, A., Zhao, Y., Poudel, P., Elbohy, H., Vaagensmith, B., Zhang, Z., Fong, H., & Qiao, Q. (2013). Evaluation of counter electrodes composed by carbon nanofibers and nanoparticles in dye-sensitized solar cells. *IEEE Transactions on Electron Devices*, *60*(11), 3883–3887. doi:10.1109/TED.2013.2279518

Threeasfour. (2016). https://threeasfour.com/ /

Tiru, B. (2015). Exploiting power line for communication purpose: Features and prospects of power line communication. In Proceedings of Intelligent Applications for Heterogeneous System Modeling and Design (pp. 320–334). doi:10.4018/978-1-4666-8493-5.ch014

Tiru, B., & Boruah, P. K. (2012). Modeling power line channel using ABCD matrices for communication purposes. In *Proceedings of International Conference on Future Electrical Power and Energy Systems Lecture Notes in Information Technology* (vol. 9, pp. 374–379). Academic Press.

Tiru, B., Baishya, B., & Sarma, U. (2015). An analysis of indoor power line network as a communication medium using ABCD matrices effect of loads on the transfer function of power line. Lecture Notes in Electrical Engineering. *Advances in Communication and Computing.*, *347*, 171–181. doi:10.1007/978-81-322-2464-8_14

Tsai, C. L., Chen, C. J., & Zhuang, D. J. (2012). Trusted M-banking Verification Scheme based on a combination of OTP and Biometrics. *JoC*, *3*(3), 23–30.

Tsekouras, G., Miyashita, M., Kho, Y. K., Teoh, W. Y., Mozer, A. J., Amal, R., Mori, S., & Wallace, G. G. (2010). Charge transport in dye-sensitized solar cells based on flame-made. *IEEE Journal of Selected Topics in Quantum Electronics*, *16*(6), 1641–1648. doi:10.1109/JSTQE.2010.2049734

Valverde, Campos, & Nelson. (2005). Artificial Neural Network Technique for Rainfall Forecasting Applied to the Sao Paulo Region. *Journal of Hydrology (Amsterdam)*, *301*, 146–162.

Vanderploeg, A., Lee, S. E., & Mamp, M. (2017). The application of 3D printing technology in the fashion industry. *International Journal of Fashion Design, Technology and Education*, *10*(2), 170–179.

Varma, S. J., Sambath Kumar, K., Seal, S., Rajaraman, S., & Thomas, J. (2018). Fiber-type solar cells, nanogenerators, batteries, and supercapacitors for wearable applications. *Advancement of Science*, *5*(9), 1800340. doi:10.1002/advs.201800340 PMID:30250788

Venkatraman, Daniel, & Murugaboopathi. (2013). Various Attacks in Wireless Sensor Network: Survey. *IJSCE, 3*(1).

Verbeek, H. B., Henry, C. H., Olsson, N. A., Orlowsky, K. J., Kazarinov, R. F., & Johnson, B. H. (1988). Integrated four-channel Mach-Zehnder multi/demultiplexer fabricated with phosphorous doped SiO/sub 2/ waveguides on Si. *Journal of Lightwave Technology*, *6*(6), 1011–1015. doi:10.1109/50.4092

Verma, G., Liao, M., Lu, D., He, W., & Peng, X. (2019). A novel optical two-factor face authentication scheme. *Optics and Lasers in Engineering*, *123*, 28–36. doi:10.1016/j.optlaseng.2019.06.028

Vesce, L., Riccitelli, R., Mincuzzi, G., Orabona, A., Soscia, G., Brown, T. M., Di Carlo, A., & Reale, A. (2013). Fabrication of spacer and catalytic layers in monolithic dye-sensitized solar cells. *IEEE Journal of Photovoltaics*, *3*(3), 1004–1011. doi:10.1109/JPHOTOV.2013.2262374

Virgala, I., Frankovský, P., & Kenderová, M. (2013). Friction Effect Analysis of a DC Motor. *American Journal of Mechanical Engineering*, *1*(1), 1–5. doi:10.12691/ajme-1-1-1

Wadi, A., Lee, J.-H., & Romdhane, L. (2018). Nonlinear sliding mode control of the Furuta pendulum. In *2018 11th International Symposium on Mechatronics and Its Applications (ISMA)* (pp. 1–5). IEEE Xplore. 10.1109/ISMA.2018.8330131

Wagih, H. M., & Mokhtar, H. M. O. (2021). Ridology: An Ontology Model for Exploring Human Behavior Trajectories in Ridesharing Applications. In M. Al-Emran, K. Shaalan, & A. Hassanien (Eds.), *Recent Advances in Intelligent Systems and Smart Applications. Studies in Systems, Decision and Control* (Vol. 295). Springer. doi:10.1007/978-3-030-47411-9_30

Wang, G., Hou, C., & Wang, H. (Eds.). (2020). *Flexible and wearable electronics for smart clothing.* John Wiley & Sons. doi:10.1002/9783527818556

Wang, N., & Li, J. (2019). Shortest Path Routing With Risk Control for Compromised WSN. *IEEE Access: Practical Innovations, Open Solutions, 7,* 19303–19311. doi:10.1109/ACCESS.2019.2897339

Wang, Y. X., & Liu, Z. D. (2020). Virtual clothing display platform based on CLO3D and evaluation of fit. *Journal of Fiber Bioengineering and Informatics, 13*(1), 37–49. doi:10.3993/jfbim00338

Wang, Y., Attebury, G., & Ramamurthy, B. (2006). *A Survey of Security Issues in Wireless Sensor Network.* IEEE Communication Surveys.

Warjri, S., Pakray, P., Lyngdoh, S., & Kumar Maji, A. (2018). Khasi language as dominant part-of-speech (pos) ascendant in NLP. *International Journal of Computational Intelligence & IoT, 1*(1).

Weber, R. H. (2010, January). Internet of Things-New security and privacy challenges. *Computer Law & Security Review, 26*(1), 23–30. doi:10.1016/j.clsr.2009.11.008

Wen, D., Han, H., & Jain, A. K. (2015). Face spoof detection with image distortion analysis. *IEEE Transactions on Information Forensics and Security, 10*(4), 746–761. doi:10.1109/TIFS.2015.2400395

Westbroek, P., Priniotakis, G., & Kiekens, P. (2005). *Analytical electrochemistry in textiles.* Elsevier.

Willems, J. (1971). Least squares stationary optimal control and the algebraic Riccati equation. *IEEE Transactions on Automatic Control, 16*(6), 621–634. doi:10.1109/TAC.1971.1099831

Williams, J. T. (Ed.). (2009). *Textiles for cold weather apparel.* Elsevier. doi:10.1533/9781845697174

Willmott, S. (2004). Deploying intelligent systems on a global scale. *IEEE Intelligent Systems, 19*(5), 71–73. doi:10.1109/MIS.2004.39

Winzer, J. P. (2010, July). Beyond 100G ethernet. *Comm. Mag, 48*(7), 26–30. doi:10.1109/MCOM.2010.5496875

Winzer, J. P., & Essiambre, J.-R. (2006). Advanced Modulation Formats for High-Capacity Optical Transport Networks. *Journal of Lightwave Technology, 24*(12), 4711–4728. doi:10.1109/JLT.2006.885260

Wool, R. P. (2008). Self-healing materials: A review. *Soft Matter, 4*(3), 400–418. doi:10.1039/b711716g PMID:32907199

Wu, Z., & Palmer, M. (1994). Verbs semantics and lexical selection. *Proceedings of the 32nd annual meeting on Association for Computational Linguistics–Association for Computational Linguistics.*

Xie, H. (2018). *Data Collection for Security Measurement in WSN: A Survey.* IEEE IoT Journal.

Xie, H., Yan, Z., Yao, Z., & Atiquzzaman, M. (2018). Data Collection for Security Measurement in Wireless Sensor Networks: A Survey. *IEEE Internet of Things Journal.*

Xie, M., Han, S., Tian, B., & Parvin, S. (2011, July). Anomaly detection in wireless sensor networks: A survey. *Journal of Network and Computer Applications, 34*(4), 1302–1325. doi:10.1016/j.jnca.2011.03.004

Xie, S., Zhang, F., & Cheng, R. (2021). Security Enhanced RFID Authentication Protocols for Healthcare Environment. *Wireless Personal Communications, 117*(1), 71–86. doi:10.100711277-020-07042-6

Xi, K., Hu, J., & Han, F. (2012). Mobile device access control: An improved correlation based face authentication scheme and its java me application. *Concurrency and Computation, 24*(10), 1066–1085. doi:10.1002/cpe.1797

Xu, C., Cao, L., Lin, B., Liang, X., & Chen, Y. (2016). Design of self-healing supramolecular rubbers by introducing ionic cross-links into natural rubber via a controlled vulcanization. *ACS Applied Materials & Interfaces, 8*(27), 17728–17737. doi:10.1021/acsami.6b05941 PMID:27337545

Xu, C., Gao, G., Chen, S., & Zhang, J. (2018). Pulse-overlapping super-Nyquist WDM system. *Journal of Lightwave Technology, 36*(18), 3941–3948. doi:10.1109/JLT.2018.2833120

Xu, F., Wu, Y., Zhang, X., Gao, Z., & Jiang, K. (2012). Controllable synthesis of rutile. *Micro & Nano Letters, 7*(8), 826–830. doi:10.1049/mnl.2012.0398

Yang, L., Li, J., & Zhang, J. (2017). Hybrid visible light communications (VLC) and PLC system. In *Proceedings of Opto-Electronics and Communications Conference (OECC) and Photonics Global Conference (PGC)* (pp. 1-2). 10.1109/OECC.2017.8114968

Yang, J., Gao, Z., Tian, L., Ma, P., Wu, D., & Yang, L. (2011). Spindle-like. *Micro & Nano Letters, 6*(8), 737–740. doi:10.1049/mnl.2011.0317

Yang, J., Keller, M. W., Moore, J. S., White, S. R., & Sottos, N. R. (2008). Microencapsulation of isocyanates for self-healing polymers. *Macromolecules, 41*(24), 9650–9655. doi:10.1021/ma801718v

Yang, L., Karim, R., Ganapathy, V., & Smith, R. (2011). Fast Memory-Efficient Regular Expression Matching with NFA-OBDDs. *Computer Networks: The International Journal of Computer and Telecommunications Networking, 55*(15), 3376–3393.

Yilmaz, N. D. (Ed.). (2018). *Smart textiles: Wearable nanotechnology.* John Wiley & Sons. doi:10.1002/9781119460367

Ying, B., Makrakis, D., & Mouftah, H. T. (2013). Privacy preserving broadcast message authentication protocol for VANETs. *Journal of Network and Computer Applications, 36*(5), 1352–1364. doi:10.1016/j.jnca.2012.05.013

Young, P. C. (2002). Advances in real-time flood forecasting. Philos Trans R Soc London. *Ser A, 360,* 1433–1450.

Yu, F., Chen, Z., Diao, Y., & Lakshman, T. (2006). Fast and Memory- Efficient Regular Expression Matching for Deep Packet Inspection. *Proceedings of the ACM/IEEE Symposium on Architecture for Networking and Communications Systems,* 93-102.

Yu, F., Chen, Z., Diao, Y., Lakshman, T. V., & Katz, R. H. (2001): Fast and Memory-Efficient Regular Expression Matching for Deep Packet Inspection. *Proceedings of the ACM/IEEE Symposium Architecture for Networking and Communication Systems,* 93-102.

Zaki, H. (2018). Analysis of cross-layer design of quality-of-service forward geographic wireless sensor network routing strategies in green internet of things. *IEEE Access: Practical Innovations, Open Solutions, 6,* 20371–20389. doi:10.1109/ACCESS.2018.2822551

Zeng, L., O'Brien, D., Minh, H. L., Lee, K., Jung, D., & Oh, Y. (2008). Improvement of Date Rate by using Equalization in an Indoor Visible Light Communication System. In *Proceedings of 4th IEEE International Conference on Circuits and Systems for Communications* (pp. 678-682). 10.1109/ICCSC.2008.149

Zenkour, A. M., & El-Shahrany, H. D. (2021). Hygrothermal forced vibration of a viscoelastic laminated plate with magnetostrictive actuators resting on viscoelastic foundations. *International Journal of Mechanics and Materials in Design, 17*(2), 301–320. doi:10.100710999-020-09526-6

Zhang, C., Lin, X., Lu, R., & Ho, P.-H. (2008). RAISEan ficientRS SU-aided message authentication scheme in vehicular communication networks. *Proceedings of the IEEE ICC '08*, 1451–1457.

Zhang, C., Lu, R., Lin, X., Ho, P.-H., & Shen, X. (2008). An efficient identity-based batch verification scheme for vehicular sensor networks. *Proceedings of the 27th INFOCOM '08*, 246–250. 10.1109/INFOCOM.2008.58

Zhang, M., Gao, T., Wang, J., Liao, J., Qiu, Y., Yang, Q., Xue, H., Shi, Z., Zhao, Y., Xiong, Z., & Chen, L. (2015). A hybrid fibers based wearable fabric piezoelectric nanogenerator for energy harvesting application. *Nano Energy*, *13*, 298–305. doi:10.1016/j.nanoen.2015.02.034

Zhang, S., Huang, Y., Yaman, F., & Inada, Y. (2015). Performance study of 100-Gb/s super-Nyquist QPSK and Nyquist 8QAM over 25-GHz spacing. *IEEE Photonics Technology Letters*, *27*(13), 1445–144. doi:10.1109/LPT.2015.2425352

Zhang, X., & Tao, X. (2001). Smart textiles: Passive smart. *Textile Asia*, *32*(6), 45–49.

Zhang, Y., Qi, T., Wang, Q., Zhang, Y., Wang, D., & Zheng, W. (2016). Preparation of. *IEEE Journal of Photovoltaics*, *7*(1), 399–403. doi:10.1109/JPHOTOV.2016.2627620

Zhan, Y., & Shen, D. (2005). Design efficient support vector machine for fast classification. *Pattern Recognition*, *38*, 157–161. doi:10.1016/j.patcog

Zhi, C., & Dai, L. (Eds.). (2018). *Flexible energy conversion and storage devices*. John Wiley & Sons. doi:10.1002/9783527342631

Zhou, Fang, & Zhang. (2008). Security Wireless Sensor Networks: A Survety. *IEEE Communication Surveys*.

Zhou, D. H., Yan, Z., Fu, Y. L., & Yao, Z. (2018, August). A Survey on NetworkData Collection. *Journal of Network and Computer Applications*, *116*, 9–23. doi:10.1016/j.jnca.2018.05.004

Zhou, Q., Yang, G., & He, L. (2014). A secure enhance data aggregation based on ecc in wireless sensor network. *Sensors Journal*, *14*(4), 6701–6721. doi:10.3390140406701 PMID:24732099

Zhou, X., & Tang, X. (2011). Research and implementation of RSA algorithm for encryption and decryption. In *Proceedings of 2011 6th International Forum on ST* (vol. 2, pp. 1118-1121). IEEE. 10.1109/IFOST.2011.6021216

Zhou, Y., Yang, L., Lu, J., Wu, Y., Li, C., Liu, Y., & Li, M. (2016). Photoelectric properties of three-dimensional urchin-like zinc oxide/titanium dioxide composite micronanostructures. *Micro & Nano Letters*, *11*(5), 277–280. doi:10.1049/mnl.2015.0394

Zhu, X., Xu, F., Novak, E., Tan, C. C., Li, Q., & Chen, G. (2017). Using wireless link dynamics to extract a secret key in vehicular scenarios. *IEEE Transactions on MC*, *16*(7), 2065–2078. doi:10.1109/TMC.2016.2557784

Zubair, L., & Ropelewski. (2006). The strengthening relationship of ENSO and the North East Monsoon rainfall over Sri Lanka and Southern India. *Journal of Climate*, *19*(8), 1567–1575.

About the Contributors

Kandarpa Kumar Sarma is currently a Professor in Department of Electronics and Communication Engineering, Gauhati University, Guwahati, Assam, India. He has over twenty five years of professional experience and has covered all areas of UG/PG level electronics courses including deep learning, cognitive radio, soft computing, mobile communication, digital signal and image processing. He obtained M.Tech degree in Signal Processing from Indian Institute of Technology Guwahati in 2005 and subsequently completed PhD programme in the area of Soft-Computational Application in Mobile Communication in 2012. He has authored eleven books, several book chapters, and peer reviewed research papers in international conference proceedings and journals. His areas of interest are Cognitive Radio, Software Defined Radio, Deep Learning, Mobile Communication, Antenna Design, Speech Processing etc. He has been conferred upon the IETE N. V. Gadadhar Memorial Award 2014 for his contribution towards wireless communication. He is a senior member of IEEE (USA), Fellow IETE (India), Member International Neural Network Society (INNS, USA), Life Member ISTE (India) and Life Member CSI (India). He serves as an Editor-in-Chief of the International Journal of Intelligent System Design and Computing (IJISDC, UK), guest editor of several international journals, and reviewer of over fifty international journals and over two hundred international conferences.

* * *

Rubi Baishya is a teaching faculty in Behali Degree College, Assam, India. She has done her PhD from Gauhati University in Power Line Communication.

Prasanta Bhattacharya obtained PhD from Gauhati University, India. He is serving the Department of Geography, Gauhati University, India as an Associate Professor.

Jonathan Bishop is an information technology executive, researcher and writer. He founded the Congress of Researchers and Organisations for Cybercommunity, E-Learning and Socialnomics in 2005, which works with the Crocels Community Media Group members. Jonathan's research & development work generally falls within human-computer interaction. He has over 100 publications in this area, including on Internet trolling, digital addiction, affective computing, gamification; cyberlaw, multimedia forensics, cyber-stalking; Classroom 2.0, School 3.0, Digital Teens. In addition to his BSc(Hons) in Multimedia Studies and postgraduate degrees in law, business, economics and e-learning, Jonathan serves in local government as a councillor, and has been a school governor and contested numerous elections, including to the UK and Welsh parliaments. He is a an FBCS, FCLIP, FInstAM, FInstLM, FAPM, FRAI, FRSS,

FRSA, SMIEEE, MIET, MACM, MIITP, MIMarEST MarTech CITP. He has prizes for literary skills and was a finalist in national and local competitions for his environmental, community and equality work, often forming part of action research studies. Jonathan enjoys music, swimming and chess.

Sujit Chatterjee is doing his PhD in the Department of Physics, Gauhati University. His research interest is development of hybrid communication using power line communication and Visible Light Communication.

Wendy Flores-Fuentes received the bachelor's degree in electronic engineering from the Autonomous University of Baja California in 2001, the master's degree in engineering from Technological Institute of Mexicali in 2006, and the Ph.D. degree in science, applied physics, with emphasis on Optoelectronic Scanning Systems for SHM, from Autonomous University of Baja California in June 2014. By now she is the author of 36 journal articles in Elsevier, IEEE, Emerald and Springer, 18 book chapters and 8 books in Springer, Intech, IGI global Lambert Academic and Springer, 46 proceedings articles in IEEE ISIE 2014-2021, IECON 2014, 2018, 2019, the World Congress on Engineering and Computer Science (IAENG 2013), IEEE Section Mexico IEEE ROCC2011, and the VII International Conference on Industrial Engineering ARGOS 2014. Recently, she has organized and participated as Chair of Special Session on "Machine Vision, Control and Navigation" at IEEE ISIE 2015-2021 and IECON 2018, 2019. She has participated has Guest Editor at Journal of Sensors with Hindawi, The International Journal of Advanced Robotic Systems with SAGE, IEEE Sensors, and Elsevier Measurement. She holds 1 patent of Mexico and 1 patent of Ukraine. She has been a reviewer of several articles in Taylor and Francis, IEEE, Elsevier, and EEMJ. Currently, she is a full-time professor at Universidad Autónoma de Baja California, at the Faculty of Engineering. She has been incorporated into CONACYT National Research System in 2015. She did receive the award of "Best session presentation" in WSECS2013 in San-Francisco, USA. She did receive as coauthor the award of "Outstanding Paper in the 2017 Emerald Literati Network Awards for Excellence". Hers interests include optoelectronics, robotics, artificial intelligence, measurement systems, and machine vision systems. https://www.emeraldgrouppublishing.com/authors/literati/awards.htm?year=2017 https://scholar.google.es/citations?user=STZq6TYAAAAJ&hl=es&oi=ao https://www.scopus.com/authid/detail.uri?authorId=55955051400.

Mark Goode has been teaching in UK Universities for over 35 years and has taught over 35,000 University students at all levels (from undergraduate year 1 to PhD). Mark has two degrees in Economics and a PhD by published works in Digital Marketing. He has written over 40 journal articles, books and over 50 conference papers, based around consumer satisfaction and loyalty, consumer behaviour on the Internet and the application of new statistical and mathematical models to consumer behaviour.

Hirakjyoti Goswami received his M.Sc. in Physics from Gauhati University in 2009. He joined the Society for Applied Microwave Electronics Engineering & Research, Ministry of Electronics & IT, Government of India as a Sr. Research Scientist in 2012. In 2014 he was awarded Ph.D. degree by Gauhati University and is currently working as an Assistant Professor in the Department of Physics, Gauhati University. He has published and presented many research papers in National and International levels. He also acted as a reviewer for many international journals. His area of interest includes Signal Processing, Lower Atmospheric Dynamics and Atmospheric Modeling.

Risanlang Hynniewta is with the Department of Information Technology, North Eastern Hill University, Meghalaya, India.

Vinodha K. is working as an Associate Professor in Department of Computer Science at PES University, India.

Merve Küçükali Öztürk is with the Istanbul Bilgi University, Turkey.

K. Vinoth Kumar is a Professional Senior IEEE member and he received the B.E degree in Electrical & Electronics Engineering from Anna University, India in 2006. He has completed his Master of Technology from Vellore Institute of Technology and Ph.D Degree in Electrical & Electronics Engineering from Karunya Institute of Technology and Sciences, India in 2008 and 2017 respectively. Currently, he is working as an Associate Professor in Electrical and Electronics Engineering Department of New Horizon College of Engineering, Bengaluru, Karnataka, India. His main research areas are intelligent control, Instrumentation, automation & process control, condition monitoring, fault analysis, Power Electronics and AC/DC Machines. He published research papers in both international and national journals as well as in conferences. He is authored the Book titled "Basic Electrical and Electronics Engineering" published by John Wiley & Sons India and Neural Networks, Soft Computing textbooks, Special Electrical Machines, Power Electronics.

Lars Lindner was born on July 20th 1981 in Dresden, Germany. He received his M.S. degree in mechatronics engineering from the TU Dresden University in January 2009. After finishing his career, he moved to Mexico and started teaching engineering classes at different universities in Mexicali. Since August 2013 he began his PhD studies at the Engineering Institute of Autonomous University of Baja California in Mexicali with the topic "Theoretical Method to Increase the Speed of Continuous Mapping of a Three-dimensional Laser Scanner using Servomotor Control", in which he worked in the development of an optoelectronic prototype for the measurement of 3D coordinates, using laser dynamic triangulation. His academic products include 22 original research articles, 3 articles in national congresses, 21 articles in international congresses, 11 book chapters and 1 book as editor. In September 2017, he was appointed as a Level 1 National Researcher by the National System of Researchers CONACYT for the period 2018-2020. Right now he is working as a technician assistant at the Engineering Institute of Autonomous University of Baja California for the department of applied physics.

Arnab Kumar Maji is with the Department of Information Technology, North Eastern Hill University, Meghalaya, India.

Horacio Alain Millan-Guerrero was born on December 14th, 1996 in Mexicali, Baja California, Mexico. He received his B.S. degree with honors in Electronics Engineering from the Autonomous University of Baja California in 2019. He also received an outstanding performance testimony from the National Center of Evaluation for Higher education in June 2019. He is currently a licensed Electronics engineer in Mexico and is also a certified Electrical & Computer Engineer-in-Training in California, USA. During his bachelor's studies, he worked on a Bode Plotter project using LabVIEW and an oscilloscope/fgen. He also worked on a Hardware-in-the-Loop advanced control project at the applied physics department of the Autonomous University of Baja California. He is currently working on his Engineering

Master's degree at the Engineering Institute of the Autonomous University of Baja California. Some of his topics of interest are electronics, advanced control, physics, applied mathematics, robotics, informatics, artificial intelligence, embedded systems, and cloud computing.

Fabian N. Murrieta-Rico received B.Eng. and M.Eng. degrees from Instituto Tecnológico de Mexicali (ITM) in 2004 and 2013 respectively. In 2017, he received his PhD in Materials Physics at Centro de Investigación Científica y Educación Superior de Ensenada (CICESE). He has worked as an automation engineer, systems designer, as a university professor, and as postdoctoral researcher at Facultad de Ingeniería, Arquitectura y Diseño from Universidad Autónoma de Baja California (UABC) and at the Centro de Nanociencias y Nanotecnología from Universidad Nacional Autónoma de México (CNyN-UNAM), currently he works as professor at the Universidad Politécnica de Baja California. His research has been published in different journals and presented at international conferences since 2009. He has served as reviewer for different journals, some of them include IEEE Transactions on Industrial Electronics, IEEE Transactions on Instrumentation, Measurement and Sensor Review. His research interests are focused on the field of time and frequency metrology, the design of wireless sensor networks, automated systems and highly sensitive chemical detectors.

Jose Antonio Nuñez-Lopez was born on November 28th, 1997, in Mexicali, Mexico. He received the Bachelor of Science degree in electronics engineering with honors from the Autonomous University of Baja California in August 2019. During his bachelor studies, he worked as a teaching assistant at the Engineering Faculty of the Autonomous University of Baja California (January 2017 to December 2018); Also, he worked as a research assistant in the Automation and Virtual Instrumentation Department at the Engineering Institute of the Autonomous University of Baja California (February 2018 to November 2018). In addition, he received the testimonial recognition of outstanding performance by the National Center of Evaluation for Higher Education in May 2019. After finishing his career, his professional experience includes managing engineering projects, industrial automation, and electronic avionics systems maintenance services in world-class companies (December 2018 to September 2020). More recently, his professional experience mainly includes computer systems maintenance services and equipment administration in the public education sector of the Baja California Government (August 2020 to the present). Since September 2020, he has been working toward a Master of Science degree in applied physics at the Engineering Institute of the Autonomous University of Baja California. His current research interests include high-performance control of electro-mechanical systems that use DC motors, dynamic friction modeling, robust adaptive control, nonlinear observer design, and friction compensation.

Chaya P. is Assistant Professor, Dept. of ISE, GSSSIETW, Mysore, India and research Scholar, Dr. Ambedkar Institute of Technology, Bangalore, VTU, Mysuru, India.

Umamaheswari P. received M.Tech in Computer Science from SASTRA Deemed University, Thanjavur, Tamil Nadu, and India in the year 2011 and M.B.A from Alagappa University, Karaikudi, Tamil Nadu, and India in the year 2006. She is pursuing Doctoral degree in Computer Science and Engineering from SASTRA Deemed University. She has 17 years of teaching experience for UG and PG courses in Computer Science and presently working as assistant professor in the department of computer science and engineering at SASTRA University, SRC Campus, and Kumbakonam. Her research interest in Data

Mining, Machine Learning and Deep learning. She published research papers in International Conferences and Scopus Indexed Journals.

Sabyasachi Pramanik is a Professional IEEE member. He obtained a PhD in Computer Science and Engineering from the Sri Satya Sai University of Technology and Medical Sciences, Bhopal, India. Presently, he is an Assistant Professor, Department of Computer Science and Engineering, Haldia Institute of Technology, India. He has many publications in various reputed international conferences, journals, and online book chapter contributions (Indexed by SCIE, Scopus, ESCI, etc). He is doing research in the field of Artificial Intelligence, Data Privacy, Cybersecurity, Network Security, and Machine Learning. He is also serving as the editorial board member of many international journals. He is a reviewer of journal articles from IEEE, Springer, Elsevier, Inderscience, IET, and IGI Global. He has reviewed many conference papers, has been a keynote speaker, session chair and has been a technical program committee member in many international conferences. He has authored a book on Wireless Sensor Network. He has edited 7 books from IGI Global, CRC Press, Springer and Wiley Publications.

Nandini Prasad K. S. is presently Professor, Dept. of ISE, Dr. Ambedkar Institute of Technology, Bangalore, VTU, Mysuru, India.

Nazreena Rahman has been awarded the Ph.D degree in Computer Science & Engineering from Tezpur University in 2021. She is an assistant professor in the Department of Computer Science & Engineering at Kaziranga University. Her research areas include text mining, natural language processing and data mining. She did her M.Tech and B.Tech from Gauhati University. She has published many research papers in international, peer-reviewed, SCIE, SCOPUS, UGC Listed and high impact factor reputed journals. She has also published papers in several book chapters in LNCS, LNNS Springer series and as well as in many reputed ACM, ACL (NLP), IEEE and Springer conferences.

Julio C. Rodríguez-Quiñonez received the B.S. degree in CETYS, Mexico in 2007. He received the Ph.D. degree from Baja California Autonomous University, México, in 2013. He is currently Full Time Researcher-Professor in the Engineering Faculty of the Autonomous University of Baja California, and member of the National Research System Level 1. Since 2016 is Senior Member of IEEE. He is involved in the development of optical scanning prototype in the Applied Physics Department and research leader in the development of a new stereo vision system prototype. He has been thesis director of 3 Doctor's Degree students and 4 Master's degree students. He holds two patents referred to dynamic triangulation method, has been editor of 4 books, Guest Editor of Measurement, IEEE Sensors Journal, International Journal of Advanced Robotic Systems and Journal of Sensors, written over 70 papers, 8 book chapters and has been a reviewer for IEEE Sensors Journal, Optics and Lasers in Engineering, IEEE Transaction on Mechatronics and Neural Computing and Applications of Springer; he participated as a reviewer and Session Chair of IEEE ISIE conferences in 2014 (Turkey), 2015 (Brazil), 2016 (USA), 2017 (UK), 2019 (Canada), IECON 2018 (USA), IECON 2019 (Portugal), ISIE 2020 (Netherlands), ISIE 2021 (Japan). His current research interests include automated metrology, stereo vision systems, control systems, robot navigation and 3D laser scanners.

Palanivel S. received B.E (Honours) degree in Computer Science and Engineering in the year 1989 from Mookambigai College of Engineering. He obtained M.E degree in Computer Science and Engineering in the year 1994 from Govt. College of Technology (GCT), Coimbatore. He joined Annamalai University in the year 1994. He obtained Ph.D in Computer Science and Engineering from Indian Institute of Technology. His areas of interest are speech, image and video processing, and Machine Learning. He published 86 papers in international journals, 26 papers in international conferences and 40 papers in national journals and conferences. He has produced ten Ph.D's in Computer Science and Engineering. He is currently guiding two research scholars in the Department of Computer Science and Engineering for Ph.D. He received Rs. 30 lakhs from AICTE to carry out research projects. He is Professor & Head in the Department of Computer Science and Engineering at Annamalai University, Chidambaram.

Debashis Saikia is a faculty member in the Department of Instrumentation and USIC, His research interest is Smart Sensor, Soft Computing. Sensor Network and Instrumentation for tea processes monitoring.

Prithi Samuel received the Ph.D Degree in Electrical & Electronics Engineering from PSG College of Technology, Coimbatore, India in 2020 respectively.

Oleg Sergiyenko received the B.S. (Honoris Causa) and M.S. degrees in Kharkiv National University of Automobiles and Highways, Kharkiv, Ukraine, in 1991, 1993, respectively. He received the Ph.D. degree in Kharkiv National Polytechnic University on specialty ''Tools and methods of non-destructive control'' in 1997. He received the PostDoc degree (DsC, or habilitation thesis) in Kharkiv National University of Radioelectronics in 2018. He has been the author of 1 book, editor of 8 books, and has written 23 book chapters, 160 papers indexed in SCOPUS (h-index 22), holds 2 patents of Ukraine, and 1 patent of Mexico. Since 1994 until the present time, he is represented by his research works in several International Congresses of IEEE, ICROS, SICE, IMEKO in USA, England, Japan, Italy, Austria, Scotland, Portugal, Canada, Ukraine, Turkey, Brazil, and Mexico. He is currently the Head of Applied Physics Department of Engineering Institute of Baja California Autonomous University, Mexico, director of several master's and doctorate thesis. He was a member of Program Committees of various international and local conferences, participating annually as Session Chair of IEEE ISIE and IECON conferences in 2014 - 2022. He is Recognized Reviewer of Elsevier, constant reviewer of IEEE Transaction on Industrial Electronics, etc. He is a member (Academician) of Academy of Applied Radioelectronics of Ukraine, Russia and Belorussia. He did receive the award of "Best session presentation" in IECON2014 in Dallas, USA, IECON2016 in Florence, Italy and ISIE2019 in Vancouver, Canada. He did receive as coauthor the award of "Outstanding Paper in the 2017 Emerald Literati Network Awards for Excellence": https://www.emeraldgrouppublishing.com/authors/literati/awards.htm?year=2017. He was Editor and author of several books in international Editorials, including his last book of Springer Nature: https://www.springer.com/gp/book/9783030225865.

Neeraj Sharma received his Ph.D. from Faculty of Engineering and Technology, Panjab University Chandigarh, India in 2021 and M.E. in Electronics and communication Engineering from the Panjab University, Chandigarh, India in 2007.He worked as an Assistant Professor at Thapar University Patiala, India from 2007 to 2008. Since 2008, he has been working as an Assistant Professor in E.C.E. department of University Institute of Engineering and Technology, Panjab University, Chandigarh, India. His research interest includes high-speed WDM systems, free space optic communication and MEMS & Microsystems.

Seuji Sharma is an Assistant Professor in the Department of Linguistics, Gauhati University, Guwahati, India.

Salma Sultana is with the Department of Computer Science & Engineering, Kaziranga University, India.

Banty Tiru is a faculty member in the Department of Physics, Gauhati University. Her research interest is signal processing, communication and atmospheric physics.

Sunita Warjri is with the Department of Information Technology, North Eastern Hill University, Meghalaya, India.

Index

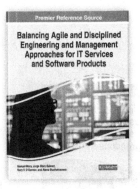

Ensure Quality Research is Introduced to the Academic Community

Become an Evaluator for IGI Global Authored Book Projects

Premier Reference Source

Stabilizing Currency and Preserving Economic Sovereignty Using the Grondona System

Patrick Collins

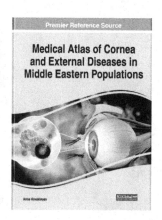

Premier Reference Source

Medical Atlas of Cornea and External Diseases in Middle Eastern Populations

Anna Hovakimyan

Premier Reference Source

Examining Biophilia and Societal Indifference to Environmental Protection

Mary Ann Markey and Lenny Douglas Steinecke

Premier Reference Source

Using Narratives and Storytelling to Promote Cultural Diversity on College Campuses

T. Scott Bledsoe and Kimberly A. Setterlund

The overall success of an authored book project is dependent on quality and timely manuscript evaluations.

Applications and Inquiries may be sent to:
development@igi-global.com

Applicants must have a doctorate (or equivalent degree) as well as publishing, research, and reviewing experience. Authored Book Evaluators are appointed for one-year terms and are expected to complete at least three evaluations per term. Upon successful completion of this term, evaluators can be considered for an additional term.

If you have a colleague that may be interested in this opportunity, we encourage you to share this information with them.

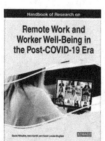

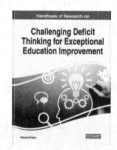

Printed in the United States
by Baker & Taylor Publisher Services